Debt, Adjustment and Recovery

Debt, Adjustment and Recovery

Latin America's Prospects for Growth and Development

Edited by
Sebastian Edwards and Felipe Larraín

Basil Blackwell

British Library Cataloguing in Publication Data

Debt, adjustment and recovery: Latin America's prospects for growth and development.
1. Latin America, Governments. External debts
I. Edwards, Sebastian 1953- II. Larraín, Felipe
336.3'433'8

ISBN 1–55786–019–X

Library of Congress Cataloging in Publication Data

Debt, adjustment and recovery: Latin America's prospects for growth and development/edited by Sebastian Edwards and Felipe Larraín.

p.   cm.

Articles and commentaries presented at a conference held in Viña del Mar, Chile in Dec. 1987, organized by the Instituto de Economía of the Pontificia Universidad Católica de Chile.
Includes index.
1.   Debts, External–Latin
America–Congresses.   2.   Debt relief–Latin
America–Congresses.   3.   Economic
stabilization–Latin America–Congresses.   I.   Edwards,
Sebastian, 1953– .   II.   Larraín B.,
Felipe.   III.   Universidad Católica de
Chile.   Instituto de Economía.

HJ8514.5.D437 1989	336.3'435'098–dc19	88–38150
		CIP

ISBN 1–55786–019–X

Typeset in 10 on 12 pt Times
by Vera-Reyes Inc., Philippines
Printed in Great Britain by
TJ Press, Padstow

Contents

Contents

Contributors

Eduardo Aninat Partner and Director of the consulting firm of Aninat, Mendez & Assoc. (Santiago, Chile). Formerly Professor of Economics at Pontificia Universidad Catolica de Chile. He has also taught at Boston University.

Mario I. Blejer Division Chief, International Monetary Fund. Has been a faculty member at the Hebrew University of Jerusalem and New York University.

Guillermo Calvo Professor of Economics, University of Pennsylvania. Has been a consultant for the International Monetary Fund. Formerly Professor of Economics, Columbia University, New York.

Eliana A. Cardoso Professor of Economics, Fletcher School of Law and Diplomacy, Tufts University.

William R. Cline Senior Fellow, Institute for International Economics (Washington, DC). Formerly Senior Fellow at the Brookings Institution.

Rudiger Dornbusch The Ford Professor of International Economics, Massachusetts Institute of Technology, and Research Associate, National Bureau of Economic Research. Has also taught at the University of Chicago and the University of Rochester.

Sebastian Edwards Professor of Economics at the University of California, Los Angeles, and Research Associate at the National Bureau of Economic Research. He has been a consultant for the World Bank, the International Monetary Fund and the government of Indonesia. He has published extensively on international economics, economic development and the economics of Latin America. His books include *Economic Adjustment and Exchange Rates in Developing Countries* (co-editor), *Monetarism and Liberalization: The Chilean Experiment* (co-author) and *Exchange Rate Misalignment in Developing Countries*.

Barry Eichengreen Professor of Economics, University of California, Berkeley and Research Associate, National Bureau of Economic Research. Has also taught at Harvard University.

Juan A. Fontaine Director of Research, Banco Central de Chile.

Francisco Gil-Diaz Director, Banco de Mexico.

Dominique Hachette Professor of Economics, Pontificia Universidad Catolica de Chile. Formerly an economist with the World Bank.

Deepak Lal Professor of Political Economy, University College, London.

Felipe Larraín Associate Professor of Economics at Pontificia Universidad Católica de Chile, currently on leave at Harvard University. He has been a consultant to the World Bank and the Government of Bolivia. His research concentrates on international economics with particular emphasis on Latin America and his work has appeared in scholarly journals. He is the editor of *Desarrollo Economico en Democracia* (Economic Development for Democracy), recently published in South America.

Jorge Marshall R. Assistant Professor, ILADES-Georgetown Postgraduate Program in Economics (Santiago, Chile).

Jorge Marshall S. Professor of Economics, Universidad de Chile.

Patricio Meller Senior Economist, CIEPLAN (Santiago, Chile). He also taught at Pontificia Universidad Catolica de Chile and at Universidad de Chile.

Felipe Morandé Assistant Professor, ILADES-Georgetown Postgraduate Program in Economics.

Jose Antonio Ocampo Executive Director, FEDESARROLLO (Bogota, Colombia).

Carlos A. Rodriguez Professor of Economics, Centro de Estudios Macroeconomicos Argentinos (CEMA). Formerly Professor of Economics, Columbia University, New York.

Francisco Rosende Senior Economist, Banco Central de Chile.

Andres Solimano Economist, Programa de Empleo para America Latina y el Caribe (PREALC).

John Williamson Senior Economist, Institute for International Economics (Washington, DC).

Roberto Zahler Regional Adviser on Monetary and Financial Policy, ECLAC/CEPAL.

Preface

The debt crisis that erupted in August 1982 greatly changed the economic circumstances of the Latin American nations. Until the early 1980s the region faced fairly rosy prospects. Between 1970 and 1981, and in spite of the two oil shocks, the nonoil exporting countries experienced healthy rates of growth that were achieved, in part, thanks to large inflows of foreign capital facilitated by the international financial community. For the oil exporting countries things fared even better during that period. They not only capitalized on the improved terms of trade, but they also had access to ample foreign funds. In late 1982 all of this came to an end, as these countries found themselves in the midst of the worst recession since the 1930s. Real incomes plummeted, unemployment soared and, for all practical purposes, these countries were declared financially insolvent.

In the late eighties the countries in the region are struggling to get back on their feet. Although there is no doubt that they have made substantial progress in adjusting, there is still much to be done. At this point some particularly pressing questions include: how well will these countries fare in the longer run? What will be the most adequate mode of development for the region? And how will growth be financed over the years to come?

The main chapters and commentaries collected in this volume were presented at a conference held in Viña del Mar, Chile in December 1987, and deal with several aspects of the Latin American debt crisis. They address some of the key questions mentioned above, and at the same time analyze what the region's prospects for growth and development are. The volume has been divided into two parts. The first includes five chapters – by William Cline, Barry Eichengreen, Deepak Lal, John Williamson, and Guillermo Calvo – that deal with global issues related to the crisis. This part also includes comments by Patricio Meller, Jorge Marshall S., Roberto Zahler, Mario Blejer and Felipe Morandé. The second part of the book contains five country studies that cover the three major debtors – Argentina (Carlos A. Rodriguez), Brazil (Eliana Cardoso and Rudiger Dornbusch) and Mexico (Francisco Gil-Diaz) – plus Chile (Juan A. Fontaine) and Colombia (Jose A. Ocampo). This part contains comments by

Andres Solimano, Eduardo Aninat, Dominique Hachette, Jorge Marshall R., Francisco Rosende and William Cline. The first chapter is by the editors and provides a general framework for the analysis, as well as a brief reader's guide.

The Viña del Mar conference was organized by the Instituto de Economia of the Pontificia Universidad Católica de Chile. We are grateful to the Instituto's Director Sergio de la Cuadra for enthusiastically supporting the project from the very beginning. We also thank Juan Ignacio Varas, Dean of the Facultad de Economia y Administración, for his support. The conference was possible thanks to a grant from the Banco Central de Chile to the Instituto de Economia. Finally, we are grateful to all the authors and discussants for taking part in this project.

Sebastian Edwards
Felipe Larraín

1

Debt, Adjustment, and Recovery in Latin America: an Introduction

Sebastian Edwards and Felipe Larraín

1 Introduction

More than half a decade has gone by since Mexico's announcement in August 1982 that it could no longer service its debt under the previously agreed conditions. Latin America is still searching for ways to cope with a debt burden that has become the most serious threat to the economic development of the region. For the world as a whole, even if the collapse of the financial system has not materialized, the collateral effects and uncertainty provoked by the debt overhang are far from over. In retrospect, what has been perplexing is the generalized nature of the crisis. It has affected both oil importers and oil exporters; both countries pursuing mostly orthodox economic policies (i.e., those of the Southern Cone) and those undergoing heterodox policies (i.e., Brazil).

Some traditional creditworthiness indicators, such as the debt–export ratio, suggest that between 1982 and 1986 no significant improvement has occured in Latin America (see, however, Cline's chapter (ch. 2) in this volume). Preliminary data for 1987 nonetheless indicate that some progress was made during that year (see table 1.1). In spite of this improvement, it has by now become clear that a long-term solution to the debt problem will be a painful and protracted process. This solution will require extensive negotiations between debtor and creditor governments, multilateral institutions and the banks, as well as additional adjustment efforts by indebted countries.

The challenge that the region will face in the late 1980s and in the 1990s is to make further progress on the adjustment front, while at the same time vigorously resuming growth. Clearly, the situation created by the significant decline in the region's real GDP per capita since 1980 is not sustainable.

Table 1.1 Creditworthiness indicators (%)

	1980	1981	1982	1983	1984	1985	1986	1987
1 Interest Payments as % of Exports								
Argentina	22.0	35.5	53.6	58.4	57.6	51.1	53.0	56.2
Brazil	34.1	40.4	57.1	43.5	39.7	40.0	41.4	34.5
Colombia	11.8	21.9	25.9	26.7	22.8	26.3	19.7	25.2
Chile	19.3	38.8	49.5	38.9	48.0	43.5	38.6	26.7
Mexico	23.3	29.1	47.3	37.5	39.0	36.0	37.9	27.9
Peru	16.0	24.1	25.1	29.8	33.2	30.0	26.7	22.4
Venezuela	8.1	12.7	21.0	21.6	20.1	26.3	32.8	26.3
Latin America	20.2	28.0	41.0	36.0	35.6	35.2	36.0	30.6
2 Total Debt as % of Exports								
Argentina	275.0	329.0	475.0	385.0	488.0	481.0	636.0	712.0
Brazil	320.0	313.0	414.0	404.0	345.0	372.0	454.0	420.0
Colombia	128.0	199.0	232.0	302.0	237.0	295.0	232.0	246.0
Chile	188.0	311.0	370.0	390.0	438.0	454.0	411.0	343.0
Mexico	216.0	259.0	335.0	345.0	321.0	353.0	457.0	377.0
Peru	206.0	241.0	278.0	334.0	351.0	377.0	438.0	445.0
Venezuela	148.0	160.0	200.0	227.0	207.0	226.0	341.0	300.0
Latin America	212.0	247.0	321.0	345.0	321.0	346.0	416.0	387.0
3 Trade Balance in Goods and Services as % of Interest Payments								
Argentina	−146.7	−19.7	54.1	63.9	58.0	84.8	48.8	
Brazil	−79.6	−16.3	−22.3	39.7	99.1	97.0	88.0	
Colombia	−20.0	−184.2	−197.8	−194.9	−16.2	−26.6	76.6	
Chile	−91.6	−167.0	−16.5	35.0	−6.5	26.2	31.2	
Mexico	−40.6	−55.6	50.9	40.9	118.8	89.8	43.0	
Peru	102.7	−89.6	−72.5	3.5	62.1	86.4	−19.5	
Venezuela	300.0	144.3	−56.2	196.9	205.0	136.7	−0.9	

Source: ECLA (1987)

The debt crisis has generated a large interpretative literature. During the early years most of it focussed on the causes of the crisis, trying to assign responsibility. More recently, however, a number of authors have discussed medium-term issues related to the adjustment undertaken by these countries and to the requirements for the resumption of growth. A large proportion of this literature has recommended conventional measures that economists had been advocating for a long time prior to the debt problem, including trade liberalization, financial reform, major devaluations and a reduced role for the government (Balassa et al., 1986; Krueger, 1987). For example, this type of policy package is at the core of the conditionality contemplated in the US Secretary Baker Plan.[1]

The chapters making up this volume try to incorporate some forward-looking elements into the debt crisis discussion. When we contacted the prospective authors we pointed out that we wanted them to frame their specific papers within the following broad question, "What are Latin America's prospects for growth and development, once the most immediate aspects of the crisis are solved?" This preoccupation about the future was in fact reflected in the title of the conference held in Vina del Mar (Chile) in December 1987: 'The Aftermath of the Debt Crisis: Latin America's Prospects for Growth and Development'. Naturally, it is possible to discuss the future in a meaningful way only if we understand the lessons from similar historical experiences, and if we know what are the initial conditions. For this reason we asked Barry Eichengreen to write an historical chapter dealing with the debt crisis in the 1930s, and we took it as our own responsibility to provide a general account on where the region stood in late 1987. We also asked William Cline to write a chapter on medium-term prospects.

How successful were we in our effort to incorporate a forward-looking perspective into the debt crisis discussion? While the volume as a whole has a forward-looking flavor, many of the chapters focused on shorter- and medium-term issues. This vividly reflects how important – and in fact how unresolved – is the debate on the causes of the debt crisis, and on the immediate strategies to be followed.

The purpose of this first introductory chapter is two fold. First, we provide a general framework that will be helpful when reading the chapters that follow. This framework is presented in sections 2 through 4: in section 2 we discuss the origins of the crisis; in section 3 we analyze the main characteristics of the adjustment path followed during the first five years; and in section 4 we discuss some of the medium-term solutions currently debated. The second purpose of this chapter is to provide a brief reader's guide to the volume. This is done in section 5.

2 The Origins of the Crisis

The adverse external conditions faced by Latin America in the early 1980s, coupled with some serious economic mismanagement, detonated a crisis of vast proportions. In this section we briefly discuss the contribution of each of these factors to such a disastrous outcome.

External shocks

The increase in world real interest rates in the early 1980s proved to be a major shock to Latin American nations, since most foreign debt (65 percent on average) had been contracted at variable rates. The deterioration of the terms of trade for most of the region's countries constituted the second major external shock. To get an idea of the magnitude of the external shocks, we can compute the relevant real interest rate faced by the Latin American countries as the nominal London Interbank Offer Rate (LIBOR) deflated by the rate of change of an index of the region's export prices. This variable combines in one indicator the effects of both the higher nominal interest rates and the lower commodity export prices. After being negative during most of the 1970s, with an average of −3.4 percent for the decade, this real rate climbed to 19.9 percent in 1981, 27.5 percent in 1982 and 17.4 percent in 1983 (Bianchi et al., 1987). As a result, even those countries with a large percentage of their debt contracted at fixed interest rates – such as Colombia and Peru – experienced significant increases in their debt burden. In fact, Bianchi et al. (1987) have estimated that the deterioration of nonoil export prices and the surge in world interest rates account for almost 50 percent of the increase in Latin America's current account deficit during 1981 and 1982.

The sudden halt in foreign lending coincided with a sharp decline in the flows of foreign investment to the region. Total net capital inflows to Latin America, which reached an all-time high of $37.5 billion in 1981, declined to $20 billion in 1982 and $3.2 billion in 1983; a drop of over 90 percent in two years!

Domestic policies

The inconsistency of domestic policies also played an important role in the generation of the debt crisis. Although the conditions varied from country to country, it is possible to say that at a broad level internal responsibility for this development should principally be placed on exchange rate policies and on broadly defined fiscal policies.[2]

Exchange rate policies The adoption of inappropriate exchange rate policies constitutes one of the most important domestic causes of the crisis.[3] Most of the countries that eventually experienced payments difficulties allowed their currencies to become highly overvalued during the late 1970s and early 1980s. The countries of the Southern Cone of Latin America provide a primary example of inadequate exchange rate policies. In Chile, for example, after a brief experience with a passive crawling peg, the peso was fixed to the US dollar in June 1979. At the same time wages were indexed to past inflation and capital controls were relaxed. As a result, the real exchange rate appreciated by more than 30 percent between 1979 and mid-1982, provoking a major deprotection of the domestic tradables sector and a gigantic current account deficit that exceeded 14 percent of GDP in 1981 (Edwards and Cox-Edwards, 1987). Argentina and Uruguay also adopted a declining pre-announced rate of devaluation (*la tablita*), as a way to reduce inflation (Corbo, de Melo and Tybout, 1986; Larraín, 1988). However, contrary to the case of Chile, in these countries the predetermined rate of devaluation was clearly inconsistent with the magnitude of the fiscal deficit. This resulted not only in a substantial real appreciation, but also in a steady loss of credibility in the sustainability of the stabilization and liberalization programs, and in major capital flight.

In Mexico, the combination of a highly expansive fiscal policy with a quasi-fixed nominal exchange rate provoked a real appreciation that exceeded 40 percent between 1976 and February of 1982 – this in spite of the almost 80 percent nominal devaluation of the Mexican peso that took place in 1976–7. In effect, by 1981 the real value of the peso was already below its 1976 level; in less than 5 years more than 100 percent of the real effect of the devaluation had been fully eroded. This case is particularly interesting since it clearly illustrates the difficulties that developing nations have faced many times when trying to engineer a real devaluation (Edwards, 1987a).

Not in every country of the region, however, was the exchange rate policy inadequate. In Colombia, for example, the adoption of an active exchange rate management characterized by a crawling peg was an important component in an overall strategy aimed at reducing the effects of world economic fluctuations. Colombia's pragmatic exchange rate regime allowed the country to avoid the deprotection effects of the coffee boom of 1975–9 and to maintain a reasonable macroeconomic equilibrium.

The tendency towards overvaluation observed in a large number of countries had two devastating macroeconomic effects in Latin America: it fueled massive capital flight and gave an additional push to the region's current account deficit.

In terms of capital flight, the magnitudes differ from country to country. However, in most cases after it became increasingly clear that the overvaluation was unsustainable in the medium run, private agents began to speculate against the local currency and moved a sizeable portion of their assets abroad. Even if it is impossible to find direct measures of capital flight, there are indirect ways of obtaining them. Table 1.2 presens a set of estimates based on the unexplained portions of the balance of payments.[4] It is indeed remarkable that this indicator of capital flight accounts for over 100 percent of the increase in Venezuelan external debt from 1976 to 1985. In fact, this implies that domestic residents channeled abroad all of the

Table 1.2   Capital flight out of Latin America ($b and %)

	Capital flight			Capital flight /
	1976–82	1983–85	Total 1976–85	Change in external debt
Argentina	27	–1	26	62.7
Brazil	3	7	10	12.0
Chile	0	1	1	6.4
Mexico	36	17	53	64.8
Peru	–1	1	0	0.0
Venezuela	25	6	31	101.3

Sources: *World Financial Markets* (1986), ECLA (1986) and World Bank tables

incremental foreign debt and a portion of their previous wealth stock. In Argentina and Mexico, capital flight explains over 60 percent of the increase in their external indebtedness, while in Brazil, Chile and Peru the importance of capital flight seems to have been low or negligible.

An empirical study by Cuddington (1986) has shown a significant relation between overvaluation and capital flight. In this respect there is an important contrast between Latin American and East Asian economies. In Korea, a country that by and large avoided the temptation of supporting an overvalued currency, the accumulated capital flight between 1976 and 1985 was negative. The only Asian nation which experienced significant capital flight during this period was the Philippines.

In some countries, such as Argentina and Chile, the overvaluation cast doubt on the continuity of the overall development strategy based on liberalization and open markets. However, in contrast with the rest of Latin America, in Chile the problem was not capital flight, but rather an unsustainable current account deficit due to private sector overspending, at a time when the public sector was running a surplus. The external deficit was partially due to the expectations of devaluation and of tariff increases (both of which turned out to be correct) that induced private agents to acquire record quantities of imported durables. (Dornbusch, 1985; Edwards and Cox-Edwards, 1987).

Fiscal policies   Except for Chile and Venezuela, all major debtors of the region experienced substantial fiscal deficits during the late 1970s. Although comparable consolidated public sector data are extremely hard to find – or even nonexistent – available information gives a broad picture of the importance of fiscal deficits for a number of countries during this period, most notably for the biggest debtors of the region: Argentina, Brazil and Mexico.[5]

In Brazil, for example, the increased reliance on external credits stemmed from a deliberate development strategy adopted after the 1973 oil shock. This policy was based on the accomplishment of major public sector investment projects throughout the economy (on the export, import substituting and service sectors) which needed to be financed from abroad.

Mexico witnessed the populist policies of the Echeverria and Lopez-Portillo administrations, with a spectacular growth in the public sector and the fiscal deficit lying behind the crisis. Part of this surge is explained by heavy investment in the oil sector, based on overly optimistic expectations about future oil prices. In Argentina, public sector deficits in the 1970s and early 1980s were principally the result of high and increasing inflation rates (via the Tanzi effect), of growing deficits in public sector enterprises and of a surge in defense spending, especially during the Falklands/Malvinas war.

What is perhaps surprising is that both oil importers and oil exporters, facing radically different external conditions, followed expansionary fiscal policies. Larraín and Selowsky (1988) have suggested that this could be labeled the "best expectations approach". Oil importing countries opted for external financing, rather than for adjustment, because they probably considered the terms of trade shock as being of a transitory nature. Oil exporters viewed it more as a permanent phenomenon, and decided to act according to their perceived higher level of wealth. Thus most countries in both groups ended up with higher public sector deficits, which were in turn translated into larger current account deficits.

3 The Adjustment Process: 1982–6

The brutal drying-up of external finance for Latin America as a whole that followed Mexico's suspension of debt service in 1982, provoked a desperate need for adjustment throughout the region. Even some countries, such as Colombia, which in no way faced payments problems, nor had serious macroeconomic disequilibria, nor had accumulated debt at a very fast pace, were affected by the reduction in foreign credits. This section will discuss the major adjustments in the external and domestic sectors of the indebted countries that were prompted by this abrupt shock.

Current account adjustment

The second half of 1982 marked a serious turning point in the financial relations between the industrial and developing nations. The reduction in capital flows to the developing countries was particularly severe for Latin America. While the average nonindustrialized country experienced a decline of about 40 percent in external financing between 1981 and 1983,

Table 1.3   Capital inflows and net transfer of resources to Latin America: 1976–86 ($b)

Year	Net capital inflows	Net interest payments	Net transfer of resources
1976	17.9	6.8	11.1
1977	17.2	8.2	9.0
1978	26.2	10.2	16.0
1979	29.1	13.6	15.5
1980	29.4	17.9	11.5
1981	37.5	27.1	10.4
1982	20.0	38.7	−18.7
1983	3.2	34.3	−31.2
1984	9.2	36.2	−27.0
1985	2.4	35.3	−32.9
1986	8.6	30.7	−22.1
Total 1976–81	157.3	83.8	73.5
Total 1982–86	43.4	175.2	−131.8

Source: ECLA (1986)

the average Latin American country witnessed approximately a 90 percent drop in net capital inflows during the same period. Table 1.3 presents data on the flows of resources to the region between 1976 and 1986. After having experienced significantly positive net transfers throughout 1981, Latin America has been consistently a net exporter of funds to the rest of the world since 1982. In fact, the accumulated net transfer between 1976 and 1981 amounted to $73.5 billion while its counterpart for the period 1982–6 was in the order of US$−131.8 billion.

Such a dramatic change in the availability of foreign resources forced Latin America to rapidly reduce its current account deficit, which was larger than $40 billion by 1982. By 1984 the deficit was reduced to a mere $0.2 billion. The speed and magnitude of this change were more significant than in the rest of the highly indebted developing countries.

This major adjustment in the external accounts was achieved through an unprecedented reversal in the trade balance, which went from an aggregate deficit of $2 billion in 1981 to a surplus of $40 billion in 1984. However, after reaching this high positive level, the trade balance has experienced a steady decline until 1986 when it stood at $18 billion. Preliminary information for 1987 indicated that in that year an improvement in this account was accomplished, with the trade surplus reaching $23 billion, still substantially below the level achieved in 1984. The region's inability to sustain a high trade surplus has been principally due to two sets of factors: (1) the negative impact on oil exporters (Ecuador, Mexico and Venezuela) of the sharp decline in oil prices; and (2) the large increases in aggregate demand in some countries, Brazil and Peru being the primary example.

It is worth noticing that the rapid improvement in the current account was mainly achieved by a drastic compression of imports. Indeed, regional imports decreased by almost $40 billion between 1981 and 1986, while the trade balance improved by slightly over $20 billion during the same period. On the other hand, the nominal dollar value of Latin American exports was lower in 1986 than in 1980, the magnitude of this decline reaching almost 13 percent. This drop was basically the result of a fall in the prices of the region's exports of almost 30 percent between 1980 and 1986. In fact, the deterioration of the terms of trade was so severe that the value of exports went down in spite of more than 25 percent increase in the amount of exports during the same period.

Despite these major adjustment efforts, the trade surpluses have not been large enough to meet the interest bill of the region. In 1986, domestically generated foreign resources could not cover even half the interest service, most dramatically in Peru and Venezuela.[6] In 1987 the situation has somehow improved for oil exporters, with Mexico having been additionally helped by a spectacular increase in nontraditional exports. On the other hand, although Chile has benefitted from a recent increase in copper prices, it is still unable to cover half its interest bill with domestically generated resources.

Inflationary adjustment and public sector deficits

The large Latin American debtors can be divided, for analytical purposes, into two groups: those that carried out an inflationary adjustment (Argentina, Brazil, Mexico and Peru – ABMP for short) and those which adopted non-inflationary paths (Colombia, Chile and Venezuela – CCV). As table 1.4 indicates, all the countries that adopted an inflationary adjustment had public sector deficits in the neighborhood of 10 percent of GDP during most of the period 1981–6. This contrasts with the significantly lower fiscal deficits of the CCV group, particularly those of Chile and Venezuela.

The relation between the public deficit and inflation in Latin America has been extensively documented. What is more interesting is the effect that the recent debt crisis has had on fiscal budgets. It is somehow surprising that relatively little has been written on this subject, especially considering the vast amount of literature that has advocated long-term structural reforms as a way to solve the debt problem.[7]

The debt crisis has caused the region's government budgets to deteriorate in several ways. The most important one has been the increase in the

Table 1.4 Inflation and public sector deficits in Latin America (% of GDP)

	1980	1981	1982	1983	1984	1985	1986	1987
Inflationary Adjustments								
Argentina								
Inflation	87.6	131.2	209.7	433.7	688.0	385.4	81.9	178.3
(PSD/GDP)	8.5	14.5	16.0	17.3	11.5	7.0	5.9	4.6
Brazil								
Inflation	95.3	91.2	97.9	172.8	203.3	228.0	58.6	396.0
(PSD/GDP)	12.2	3.9	5.9	5.6	6.9	12.1	n.a.	n.a.
Mexico								
Inflation	29.8	28.7	98.8	80.8	59.2	63.7	105.7	143.6
(PSD/GDP)	7.9	14.7	17.7	8.8	9.0	10.5	16.4	16.6
Peru								
Inflation	59.7	72.7	72.9	125.1	111.5	158.3	62.9	104.8
(PSD/GDP)	4.7	8.4	9.3	12.1	7.6	3.0	6.0	n.a.
Noninflationary Adjustments								
Colombia								
Inflation	26.5	27.5	24.1	16.5	18.3	22.3	21.0	24.7
(PSD/GDP)	2.5	3.3	7.6	7.5	6.3	3.5	–0.6	2.5
Chile								
Inflation	31.2	9.5	20.7	23.6	23.0	26.4	17.4	22.9
(PSD/GDP)	–5.4	–0.8	3.4	3.0	4.3	2.6	1.8	0.8
Venezuela								
Inflation	19.6	11.0	7.3	7.0	18.3	5.7	12.3	36.1
(PSD/GDP)	–0.6	0.3	10.4	3.5	–4.8	–3.3	6.1	n.a.

n.a. not available
Sources: World Development Report (1987); ECLA (1987); and Barandiarán
       (1988)

interest bill on foreign obligations, due both to the rise in international
interest rates and to the sharp real devaluations that have increased the
domestic cost of obtaining foreign exchange. This has forced many governments either to implement relief measures to private sector debtors (such
as preferential exchange rates) or to directly bail out private sector obligations. The increase in interest payments on domestic debt has also
contributed to the deterioration of the fiscal position of these countries.
This increase has been the result of both higher inflation rates and the
increase in domestic real interest rates generated by restrictive aggregate
demand policies. The last effect has been particularly important in Mexico,
which has a significant stock of outstanding domestic debt. Furthermore, in
some countries public revenues were significantly hurt by the slowdown in
output that followed the debt crisis. Overall, the combined effect of all

these factors was a sharp increase in public sector deficits in many countries of the region.

In countries like Argentina, Mexico and Peru, the external interest bill accounts for approximately 20 percent of public spending. Naturally, it is very difficult to stabilize the economy if such a large proportion of government resources is precommitted to paying interest on public debt. A case in point is Bolivia, which pursued a successful stabilization that reduced inflation from an annual rate close to 50,000 percent in 1985 to almost 10 percent in 1987. A prerequisite for this achievement was the Bolivian decision to suspend commercial debt service. Since the payment of interest on bank debts would have absorbed about 50 percent of the government budget, it would have been impossible to stabilize while at the same time meeting this obligation (Sachs, 1987).

In spite of all these obstacles, the Latin American governments have still managed to engineer substantial cuts in spending. According to a recent study at ECLA (1986), following the crisis government spending was cut by more than 20 percent in real terms in Argentina, Ecuador, Mexico, Uruguay and Venezuela. Most of these cuts were concentrated on public investment and public sector wages. In the countries of the ABMP group, however, these reductions were insufficient to avoid the budget deterioration. Some of these governments also increased taxation on exports and raised the price of public enterprise goods and services. However, these measures brought about strong opposition and some of them have already been reversed. Given these difficulties, the only alternative left to these governments was to close the fiscal gap by relying on inflationary finance.

As pointed out above, the countries of the CCV group did not carry out an inflationary adjustment. Chile was able to avoid inflationary pressures mostly because its public sector had already gone through a major adjustment process; at the outbreak of the crisis the Chilean fiscal accounts were in surplus. Venezuela also faced the debt shock with a public sector surplus generated mainly by devaluation of the bolivar. Finally, Colombia did not experience a substantial deterioration in its fiscal position.

Overall, then, even though the need is clear to adjust the public sector in Argentina, Brazil and Peru further, it is also clear that with little foreign finance available, this is likely to be a long and painful process. In the meantime, these countries will face a difficult dilemma as the full compliance of foreign obligations will undermine macroeconomic and political stability at home.

Interest rates, exchange rates and real wages

In several countries the adjustment also relied on higher real interest rates that helped to keep expenditure, and in particular investment, in check. It should be noted, however, that in some cases the rise in real interest rates began some time before the "official" unleashing of the debt crisis in August of 1982. For example, in the countries of the Southern Cone real interest rates started to climb rapidly in mid-1981 as these economies became clearly overheated; these higher interest rates were in fact an indicator of the proximity of the required adjustment. In Argentina the annual real lending rate reached as much as 19.3 percent in 1981, a rate significantly higher than the average of 1.5 percent prevailing during 1978–80. In 1982 and 1983, when the effects of the debt crisis *per se* were reflected, the real lending interest rates remained high (around 12 percent per annum) but were below the level attained in 1981. Chile presents a similar picture: in 1981 the annual real interest rate reached 58.1 percent, a much higher rate than the average of the previous two years (8.5 percent). During 1982 and 1983 the real lending rate also declined, but only to reach the still remarkable level of 16 percent per annum. Most of these experiences with persistently high real interest rates ended up in financial crises (Díaz Alejandro, 1985; Edwards and Cox-Edwards 1987; Larraín (1988)).

Another characteristic of the adjustment to the debt crisis was the reliance, in most countries, on some expenditure switching policies. These policies consisted in most cases of a combination of nominal devaluations and, at least initially, a major escalation in the degree of trade restrictions. The extent of the devaluations varied from country to country. Moreover, as a way to avoid the erosion of the effects of the nominal devaluations on the real exchange rate, most countries adopted some kind of active exchange rate management where the exchange rate continued to be adjusted after the initial parity change.

The adoption of multiple exchange rates was also an important feature of the exchange rate policy followed by many countries. This basically served three purposes. First, by implementing differential exchange rates for capital and current account transactions – as in Venezuela – the authorities hoped to separate real transactions from the presumably extreme volatility of capital movements. More importantly, however, by imposing a free floating exchange rate on unregistered capital flows, these countries' authorities tried to discourage capital flight without greatly affecting the current acount. Second, multiple rates were also applied as a way to supplement the protective system, as in the cases of Mexico and Venezuela. Third, in some countries – such as Mexico, Chile and Venezuela – a lower "preferential" exchange rate was applied to the repayment of the private sector foreign debt, as a way of avoiding the generalized bankruptcy of these heavily indebted agents.

The devaluation component of the adjustment packages in some cases more than corrected the real exchange rate overvaluation that preceded the crisis. As a result of these large nominal devaluations most countries experienced important increases in their price levels. As noted above, in an effort to avoid the eroding effects of these price increases these countries' authorities decided to resort to further devaluations as a means of maintaining a high real exchange rate. Naturally, this practice added fuel to the already accelerated rate of inflation.

In an attempt to compensate workers for the price increases in public firms' goods and services and for the effects of devaluation, some countries designed policies to hold – and even increase – the real wage rate. The most notable example of the policy was Argentina during the final year of the military dictatorship and the first 18 months of the Alfonsin government. More recently, the Cruzado Plan prompted a substantial real wage rate increase in Brazil that proved to be unsustainable later on and had to be corrected by early 1987. Sooner or later, however, wage restraint had become an important component of the adjustment package of the region. In fact, as table 1.5 shows, with the exception of Argentina, Brazil and Colombia, the decline in real wages throughout Latin America after 1981 has been significant.

Output effects of the adjustment

The significant costs of the adjustment are reflected by the consecutive decrease in Latin America's GDP in 1982 and 1983. Moreover, by the end of 1987 only two of the major debtor countries – Brazil and Colombia – had achieved levels of per capita income higher than the ones prevailing at the beginning of the decade, while Argentina and Uruguay were worse off than in 1970 (see table 1.5).

On the other hand, the decline in aggregate spending brought about by the crisis was unevenly distributed between consumption and investment within the region. In Chile and Peru the bulk of the adjustment fell on consumption, while in Argentina, Brazil, Venezuela and in Mexico it was centered on the reduction of investment (Barandiaran, 1988). Furthermore, most of the reduction, both in investment and consumption, was borne by the private sector.

The drop in disposable income also had an important effect on the level of savings throughout the region. Except for Brazil and Mexico, Latin American countries have experienced sharp drops in national savings. Given the critical role of the savings constraint on investment and the obstacles for increasing foreign savings from their current levels, most of the additional effort to finance domestic capital accumulation will have to come from national savings. If these do not increase, the evolution of investment will continue to be sluggish. Indeed, with the exception of

Introduction

Table 1.5 Real GDP per capita (1970=100) and real wages (1980=100) in selected Latin American countries

Country	1970	1975	1980	1981	1982	1983	1984	1985	1986	1987
Argentina										
GDP	100	105.9	100.7	99.2	92.6	93.9	94.3	88.7	92.2	92.8
wages			100.0	89.4	80.1	100.5	127.1	107.8	109.5	100.3
Brazil										
GDP	100	145.1	179.5	172.8	170.4	161.5	165.0	174.7	184.7	186.0
wages			100.0	104.7	107.2	94.0	96.7	118.9	149.8	142.0
Colombia										
GDP	100	118.2	137.9	138.0	136.4	134.7	136.1	136.6	140.7	145.1
wages			100.0	101.4	104.8	110.3	118.5	114.9	120.2	121.9
Chile										
GDP	100	81.8	109.1	113.4	95.8	93.6	98.1	98.8	101.9	105.6
wages			100.0	108.9	108.6	97.1	97.2	93.5	95.1	93.7
Mexico										
GDP	100	116.8	139.8	146.8	142.3	131.3	132.4	132.6	124.3	122.8
wages			100.0	103.5	104.4	80.7	75.4	76.6	72.3	72.8
Peru										
GDP	100	108.9	104.7	105.9	103.6	89.9	91.8	90.9	96.2	100.5
wages			100.0	98.3	100.5	83.7	70.1	59.6	75.5	80.6
Uruguay										
GDP	100	106.5	105.7	102.3	100.0	91.8	88.3	83.7	82.9	87.0
wages			100.0	107.5	107.1	84.9	77.1	88.1	94.0	97.5

n.a. not available
Sources: ECLA (1987) and Barandiaran (1988)

Brazil and Colombia, investment rates have declined strongly in Latin America in recent years. If this situation is not reversed, the costs in terms of future income of the current adjustment process will be overwhelming.

4 Debt Strategies and Adjustment with Growth

The annual net transfer of resources from the region averaged 4.2 percent of GDP between 1982 and 1985; this was almost double the war reparations that Germany had to pay to the Allied countries after World War I (Bianchi et al., 1987). In spite of this staggering effort the region's trade surplus covered only half of the interest bills due during 1986. Up to now this financing gap has had to be closed, year after year, with resources provided by the multilateral institutions and (reluctantly) by the creditor banks. However, the latter have provided debt relief only in the form of lower spreads and fees, and through the extension of repayment periods for the principal.

In this context, commercial banks have relied on the policing activities of the multilateral institutions – in particular of the IMF – to assess whether a particular country is making a "sufficient" effort to adjust and is thus eligible to obtain new funds. It is interesting to note that the IMF has shown a significant degree of flexibility in monitoring these programs. Indeed, it is possible to argue that the IMF-sponsored programs have been somewhat unconventional after the debt crisis (Edwards, 1987b). Contrary to historical experience, these have been stabilization programs with acceleration in monetary expansion, persistently high fiscal deficits that have largely exceeded the levels that prevailed before the crisis, and very high inflation rates.

Overall, the debt strategy followed since the beginning of the crisis has permitted the generation of large trade surpluses, but so far has failed to promote sustained growth and, thus to offer a long-term solution to the debt problem. In particular, the uncertainty implicit in the yearly negotiations by which the countries have been obtaining additional financing have damaged future growth prospects. Until now, the banks have not made a long-term commitment to provide additional resources to support sustained growth in the region.

The dim prospects of the debt problem forced a reorientation of the global strategy. In October 1985 US Secretary James Baker proposed a plan to increase the availability of resources for those debtor countries willing to pursue long-term structural adjustment programs. From the outset, many analysts pointed out that the additional financing offered by the plan was not enough to achieve the desired objectives.

The growing perception that the Baker Plan was not working gave way to two major developments during 1987. On the one hand, there was a substantial increase in the number of countries in the region which partially or totally suspended the service of their foreign debt. This group includes Bolivia, Brazil, Costa Rica, Cuba, Ecuador, Honduras, Nicaragua and Peru. On the other hand, the commercial banks, following Citibank's lead, increased their loan-loss provisions, recognizing that their credits were not worth 100 percent of par value.

These two developments activated significantly the secondary markets for Latin American debt and increased the discounts at which debt was traded. In fact, total transactions on these secondary markets were around $12 billion between 1982 and 1986, with 42 percent of the total being traded in 1986. Also, preliminary data indicate a volume of transactions of approximately $15 billion for 1987. Although these markets are still thin compared to a foreign debt that exceeds $350 billion for Latin America, it is to be expected that they will continue to grow in the near future.

Another characteristic of the current environment has been the difficulties in completing previously agreed financial packages for the debtors. This has been a consequence of the recent practice by large banks of provisioning a fraction of the new money directed to the region; in this way the financial results of commercial banks have become negatively affected by new loans to Latin America. Additionally, the participation of banks with a smaller exposure to these countries has been increasingly difficult to obtain. In general, the well-known free rider problem has prevailed, in the sense that, although it may be in the best interest of the foreign creditors as a group to provide new financing that can keep a debtor "alive", each one of them has decided to curtail its contribution.[8]

Within this context some interesting new features in the rescheduling agreements of three Latin American debtors emerged in 1987. For example, Mexico's financial package contained some contingency clauses. According to these, the banks were willing to provide additional funds of $1.2 billion if an oil price deterioration created a foreign exchange shortage for the country, and an additional $500 million if the growth rate of the economy failed to reach the 3–4 percent range set as a target by the Mexican authorities. (Barandiarán, 1988; Cline, 1987).

Chile's financial package, signed in June, included the repricing of old loans and a retiming of interest payments. The latter clause implied that interest payments would have to be made every 360 days instead of biannually, as was established before. This was a way of providing new money for the country in a nontraditional form.

Finally, in the Argentinian package of August 1987 new funds were granted both through the repricing of old debt and through shared lending schemes. In order to provide an alternative for banks with a low exposure, the agreement included the option of an "exit bond" for creditors willing to convert a maximum of $5 million of their loans. This bond was not subject to future restructuring and granted a 4 percent interest for 25 years, with 12 years of grace. It was accepted by only two small banks.

Of all the innovations outlined above, the contingency clauses are the most interesting. However, until early 1988 they have not been extended to other agreements different from that of Mexico. The relatively better treatment received by Mexico is probably explained by the intense US pressures in support of this country. On the other hand the Brazilian suspension of interest payments in February 1987 generated expectations of a generalized suspension of payments from all the other debtors of the region and negatively affected the willingness of the banks to include contingency clauses in debt negotiations.

Contigent financing is, however, an efficient way of reducing uncertainty in highly indebted countries and sharing risks between creditors and debtors. In particular, by linking financial obligations to the evolution of the external interest rate – the variable to which highly indebted countries are more vulnerable – the commercial banks can provide significant relief to Latin American debtors. It is interesting to note also that the indebted countries can use the existing futures markets to hedge their interest payments. During 1988, for example, Chile and Mexico have used this mechanism.

Proposed solutions

No consensus has yet been reached on a new and global approach to the debt problem, and the range of views in this respect is quite broad. There are essentially two different positions on this subject. Some analysts think that the current debt strategy is basically sound, but needs to mobilize additional financing to the debtors. Others consider that debt reduction – either in the form of relief on interest payments or on the principal – is an essential component of a long-run solution.

Among the former group stands Feldstein (1987), who has said "the world has been muddling through the Latin American debt problem with reasonable success for nearly five years now" (p. 21). Although he recognizes the importance of increasing foreign finance for debtor countries, his principal conclusion is that countries can grow out of the debt problem and that it will become more manageable as time goes by. Not surprisingly, the banking community can also by included in this group, although they certainly want to shift the burden of providing new financing to the multilateral and other official institutions. According to their view, "realism demands an increased share of new money be furnished by official sources during the next several years" (Morgan Guaranty, 1987, p. 2).

William Cline (1987) is another prominent representative of the "muddling through" strategy. He has recently argued that "the international community has achieved considerable success in managing the debt crisis since its outbreak in 1982," (p. 1) but still recognizes the need to channel additional resources to debtor countries. He has also stressed the need to provide a wider menu of options for banks to mobilize funds to highly indebted countries, following the idea laid out by US Secretary Baker. His proposal hinges on two basic principles: first, to grant preferred status for new loans, which should ideally take the form of bonds in order to be securitized instruments; and, second, to offer a wider variety of ways in which banks could participate in new credits, so that each financial institution could find some kind of "tailor-made" solution for its own needs.

However, the lengthy and protracted nature of debt negotiations and the many uncertainties surrounding them, together with the unstable macro-economic scenarios of most debtor countries and the failure of the current debt strategy to promote sustained growth have led other groups of analysts to search for alternative solutions. These proposals amount, in one way or another, to some form of debt reduction.

As can be expected, banks have in general been quite reluctant to provide debt relief on an international scale, even though they have adopted this type of measure at a domestic level (Morgan Guaranty, 1987, pp. 5–6). Whether banks are simply reluctant to bear the losses implied by the relief, or whether they cannot afford to, is an important issue. There is little doubt that banks are now in a much stronger position than in 1982. When loans are measured as a proportion of the capital base, the exposure of US banks to Latin America has decreased from almost 120 percent in 1982 to 68 percent in late 1986 (Sachs and Huizinga, 1987). This has been due not only to an important rise in the capital of the banks, but also to a sharp decline in their new loans to the region. Furthermore, the banks were able to cope with the increased provisions of Citibank and other major banks in the second quarter of 1987 – which raised loan-loss reserves to 25 percent of developing country debt – without provoking a financial crisis.[9]

In general, banks might be unwilling to provide debt relief in forms other than lower spreads and longer repayment periods. However, the discounts that have prevailed for some time now in the debt secondary markets suggest that they have anticipated that some kind of relief will indeed take place. Moreover, the fact that interest payments continue to be accrued at 100 percent of the nominal value of the loans, while the secondary market price of the region's debt is below 50 percent on average constitutes a serious problem. The issue is, then, how to translate these discounts into a scheme that benefits the debtor countries directly. Three types of alternatives are available in this respect.

1   *A global strategy.* The establishment of an international financial institution which could purchase, at some discounted value, the loans of commercial banks to highly indebted countries is a possibility that has been discussed for some time. The facility has been suggested as a negotiated process between creditor banks and this institution, for which the price of debt on secondary markets can be a useful reference point. Under this proposal, the international institution would give its own bonds in exchange for the loans. The discount would be reflected either in a lower nominal value of the bonds relative to the debt – valued at market interest rates – or in a return on the bonds lower than the market rate maintaining the nominal value of the debt. This change from bank debt to bonds can make the new instrument attractive to a broad range of investors. This proposal amounts to a global solution to the debt problem, which is beyond the range of options of individual countries and involves a number of

unresolved operational issues. Among these the most important are, determining the proportion of each country's debt that will be subject to this scheme, and designing the appropriate system of incentives to avoid the generation of a typical "moral hazard" problem.

2 *A direct, case-by-case mechanism.* The second alternative is a direct negotiation between each debtor country and its foreign creditors, either to repurchase its own debt or to convert the debt in bonds – in both cases at a discount. The former strategy is currently being pursued by Bolivia, who has obtained transfers from foreign governments for this purpose. The discount at which Bolivia has made these purchases is close to the one that prevailed on the secondary market, i.e., around 90 percent. Such buyback strategy is likely to work only for those small debtors which – as Bolivia – have been subject to drastically adverse conditions, and for whom the renewal of debt service is unlikely in the foreseeable future.

The second strategy – the conversion of debt into bonds – has been attempted by Brazil. In September 1987 the Brazilian authorities offered to convert half of their $68 billion stock of bank loans into 35-year bonds yielding a 6 percent fixed interest rate per year. This was equivalent to a discount of almost 50 percent on the nominal value of their debt. The proposal did not materialize, but the doors do not seem to be closed for a mechanism of this sort. The crucial point, apparently, is the size of the discount that the bonds will carry in relation to the debt. The Mexican attempt in early 1988 to exchange existing debt for bonds guaranteed by the Federal Reserve is another innovative attempt that was not received with much enthusiasm by the international financial community.

3 *The use of secondary markets.* The growing importance of secondary markets for Latin American debt has led some countries in the region to implement mechanisms – widely known as debt swaps – by which old liabilities are exchanged by new ones at a discount. Not all debt swaps, however, amount to a reduction in the stock of foreign debt. For instance, the so called debt-debt swaps are just an exchange of loans between foreign creditors. Only debt-equity swaps and debt repurchases have the effect of reducing a country's external debt.

Debt-equity swaps convert a foreign loan into domestic equity of the debtor country. Although the country's external debt is reduced, this operation amounts to a replacement of one type of obligation for another, and does not necessarily imply a reduction in the present value of foreign liabilities. This replacement involves benefits and costs for the debtor country, and the net balance between them will generally depend on the specific operation being considered. A critical issue is, how much of the secondary market discount is captured by the debtor country. A domestic distributional issue is also present; if the government is the major debtor and a large fraction of the discount is captured by the private sector, there will still remain the difficult problem of transferring resources from private agents to the public sector.

The main benefits of debt-equity swaps for the debtor country are: (1) if new foreign investments face restrictions on profit and capital repatriation initially, the outflow of financial services will be temporarily reduced; (2) profit repatriation normally bears more relation to the country's economic activity than interest payments. Notice, however, that profit repatriation tends to be less procyclical than total profits, due to the behaviour of reinvested earnings; (3) new investments may help to increase capital formation in the host country. This will not be the case if the operation implies just a change in the ownership of assets between residents and nonresidents.

However, debt-equity swaps normally impose costs to the debtor country: (1) there is substitution between investment with fresh resources and debt-equity conversions; (2) these transactions can generate inflationary pressures when the local debtor is the Central Bank and it redeems the debt in local currency, although this need not be the case if redemption is made using other financial instruments; and (3) similar pressures can occur in domestic interest rates if the local debtor issues bonds, uses its available liquidity or increases its demand for credit in order to redeem the foreign debt.

Debt repurchases, on the other hand, involve the exchange of debt for cash, either directly by the debtor or through an intermediary. The local debtor then uses existing assets or increases in domestic liabilities to redeem the foreign debt. In any event, the crucial issue is the provision of foreign exchange to carry out the operation. If access to the official reserves of the country for this pursose is denied, the dollars will normally be obtained through the parallel – or black – market. The major benefits of debt-repurchases are: (1) unlike the case of debt-equity deals, an official foreign liability is extinguished for the country, and (2) these operations may constitute a vehicle for the repatriation of offshore capital held by residents, who would ultimately provide the dollars required by the transaction.

The costs which the country can incur if this strategy is followed are higher domestic interest rates or increased inflation, which are qualitatively analogous to the costs involved in debt-equity conversions. Additionally, in those cases in which the foreign exchange is obtained in the parallel market, these operations could increase the spread between the official and parallel exchange rates. As a result, the well-known incentives for over-invoicing of imports, under-invoicing of exports and outright smuggling would take place, as well as the potentially destabilizing influences on expectations. However, if the rights to make these transactions are carefully regulated by the economic authorities, some of the undesired effects may be avoided.

Both types of operations have already been implemented in some countries of the region. Chile has so far established th most liberal schemes for debt conversion and debt repurchase. Argentina and Mexico have institutionalized mechanisms for debt–equity swaps. The extension in the use of these schemes will depend on the future evolution of the global debt strategy.

5   A Reader's Guide to the Volume

Chapters making up this volume can be classified into two broad groups. The first, consisting of chapters 2 through 6, deals with global problems and discusses cross-country issues; the second group – chapters 7 through 11 – analyzes in detail five country cases: Argentina, Brazil, Chile, Colombia, and Mexico. In this section we provide a brief reader's guide to the book, including a brief summary of each chapter.

Global issues

William Cline analyzes the medium-term prospects for the highly indebted Latin American nations. He starts by pointing out that when the relevant indicators are used it is possible to see that in the last few years there has been significant progress on the debt front. He points out that the weakest area corresponds to inflation, where little improvement has taken place since 1982. After reviewing different proposals based on providing (partial) relief, Cline argues that the advocates of those strategies have not demonstrated that the benefits of relief outweigh its costs in terms of long-run loss of reputation. He further argues that from a cash flow perspective relief is equivalent to bank refinancing.

Cline also discusses issues related to conditionality and to the use of secondary markets. Towards the end of his chapter, he acknowledges that there are a number of nonviable and insolvent (very poor) countries for which debt relief or forgiveness may be the only solution. In sum, the overall tone of Cline's chapter is one of optimism.

Only by understanding the lessons from history can we correctly evaluate the subtleties of the current crisis. In chapter 3 Barry Eichengreen investigates the history of the Latin American debt crisis of the 1930s. He starts by pointing out that there are important similarities between the 1930s and the current crisis. Then, as now, the intensity of the crisis was magnified by disarray in international financial markets. Also, in the 1930s there were basically two positions regarding the best strategy to follow. On the one hand there were those that favored a global solution; on the other, there were those that advocated a case-by-case approach. At the end global solutions were not implemented. One of Eichengreen's aims in this chapter is to analyze why global approaches were abandoned in the 1930s. A first crucial characteristic has to do with the nature of the debt. Then, contrary to the current case, the overwhelming majority of the Latin American debt was in the form of bonds. Eichengreen argues that this made negotiations extremely protracted and difficult. He describes in detail four global plans, underlining the stumbling blocks found by their proponents. He then looks at the case-by-case approach focusing on government to government negotiations as well as on negotiations between boldholder groups and the debtor countries. Eichengreen concludes that the history of the 1930s, and in particularly the failure to implement creative global solutions, carry important lessons for the 1980s and 1990s.

In chapter 4 Deepak Lal discusses possible modes of development over the longer run for Latin America. He begins by stating that a precondition for solving the crisis and resuming growth is that the countries in the region adopt a more *outward-oriented* development strategy that would rely on comparative advantages and on export growth. Why, Lal asks, has Latin America failed to adopt such a strategy early on? And, what is the probability of its moving in that direction in the future? The answers to these important questions lie in the realm of political economy. Lal develops a typology of state where he distinguishes between what he calls a "benevolent" state, a "predatory" state, and a "factional" state. From here he moves to develop an interpretation of the development strategies observed in the region. In doing this he focuses on income distribution consequences of different trade orientations. For this he uses three factors of production and multiple goods model of international trade. He argues that because of the abundance of natural resources, Latin America suffers a sort of embarrassment of riches. According to him Latin America's factor endowment implies that the pursuit of an outward oriented development strategy will result in a decline in (relative) wages. This, indeed, will generate serious political problems. He then discusses several possible ways to overcome these difficulties.

Chapter 5 deals with the role of the international economy in the future development prospects in Latin America. John Williamson focuses on the role of the international capital markets as a source of future funds for the region and on the role of international monetary arrangements. Williamson argues that the fact that Latin America was cut off from the international financial market in 1982 cannot be considered a sign of the failure of those markets. It was cut off because it was considered not to be creditworthy. Williamson argues that the return to voluntary lending will be slow.

The many new modes of financing developed after the crisis are mainly directed towards solving the current impasse, and will not have a major effect over the longer run. This means that in the future the region will have to rely more extensively on equity financing. According to him it is naive, however, to think that in the future banks will play no role in the process of intermediating funds to Latin America.

Williamson also argues that excessive exchange rate volatility among the currencies of industrial countries has generated a highly unstable global environment that has negatively affected the developing nations. He discusses in detail a number of scenarios and policies that could, in principle, reduce such global volatility, and he analyzes the ways in which such developments could help the Latin American nations.

Inflation has had a long and traumatic history in Latin America. There is generalized agreement that in the longer run any efforts to develop a strong economic environment in the region will require coming to grips with the inflationary problem. In chapter 6 Guillermo Calvo develops a model to analyze the important problem of controlling inflation in the presence of (domestic) public debt. In Calvo's model, if there is nominal debt the government is constantly tempted to use inflation as a means of reducing its outstanding liabilities. Calvo shows that in this setting there will be two equilibria: a high inflation equilibrium and a low inflation equilibrium. This multiple equilibria would be solved if instead of nominal debt the government issues indexed debt. An interesting implication of this is that, according to this model, it is not obvious that a de-indexation process, as followed in the recent heterodox stabilization programs in Argentina and Brazil, will help the anti-inflationary effort. Calvo then discusses alternatives to issuing indexed debt, including interest caps and price controls.

Country studies

Chapters 7 through 11 deal with five country studies. In chapter 7 Carlos Rodriguez analyzes the Argentinian case. He starts by developing a portfolio framework to analyze the origins of the crisis. He does this by tracing asset accumulation and decumulation in Argentina. He shows that net indebtedness amounted to only 25 percent of gross indebtedness. Rodriguez argues that this situation resulted from the fact that in the late 1970s different agents had different perceptions of the cost of credit and the future evolution of exchange rate policy. Rodriguez points out that since about one half of the debt was of government origin, any attempt to fully elucidate these issues should focus on government behavior, including that of public enterprises. Rodriguez then analyzes possible solutions. After weighing the pros and cons of a number of alternatives, he argues that any lasting solution should start by acknowledging that Argentina is not in a viable position to undertake the total payment of its foreign debt. He then discusses a number of possible scenarios that would lead to an improvement in the Argentinian situation.

In chapter 8 Juan A. Fontaine deals with the Chilean case. He analyzes the adjustment after 1983 and argues that the Chilean experience can be labeled as one of adjustment with growth; since 1984 real GDP has grown at an average annual rate of 4.8 percent. According to Fontaine this performance was aided by the adjustment packages implemented with the support of the IMF and the World Bank, and was helped by the implementation of fairly orthodox macroeconomic policies. The chapter includes a long and detailed discussion on the debt conversion schemes implemented by Chile since 1985. Fontaine's conclusion is that the Chilean case is a prime example of how far the "muddling through" approach can go.

In chapter 9 Jose Antonio Ocampo analyzes the Colombian experience. Colombia has been considered a rare example of a Latin American nation that in the late 1970s and early 1980s managed its economy soundly, without succumbing to the "temptations" of the easy monies provided by the international financial community. In this way, Colombia was the only large Latin American country that was not strongly hit by the debt crisis. Ocampo devotes this chapter to analyzing the evolution of the Colombian economy since the mid-1970s; he also provides an assessment of the prospects for growth until 1992. He pays particular attention to the macroeconomic and exchange rate policies pursued during the last 15 years or so. Ocampo argues that in spite of Colombia's prudent behavior it has not been spared from the negative effects of the debt crisis. Foreign funds have become increasingly difficult to obtain and when they are negotiated they are available at a relatively high cost. In fact, Ocampo argues, the prospects are not very rosy for the next few years; in one of his scenarios high repayments and the difficulty in obtaining truly "voluntary" funds can indeed result in a severe crisis.

In chapter 10 Francisco Gil-Diaz discusses the Mexican debt. His analysis focuses on two issues: first, he measures the current magnitude of the debt burden in Mexico. Second, he discusses future perspectives. An interesting aspect of Gil-Diaz's chapter is his analysis of Mexican debt problems during the 1930s. An important, indeed crucial, question that Gil-Diaz asks is why so many initiatives have had only partial success in Mexico. The answer to this, he argues, rests on the fact that as soon as any improvement is seen on the debt front the macro picture begins to show new signs of disequilibrium. He then discusses the prospects of Mexico regaining macroeconomic equilibrium and defeating inflation. Only to the extent that stabilization is indeed accomplished will Mexico's prospects for growth become brighter.

In the last chapter Eliana Cardoso and Rudiger Dornbusch analyze the Brazilian case. They begin by looking at the historical evidence, concentrating on the Brazilian debt crisis of 1889, and placing particular emphasis on the rescheduling process that began in 1898. This historical discussion focuses on Brazil's successful scheme implemented in 1943 to reduce the debt by exchanging existing bonds by new bonds with a lower face value. In analyzing the current debt crisis Cardoso and Dornbusch first go through the origins of the Brazilian crisis, pointing out the main differences between this case and the rest of the Latin American nations. They then argue that in the case of Brazil the so-called "muddling through" strategy has already failed and that the only realistic way to find a longer-term solution to the Brazilian debt problem is to recycle a large portion of the interest payments back into the country. One way of doing this would be to pay the bulk of the debt in domestic currency bonds. Creditor banks would then relend these funds (in cruzados) to the government.

NOTES

This is a revised version of a paper presented at the Conference "The Latin American External Debt: Perspectives and Solutions", Vina del Mar, Chile, December 14–15, 1987. Edwards gratefully acknowledges financial support from UCLA's Academic Senate and from the National Science Foundation.

1 There have been few attempts, however, to evaluate whether the design of these traditional policies, and in particular their speed and sequence, should be altered in the current context of significant macroeconomic disequilibria caused by the debt crisis. It is fair to say that, to a large extent, most of the literature on the debt crisis has concentrated on short- and medium-term issues.

2 Naturally, there were important differences across countries in the conduct of domestic policies. In what follows we try to draw a broad picture, making, when necessary, distinctions across countries.

3 This section draws partially on Edwards (1987b).

4 The estimates in table 1.2 cannot account for the over-invoicing of imports, the under-invoicing of exports and outright smuggling.

5 A recent World Bank project has put together a substantial set of public sector data for the most heavily indebted countries of Latin America in the period 1970–85 (Larraín and Selowsky, 1988).

6 Venezuela is the most oil-dependent country of the region; 90 percent of its exports proceeds come from oil.

7 Sachs (1987) and Edwards (1987b) are exceptions.

8 Mexico's financial package of March 1987 did provide the $3.5 billion initially agreed, but 139 creditor banks did not participate in the agreement and, thus, the

rest of the group had to put up more than their share. Moreover, some of the more innovative ideas, such as the Mexican bond of 1988, have generated a very timid response by the international financial community.

9 Ironically, stock prices of some banks increased after this move, implying that the markets had already discounted these losses.

REFERENCES

Balassa, B., Bueno, G. M., Kuczynski, P. P. and Simonsen, M. H. (1986), *Toward Renewed Economic Growth in Latin America*, Washington, DC: Institute for International Economics.

Barandiaran, E. (1988), "The Adjustment Process in Latin America's Highly Indebted Countries," mimeo, Washington, DC: World Bank, March.

Bianchi, A., Devlin, R. and Ramos, J. (1987), "The Adjustment Process in Latin America, 1981–1986," mimeo, Washington, DC: Symposium on Growth Oriented Adjustment Programs, February.

Cline, W. (1987), "Mobilizing Bank Lending to Developing Countries," *Policy Analyses in International Economics*, 18, Washington, DC: Institute for International Economics, June.

Corbo, V., de Melo, J. and Tybout, J. (1986), "What Went Wrong in the Southern Cone," *Economic Development and Cultural Change*, April.

Cuddington, J. (1986), *Capital Flight: Estimates, Issues and Explanations*, Princeton, NJ: Princeton Studies in International Finance.

Díaz-Alejandro, C. (1985), "Good Bye Financial Repression, Hello Financial Crash," *Journal of Development Economics*, January.

Dornbusch, R. (1985), "External Debt, Budget Deficits and Disequilibrium Exchange Rates," in G. Smith and J. Cuddington (eds.), *International Debt and the Developing Countries*, Washington, DC: World Bank.

ECLA (1986), *Balance Preliminar de la Economia Latinoamericana 1986*, Santiago, Chile.

ECLA (1987), *Balance Preliminar de la Economia Latinoamericana 1987*, Santiago, Chile, September.

Edwards, S. (1987a), "Exchange Rate Misalignment in Developing Countries," UCLA Working Paper N° 432.

Edwards, S. (1987b), "Structural Adjustment Policies in Highly Indebted Countries," mimeo, Washington, DC: Conference on Developing Countries Debt, September. Forthcoming in J. Sachs (ed.) conference volume.

Edwards, S. and Cox-Edwards, A. (1987), *Monetarism and Liberalization: The Chilean Experiment*, Cambridge, MA: Ballinger.

Feldstein, M. (1987), "Latin America's Debt. Muddling Through Can Be Just Fine," *The Economist*, June 27.

Krueger, A. O. (1987), "The Problems of LDC Debt," paper presented at the NBER Conference on the US in the World Economy, West Palm Beach.

Larraín, F. (1987), "Desarrollo Economico para Chile en Democracia," in F. Larraín (ed.) *Desarrollo Economico en Democracia. Proposiciones para una*

Sociedad Libre y Solidaria, Santiago, Chile: Ediciones Universidad Catolica de Chile, December.

Larraín, F. (1988), "La Reforma Financiera Uruguaya de los Setenta: de la Liberalizacion a la Crisis," *El Trimestre Económico*, July-September.

Larraín, F. and Selowsky, M. (1988), "Public Sector Behavior in Latin America's Biggest Debtors," mimeo, Washington, DC: World Bank, December.

Morgan Guaranty Trust Co. (1987), "LDC Debt Realities," *World Financial Markets*, June/July.

Sachs, J. (1987), "Trade and Exchange Rate Policies in Growth Oriented Adjustment Programs," Washington, DC: Symposium on Growth-Oriented Adjustment Programs, February.

Sachs, J. and Huizinga, H. (1987), "U.S. Commercial Banks and the Developing Country Debt Crisis," Brookings Papers on Economic Activity 2.

Part I

The Latin American Debt Crisis: Global Issues

2

Latin American Debt: Progress, Prospects, and Policy

William R. Cline

1 Introduction

At the end of November 1987, the presidents of eight Latin American nations issued a declaration at Acapulco, Mexico, that was the harshest critique yet of the past strategy of dealing with the debt problem. Brazil had been in moratorium for months, and rumors of an Argentine moratorium threat surrounded hasty IMF approval of a new lending program. Even Phoenix-like Mexico, with its cache of $16 billion in reserves, was under new strain from the collapse of its stock market and free exchange rate.

Despite the apparent grounds for pessimism, there has been more progress on the Latin American debt problem than is generally recognized. Increasingly the lesson seems to be that those nations with the political conditions for pursuing sound economic policies have been able to make progress even in the face of renewed external shocks, while those lacking these political conditions have lost important opportunities to advance. The pattern that appears to be emerging is that, barring severe world recession or an explosion of interest rates, the "serious" countries will continue to emerge gradually from the debt crisis, while those whose political environments are too unstable to permit "serious" economic policies may well fail to do so even though favorably positioned in terms of underlying economic strength. Lest this judgement seem too harsh, it should be acknowledged at the outset that the United States itself has come perilously close in recent years to falling into the category of lacking a serious economic policy because of its political taboos, primarily fiscal.

2 Progress or Retrogression?

In view of growing political (and academic) calls for concessional debt relief, it may come as a surprise to many that on the most germane measures there has been significant improvement in the debt problem since 1982. The best measure of relative debt burden is the ratio of net interest payments (deducting earnings on reserves and other interest income from interest paid on debt) to exports of goods and services. Data are more readily available for gross interest payments as a ratio of exports of goods and services. These data appear in table 2.1. For Latin America as a whole they indicate a decline from 41 percent in 1982 to 35.1 percent in 1986. The estimates by the IMF for developing countries in the Western hemisphere show a decline from a peak of 32.6 percent in 1982 to 30.5 percent in 1986 and 26.9 percent estimated for 1987.

The interest–exports ratio declined modestly for oil-exporting countries from 1982 to 1985, but then reversed in 1986 as oil prices collapsed. However, the partial recovery of oil prices in 1987 and the strong performance of at least Mexican nonoil exports points to a return to an improving trend for 1987. In the Mexican case, there is a dramatic decline in the interest–exports ratio for 1987, from 40 percent to 25.6 percent. And if interest income on the large stock of reserves and on private assets abroad is deducted, the ratio is only 20 percent. Even on the gross interest–exports criterion, Mexico's situation has improved markedly, from 47.3 percent in 1982 to 25.6 percent in 1987.

The nonoil-exporting Latin American countries have shown greater progress than the oil exporters. Their ratio of interest payments to exports of goods and services has declined from 46.7 percent in 1982 to 34.2 percent in 1986 and should decline further in 1987. For Brazil, the decline has been from 57.1 percent in 1982 to 33.6 percent in 1987. Even for Argentina, the country with the highest relative debt burden among major debtors, the ratio has fallen from a peak of 58.4 percent in 1983 to only 46.9 percent in 1987.

Trends in the ratio of debt to exports of goods and services are less favorable. However, the decline in interest rates from their extraordinary levels in the early 1980s makes simple observation of the debt–export ratios misleading. Even on the debt/export criterion, the nonoil Latin American countries have managed to avoid further increases, as their debt ratio in 1986 (374 percent) was only marginally higher than in 1982 (363). The ratio in 1986 was especially unfavorable for oil exporters, but their 1985 ratio is probably more representative (given the partial recovery of oil prices and the strong Mexican performance), and in that year their debt/export ratio was also only modestly higher (at 311 percent) than in 1982 (278 percent).

The cost of debt has declined sharply. Thus, in 1982 LIBOR (with a six-month lag) was 15.6 percent and the typical spread perhaps 1.75, for total cost of 17.3 percent. For 1987, LIBOR (6-month lag) will average 6.4 percent and the spreads, which have been renegotiated, under 1 percent, for a total debt cost of some 7.4 percent. When the cost of debt has fallen

Table 2.1 Indicators of external debt and adjustment

	1980	1981	1982	1983	1984	1985	1986	1987
Gross Interest/Exports of Goods and Services XGS (%)								
IMF:WH	18.4	24.8	32.6	31.6	30.8	30.2	30.5	26.9
ECLA:LA	20.2	28.0	41.0	36.0	35.6	35.2	35.1	.
LA-OX	16.6	22.6	35.6	31.4	32.5	32.3	36.5	.
LA-NOX	23.7	33.6	46.7	40.7	38.7	37.9	34.2	.
ARG	22.0	35.5	53.6	58.4	57.6	51.1	51.8	46.9[a]
BRZ	34.1	40.4	57.1	43.5	39.7	40.0	37.7	33.6[a]
MEX	23.3	29.0	47.3	37.5	39.0	36.0	40.0	25.6[a]
CHL	19.3	38.8	49.5	38.9	48.0	43.5	39.2	.
COL	18.0	28.0	36.1	33.0	26.6	27.3	22.7	.
PER	16.0	24.1	25.1	29.8	33.2	30.0	27.3	.
VEN	8.1	12.7	21.0	21.6	20.1	26.3	33.3	.
Current Account ($b)								
IMF:WH	−30.2	−42.7	−42.5	−10.9	−2.6	−4.3	−17.5	−13.1
ARG	−4.8	−4.7	−2.4	−2.5	−2.4	−1.0	−2.6	−3.3[a]
BRZ	−12.8	−11.7	−16.3	−6.8	0.5	0.3	−4.1	−3.1[a]
MEX	−6.8	−11.8	−4.9	5.3	4.2	1.2	−1.3	5.1[a]
Debt/XGS (%)								
IMF:WH	183.3	209.7	273.0	291.9	277.4	298.5	360.7	362.2
ECLA:LA	214.0	248.0	321.0	343.0	322.0	342.0	401.0	.
LA-OX	186.0	219.0	278.0	303.0	215.0	311.0	447.0	.
LA-NOX	240.0	276.0	363.0	381.0	355.0	369.0	374.0	.
ARG[b]	213.3	299.6	421.8	472.9	460.8	458.5	523.3	596.0
BRZ[b]	260.0	252.0	360.0	362.0	311.0	335.0	410.0	408.0
MEX[b]	208.0	237.0	311.0	327.0	295.0	332.0	416.0	300.0

LA: Latin America; LA-OX: oil exporters; LA-NOX: nonoil-exporters; WH:
Western hemisphere LDCs; XGS: exports of goods and services
ARG: Argentina; BRZ: Brazil; MEX: Mexico; CHL: Chile; COL: Colombia;
PER: Peru; VEN: Venezuela
[a] Forecast, *Latin American Economic Outlook (LAEO)*
[b] Net debt/XGS
Sources: IMF, *World Economic Outlook*, October 1987; ECLA, *Preliminary
Balance of the Latin American Economy in 1986*; and *LAEO*

by more than half, the debt burden is lighter even if the ratio of debt to
exports of goods and services has not declined.

Nor is the alleviation of the burden reversed by considering the real
instead of nominal interest rate. The IMF index of dollar unit values of

exports from industrial countries fell from 100 in 1980 to 96.2 in 1981 and 92.8 in 1982; in contrast, from 1985 to 1986 it rose from 87.2 to 99.2, and the index reached 110.4 by May 1987. At least on this index, inflation in traded goods was -3.5 percent in 1982 and +10 percent in 1987, and the real interest rate for external debt thus shifted from 21.4 percent in 1982 to -2.7 percent in 1987. Similarly, if the deflator is the IMF's index of nonoil commodity prices, world trade inflation was -4.7 percent in 1982 and +6.6 percent for the year ending June 1987, meaning that the real cost of Latin American debt shifted from 22.8 percent in 1982 to 0.7 percent in 1987. These low or negative real interest rates for 1987 mean that, ironically, President Alfonsin's demand for a return to the low real rates of the 1970s has already been granted, albeit temporarily. More generally, even if there is no decline in the real interest rate, a falling nominal interest rate provides cash-flow benefits by reducing premature amortization through inflationary erosion of real debt.

There is of course a relationship between the nominal interest rate and the debt–export ratio. If inflation in industrial countries had not fallen sharply since the early 1980s, nominal rates would have been higher, but so would export prices, so that there would have been lower debt–export ratios but no more (and perhaps less) progress in reducing interest–export ratios. As discussed below, the persistence of high debt–export ratios does pose the risk of greater difficulty if interest rates rise again, and a major challenge to international macro-management is to avoid a serious rise in these rates.

Tables 2.1 through 2.3 provide other indicators of progress on the debt problem as well. As indicated in table 2.1, Latin America has cut its external current account deficit from $42.5 billion in 1982 to $13 billion in 1987, and had almost eliminated the deficit in 1984–5 before the oil price collapse of 1986. Table 2.3 shows that there has been progress in reducing fiscal deficits as well. Argentina has cut the deficit from nearly 17 percent of GNP to about 6 percent, and Mexico from nearly 9 percent to zero (real, or operational, deficit) despite the severe fiscal loss from the 1986 oil shock. Brazil's progress has been more uneven, as the deficit had fallen from a peak of near 8 percent to less than 3 percent by 1984 but is now near 6 percent again. And even Argentina's gains, from an extraordinarily high initial deficit, have left the fiscal gap still too large to achieve low inflation.

The most important indicator is economic growth. While adjustment to the debt cirsis (as well as internal imbalances) caused severe recession in 1982–3, since 1984 there has been broadly positive growth, and by 1986 the nonoil countries achieved a strong 6.5 percent growth average. Moreover, several countries participated in high growth, not just Brazil; Colombia, Peru, Chile, and Uruguay all had growth over 5 percent in 1986. Mexico's oil-related recession in 1986 is yielding to slow but positive growth this year.

Table 2.2 Main LDCs' exports ($b)

	1980	1981	1982	1983	1984	1985	1986	1987
IMF:WH	93.6	99.7	90.3	91.8	101.6	96.1	80.4	88.5
ECLA:LA	88.1	96.6	87.3	87.5	97.7	92.0	78.3	.
LA-OX	43.0	48.9	45.4	43.0	46.7	42.5	28.0	.
LA-NOX	46.1	47.7	41.8	44.4	51.0	49.5	50.3	.
ARG	8.0	9.1	7.6	7.8	8.1	8.4	7.0	6.7[a]
BRZ	20.1	23.3	20.2	21.9	27.0	25.6	22.4	24.1[a]
MEX	15.3	19.4	21.2	22.3	24.2	21.7	16.0	20.9[a]
CHL	4.7	3.9	3.7	3.8	3.7	3.8	4.2	.
COL	3.9	3.0	3.1	3.1	3.5	3.6	5.1	.
PER	3.9	3.8	3.7	2.7	3.1	3.0	2.5	.
VEN	19.2	20.1	16.5	15.2	14.0	12.5	10.0	.
IMF								
Asia LDCs	154.6	167.5	161.9	171.5	198.6	196.2	216.1	265.6
FUELX	328.1	310.6	251.4	215.0	213.2	192.6	125.3	146.8
NON-FUELX	302.4	309.2	294.9	306.1	342.8	341.4	370.5	430.4
PRIM PRODX	133.4	127.8	117.0	120.6	133.1	128.9	130.4	140.3
MFX	149.3	161.5	159.1	166.8	189.7	192.1	217.9	265.7

FUELX: Fuel exporters (LDCs); PRIM PRODX: Exporters of primary products;
MFX: Exporters of manufactures (LDCs)
[a] *LAEO* forecast
Source: ECLA, *Preliminary Balance*, various years; IMF, *International Financial Statistics* and *World Economic Outlook*, Oct. 1987

The principal area of failure to consolidate improvement is in inflation. The hopeful Austral and Cruzado Plans did break hyperinflation, but high rates of inflation are back again in both Brazil and Argentina. Annual rates in the range of 100 percent to 200 percent now afflict these two countries as well as Mexico. However, there is evidence from other countries in the region that external debt management does not inevitably mean high inflation. Chile, Colombia, and Venezuela have all maintained relatively low inflation. The role of external debt in inflationary problems is examined below.

There is another area in which Latin American adjustment has been less than impressive: export expansion. As indicated in table 2.2, the region's exports for 1987 are almost identical to the dollar level achieved in 1982 (approximately $90 billion), and last year with low oil prices they troughed at 11 percent below the 1982 level. Weak oil prices have played a major role in this stagnation; exports by the oil-exporting countries declined by 38

Table 2.3 Indicators of growth and internal adjustment

	1981	1982	1983	1984	1985	1986	1987
GDP Growth (%)							
LA	0.5	−1.4	−2.4	3.2	2.7	3.4	.
LA-OX	5.6	−0.3	−5.6	2.5	1.8	−1.9	.
LA-NOX	−2.4	−2.1	−0.5	3.7	3.2	6.5	.
ARG	−6.8	−4.2	2.8	2.6	−4.5	5.7	2.9[a]
BRZ	−3.4	0.9	−2.5	5.7	8.3	8.2	4.5[a]
MEX	8.0	−0.5	−5.3	3.7	2.7	−3.8	1.5[a]
CHL	3.5	−14.5	−2.2	4.3	0.7	5.7	6.0[b]
COL	2.3	1.0	1.9	3.6	2.6	5.0	5.0[b]
PER	4.0	0.1	−11.9	3.8	1.6	8.5	6.5est
VEN	−1.0	−1.3	−5.6	−1.1	−0.6	5.0	.
INFLATION (CPI, %)							
ARG	131.2	208.7	433.7	688.0	385.4	81.9	126.2[c]
BRZ	95.2	99.7	211.0	223.8	235.1	65.0	210.0[d]
MEX	28.7	98.8	80.8	59.2	63.7	105.7	133.9[c]
CHL	9.5	20.7	23.6	23.0	26.4	17.2	20.8[c]
COL	27.5	24.1	16.5	18.3	22.3	19.6	24.9[e]
PER	72.7	72.9	125.1	111.5	158.3	60.6	82.2[e]
VEN	11.0	7.3	7.0	18.3	5.7	13.1	27.3[f]
FISCAL DEFICIT (% of GDP)							
ARG	13.3	15.1	16.8	10.8	6.3	4.3	6.5[g]
BRZ[h]	6.2	7.7	4.4	2.7	4.3	3.7	5.5[i]
MEX[h]	8.8	5.2	1.9	0.6	1.1	1.5	0.0[g,i]

Abbreviations: see table 2.1
[a] *LAEO* forecast
[b] First half over same period 1986
[c] 12 month ending August
[d] Jan-July, GPI
[e] 12 month ending July
[f] 12 month ending June
[g] First half
[h] Real
[i] Estimate
Source: *LAEO*; ECLA *Preliminary Balance* and *Economic Panorama of Latin America*

percent from 1982 to 1986 (but should rise again in 1987). In contrast, the nonoil-exporting Latin American countries raised the dollar value of their exports by 20.3 percent from 1982 to 1986.

While nominal export growth of some 5 percent annually by nonoil Latin American countries was not a bad performance, neither was it particularly good. In this same period the Asian developing countries (not just the East Asian Newly Industrialized Countries (NICs) but including such countries as India) raised their exports by 33.5 percent. Developing countries that export primarily manufactured goods increased their exports by 37 percent. And while the developing countries that export mainly primary products increased their export earnings only 11 percent, that group (which includes most of Africa) as a whole has much less underlying potential for manufactured export expansion than do countries such as Argentina, Brazil, and Mexico.

While the export performance of Mexico has been stunning (with manufactured exports growing at over 40 percent in both 1986 and 1987), that of Argentina and Brazil has been poor to mediocre. Argentina's decline in exports cannot be blamed wholly on falling grain prices; its manufactured export earnings have also fallen, by 8 percent from 1982 to 1986. Brazil's manufactured exports rose briskly in 1984 (from $11.3 billion to $14.9 billion) but then stalled and proceeded to decline by 16 percent by 1986 (to $12.5 billion). Compared to either the Mexican performance or to that of developing country exporters of manufactures, the growth of Argentinian and Brazilian industrial exports has been seriously disappointing. Considering the dynamism elsewhere, this record can hardly be blamed on the international economy.

Overall, despite areas of weakness, the record since the outbreak of the debt crisis in 1982 is one of progress rather than further deterioration. It is true that the *pace* of this progress has been slower than had initially been hoped. The rapid improvement through 1984 proved to be cyclically above the sustainable rate of progress. As with the origins of the debt crisis itself, there were both external and domestic reasons for the deceleration of improvement after 1984. On the external side, the dollar continued to strengthen through early 1985, and the large rise of the dollar depressed dollar prices of internationally traded goods, especially commodities. Thus, from 1982 to 1986 the IMF index of nonoil commodity prices fell from 85.2 to 73.1 (1980=100), or by 14.2 percent, rather than rising as had been anticipated on the basis of past positive response to global recovery. Structural trends in demand and supply, lagged effects of the strong dollar, and the easing of industrial country growth appear to have driven the commodity price erosion. In addition, in 1986 the collapse of oil prices imposed a new shock on the debt problem, considering that oil bulks larger in the exports of the oil-exporting debtor nations than in the imports of the oil-importing ones.

Against these external trends on the negative side, economic growth in industrial countries was approximately the 3 percent average that had been seen as necessary for emergence from the debt crisis, although the distribution of growth was uneven, with a strong surge in 1984 and moderate growth thereafter. Thus, after brisk recovery from the global recession in 1982 (when industrial country growth was -0.3 percent) in 1983 (2.7 percent) and especially 1984 (5.0 percent), growth in industrial countries slowed to 3.1 percent in 1985, 2.7 percent in 1986, and 2.4 percent in 1987 (IMF), for an average of 3.2 percent in 1983–87 (IMF, 1987a). The moderation of OECD growth after 1984 was compensated for by the highly favorable downward trend of the international interest rate, as reviewed above. At least for those debtor countries not highly dependent on oil or a few commodities with especially unfavorable price trends, the net effect of external factors in the period 1983–6 as a whole was broadly neutral and certainly consistent with the basic debt strategy premised on export expansion. The dynamic export performance of the Asian countries (and Mexico in 1986–7) demonstrates the opportunities that existed given the global economic environment. Moreover, by 1987 commodity prices began to turn around. The nonoil commodity price index of the IMF reached a trough in August of 1986 (at 68.9); by September of 1987, it had risen by 14.8 percent. One of the largest increases has been in the price of copper, which rose from 59 cents per pound in August 1986 to 82 cents by September of 1987, and by early December had reached $1.22 per pound (IMF, 1987b; *Wall Street Journal*, 1987a). With the price of copper now more than twice the level at its 1986 trough, both Chile and Peru should experience large gains in export earnings.

In sum, if a strong dollar, weak commodity prices, moderating industrial country growth, and lower oil prices contributed to a somewhat less favorable external environment for the debt problem than had been anticipated in 1984, the negative effects were broadly neutralized (except for the oil exporters) by a decline in interest rates further than had been expected, and for more than a year now the adverse trend in commodity prices has been reversed. Overall, the international economic environment remained one in which countries following appropriate policies could continue to expand imports and reduce their relative debt burden.

Internal policies thus have played an important role in the slower than expected pace of recovery from the debt problem. Brazil made a good beginning with major devaluation in 1983 and a strong increase in exports in 1984. But by 1986 its excess domestic demand, repressed inflation, and increasingly overvalued exchange rate (frozen for nine months) choked off its trade surplus. External sector performance for 1986 was thus unfavorable despite a large windfall gain of lower oil prices and interest rates. While by mid-1987 the trade surplus had rebounded to a rate of some $12 billion annually or more, precious time had been lost and the expansion path of exports was behind schedule, so that for a given trade surplus the export base (and thus the level of imports) was lower than otherwise would have been possible.

Conscious policy decisions led to the derailing: the boost in real wages on the eve of the Cruzado Plan, the failure to take the advice of economists within the administration to implement demand-cooling measures by the second quarter of 1986, and the excessive duration of the price freeze (with resulting shortages and emergency imports). Above all there was the failure to deliver on the intellectual premise of the heterodox shock approach: that the fiscal fundamentals would be in place with a zero real fiscal deficit. Although a zero real deficit was widely announced to be at hand early in the Cruzado Plan on the strength of fiscal reforms late in 1985 and the "Tanzi effect" (termination of inflationary erosion of taxes due but not yet collected), in practice the real deficit turned out to be in the range of 4–6 percent of GNP (table 2.3). Compounding the economic problem, the search for a political quick fix to offset the failure of the Cruzado Plan induced the government to declare a debt moratorium in early 1987, whereas an emergency lending arrangement with the banks could have dealt just as well with the problem of declining reserves without causing the same damage to Brazil's longer-term image as a credit risk. Without a single public demonstration in favor of the moratorium, the stratagem appears to have failed even in terms of domestic politics.

In Argentina as well, the Austral Plan has essentially foundered on the failure to reduce the fiscal deficit as promised. Alfonsin pledged to limit the fiscal deficit to what could be financed abroad, initially set at 2.5 percent of GNP. The initial rise in real revenue associated with reversal of the Tanzi effect and with imposition of temporary measures such as high export taxes on agricultural goods and voluntary savings were not followed up by fundamental measures to slim down the state sector, and a fiscal deficit in the range of 6 percent of GNP has proved incompatible with internal and external balance. As noted above, the decline of Argentina's manufactured exports since 1982 cannot be attributed to external factors, but instead reflects exchange rate and regulatory policies (particularly in the oil sector).

Mexico's external sector performance in 1986–7 provides a vivid illustration of the difference that energetic policy measures can make even in the face of severe external shock (or, if one subscribes to the theory that politicians can act only when matters reach a crisis stage, perhaps because of external shock). The collapse of oil prices in 1986 cost Mexico $8 billion in export earnings and 6 percent of GNP in fiscal revenue. By forceful fiscal measures, the government held the net rise in the fiscal deficit to 0.4 percent of GNP. Through a 32 percent real devaluation of the peso (trade-weighted), the authorities launched an export expansion that increased manufactured exports by 42.9 percent in 1986 and by approximately 40 percent again in 1987. By applying a tight monetary policy, the government induced firms to transfer working capital from abroad, and brought a swing in the categories of "short-term capital" and "errors and omissions" from an outflow of $3.9 billion in 1985 to an inflow of $1.2 billion in 1986. With the help of partial recovery of oil prices in 1987, by September the President could announce that Mexico had $15 billion of reserves in hand. As indicated in table 2.1, the ratio of net debt to exports of goods and services improved sharply, falling from 416 percent in 1986 to 300 percent in 1987.

The cases of Chile and Peru further illustrate the importance of domestic policy. Both countries had experienced severe recession in 1982–3 (table 2.3). Both have a considerable dependence on copper exports. Yet Chile chose a relatively orthodox set of policies and co-operation with foreign lenders, while Peru openly confronted external creditors and pursued a mix of policies with numerous internal contradictions, including the lagging of devaluation behind inflation and wage increases in the face of price controls. In the external sector, the results may be seen from table 2.2. In 1982, the two countries had identical export earnings ($3.7 billion); by 1986, Chile's exports had risen by 13.5 percent while those of Peru had declined by 32.4 percent. Ironically, Peru's limitation of debt servicing to 10 percent of exports appears to have had a more negative cash-flow effect even on the capital and interest accounts than a more conventional policy might have achieved, as cutbacks in short-term credit by lenders scared by a confrontational approach meant an unintended amortization of debt. While growth from 1984 through 1987 was somewhat higher in Peru (cumulative 22 percent) than Chile (18 percent, table 2.3), there is every indication that the surge of growth in 1986–7 in Peru was at the cost of future growth because of the distortions involved, whereas the Chilean economy now seems positioned to continue favorable growth into the future.

Some analysts dismiss the Chilean experience out of hand on grounds that it is the work of a dictatorship and therefore irrelevant for policy-making in democratic Latin American countries. Even within the Chilean context alone this reflex reaction seems unjustified. The dictatorship charge conjures up images of enormous sacrifice by a cowed public; yet the trends in per capita income show no such repression for the sake of servicing foreign debt. The fact is that from 1984 to 1987, per capita income in Chile has risen faster than in a long list of other Latin American countries. Moreover, there are clearly examples of democratic regimes that have successfully adopted appropriate economic policies and managed external debt on a relatively conventional basis. The Mexican case just reviewed is one, and Mexico remains a democracy despite instances of probable election fraud. The case of Colombia is another. The Colombian government has consistently exercised remarkable fiscal responsibility. In 1985, it was even able to carry out a large corrective devaluation (51 percent) without creating a surge in inflation (table 2.3), because tight monetary and fiscal policies accompanied the measure. Nor should Colombia be considered irrelevant because it is exempt from the debt crisis. While Colombia has successfully avoided rescheduling as such, it applied all the techniques of co-ordinated lending to mobilize a "jumbo" loan in 1984 that covered all of the principal and half of the interest owed to the banks; and, ironically, its ratio of interest to exports of goods and services is not much lower than that of Peru (and Colombia's ratio was actually higher than that of Peru in 1980–3).

In sum, there has been gradual progress in dealing with the debt problem. The international economic environment has been broadly adequate for improvement. However, there has been substantial variation in the extent to which individual countries have taken advantage of this environment. The coherence of domestic economic policies, which has been primarily a function of the strength of political leadership and the underlying political stability in each country, has been a dominant factor in determining the outcome for each country.

3 Challenges to the Debt Strategy

The critiques of the mainstream debt strategy are well known. A major criticism has been that the banks have failed to make good on their assignment under the Baker Plan. Rather than expanding their exposure to the 15 highly indebted countries by 2.5 percent annually (or $7.5 billion per year), they had a combined reduction of exposure to these countries by approximately 1 percent from the end of 1984 to 1986, and for the US banks the reduction was 10 percent (Cline, 1987b, pp. 3–5).[1] However, the strength of external accounts of major debtors in 1984–5 meant that the largest debtors were not requesting new money. For 1987, the large flows of new lending to Mexico and Argentina alone should mean a significant rise in bank exposure, at a rate not far from the Baker Plan target.

The underlying critique of the existing strategy, however, is the view that even if the banks do their part, there remains an outward resource transfer that is incompatible with acceptable rates of economic growth in Latin America. Based on this premise, Senator Bill Bradley has proposed that banks forgive 3 percentage points of interest and 3 percentage points of principal over a period of three years; Professor Jeffrey Sachs of Harvard has proposed five years of interest forgiveness for a wide range of debtor countries that have experienced sharp reductions in per capita incomes; Professor Rudiger Dornbusch of MIT proposes that countries such as Brazil make payments exclusively through local currency obligations (of which some would be convertible into equity) over a period of several years; and numerous proposals suggest that in some way the existing discount between the secondary market price of the loans and their face value be conveyed to the debtor countries as outright relief.[2]

It is by no means clear that the capital constraint (and domestic savings) is the binding limit to growth, such that the "outward resource transfer" model is the proper framework for analysis. Domestic savings and investment have indeed declined, but it is likely that there would be considerable scope for both to rise if the domestic economies presented more stable outlooks and thus better prospects for new investment. Domestic fiscal and monetary imbalance may thus be more germane than inadequacy of total potential resources as the obstacles to growth. As for the foreign exchange constraint, there is ample evidence since the debt crisis that proper policies can break it through stimulating the expansion of exports, especially in manufactured goods.

But even if a framework of resource constraint is adopted, few of the advocates of concessional debt relief seem to realize that the actual resource transfers that would be mobilized under such proposals would be unlikely to differ much from those under refinancing at market-related terms. The choice is essentially between new lending, on the one hand, and debt forgiveness, on the other. Considering that few if any of the proposals for concessional relief amount to forgiveness of more than half of the debt, the two alternative options can produce identical cash-flow results as long as banks can be induced to roll over principal entirely and refinance up to half of the interest coming due. This target is somewhat more ambitious than the Baker Plan (which amounts to refinancing all the principal and about one-third of the interest), but it seems likely to be necessary in many cases if the existing approach is to succeed, and in the experience of 1987 banks have in fact gone considerably further by financing closer to two-thirds or three-quarters of the interest coming due for Mexico and Argentina.

Once it is recognized that bank refinancing (new money packages) can accomplish the same cash-flow and thus resource transfer as schemes for concessional relief, the latter lose much of their allure. Concessional relief provides the additional benefit only of reducing the balance sheet obligation of the country, without affecting the current resource transfer. While the balance sheet reduction does eliminate "piling new debt on top of old," increasing debt is not by itself inappropriate as long as the country's exchange rate and other policies (and the state of international markets) lead to a rate of export growth that significantly exceeds the rate of growth of debt. On the cost side, concessional relief has the negative effect of undermining the country's long-term credit reputation and delaying the day when the country can re-establish normalized relations with the capital markets on a basis of voluntary lending.

Even if schemes of concessional relief could generate a significantly greater cash flow than refinancing (either because they concentrated relief wholly on current interest rather than principal, or because banks proved unwilling to provide new loans but somehow willing to accept concessional relief), it is important not to overestimate the favorable growth effects of the resulting increase in resource availability. One of the striking features of the long array of proposals for concessional debt relief is that virtually none of their authors has demonstrated through the use of traditional economic modeling the magnitudes of the growth benefits that debtor countries would be able to purchase at the expense of the erosion in their long-term credit reputations through relief programs.

Consider Brazil. Suppose that through quasi-forced concessional relief it could mobilize resources equal to, say, one-third of its bank interest obligation. For example, a relief program might forgive two-thirds of interest while refinancing might be able to come up with coverage for only one-third. (The plan by Finance Minister Bresser Pereira to cut half the debt in half on the basis of the secondary market, although withdrawn when declared a "nonstarter" by US Treasury Secretary James Baker, would have saved only one-quarter, or half of half, of the interest due.) On its $77 billion in debt owed to foreign banks, and with LIBOR higher than in 1987, so that total debt cost is about 9 percent, Brazil pays close to 3 percent of GNP annually in interest to banks. Forcing concessional relief to save one third of this amount (above and beyond what might be the limits on more conventional refinancing) would reduce the resource transfer by one percentage point of GNP. Using the traditional capital constraint and an incremental capital – output ratio of 3.0, the result would be an increase in the growth rate by 0.3 percent annually. If instead a foreign exchange constraint is applied, and a shadow price of foreign exchange of 2.0 is assumed (so that Brazil would be prepared to pay 100 cruzados to the dollar, even though the going exchange rate were only 50 cruzados), these savings would translate into a one-time increase of 1 percentage point in the level of GNP.[3] (The rise would be once-and-for-all because the higher level of imports would, through the foreign exchange constraint, permit a higher absolute level of domestic production as long as it were sustained, but not still further subsequent additions to output.) These calculations suggest that the growth benefits of concessional relief for a country such as

Brazil would be limited, and could relatively easily be turned negative by adverse effects on future growth resulting from any resulting isolation of the economy from international capital and trade markets.

An important recent line of thinking adds a third growth constraint, however: a domestic fiscal constraint. In this approach, whereas the external debt might be manageable in terms of the resource transfer in view of either the capital or the foreign exchange constraint, it becomes unmanageable after taking into account a fiscal constraint. Although this approach[4] is less than fully formulated, it essentially maintains that major debtor countries are unable to reduce high inflation because of a domestic fiscal gap; that growth will be unsustainable without reducing inflation; and that it is unlikely the fiscal gap can be sufficiently closed in the absence of a reduction in the fiscal burden associated with interest on external debt.

Former Brazilian Planning Minister Mario Simonsen has satirized this viewpoint by noting that it is impossible to separate the "molecules" of the fiscal deficit into those branded "external debt" and all others, and that the notion that the government can renege on part of its debt presumes that future creditors will have amnesia (Simonsen, 1987, pp. 24–35). An examination of the "fiscal constraint" argument suggests that it too provides little basis for advocating concessional relief over refinancing through new money programs.

One reason a fiscal constraint might be relevant is with respect to the mobilization of resources for investment. The government's deficit pre-empts resources otherwise available for private investment; and, the argument would run, cutting the deficit by reducing the foreign debt obligation would free resources for investment. This argument is not germane, however, if the alternative to the forgiveness of the interest is new money from the banks. The new lending provides the resources in question so that they do not have to be wrested from the private sector and from domestic investment.

A second reason the fiscal constraint might be of concern is high domestic inflation. But again, if the alternative is foreign refinancing, there is no net benefit from forgiveness of the interest. In the Keynesian sense of the influence of the fiscal deficit on inflation, working through excess real demand, the provision of new money from abroad means that payment of the interest (as opposed to having it forgiven but with a corresponding drop in foreign financing) does not cause inflation – it has no net effect on resource availability and therefore the degree of excess demand. In the monetarist sense of the role of the fiscal deficit, its monetization and therefore inflationary pressure from the standpoint of money supply, the payment of interest on external debt refinanced by banks is similarly irrelevant. The provision of foreign finance for payment of the interest means that this source of the fiscal deficit can be financed rather than monetized, and moreover that it is financed through a vehicle that, unlike domestic short-term government paper, does not become quasi-money in the domestic economy.

In short, the notion of a fiscal constraint provides no case for concessional debt relief rather than bank refinancing for the coverage of a given amount of interest obligations on foreign debt. If more of the interest could be covered by concessional relief than by refinancing, then the argument becomes more relevant, although there is no immediate reason to believe that the shadow price on amounts entering the fiscal deficit is greater than that on foreign exchange, or that fiscal crowding-out changes the essential case based on resource transfer and the capital constraint (both analyzed above). In practice, the argument probably does not need to be extended this far. Few are proposing debt forgiveness in excess of half of the outstanding debt (except for the most extreme cases), and it is likely that half of interest coming due can in fact be refinanced by the banks under appropriate policy performance.

The cases of Chile, Venezuela, and Colombia provide empirical support for rejecting the argument that fiscal balance and internal stability are impossible without concessional relief on external debt. Indeed, in Venezuela the government has even eschewed new money and has pursued some amortization of the debt (and voluntary lending is beginning to return on specific projects). Ironically, Mexico also illustrates that fiscal balance is possible without concessional debt relief. Even though Mexico's inflation is now a high 140 percent, in real terms the deficit is zero and if the authorities decided to adopt a heterodox shock (along the Israel/Austral Plan lines), it is likely that inflation could be brought down relatively quickly and on a sustainable basis.[5]

Jeffrey Sachs has stressed a quite different interpretation of the benefits of concessional debt relief.[6] Sachs argues that the main cause of the debtor countries' growth and debt problems may be found in misguided domestic policies. However, because these policy flaws, and excessive fiscal deficits in particular, are the consequence of fundamental political conflicts within the societies, what is lacking is a strong incentive that will help the country overcome these conflicts and adopt policy reform. Sachs proposes concessional debt relief as precisely the carrot that can be used to cause this political turnaround.

This "policy bribe" thesis is speculative. The strong tendency in such countries as Brazil and Argentina is in just the opposite direction, toward rejection of external conditions. That the domestic political factions would throw over their conflicts and adopt fiscal and other economic reforms insisted on by an international entity in return for the extinction of some of the debt on the country's balance sheet (but with little if any cash flow effect as compared with new lending) seems less than likely. There is at least as much likelihood that any net relief would be used by the country on questionable expenditures, such as President Sarney's proposed railway from Brazilia to his home state of Maranhao, or President Alfonsin's project for a new capital in the South of Argentina (at Viedma).

4 Automaticity

The Acapulco meeting confirmed two trends in the objectives (demands?) of the Latin American debtor countries: a need for greater automaticity in the refinancing of a portion of their interest coming due, and the goal of obtaining for the country's benefit some part of the discount from face value that exists in the secondary market for the bank claims. The first of these trends was already present in the Mexico bank agreement of 1986, which provided for automatic increases in financing if the price of oil fell below $9 per barrel (and, in a smaller amount, if domestic growth was below target).

It is becoming increasingly clear that subjugation of domestic policy freedom to the requirements of an outside entity, particularly the IMF, is chafing the large debtors. Argentina temporarily circumvented the problem by mobilizing sufficient political support abroad to obtain a new IMF loan in the winter of 1987 without first completing the policy steps the IMF staff had sought (in particular, actual passage through congress of the proposed new fiscal measures). Carefully staged leaks of the threat of an Argentine moratorium in the middle of November 1987 provided the needed spur to this action. Brazil more transparently simply seeks to delink all bank disbursements from any IMF disbursements, and thus from policy conditions set down by the IMF. In Finance Minister Bresser Pereira's argument, because the new money from the banks is being used to pay only interest owed to them rather than, for example, for the construction of new dams and factories, there is no justification for applying policy preconditions to the disbursement of these loans.

There is an element of validity in the petitions for greater automaticity. The leash of the IMF review is at times simply too short (in the Argentine case in mid-1987, down to bi-monthly reviews). Treasury Secretary Baker acknowledged as much in his speech to the IMF–World Bank annual meetings in September 1987, when he called for IMF reviews on a bi-annual rather than quarterly or shorter basis. At a much more fundamental level, however, there is a basic tension inherent in the current process. IMF tutelage was traditionally designed for limited periods, of 18 months to three years. Yet managing the debt problem has proved to be a longer-term task. It is unclear that any of the founders of the IMF envisioned that the agency would be in a situation of exercising tight surveillance over country policy for years on end, or that national governments would accept such an arrangement.

One of the benefits of a return to voluntary lending, of course, is that the country would no longer be asking for new money on a co-ordinated, or involuntary basis, and as such would no longer be asked for the *quid pro quo* of a policy reform package endorsed and financed by the IMF. The question is whether some greater scope for automaticity is warranted in new lending to countries still requiring new money and not yet capable of obtaining it on a voluntary basis.

It seems clear that the complete absence of policy conditions, as apparently sought by Bresser Pereira, amounts to a blank check that the banks cannot be expected to sign. The banks have fiduciary responsibilities, and could not in good conscience call the new loans legitimate claims if there were no basis for believing that they would be used in a way that would ultimately firm up the value of loans to the country. At the same time, there is no reason that the disbursements of the banks have to be tied to those of the IMF. In particular, the banks could establish annual reviews keyed to IMF surveillance, rather than making each quarterly disbursement contingent on the simultaneous disbursement of the IMF. For longer-term agreements, the intervals could perhaps be stretched out to 18 months or two years.

If even more infrequent reviews linking bank disbursements to those of the IMF are unacceptable to Brazil or other countries, the borrowers could well have to accept conditions developed by the banks themselves (for example, through their Institute of International Finance), or, more plausibly, by other entities, in particular the World Bank. In the specific Brazilian case, however, it seems doubtful that the alleged political anathema of dealing with the IMF can be split so finely that the public could tell the difference between an IMF program not linked to bank disbursements and one linked; yet Brazilian authorities by late 1987 had already agreed in principle to return to the IMF. Few riots may be expected over the issue of whether, in addition to going back to the IMF, Brazilian authorities accept bank linkage of their disbursements to those of the IMF, especially if the bank reviews of policy are generously spaced.

More complete automaticity seems of doubtful value for the system. Would it be favorable either for the debtor countries or for the banks to agree that for the next five years, for example, 60 percent of all interest coming due must automatically be refinanced, whether by new loans or through interest capitalization, with no conditions on the quality of country policy and economic performance whatever? The answer as almost certainly no. In the extreme case, automatic refinancing of all interest with no policy conditions is practically equivalent to complete debt forgiveness, because there would be little credibility to the valuation of the rising obligation over time.

In terms of strategic behavior, it is unrealistic to expect banks to provide condition-free refinancing of a large portion of interest over a long period of time. They have negative sanctions they may employ if they have not signed away the right to any policy review. The first of these is merely to continue to leave the situation unresolved, so that after a period of some six months to a year of unpaid interest the regulatory authorities classify the country as "value impaired" (in the United States). The Brazilian authorities decided to reach an interim agreement with banks that narrowly averted this classification in October 1987, even though the arrangement involved a pledge by Brazil to go to the IMF (albeit on an unlinked basis) after persistently harsh rhetoric that it would not do so, and required a payment of $500 million by Brazil even though the authorities had insisted that no payment would be made until a long-term agreement was fully in hand. This demonstrates the considerable power of suasion of the specter of this official down-grading of debt (which requires specific allocation of loan loss reserves against the country). Banks also have the option of working down their short-term credit to the country (and the disparity between Brazil's cumulative trade balance in March through September and its stagnant reserves suggests that short-term credits had indeed run down by as much as $2 billion). It is hardly necessary to envision stiffer sanctions such as attempted legal seizures of reserves or export shipments to recognize that the banks do have options for pressure that they are unlikely to sign away lightly through commitment to unconditional refinancing of a major portion of interest over a period of several years.

As for the impact of policy conditions on debtor country policies, it would be difficult to argue that the country's economic policies would be superior in the absence of any external conditions.[7] There is considerable room for re-evaluation of the content of IMF (or, under a new regime, World Bank) conditionality. There are grounds for shifting its emphasis more fully toward external sector performance, especially maintenance of a real exchange rate that provides sufficient incentive to continued expansion of exports, while providing more latitude for the country to choose its own approach to internal balance.[8] In some countries, an inflation tax may be necessary to meet fiscal needs because of the political weakness of dealing with the fiscal problem more directly; as long as offsetting devaluation avoids deterioration in the external sector, the direct interests of foreign creditors are not necessarily threatened by the absence of more othodox internal policies. But there is little basis for the abolition of policy conditions, and indeed one school of debt-forgiveness advocates (Sachs et al.) calls for superconditionality.

The best conditionality, of course, is that which codifies a coherent plan drawn up by the authorities of the country itself, and provides external reinforcement for the domestic political implementation of that plan. Successful IMF programs in India, Turkey, and South Korea in recent years are the classic examples. Within Latin America, the early months of Argentina's Austral Plan and the 1986 IMF agreement with Mexico are examples of such plans. Brazil's mid-1987 Plan of Macro-Economic Control could have provided a basis for an IMF program. There is good reason to believe that in most cases where essentially sound plans are developed domestically, the IMF will sign on to them rather than hold out for its own alternatives on a rigid ideological basis. Moreover, as noted, other entities could assume the IMF's policy monitoring role, although where the country owes considerable repayments to the IMF (as in the case of the $1 billion annually now due from Brazil), the banks will strongly prefer IMF involvement so that the Fund can relend and new money from the banks will not have to be augmented to finance amortizations to the IMF.

5 Secondary Market Relief

Another salient theme in recent debt negotiations, in the Acapulco statement, and even in the draft omnibus trade bill before the US Congress, is that debtor countries should enjoy outright forgiveness of a portion of their debt obligation related to the discount on their paper in the secondary market. Appropriately interpreted and implemented, this approach could indeed help provide some useful flexibility in the system. Inappropriately conceived and implemented, it could do great damage.

The key distinction, as Secretary Baker told his Brazilian counterpart at their meeting in late September, is whether the forgiveness is mandatory (with apologies to semanticists) or at the choice of the creditor bank. If the former, there will be lasting damage to the country's credit relationship with capital markets, and it is rather late in the game for major debtor countries to throw away their longer-term creditworthiness image that they have paid so much to maintain. If the latter, there could be a useful lubrication of the system to permit the "impatient banks" to exit at a cost while the patient banks are not required to experience losses but instead can aspire to eventual normalization of credit relations with the country.

Mandatory concessional relief keyed to the secondary market discount has numerous problems. A major one is moral hazard: aggressive actions by the debtor will be rewarded. The course of the secondary market's quotation of Brazil's debt in 1987 illustrates the point. From July 1985 until January 1987, Brazil's debt sold on the secondary market at about 75 cents on the dollar. Then, after the country declared a moratorium at the end of

February, it had fallen to 64 cents by May. With the passage of time and the corresponding shift to non-accrual status, and as Citibank and other banks set aside unallocated loan loss reserves that increased the likelihood that some banks would try to dump debt on the secondary market, the quotation fell to 57 cents by July and only 39 cents by September (on the eve of possible value-impaired classification).[9] Some economists and politicians (from both creditor and debtor countries) contend that the secondary market is the only "fair" measure of the value of the debt, and therefore that claims should be written down to the level it dictates. The Brazilian case demonstrates, however, that aggressive behavior rather than long-term economic fundamentals can be the greater influence driving the secondary market price. From January to September Brazil actually revived its trade surplus from zero to an annual rate of some $10 billion, so on the fundamentals the secondary market price should have risen. But the escalating demands for relief and ever longer extension of the moratorium swamped the economics.

There are other reasons for suspicion about the secondary market as the arbiter for valuation in a scheme of concessional relief. Like some fashion models, the secondary market is extremely thin and fickle. Trading in Brazilian paper is reported to have exceeded $1 billion in 1986 but to have virtually dried up in 1987, and quotations on what may be nearly a non-market must be subject to doubt.

There is a positive role for relief based on the secondary market, however. It may take various forms, but its central principle is that by voluntary commercial action, some banks may be prepared to dispose of their claims at the secondary market price in a manner that does succeed in conveying the discount to the country. Such banks would be paying a substantial price for benefit of liquidity. Their action would be market-based rather than imposed on them by political authorities. As such, it would be a useful escape valve that should be viewed as a means of flexibility in the process of debt management rather than as a failure of the basic strategy.

Debt–equity conversion is one instrument for this process. When a multinational firm purchases debt at 50 cents on the dollar and agrees with the debtor government to convert it into pesos at 75 centavos on the peso for equity investment, the firm is an intermediary in a transaction that conveys some of the secondary market discount to the country as debt relief. When a bank holding claims agrees to a similar conversion, it is doing so as well. Much has now been written on the advantages and disadvantages of debt–equity conversion (Cline, 1987b; Roberts and Remolona, 1987; Fischer, 1987), and it need not be repeated here. In essence, there is a benefit of debt replacement by the more flexible equity obligation (on which remittance limits may be placed), while there are potential costs in terms of monetary expansion, real interest burden if the government borrows at higher rates domestically than abroad, possible substitution for investment flows that would have entered at full price, and the general problem of potential resource misallocation through the creation of a particular vehicle with an exchange rate that diverges from the central rate. In practice, despite relatively large use in Chile (where, however, the atypical objective of arranging foreign bailouts for a large group of near-bankrupt companies was the dominant motive), it appears likely that the role of debt–equity swaps will be limited in magnitude, although important as a vehicle for increased flexibility.

Discounted debt repurchase is another instrument. Portes finds that loan buybacks were a dominant form of *de facto* debt relief after the defaults of the 1930s (Portes, 1987). This mechanism is perhaps the purest form of market-based concessional debt relief, and it most directly exemplifies the principle of a mutually beneficial transaction between debtor and creditor that places a high priority on immediate liquidity rather than ultimate collection of full value. There are obstacles to repurchase in the form of "sharing" clauses in many loan contracts with Latin American governments. Technically a bank selling back its claims to the debtor could be faced with lawsuits from other banks claiming a share in the funds received. However, it would be appropriate policy both at the public and bank advisory committee level to establish that no such impediments will in fact be exercised. When a class of more impatient banks sells out at a sizeable discount, the expected value of the claims held by the more patient banks should rise because of the reduction in the remaining debt burden.

Mexico is the principal country now in a position to buy back substantial amounts of its debt at a discount. By early 1988 Mexico could have some $20 billion in reserves, and allocation of half of this amount to repurchases at perhaps 50 cents on the dollar would provide the basis for a major reduction in the external debt. Indeed, this process already appears to have been occurring, as September estimates revealed that private debt had fallen since 1982 by some $7.5 billion in what is presumably a process of private buybacks at favorable discounts (de la Madrid, 1987).

Few other countries are likely to be in a position to make major repurchases at a discount (although with the help of foreign assistance Bolivia is expected to buy back all of its bank debt at some 20 cents on the dollar). Moreover, there is a delicate interrelationship between buybacks and new money. Governments can hardly ask for large amounts of new money at 100 cents on the dollar for use in the repurchase of debt at 50 cents. Indeed, the recent silence of Mexican authorities on possible buyback operations is wholly understandable in view of the fact that the banks have still to disburse the second half of the $6 billion in new money from the 1986 package. However, there is every reason for banks to be co-

operative with a basic strategy that would provide that new money requirements to finance a reasonable portion of interest coming due would first be
established on grounds of the central expected path of external accounts
over a two- or three-year period, but that additional funds obtained by the
country through above-plan performance of exports could be free for use
in discounted loan repurchases without reductions in the initially envisioned magnitudes of new lending.[10]

There is a critical need to avoid moral hazard in programs for discounted
debt repurchases, as in any approach seeking a market solution based on
the secondary market. In particular, authorities of the debtor country
could take a highly aggressive position and threaten that either creditors
could sell out now at a large discount or else expect total default in the
future. This moral hazard illustrates once again the need for arrangements
that take place within a broad framework of negotiated, co-operative
solutions and with some structure providing for the monitoring of country
policy performance.

Various proposals for a public entity to buy debt at a discount and
convey the discount to the debtor country, including those in the draft US
trade bill, are not credible. The hard fact is that the public sector has no
intention of appropriating billions of dollars for this purpose. Yet if a
public entity were to purchase the debt and then hold it, while reducing the
interest rate to the debtor, it would have to immobilize large amounts of
capital. Contrary to some formulations in the draft US trade legislation (on
the House side), there is no magic whereby the public entity could buy debt
from party A at 50 cents on the dollar, somehow repackage the instrument
with a sharp reduction in its face obligation (such as the 50 cent discount),
and then resell at 100 cents on new face value. Because sovereign risk
would remain with the new, repackaged instrument, it in turn would sell
only at a discount, unless the public entity were prepared to offer a
guarantee. In short, the public entity either would have to call on large
amounts of capital to purchase and hold the debt, or would have to extend
a guarantee that would put the public at risk on a contingent basis. The
latter approach is more feasible in terms of budget constraints than the
former, but would still face political difficulties.

The *exit bond* is a potential vehicle for conveying relief through sharing
the secondary market discount. Originally conceived by bank negotiators
as an instrument for streamlining negotiations by permitting the smallest
banks to exit from the process of new money packages, the exit bond could
be generalized to be available even in large amounts to those (impatient)
banks with a high priority for liquidity and a willingness to pay a corre-
spondingly high price in terms of immediate loss. The Argentine new
money package of Spring 1987 contained a 25-year, 4 percent interest exit
bond that turned out to have virtually no takers. In retrospect, it seems

clear that the problem was that of the "double discount." The specified terms directly applied the first discount, but the discounted present value of the instrument was above the secondary market price so that if that were the only discount the option should have been taken by many banks. The problem was that a second discount remained: sovereign risk. That is, takers of the exit bond had no guarantee that Argentina would honor the full terms of the new instrument over its 25-year life.

The experience of the Argentine exit bond highlights the misconception behind the general notion that somehow "securitization" is the solution to the debt crisis. Securitization has come to be understood as a means of dispersing the claims widely among the public by transforming them from traditional loans into securities. The notion is common that, because the secondary market has a large discount, this process would provide room for reducing either the face value of the claim or its interest rate, thereby providing some concessional relief to the country. The problem, however, is that potential investors in securitized debt have to be compensated for the high risk they take by retaining full claim to 100 cents on the dollar. If the instrument sells at 50 cents on the dollar, the reason is that there is a 50 percent probability that the debtor will not pay (or even a lower risk of nonpayment, if the market is broadly risk averse).

Securitization, therefore, can provide dispersion of the risk. But it cannot provide real relief to the debtor without the introduction of another element: guarantee. If some international authority is prepared to guarantee the securitized instrument, then the second discount of the "double discount" – sovereign risk – can be stripped away. Then the specified interest and face value, themselves incorporating the now single discount, will be valued by the market without a further risk discount. Guaranteed exit bonds, in short, would be a credible vehicle for mobilizing the secondary market discount on behalf of reduction in the debtor's burden. Unguaranteed exit bonds are highly unlikely to do so.

There is perhaps a small degree of margin for unguaranteed exit bonds if they carry relatively high interest rates and if the country itself does all it can to provide a guarantee on its own, for example by stating that the instruments have senior status over all other debt.[11] Because it is difficult for the country credibly to "bind" itself, however, it is unlikely that such instruments will be able to marshal much relief in the form of a substantial discount on interest terms below what the original debt carries.

Serious consideration should be given to the development of a significant program of international guarantees for exit bonds. The World Bank has loan guarantee authority, which probably could be leveraged against its capital backing. Even without leveraging, the allocation of World Bank lending capacity to the guaranteeing of exit bonds could be a high-return use of the institution's resources. Thus, funds so earmarked would immedi-

ately earn a return of 100 percent if they permitted the country to extinguish $1 of debt in return for an exit bond worth 50 cents. (Note that
more normal World Bank loans could accomplish the same broad result
through the use of the funds for discounted loan repurchases.)

In sum, reliance on market-based "relief" related to the secondary
market has some potential for alleviating the burden of debt, and could be
systemically favorable so long as the mechanisms are strictly voluntary and
careful attention is paid to the avoidance of moral hazard. It should be
noted that the more of this type of transaction that takes place, the more
the secondary market price could be expected to rebound. The most
nervous banks would be taken out of the market, and the increased volume
on the demand side of the market through loan repurchases would tend to
bid up the price. This process would be all to the good, because closure of
the gap between the secondary market price and the face value will at some
point be essential if a return to a normalized, voluntary capital market is to
occur. New loans at 100 cents on the dollar are unlikely to be offered on a
voluntary basis (and especially by third parties without existing exposure)
as long as the secondary market price is in the range of 50 cents rather than
90–100 cents.

An important qualification of the range of instruments for market-based
debt relief is that the resulting total magnitude of real reduction of the
external debt obligation seems likely to be limited. For a country with a
strong base of human and natural resources and favorable economic
potential under proper policy, the major creditor banks are unlikely to be
willing to sell off claims at discounts as large as currently exist in the
secondary market. These "patient" banks are likely to account for the
greater part of debt. Perhaps only one-third of the volume of outstanding
bank debt would be represented by impatient banks willing to exit at a cost
anywhere near the present secondary market discount. While alleviation
reaching one-third of the debt would be helpful, it would not be overwhelming. Suppose that the relief on this portion of the debt amounted to
one-half of the face value. The effect would be to reduce the country's debt
obligation by one-sixth, an amount that is of secondary significance compared to underlying economic factors such as the country's policy and the
course of international economic events.

6   Insolvent Countries

The discussion so far concerns countries judged to be solvent in the sense
that they can plausibly be expected to pay full interest obligations, with the
help of partial refinancing of interest, over a period of five to ten years,
while achieving politically acceptable rates of economic growth (perhaps in

the range of 3–6 percent annually). The judgement of a country's capacity to make interest payments depends on prospective export earnings, the relative debt burden, domestic savings capacity, and so forth. The central presumption that the large debtor countries such as Brazil, Mexico, Venezuela, Argentina, Colombia, and Chile remain solvent under this broad definition remains valid. The internal revolutionary pressures in Peru and the actual behavior of its government pose obvious questions about the solvency of this country. Among the largest debtors, Argentina's high relative debt burden raises some questions about solvency as well, although the debt ratios could quickly look far better under certain plausible circumstances (such as significant recovery in agricultural prices).

For some other countries, presumably including Bolivia and perhaps some Central American nations (and many in sub-Saharan Africa), the judgement is more likely to be that the problem is one of insolvency. For these countries, outright forgiveness of a significant portion of the debt may be the eventual policy required. The example of Bolivia indicates that the banking community is not necessarily unwilling to consider forgiveness when it shares the judgement that the country is insolvent. I shall not elaborate mechanisms for forgiveness of the debt of insolvent countries because they do not constitute the bulk of the problem, either in total value of the debt or in share of the population of debtor countries. It should be noted, however, that there will be a greater feasibility of forgiveness where the country has a low per capita income and is eligible on grounds of international equity for access to concessional funds from such sources as the International Development Association. A higher income country not so eligible would tend to find itself isolated from all sources of finance after implementation of a concessional debt relief scheme, because private sector finance would be unlikely to continue.

It should be underlined that for those countries not clearly insolvent, shifting from a basis of market-related debt management (with co-ordinated new lending until voluntary capital market access can be re-established) to one of quasi-forced forgiveness of a substantial portion of debt by all creditors on a mandatory basis has potentially large long-run costs. The less amicable the workout, the more the country is likely to be isolated for a long period of time from foreign capital markets. In addition, isolation from trading markets is a likely outcome. Trade credit may be expected to dry up, and the potential for export expansion is likely to be substantially reduced. In truly conflictual cases, explicit trade retaliation in terms of foreign protection could not be ruled out.

On the positive side, gradual reduction of debt/export and interest/export ratios should permit eventual return to voluntary borrowing. As noted above, Venezuela has already had some success in obtaining voluntary financing for specific projects. Turkey re-entered the capital markets after debt rescheduling in the late 1970s; because its outward resource transfer was comparable to levels experienced in Latin America, even though the country did receive aid from OECD countries (that is, Turkish exports rose so much that the outward transfer was high despite this aid), Turkey is a relevant example. In short, there are major reasons for countries not to self-classify themselves as insolvent when the international community does not consider them to be so.

7   Prospects

One of the reasons a pall hangs over Third World debt today is the widespread anxiety that the international economy is on the verge of a new round of global recession. The Stock Market crash of October 16 seemed to many to be the signal portending the downturn. There is no doubt that global recession would wreak havoc with the debt strategy. Although longer-term horizons of ten or even five years should not necessarily be altered by a brief recession, political patience in debtor countries could buckle under the pessimism that even a short international recession would bring.

The stock market crash itself was hardly the source of a new recession, however. It was the reversal of a speculative bubble that had carried the market too far too fast.[12] Significantly, the US market today still remains above its level of 1986. While the propensity to consume out of wealth is an important factor, when that wealth is purely transitory (as was the $1 trillion in stock market gains from late 1986 until October of 1987) it is unlikely that consumption patterns will change much. Most official and private forecasting entities now seem to be coming to the conclusion that the crash will shave between 0.5 and 1 percentage point off US growth for 1988. The OECD secretariat has re-estimated OECD growth at 2.25 percent in 1988 and 1.25 percent in 1989 in light of the crash, while the 49 private forecasters surveyed by the Blue Chip Economic Indicators have cut their 1988 forecast for the United States from 2.8 percent to 1.9 percent (*Financial Times*, 1987a; *Wall Street Journal*, 1987b). If there is a more severe slow-down in store, it appears more likely to come in 1989 than in 1988.

A major slowdown, let alone a world recession, is by no means certain. At the moment the signs are of economic strength. The US economy grew at 4.1 percent in the third quarter. US unemployment is down to a trough of 5.9 percent. Before the stock market crash, many analysts were expressing concern that the real risk was the overheating of the US economy, not recession. Capacity limitations are beginning to appear in certain manufacturing sectors.

In the seventies and early 1980s, global recession stemmed from oil price shock and stagflation. Today the principal risk of recessionary shock comes from the possibility that the correction of the large external imbalances among the United States, on the one hand, and Europe and Japan, on the other, will fail to be managed in a competent way. Stephen Marris emphasizes the risk of recession driven by sharply higher US interest rates, pushed up by an exchange rate crisis that dries up the supply of foreign capital to the United States before the trade turnaround has time to materialize (Marris, 1987). The failure of private capital to continue entering the United States in 1987, and its replacement primarily by intervention by foreign central banks, is disturbing evidence that this scenario could actually be under way. Much will depend on whether foreign exchange market expectations are stabilizing, in which case investors abroad could return to placing funds in the United States because the lower dollar seems cheap, or whether expectations are extrapolative, causing foreign investors to expect still greater exchange losses if they venture back into the US capital market. Similarly, the extent to which foreign central banks are prepared to build up further dollar reserves will be an important factor.

At a more general level, there is concern about slow international growth because of the fear that as the United States reduces its trade deficit with the rest of the world, there will be a Keynesian lack of effective demand because of inadequate replacement of export demand in Europe and Japan by new domestic demand. While the Japanese government has begun to take measures to address this problem, most of Europe is waiting on Germany to act (in light of the precarious external accounts of several European countries), and the German government has been moving slowly indeed. There is considerable scope for demand expansion in Europe, in view of persistently high unemployment rates and low inflation.

The required policy package is a combination of sharp reductions in the US fiscal deficit, to reduce the resource imbalance and take pressure off external accounts, combined with measures for stimulus in Europe and Japan. In the United States, growth would be largely maintained by the contribution of increased exports and the crowding in of domestic investment as the scope for monetary ease increases with fiscal correction. Such a "co-operative" international package could avert at least the worst scenarios for international recession. It is highly disconcerting, however, that so far the US political system seems incapable of dealing with its fiscal deficit. The highly advertised compromise between Congress and the President after the stock market crash does no more than freeze the deficit at $150 billion through 1989.

If OECD growth is one source of concern, international interest rates are a second. For Latin American debtors, the worst combination would be an OECD recession driven by a sharp rise in interest rates. This scenario seemed to threaten in mid-1987 as the interest rate rose. From early in the year until early October, LIBOR rose from the range 6.5–9.25 percent. By the end of November, the dampening of inflationary expectations from the stock market crash, and the ample provision of money by the Federal Reserve in light of the crash, brought LIBOR back down to 7.75 percent. If the rate remains there, for 1988 interest costs on Latin American variable-rate debt will be approximately 1.3 percentage points above the 1987 rate (6-month lagged).

The specter of sharply higher interest rates has pressed Brazilian negotiators to seek an interest cap in their negotiations with the banks, and induced Treasury Secretary James Baker to propose that the IMF compensatory finance facility be extended to cover interest rate shocks.[13] Market mechanisms would permit conversion of floating to fixed interest rates at a price, although it is unlikely that Brazil or other debtors are prepared to pay the premium above current LIBOR that would be required.

Sharply higher interest rates are not a foregone conclusion either, however. Indeed, the US strategy has recently shifted from defending the dollar at ranges set at the OECD Louvre meeting in spring 1987, including through higher interest rates, to allowing the dollar to decline further and avoiding a rise in the rate of interest. By early December there were signs that German monetary authorities were prepared to let rates there fall to limit the decline of the dollar. More generally, if Keynesian demand deficiency is the prospective tendency in the international economy, the natural trend for interest rates (apart from dollar confidence crises) would be downward.

Besides aggregate demand in the OECD and the level of international interest rates, there is concern about how the needed correction in the US external accounts (a correction likely to cut $150–200 billion off the US trade deficit) can be carried out over the next few years without an adverse effect on Latin American exports. The United States is the largest market for these exports, especially for manufactured goods. However, as long as the debtor countries do not allow real appreciation of their exchange rates on a trade-weighted basis, there should be no adverse impact on their exports from the standpoint of relative price. Indeed, because many peg to the dollar in real terms, they could depreciate in real terms on a trade-weighted basis, and their increased exports to Europe and Japan could exceed their reductions in exports to the United States. It is important, however, that the US adjustment not be based primarily on US recession. In that case, the income effect would cause reduced Latin American exports even if the price effect did not.

In the commodity area, there is cause for optimism. As noted above, the reversal of the long decline in dollar commodity prices has been under way for more than a year now. Basic theory and considerable past econometric work suggest that the sharp decline of the dollar should eventually be mirrored by a rise in dollar prices of traded goods, including commodities, in order to maintain their real value. Even against a long-term trend toward price erosion from such factors as substitution by synthetics, technological change in materials use, and outward shifting supply, there should be considerable scope for rising nominal dollar prices. Higher commodity prices, of course, would inflate the export value base supporting the debt, which is largely denominated in dollars. Moreover, because most of Latin America is in trade surplus, there would be an additional trade balance gain because a given percentage rise in dollar prices of imports and exports would cause a greater rise in the absolute value of the latter. As for oil, the likelihood is that the longer-term trend is toward a gradual increase in real price, so that a renewed collapse along the lines of 1986, with its severe destabilization for the oil-exporting debtors, is unlikely. At the same time, near-term supply pressure makes it unlikely that there will be an upward price shock that would destabilize major oil importers such as Brazil.

The international economic outlook is thus filled with risk, much of it downside, but there are also potential favorable developments for the debtor countries (especially in the commodity price area). It does seem that there is a fundamental difference between the recessionary pressures of the mid-1970s and early 1980s, arising from the real shock of oil prices and the need to reduce extremely high inflation, on the one hand, and the potential recessionary pressures today arising from mismanagement of the process of correcting international trade imbalances. Thus, in the current context, any recession would seem more likely to be shorter and shallower than that of 1982 or that of 1974. For example, a US recession would speed up the correction of the US trade deficit, and alleviate exchange market expectational pressure on US interest rates (assuming, as is reasonable, that the exchange market is now back in the mode in which trade balances affect the rate more than capital markets, as suggested by the sharp announcement effect of the unfavorable August 1987 trade data).

What are the prospects for Latin America's ability to service its debt in this environment? With average OECD growth of 3 percent and LIBOR averaging 8 percent, my own baseline forecasts show that Brazil and Mexico should be able to make considerable continued progress. Brazil should be able to reduce the ratio of net interest payments to exports of goods and services from 36 percent in 1986 to 29 percent by 1991. Mexico should be able to reduce its corresponding ratio from 31 percent in 1986 to 17 percent by 1991 (and much of the reduction already occurred in 1987, although to some extent the ratio is understated by Mexico's practice of including interest earnings abroad by private citizens in its balance of payments, even though these earnings may remain abroad). While there is considerable risk that OECD growth will fall well below 3 percent in 1989 in particular (after the US election-year push to prolong growth is over), an average of 3 percent over five years is plausible. Interestingly, my projections for Brazil are close to those published by the government in its Plan of Macroeconomic Control (Brazil, Ministerio de Fazenda, 1987). The projections allow for growth in the range of 4–5 percent in Mexico and 5–6 percent in Brazil.

For Argentina, medium-term projections are less favorable. My projections show little change in the ratio of net interest payments to exports of goods and services from its 1987 level of 45 percent through 1991. However, the assumptions are conservative on commodity prices, and moderate recovery in agricultural prices could make the outlook far more favorable for Argentina.

Even under base-case and favorable international economic scenarios, continued emergence from the debt problem will require skillful economic policy-making in the debtor countries. Once the uncertainty associated with an undetermined presidential term and constitutional reform gives way to a more predictable environment, and especially after the election of a new president, the chances are that economic policy-making will become more stable in Brazil. In Argentina, there are signs of fatigue in the adroit economic strategy that began with the change of economic ministry in early 1985, and many Peronist economists call for some form of concessional debt relief in particular. Although Alfonsin has urged a return to lower "historic" interest rates, he has carefully reiterated that Argentina will negotiate rather than act unilaterally.

So far Mexico has shown remarkable economic policy judgement in the face of adversity. President de la Madrid explained the decision to remain within the conventional debt strategy despite the 1986 oil shock in these words: 'Today, trade and financing are closely linked, and we cannot jeopardize the flows of food, inputs and capital goods, or the flow of tourism from abroad, that our economy needs to function. The vast majority of Mexicans do not want to declare economic war on the world' (Fifth State of the Nation Report, 1987). There could be intensified pressure within Mexico to seek some form of concessional interest relief to assist in dealing with the severe problem of inflation. However, as stated above, the analytical case for concessional debt relief to deal with internal fiscal and inflationary problems is weak. It remains to be seen whether the sophisticated economic expertise of the probable new President, Carlos Salinas, will dominate political pressures in the formation of future policy, although the business community's reaction to the announcement of his candidacy indicated the general expectation that it would.

The remain structural difficulties to be dealt with in the capital markets as well. The return of rescheduling countries to voluntary lending will be a delicate task even as debt indicators return to more acceptable levels. Thus, Colombia has attempted to mobilize financing just to refinance principal in 1987–8, and has had to mount an exercise called the "Concorde" of co-ordinated lending to do so rather than rely on more completely voluntary lending. Although the bulk of the money sought appears to be in hand, the program has not been completely successful in raising refinancing. "Club" loans of this sort are likely to play an important role in the transition back to voluntary lending. So will trade credit and project credits along the Venezuelan model. Among the largest debtors, the rapid improvement in Mexico's external debt indicators suggests that it may be the first to be able to restore more normal access to credit markets.

In the meantime, the process of mobilizing new lending through co-ordinated packages will have to continue to be an important element of the debt strategy. Skeptics have repeatedly announced the demise of new money packages, yet they have shown surprising resilience. The most recent evidence that this mechanism remains viable is the apparently successful mobilization by 70 banks of the $1 billion in new lending to Brazil for the $1.5 billion total package (of which Brazil is to contribute $500 million) to cover interest for the final quarter of 1987 (*Financial Times*, 1987b). Elsewhere I have examined new approaches that might bolster the new-money process (Cline, 1987b). These include the use of bonds as a means of providing *de facto* seniority for new money; the incorporation of "sweeteners" such as options for debt–equity conversion and scope for on-lending to private sector clients; and elective interest capitalization for those banks (presumably a minority primarily in some European countries) that prefer it over new lending. The important point is that, with or without major innovations, new money will have to be forthcoming to refinance somewhere in the range of one-third to one-half of interest coming due in most cases (although Colombia, Venezuela, and Mexico should be able to make do with considerably less). In the end it seems likely that banks acting in their collective self-interest will accomplish this task, lest it be accomplished for them by other less attractive means.

In sum, neither the future outlook for debt management nor the actual past record is as bleak as many believe and as recent statements at the political level in Latin America would indicate. Instead, it is likely that those countries that take serious steps to get on with the business of export expansion and fiscal correction will be able to make continued progress in dealing with their debt problems.

Other nations that use external debt as a justification for inadequate domestic policies could encounter more troublesome times. Nor would an aggressive threat posture, even of a group of two, three, or more, be likely to be productive even in a zero- (or negative-) sum game sense with the debtors as beneficiaries. With larger reserves and higher capital relative to Latin American debt, the banking systems in the industrial countries are no longer greatly vulnerable to this debt as they were in 1982.

Most of the Latin American nations have made efforts of heroic proportions so far in dealing with the debt crisis. There has been important policy slippage in some major cases, but the extent of the efforts overall has been massive. The challenge to Latin American policy-makers is to identify and pursue the soundest strategy to consolidate these costly gains, with the objective of providing the most favorable possible economic outcome for their populations five years or a decade from now. The challenge to policy-makers in the industrial countries is to navigate the macroeconomic waters that confront them, especially those associated with the correction of international trade imbalances, in such a way that global growth is sustained and the economic environment in which the Latin American debtor countries must operate remains as hospitable as possible.

NOTES

1 The total bank figures are from BIS data, adjusting flows for exchange rate changes. Note that both these data and the US data may somewhat bias downward the amount of new lending, because writedowns (on countries such as Peru) reduce the reported loans outstanding even though amortization has not taken place.

2 While Dornbusch's proposal differs in that it is not directly a recommendation of concessional relief, in practice it becomes so because the holders of obligations that may not be transferred abroad will apply deep discounts on them even if they provide for full protection against domestic inflation plus some real return.

3 The elasticity of GNP with respect to foreign exchange availability equals the shadow price of foreign exchange minus unity, multiplied by the share of imports in GNP (Cline, 1987a, Appendix A). Brazil's import share is approximately 6 percent, so the elasticity of GNP with respect to import availability is 0.06. Savings of 1 percent of GNP would permit an increase of imports by 16.7 percent. Applying the elasticity of GNP with respect to import availability, GNP would rise by 1 percent.

4 This approach may be found, for example, in Bacha (1987); and, implicitly, in recent reported statements by authorities in Argentina and Brazil to the effect that growth with price stability is incompatible with servicing of the full debt.

5 Note however that there is probably some real deficit remaining despite the zero operational deficit. The existing inflationary tax through erosion of the money supply's real value may contribute up to 3 percent of GNP in resources

to the government. Even so, this fiscal performance is much closer to closure of the fiscal gap than in Argentina and Brazil.

6 For example, in the conference presenting the results of the National Bureau of Economic Research project on Latin American debt, Washington DC, September, 1987.

7 Although Edmar Bacha did so argue with respect to Brazil in the early 1980s, on the grounds that IMF formulae would have caused more severe recession than necessary, it would appear that many Brazilian economists who took this position earlier have now reversed their views in light of the policy disarray within Brazil since mid-1986 (Bacha, 1983, pp. 31–41). In any event the issue here is broader: whether any conditions whatsoever (not necessarily those of an earlier and more rigid IMF formulation) can help ensure favorable economic policies.

8 Diaz-Alejandro favored this approach in part because of the disarray in economic theory concerning proper domestic macropolicy (Diaz-Alejandro, 1983, pp. 341–6).

9 Salomon Brothers, as cited in Cardoso and Dornbusch, 1987.

10 I am indebted to John Williamson for this point, although his formulation also incorporates a broader agreement providing for concessional relief and directed more towards countries with extremely heavy debt burdens.

11 Countries seeking to provide their own guarantees might find it desirable to experiment with zero coupon bonds as collateral. Zero coupon US Treasury bonds of 20 to 25 years maturity can be purchased at a small fraction of face value. The debtor country could set aside a modest amount of foreign exchange for the purchase of these instruments. For each dollar used, perhaps $5 or more of face value zero coupon bond could be purchased. These instruments could then be placed in depository banks abroad as the collateral on $5 face value of exit bonds. While to the economist the guaranteeing of principal, as opposed to interest stream, on a long-term instrument is of limited value, it is possible that market participants would take considerable psychological comfort from the presence of principal guarantee provided in this manner.

12 My own theory is that the US 1986 Tax Act caused the bubble. The law ended preferred tax treatment for long-term capital gains. The change created a sharp incentive for anyone planning to sell stocks to do so before the end of 1986. Many did so, as shown by the unexpectedly high fiscal revenue from capital gains taxes for that year. At the beginning of 1987, this selling pressure disappeared. Not surprisingly, the market began to rise. Once it had risen for a period of time, it gained its own band-wagon momentum. As with all bubbles, adverse information punctured it (in the instance, in the form of rising interest rates, adverse data on the trade balance and thus the fear of higher interest rates to defend the dollar). Once selling began, there was no longer a tax incentive to hold on for longer-term capital gains, and programmed portfolio insurance trading accelerated the decline.

13 As recommended in Bergsten, et al. (1985), pp. 75–6, and in my own earlier congressional testimony.

REFERENCES

Bacha, Edmar (1983), "The IMF and the Prospects for Adjustment in Brazil," in John Williamson (ed.), *Prospects for Adjustment in Argentina, Brazil and Mexico*, Washington: Institute for International Economics, June.

Bacha, Edmar (1987) "The Antechamber of Confrontation: Latin America's Debt-Crisis in the Late Eighties," mimeo, Rio de Janeiro: Catholic University, August.

Bergsten, Fred, Cline, William, and Williamson, John (1985), *Bank Lending to Developing Countries: The Policy Alternatives*, Washington: Institute for International Economics, Policy Analyses in International Economics No. 10, April.

Brazil, Ministero de Fazenda (1987), *Plano de Controle Macroeconomico*, Brazilia, July.

Cardoso, Eliana and Dornbusch, Rudiger (1987), "Brazilian Debt: A Requiem for Muddling Through," chapter 11 in this volume.

Cline, William (1987a), "Implications of Alternative Debt Strategies for Mexico," in *Economic Issues in United States–Mexican Relations: Prospects and Perspectives*, New York: Ford Foundation, April.

Cline, William (1987b), "Mobilizing Bank Lending to Debtor Countries," Washington: Institute for International Economics No. 18, June.

de la Madrid, Miguel (1987), *Fifth State of the Nation Report*, mimeo, Mexico: September.

Díaz-Alejandro, Carlos (1983), "Comments," in John Williamson (ed.), *IMF Conditionality*, Washington: Institute for International Economics.

Financial Times (1987a), November 19.

Financial Times (1987b), December 4.

Fischer, Stanley (1987), "Resolving the International Debt Crisis," in Jeffrey Sachs (ed.), *Developing Country Debt*, Cambridge, MA, NBER.

International Monetary Fund (1987a), *World Economic Outlook*, October.

International Monetary Fund (1987b), *International Financial Statistics*, November.

Marris, Stephen (1987), *Deficits and the Dollar*, Washington: Institute for International Economics.

Portes, Richard (1987), "Debt and the Market," mimeo, London: Centre for Economic Policy Research, September.

Roberts, David and Remolona, Eli, (1987), "Debt Swaps: A Technique in Developing Country Finance," in R. A. Debs, D. M. Roberts and E. M. Remolona (eds), *Finance for Developing Countries*, New York: Group of Thirty.

Simonsen, Mario H. (1987), "O Risco de Optar pelo Atraso," *Veja*, October.

Wall Street Journal (1987a), December 4.

Wall Street Journal (1987b), December 7.

Comment

Patricio Meller

William Cline has been persistently optimistic about the Latin American debt prospect. He was an optimist in 1983 when he stated that the Latin American external debt problem was only a liquidity problem which would be solved within a couple years; he is very optimistic now in stating (1) that there has been progress in the external debt situation; and (2) that future perspectives look quite good. William Cline arbitrarily uses any type of indicator which he considers useful to support his statements.

The main message of Cline's paper is the following: those countries which will implement *sound* economic policies oriented towards increasing exports and lowering the fiscal deficit will have no problems in servicing and paying the external debt. The implicit idea here is that the solution of the external debt problem is really an internal problem of the debtor countries and, therefore, they should not look for external solutions.

These comments will be divided in two parts: in the first part it will be shown that there are some economic indicators not provided by Cline, and which are quite relevant for understanding the difficulties related to the solution of the external debt problem. In the second part there will be a criticism on the focus of Cline's paper.

The following is a schematic list of indicators not provided by Cline's paper:[1]

1 Latin America's cost of adjustment: growth rates, investment, consumption and real wages have all decreased while unemployment has increased. The average annual growth of Latin America has been 1 percent in the 1981–6 period, compared to a 5 percent rate of the 1970s; Latin American income per capita of 1986 is 14 percent lower than that of 1980.

2 The amount of the transfer: the relative importance of Latin American external debt interest payments with respect to GDP or exports is *twice* as large as that of Germany's war reparations (World War I, 1925–32). It should be pointed out that Germany had important deficits in its trade balance (1925–8) while servicing its war reparation payments; moreover, payments were suspended in 1933. Latin America's real transfer has been 4.3 percent of GDP during 1982–5;[2] Germany's real transfer was 2.5 percent of GDP during 1929–32.

3 External shocks: during the 1980s, Latin America faced several adverse shocks: deterioration of the terms of trade, and increases in the
(nominal and real) international interest rates. According to Bianchi,
Devlin and Ramos (1987)[3] if Latin America had not suffered these adverse
external shocks, then the Latin American current account would have had
surpluses from 1983 on.

4 Different external debt indicators show a non-improving, and in effect
a deteriorating evolution of the Latin American debt situation. For Latin
America as a whole, interest payments over exports were 20.2 percent in
1980, increased to 41 percent 1982, and then, from 1983 on they have
stayed over 35 percent. For Latin America as a whole, the stock of the
(external) debt with respect to exports has persistently increased from 214
percent in 1980, to 321 percent in 1982, and to 401 percent in 1986.

The main message from the above indicators is the following: in spite of
all the adjustment costs incurred by Latin America in order to continue
servicing the external debt payments, the situation is at best either the
same as before, or worse. Then, why will more of the same, as Cline
suggests, make things better? Nowadays it is clear that more of the same,
i.e., the "muddling-through" scheme is not the solution; Latin America
has reached saturation point.

Cline's paper is out of focus with respect to the issues that are currently
discussed in Latin America. A recent meeting of eight presidents of Latin
American countries was held in Mexico in November 1987; it is true they
did not have a chance to read Cline's paper, but if they had I do not think it
would have made any difference. In that meeting the main outcome was
that Latin America is not able to make any more external transfers of the
size it has made so far. Therefore there should be an upper limit to the
amount of the transfer related to domestic economic conditions and
without sacrificing economic growth.

The implication of this statement is that a definitive global solution to the
Latin American external debt problem must be reached *now*, and there
should be no more postponement. Latin American countries cannot think
long terms without a solution to the external debt problem. The debt
overhang critically affects savings and investment decisions, and therefore
long term growth.

The main thrust of the problem should be the following: given the fact
that Latin America can pay only a given percentage of debt service
payments, what type of action can resolve the problem, and how will the
costs related to the lower debt service payments be distributed? In return,
Latin American countries will follow so-called sound economic policies,
and there should be an agreement that conditions are required to ensure
this process. There is no problem with the existence of conditionality; the
difficulties are related to the requirements included in the conditionality

package. In this respect, Latin American countries would be willing to accept a conditionality package similar to one that would be accepted by the more developed countries. In other words, a Latin American country would accept a conditionality policy similar to any that the United States would implement in order to reduce a fiscal and trade deficit which are about 4 percent of GDP.

Most Latin American economists agree that it is important to increase exports, and that the outwards oriented strategy is the one which will promote faster growth; here again, Cline's paper is out of focus. The main questions in this respect are: (i) all economists support the implementation of sound policies, but the discrepancies lie in agreeing which are the so-called sound policies that would promote export growth; and (ii) export promotion requires major structural adjustments which involve the use of a large amount of resources. The main problem is that, given that existing resources are scarce, Latin American countries cannot implement the required structural adjustment changes while transferring outwards huge real resources for servicing the external debt.

NOTES

1 For more detailed information and their respective references see P. Meller, "America Latina y la condicionalidad del Fondo Monetario Internacional y del Banco Mundial", *Coleccion Estudios CIEPLAN* March 1988.
2 Many Latin American economists are reviewing history in order to find out which war lost Latin America.
3 A. Bianchi, R. Devlin, and J. Ramos (1987), "El proceso de ajuste en la America Latina. 1981–1986", *El Trimestre Economico*, Vol. LIV, No. 216, October, pp. 855–911.

3

Resolving Debt Crises: an Historical Perspective

Barry Eichengreen

1 Introduction

The developing-country debt crisis recently celebrated its fifth anniversary. That more than five years have passed since the Mexican crisis of 1982 is no cause for celebration. In the intervening years, the collapse of long-term lending and the policies of austerity adopted by the borrowers have combined with global economic imbalances to depress domestic investment and economic growth through much of the developing world. As the crisis drags on, prospects for renewed growth continue to be adversely affected. This recognition has occasioned a number of ambitious plans for resolving the crisis. These range from the Baker Plan to encourage concerted bank lending to developing countries, to the Kenen Plan which would have the IMF or another international entity buy up debt at a discount and pass along the benefits to the debtor countries, the Bradley and Sachs Plans which would have the banks directly forgive developing-country liabilities, and the Dornbusch Plan which permits countries to service their debt in domestic currency.[1] In contrast, Cline (1987) and Feldstein (1987) have criticized the global approach, urging instead reliance on the market to resolve the crisis through case-by-case negotiation.

This is not the first time that foreign lending has culminated in default or that default has reached crisis proportions. Nor is it the first time that ambitious proposals have been elicited by disarray in international capital markets. In the 1930s, when some two thirds of foreign dollar bonds lapsed into default, a number of global schemes for resolving the crisis were discussed. Some, like current proposals under which the World Bank or IMF would adopt a leading role, relied on the newly-established Bank for International Settlements for mediation and liquidity. Others advocated instead the establishment of an independent facility controlled by the bankers. Some thought the solution lay in converting one asset into another, not through debt–equity swaps as today, but by transforming short- and medium-term obligations into long-term liabilities. Others emphasized instead the need to index payments to macroeconomic indicators such as the price level or the value of exports, or to permit debt to be serviced in local currency with provision for reinvesting interest payments domestically when transfer was not feasible. Like today, there were those who argued the inefficacy of all global plans, insisting on the superiority of case-by-case negotiation.

In the end, no global plan was adopted. The debt crisis of the 1930s was resolved by the "muddling-through" approach of bilateral negotiation. This observation raises two questions. First, what stumbling blocks stood in the way of the adoption of global schemes? Second, as the crisis dragged on, how did the evolution of debtor and creditor strategies permit the crisis to be resolved through bilateral negotiation?

In this chapter I analyze global and bilateral approaches to dealing with foreign default in the interwar years. Section 2 sketches the background to negotiations: the origins and characteristics of the debt crisis of the 1930s. Section 3 then describes the global schemes and bilateral negotiations. The conclusion suggests some implications for the current situation.

2   Into the Crisis

The tapestry of foreign debts

The experience with foreign lending in the 1920s has been recounted on more than one occasion (Fleisig, 1970; Eichengreen and Portes, 1986). The aspect of the episode relevant for present purposes is that the way countries got themselves into the debt crisis of the 1930s shaped their options for getting out. The nature of the shocks which pushed the borrowers into default conditioned debtor and creditor attitudes toward negotiations to restart debt service. The nature of the foreign debts incurred – their magnitude, maturity and currency composition – served as the initial conditions from which negotiations would commence. The institutional structures linking the small investor to the foreign government, notably issue houses, the secondary market for bonds, and bondholders' committees, comprised the framework within which those negotiations took place.

Frequently it is suggested that, compared to the current environment of gigantic bank syndicates, lengthy loan contracts, and complex regulatory restrictions, rescheduling in the 1930s was straightforward. The era of bond finance is portrayed as a simpler era, when bond covenants were transparent and negotiations had to surmount only the large numbers problem created by the multitude of small creditors, a hurdle which was successfully overcome with the creation of bondholders' representative committees. A central message here is that precisely the opposite was true. Progress in debt renegotiation in the 1930s was impeded by interlocking creditor–debtor relationships and by the proliferation of debt instruments ranging from short-term acceptances to long-term bonds, from war debts to reparations, from foreign commercial deposits to foreign exchange reserves. Freeing one thread from this tapestry without unraveling the fabric was the challenge for negotiators.

The first thread in the tapestry was made up of war debts, in Herbert Feis's evocative words, the "sludge left after the fires of the First World War had died down." The stance of the United States, the principal creditor, toward war debts shaped the attitudes of negotiators toward other obligations. Accounts of war debt negotiations traditionally emphasize US intransigence, an emphasis that certainly is relevant here.[2] But while insisting that war debts were business transactions to be honored like any other, by the standards of commercial creditors the US displayed considerable flexibility when negotiating the payment schedule. It did not insist on immediate repayment in the exceptional circumstances of the early postwar years. The individual agreements negotiated and ratified by Congress were adapted to the economic circumstances of the debtor. The agreement with Britain concluded in June 1923, for example, stretched out the repayment period to more than 60 years, and reduced the interest rate from the high levels at which Britain had been forced to borrow during the war. Arrears from the immediate postwar years were capitalized at concessional rates that varied with the debtor's ability to pay. These concessions reflected a realization on the part of business interests that US prospects were linked to the successful economic recovery of the heavily indebted nations of Europe (Leffler, 1972, pp. 586–9). If the US was unwilling to simply cancel these debts or even to enter into multilateral negotiations, it nevertheless exhibited some flexibility in negotiations with individual debtors and set an important precedent for subsequent debt negotiations by acknowledging the relevance of ability to pay.

The second thread in the tapestry was German reparations. Their story is depressingly familiar. In 1919 signatories of the Versailles Treaty, unable to agree on an amount, appointed a Reparations Commission which in April 1921 delivered a figure of 132,000 million gold marks, an amount roughly twice German GNP. Payments on 50,000 million of the 132,000 million mark total were to commence immediately. Like war debts, German obligations were partially indexed to economic conditions: in addition to her fixed obligation of 2,000 million gold marks annually, Germany would pay 26 percent of her export revenues. Germany's payments in foreign exchange and kind dwindled rapidly – whether due to calculated strategy or a sincere inability to pay is still disputed today – leading an exasperated France and Belgium to occupy the Ruhr in January 1923. Occupation led not to resumption of full payments but to passive resistance and hyperinflation. At the end of the year, the exhausted British, French and German governments agreed to a commission to reschedule reparations in a manner that would buttress the precariously stabilized German currency. Under the chairmanship of Charles Dawes, Director of the US Bureau of the Budget, the Commission scaled down Germany's total obligation and deferred the bulk of the payments. Annual transfers started at 1,000 million gold marks, rising gradually to 2,500 million after five years. In a significant departure from the manner in which commercial bond covenants were structured, reparations were indexed to the state of the world economy (rising or falling if the price level varied by more than 10 percent). In addition, the payments schedule was indexed to domestic economic conditions, as measured by such items as the volume of automobile sales. Germany's obligation ended with the deposit of domestic currency in the reparation authority's account; responsibility for effecting the transfer into foreign currency rested with the recipients. If transfer difficulties arose, the reparations commission was to reinvest the funds in Germany. A foreign Agent-General was appointed to monitor and enforce the provisions of the plan. To seal the agreement, a loan of 800 million marks secured by the assets of the German railway system was floated in foreign financial centers.

This capsule account conveys little sense of the complexity of negotiations. A central source of difficulty was that reparations were interwoven with other obligations, notably war debts. Notwithstanding US insistence that the two were unrelated, Britain, France, Belgium and Italy, for whom reparations receipts offset war debt expenditures, were disinclined to extend debt relief to Germany unless the US similarly relieved them of wartime obligations.[3]

The third thread in the tapestry was made up of foreign bonds floated mainly in New York in the 1920s. These were tightly interwoven with the intergovernmental debts just described. Not only had the process of large-scale foreign lending in the twenties been initiated by successful flotation of the Dawes Loan in New York and London, but a significant share of bonds subsequently sold in New York on behalf of foreign borrowers was floated on behalf of Germany and the successor states of Eastern Europe that owed reparations. Despite its disastrous denouement, the process was not without logic. Long-term borrowing was a way for these countries to defer a transfer that was difficult in the short run. A reparations obligation of, say, 1,200 million marks in 1926 could be funded by borrowing an equal amount from the United States, thereby permitting payments to be spread out over the life of the bond. While the present value of the obligation was unchanged, transfer was deferred until a time when the disorganized conditions of the 1920s could be surmounted. By delaying the transfer until the productive potential of the German and Eastern European economies was restored, these countries would have been permitted to grow out from under the burden of the debt (Feis, 1966, pp. 15–16).

The final thread in the tapestry was short-term debt: loans, foreign deposits and acceptances. Often short-term loans were extended to long-term borrowers by the syndicate of underwriting banks and issue houses over the period required to successfully market their bonds. To these should be added the foreign deposits maintained by creditor-country banks and corporations doing business abroad, for use in making payment for goods and services purchased from foreigners or receiving payment for those rendered. Acceptances, a form of trade credit on behalf of commercial borrowers, should also be included under this heading (Eichengreen and Portes, 1987). As the most volatile component of foreign lending, short-term debts had considerable capacity to interfere with the balance-of-payments position and hence with the debt-servicing capacity of foreign debtors.

Origins of debt-servicing difficulties

The debt crisis of the 1930s did not result from any single cause. As in the 1980s, it arose out of the interaction of a sequence of unanticipated disturbances with a set of fragile initial conditions. Over the period of large-scale foreign lending (1924–8), the sheer volume of debts to be serviced had increased enormously. Annual interest and amortization payments could amount to 10 percent of the debt outstanding; thus in relatively heavily indebted Latin American countries like Mexico, Bolivia, Uruguay and Chile, upwards of 15 percent of export receipts were required to service the central government's external debt alone (see figure 3.1).[4] In other countries where the absolute value of the debt was greater (such as Australia and Canada, shown in figure 3.2), the burden relative to exports was less. In Latin America, with such a large share of export revenues already going to debt service, once new lending evaporated in 1928, a significant transfer from debtor to creditor could be required to keep service current. The indebted countries were clearly vulnerable to export and price-level shocks.

Shocks came not in isolation but in rapid succession. The terms of trade of primary-product exporting countries had already been deteriorating throughout the 1920s. They then plunged downward with the onset of the Great Depression. The United States was the leading market for primary products, accounting for nearly 40 percent of the consumption of the 15 leading industrial countries, and the severity of the Depression in the US

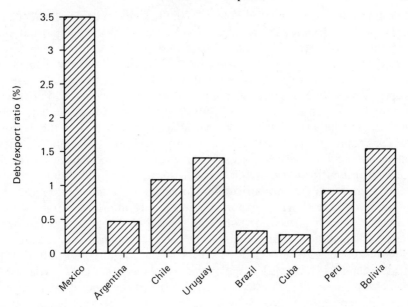

Figure 3.1 Comparative debt/export ratios, Latin America, 1928

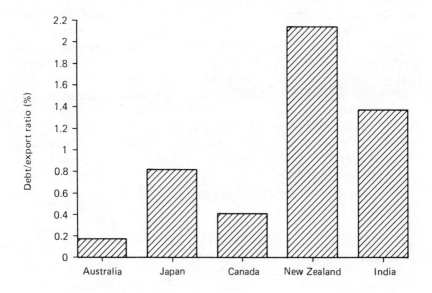

Figure 3.2 Comparative debt/export ratios, 1928

was unparalleled. Between 1929 and 1930, the terms of trade of wheat and tin exporters declined by roughly 10 percent, of cotton, sugar and silk exporters by 20 percent, of rubber exporters by 30 percent (Eichengreen and Portes, 1986, p. 612). By increasing the cost of inelastically-demanded imports, the terms-of-trade shock left a smaller trade surplus for use in debt service. That shock was reinforced by the global deflation; since external debt was denominated in foreign currency (mainly dollars) and bore fixed interest rates, the decline in wholesale prices in the United States of approximately 10 percent between 1929 and 1930 reinforced the shock to the debt-servicing capacity of borrowing countries. Sovereign debt–export ratios of most borrowing countries rose more dramatically after 1928, when foreign borrowing had virtually halted, than before. In other words, the shock to export markets contributed more dramatically than the preceding wave of borrowing to the alarming rise in the debt burden. Difficulties at the periphery were exacerbated by increased protectionism at the core, especially since the new tariffs imposed after 1929 discriminated against agricultural goods (Eichengreen, 1989). Together, depression and protectionism reduced the export revenues of 41 primary-product exporting countries by some 50 percent between 1928–9 and 1932–3. The magnitude of the shock suggests that the extent to which the indebted countries squandered the funds they borrowed on unproductive projects, even if relevant, is of secondary importance.

The weight of the debt and the magnitude of the external shock, while critically important, were not the only determinants of default. Eichengreen and Portes (1986) have presented a multivariate analysis of the incidence and extent of default in the 1930s. The probability of default was found to rise with both the debt–income ratio and the percent deterioration in the terms of trade. But in addition, domestic policy responses to the Depression, notably the change in the government budget deficit, also affected the tendency to default. Countries which adopted draconian fiscal responses to the budget deficits induced by the macroeconomic slump were less likely to default than other countries with similar debt–income ratios, similar terms-of-trade shocks, but more expansionary fiscal policies. Default depended not only on the external shock but on the domestic response.

3   Out of the Crisis

Global plans

The challenge facing those attempting to renegotiate debts in the 1930s was how to deal with the overlapping nature of different liabilities. These interdependencies were what gave special appeal to global plans.

The Bank for International Settlements (1930–2) The most straightforward global approach to the debt crisis would have been to empower the Bank for International Settlements. The BIS had been founded in 1930 as part of the Young Plan rescheduling of German reparations. France and Britain had never been satisfied with the Dawes Plan apparatus on the grounds that achieving the transfer was not properly the responsibility of Germany's creditors and their Agent-General. At the same time, they hesitated to place discretionary power in German hands. Hence the establishment of an international bank to perform these financial functions.[5]

Having been established to manage reparations, it was logical to ask whether the BIS might be used to address other debt problems. According to J. W. Beyen (Vice-President of the BIS from 1935 to 1937, President from 1937 to 1940, and author of the Beyen Plan discussed below), the BIS was initially conceived not just to administer reparations but "also for international loans floated either in connection with reparation payments or for other purposes" (Dulles, 1932, pp. 45–6). In a proposal reminiscent of those for an expanded role for the IMF today, Hubert Henderson of the British Economic Advisory Council suggested that the BIS might issue unbacked "International Certificates," to be allocated to countries in proportion to the gold value of their exports in 1928. The receipts could be used for any purpose, including presumably the maintenance of debt service.[6]

The suggestion bore no fruit, due in part to the financial position of the BIS itself. Having made unsuccessful loans in defence of the gold standard to Austria, Germany and Hungary in 1931, many of the Bank's assets were frozen. The profits derived from the everyday business of collecting German reparations in Reichsmarks (RM) and converting them to francs and sterling were eliminated by the Hoover Moratorium that suspended all payments on intergovernmental debt. The balance sheet total of the BIS fell from 2b Swiss gold francs at the beginning of 1931 to barely one-third that amount in 1933. The BIS had little liquidity of its own to inject into the international system, while creditor-country governments hesitated to entrust new foreign lending to an institution with so dismal a record of loan administration.

BIS officials took little initiative in raising additional capital or lobbying for a more active role, and concentrated instead on fostering co-operation among central banks. Exchange-rate stability rather than foreign debts became their primary concern. This is unsurprising since the BIS was creature of the creditor countries, and the governors of their central banks dominated its Board. These officials attached priority to the instability of currencies rather than to the collapse of foreign lending. Indeed, to insulate efforts to insure international currency stability from impinging political pressures, the statutes of the BIS prohibited the new institution from extending loans directly to governments (Beyen, 1951, p. 51).[7] After their unsatisfactory encounter with sovereign lending in 1931, central banks were disinclined to alter these statutes or to contemplate yet more ambitious initiatives. If a global solution to the debt crisis was in the offing, it would not originate with the BIS.

The Kindersley–Norman Plan (1931)   Attributed variously to Sir Robert Kindersley, Chairman of Lazard Brothers and a Director of the Bank of England, Sir Charles Addis, one-time British representative to the Reichsbank, and Montagu Norman, Governor of the Bank of England, this scheme came to be known as the Norman Plan once the Governor presented it at a meeting of the directors of the BIS. Resembling ideas offered previously by Hjalmar Schacht among others, the plan was to establish a special international facility, resembling the Bretton Woods institutions which were to be founded after World War II, to make loans to foreign countries and corporations incapable of obtaining them through normal channels. The facility would be independent, not a branch of the BIS (Clarke, 1967, p. 179).[8]

The corporation, with its headquarters in Holland or Switzerland for fiscal reasons, would be endowed with a board of directors on which the bankers and other financiers would be represented. While the UK and possibly also Switzerland and Holland would help fund the facility, the major contributions were to come from the US and France, the two countries running significant balance-of-payments surpluses. "World recovery will be impeded," read the original version of the Plan "by the fact that the US and France, instead of lending back to the world their surplus for a usable balance of payment, have been taking this surplus in the form of gold."[9] Significantly, however, most of the money to be lent would come not from governments but from private investors. The scheme envisaged a corporation with £25–50 million of ordinary capital, put up by governments and the BIS, and the power to issue bonds in amounts up to three times the value of subscribed capital. The corporation would lend to "such Foreign Governments, Municipalities, Mortgage Banks, Harbour Boards, Railways and Public Utility Companies, as are in need of funds which cannot be obtained at the time through customary channels, and are in a position to offer really good security." These loans would have the effect "of reestablishing the credit of the foreign Governments, corporations, etc., to whom the money is lent, to [sic] improving the price of their securities in all markets of the world, and the purchasing power of their nationals . . ."[10]

This debt would take the form of debentures purchased in the creditor countries by banks, issue houses, and corporations and companies "of any magnitude." Trust and insurance companies, as owners of existing bonds, were likely customers since they were "vitally interested" in steps that might repair the credit of foreign debtors. Industrial firms dependent on export markets similarly might be willing to subscribe. Other investors could be encouraged through moral suasion. The cost to the borrowers would be 1–2 percent over the yield to the bondholders, the margin to be placed in the corporation's reserve for contingencies.

Memos describing the plan fail to explain why banks and issue houses, otherwise disinclined to lend to illiquid debtors in 1931, might willingly contribute £100–150 million to such a facility. One possibility is that underwriting governments might have guaranteed the loans to financially embarrassed borrowers, although this would have greatly increased their financial commitment (Bennett, 1962, p. 104). Another is that new loans might be granted seniority relative to old ones.[11] By backing not specific loans but its entire portfolio with its £25–50 million of capital, the corporation might have been able to pool default risk more effectively than smaller creditors. Debtor-country authorities might have been less inclined to default on loans extended by an international facility, extending them the kind of favored treatment usually reserved for League of Nations loans. Perhaps the corporation's loans to fund private investment or public works would succeed in restarting growth, thereby reducing debt–income ratios and restoring creditworthiness.

To what extent was the Kindersley–Norman Plan a sincere effort to deal specifically with default and the collapse of foreign lending, not simply a device to prop up sterling by inducing France and the US to stimulate demand for British exports by debtor nations? The Plan was developed and presented to the BIS at the same time as other talks were underway for strengthening sterling. In November and December 1930, Norman was discussing the possibility of Britain's floating a long-term loan in France to reduce its short-term liabilities to foreigners (Clarke, 1967, p. 178). Clarke's view (p. 181) is that the proposal as presented to the BIS was at bottom an attempt to obtain "indirect support for Britain's financial position." This seems more plausible than to assume that the British were operating out of altruism. While it remains true that loans to indebted countries would have helped them keep current the service on their sterling debts, the tendency of this to buttress Britain's financial position would have been only one effect of the initiative.

Insofar as the Kindersley–Norman Plan represented an effort to deal with the problems of debtor nations, it is not entirely clear which nations British officials had in mind. Skidelsky (1967) and Kindleberger (1973) suggest that they were concerned mainly to assist Britain's traditional export markets: Germany, Eastern Europe, Australia and South America. Except for Australia (where the threat of default by New South Wales in 1931 did not turn into actuality), these were the principal regions where default ultimately took place. Hence an amply-funded institution directing foreign capital to these regions might have done much to head off the debt crisis.

In the end, the Kindersley–Norman Plan came to nothing. As early as January 1931 Norman confessed that the plan was not particularly practical, by which he meant that it was unlikely to be favorably received (Kunz, 1987, p. 35). As Thomas Lamont's Paris partner reported following the February 9, 1931 meeting of the BIS at which Norman's memo was read, "no comments were made and no special interest was shown in it."[12] Merle Cochran, the American Consul in Basle, was more blunt, describing how the plan was poorly received since it placed the blame for the collapse of foreign lending on France and the United States.[13]

A related problem, as Norman admitted to his American colleague Harrison, was "the unwillingness, which we have seen in certain quarters, to support a scheme of which the control and the funds are truly international."[14] J. E. Crane, Deputy Governor of the New York Fed in charge of foreign affairs, concluded that US reluctance to lend abroad would not be dissipated by a scheme over which New York had little control. J. P. Morgan and colleagues voiced their unwillingness to purchase foreign bonds through the agency of an international corporation over which they had only limited control, and which might be influenced by foreign politicians and attacked by populist congressmen. Rather than create artificial agencies, Morgan insisted that new loans meet the market test. The most that should be done was to appoint an advisory committee to stimulate private bankers "to go ahead with their own projects."[15] Even this modest proposal to improve the climate for lending met a mixed reception.

France's resistance was even stronger. Since the lion's share of the funds was likely to come from France, the Paris commercial banks and the Bank of France insisted that control over any new corporation rest in French hands. In the event such a scheme was adopted, the French favored several separate institutions, one for agricultural loans, one for railway construction, and so forth.[16] But the French and Belgians agreed that the initiative for formulating such a plan properly rested with bankers, not governments.[17]

The Beyen and Crena de Jongh Plans (1932) The Beyen and Crena de Jongh Plans were floated in the winter of 1931–32. Compared with other plans discussed here, their scope was limited: they were designed to address the problem of short-time debts, not default on long-term bonds.

Beyen made his proposal to the Standstill Conference in the Winter of 1931.[18] This conference arose out of the threat to creditor-country banks and acceptance houses due to the German financial crisis.[19] German banks and firms relied heavily on short-term credits from abroad.[20] The prospect that the repayment of credits might be interrupted by the German financial crisis posed a serious threat to the London acceptance houses. These institutions specialized in the extension of trade credits, advancing to foreign exporters the funds they would receive once their goods were shipped and payment was received. Payment when received was passed along to the owner of the acceptance, interest earned taking the form of the spread between the payment received and the amount advanced to the exporter. In practice, British acceptance houses resold their paper to the market, functioning as intermediaries rather than investing their own capital in the acceptance business. Their reputation served as guarantee in the event that the debtor failed to deliver the money on the date specified. So long as default on these short-term debts was exceptional, the acceptance houses could treat it as a cost of doing business. But if many debtors defaulted simultaneously or their governments imposed exchange control, the acceptance houses themselves could be pushed into default.

This delicate mechanism functioned smoothly because the acceptance houses could count on support from the Bank of England. But the Bank of England had its own regulations to obey; it could not extend loans to the acceptance houses on unacceptable collateral, or so its Governor, Montagu Norman, argued.[21] Hence for the Bank to lend in 1931 it was necessary to maintain the pretence that German credit was still good. Under the provisions of the first German Standstill Agreement concluded in Basle under the auspices of the BIS on August 19, 1931, participating bankers agreed not to call in outstanding credits nor to cancel the credit lines under which German debtors could draw bills. Bankers who refused to sign could of course call in their credit outstanding but would receive only blocked Reichsmarks under the provisions of German exchange control.[22] The governments involved put considerable pressure on the bankers to sign.

In Beyen's view, this charade would eventually be seen through, leading to runs on financial institutions. Default on short-term debts, in his view, was more serious than default on long-term loans. While not belittling the seriousness of default on bonds, he concluded that "whatever the loan contracts may say to the contrary, the capital is in fact not called for, and the default on interest payments does not seriously hamper the economic life of the debtor country until it needs to borrow again" (Beyen, 1951, p. 62). As a banker, he regarded default on short-term debts the more serious threat to financial stability.

Beyen's proposal to the second Standstill Conference that met in Berlin in December 1931, at which he was a member of the Dutch delegation, was to convert short-term credits into long-term loans repayable in installments over a period of 20 years. There was no plan for government to assume obligations incurred by the private sector or for other administrative changes. Each debtor was to be considered individually. If the problem was not one of illiquidity, which could be resolved simply by lengthening the maturity of the debt, but one of the insolvency of a foreign corporate debtor, then the remaining assets of the company should be allocated among the creditors, with natives and foreigners receiving equal treatment. But in Beyen's view the problem was mainly one of illiquidity, not insolvency. If this could be dealt with by lengthening the maturity of the debt, repayment could begin and German exchange controls could be lifted. The creditworthiness of the debtor having been restored, the normal operation of international capital markets could recommence.

In the event that a debtor country did not succeed in earning foreign exchange adequate to service the long-term debt, there would be provision for payment in local currency. In the event of a foreign exchange shortage, debtor countries would be permitted to extend preferential treatment to creditor countries who were their best customers; creditors running bilateral deficits would have first claim on the available foreign exchange.

To say that the Beyen Plan was unenthusiastically received is to put it mildly. The bankers preferred to maintain the charade of business as usual in the hope that events might turn for the better. Germany, embroiled in reparations negotiations, insisted that servicing even long-term loans was impossible in light of the limited availability of foreign exchange. Given the interlocking nature of different debt instruments, a global plan limited to short-term debts was not global enough.

An alternative to the Beyen Plan was submitted to the Standstill Committee by another Dutch banker, Crena de Jongh. It took a different approach to lengthening the maturity structure of the debt. In contrast to the Beyen Plan, creditors were to repay their short-term debts on schedule, but in local currency rather than foreign exchange. A central administrator would issue foreign-currency-denominated bonds to be serviced with the return from investing the funds stemming from the repayment of short-term loans by domestic debtors. Where the Beyen Plan relieved domestic debtors of the obligation to repay in the short run, the Crena de Jongh Plan would have required domestic debtors to make prompt payment, albeit in local currency. If Crena de Jongh viewed the crisis simply as a transfer problem, Beyen viewed it principally as a problem of domestic illiquidity that would have interrupted service even had the short-term obligations been denominated in domestic currency. In contrast to the Beyen Plan, which failed to specify the composition of the agency which would collect and administer the foreign exchange, under the Crena de Jongh Plan administration was placed firmly in the hands of creditor-country banks.

As Beyen (1951, p. 69) put it, the Crena de Jongh Plan "met with as little response from the Standstill creditors as my suggestions."

The World Economic Conference (1933)　The World Economic Conference which convened in London on June 12, 1933 was an outgrowth of the conference on intergovernmental debts held at Lausanne in 1932. Part of the rationale for the London Conference was the feeling, especially prevalent in Europe, that the problems of war debts, commercial debts, deflation, exchange-rate instability and trade warfare could be resolved only if all were addressed simultaneously. Despite or perhaps because of these interconnections, debts remained, in the view of the Europeans, one of the central issues to be taken up in London. But the United States still regarded war debts as off limits. Consequently, the agenda for London was limited to money and credit policies, exchange-rate stabilization, and tariff and nontariff barriers to trade. With the dollar's devaluation on the eve of the conference and President Roosevelt's refusal to agree to its early stabilization, European delegations increasingly focused on what they perceived as the ongoing disintegration of the international monetary system.

The heavily indebted countries of Latin America and Eastern Europe saw things differently, and did their utmost to remind creditor-country governments of the urgency of the debt crisis. In a series of preparatory meetings with US officials in Washington, DC, they advocated ambitious initiatives to restart international capital flows. The idea of a "normalization fund" to funnel capital to countries requiring foreign funds in order to restart debt service, and to fund public works programs, had been mooted by the Special British Mission (Kindleberger, 1973, p. 211). Britain proposed an international fund of $1500–2000 million, to be subscribed by creditor-country governments and designed to make loans to debtor-country central banks, which would respond by lifting trade barriers and exchange controls. One after another, debtor-country delegations endorsed the proposal. The Rumanians argued that this initiative was essential for the recovery of countries with no domestic financial market to finance deficit spending. Their representative stated "with great emphasis that it should be clear that some international arrangement simply has got to be worked out to help them" (US State Department, 1933, p. 563). Turkey proposed the establishment of an "international credit bank" to promote international capital flows (US State Department, 1933, p. 571). Czechoslovakia, though not among the most heavily indebted nations, acknowledged the dependence of its economic prospects on the recovery of its trading partners and attached great importance to "the general alleviation of the indebtedness of the Central and Eastern European agricultural countries which were formerly her best customers" (US State Department, 1933, p. 530).[23]

But with intergovernmental debts off limits, it was hard to hold a productive discussion of commercial obligations. Had it entertained Latin

American and European proposals for a wide-ranging solution to the problem of commercial debts, the US would have undermined the official position that it was inappropriate to reconsider intergovernmental debts. In private, US officials admitted that an international fund to lend to countries requiring capital inflows to aid recovery could not be pushed through Congress. As they put it to the Polish ambassador, "American experience with respect to international loans has not been sufficiently happy to encourage it to enter into additional obligations" (US State Department, 1933, p. 561). In the end, debt was not extensively discussed in London. The atmosphere was best summed up by Beyen, who again appears on the scene, this time as deputy delegate from the Netherlands. "We met in the Geological Museum at Kensington," he subsequently wrote, "and none of our activities disturbed the fossils" (Beyen, 1951, p. 82).

Negotiations between governments

With the rejection of global plans, negotiations were officially left in private hands. One wonders how the give and take between debtor and creditor would have been shaped had governments been more intimately involved. Some light can be shed on the question by considering war debts and reparations, where official involvement was inevitable because governments were both the major creditors and the major debtors.

The Dawes Plan under which German reparations had been rescheduled in 1924 was never conceived as a permanent solution. A new committee, which differed from the Dawes Committee by virtue of Germany's full and equal representation, was appointed in January 1929 to effect such a solution. Fatigued by endless disputes, those involved hoped for a settlement that would entail early evacuation of the Rhineland and elimination of the extraordinary provisions of the Dawes Plan, notably a foreign Agent-General on German soil to collect earmarked revenues and administer their transfer into foreign currency.

In line with previous policy, the US government did not participate in the conference from fear that its involvement would be seen as acknowledgement of the linkage of war debts and reparations; instead it provided the committee's neutral chairman, Owen D. Young. Negotiators eliminated those provisions of the Dawes Plan that Germany found most objectionable, notably a reparations agency to monitor German finances. Not only was the bill scaled down and pushed further into the future, but Germany's obligation was once again indexed to economic conditions: the total was split, with provision that the second, or conditional, tranche could be deferred in the event of transfer problems.

The Young Plan represented a significant reduction of Germany's reparations payments. The principal stumbling block to further steps in the direction of realism remained US intransigence on war debts. The relationship of reparations to war debts was readily acknowledged by other governments: under the Young Plan Germany's reparations bill would be reduced automatically by at least two-thirds of any war debt relief extended by the US. To circumvent US objections, this rider was contained in a separate "concurrent memorandum."

The prominent feature of the Young Plan was its short life. The Great Depression underscored the fantastic nature of the transfer schedule, swiftly rendering the plan redundant. The problem of acknowledging this reality was again the linkage with war debts. President Hoover vacillated out of fear that a moratorium on reparations and war debts would destroy once and for all US ability to deny the existence of a link (Kindleberger, 1973, p. 154). In the event, the severity of the Depression and the outbreak of financial crisis in Austria and Germany left little choice. The Hoover Moratorium announced on June 20, 1931 suspended all payments on all intergovernmental debts.

The moratorium was designed to last for a year. To negotiate a more durable solution, national delegations assembled once more in Lausanne in June 1932. The US was absent yet again, this time because Congress, in an election year, had passed a resolution prohibiting the Administration from negotiating any reduction in foreign debts. In light of the continued deterioration of economic conditions, radical concessions were made on reparations. To extinguish her obligation, Germany was required only to deliver £150 million (or RM 3 billion) of 5 percent redeemable bonds to the BIS, which amounted to about one year's transfer under the 1921 plan. But under "the Gentlemen's Agreement," ratification of this plan was made contingent upon the successful conclusion of parallel negotiations on war debts.

British officials argued that concessions were in the interest of even the United States. They regarded debt relief not simply in terms of the feasibility of repayment but in terms of global repercussions. "Experience has, in fact, shown," Sir R. Lindsay wrote, "that when dealing with international transfers of the character and of the unprecedented magnitude of the post-war intergovernmental obligations, the principle of "the capacity to pay" of the debtor – even if thus applied – can only be regarded as of secondary importance compared with an even wider principle, viz., that of the capacity of the world to endure the economic and financial consequences which those transfers would involve" (UK Government, 1932, p. 7).

By insisting on prompt payment of interest and principal, the British argued, the United States was worsening the Great Depression. Between

1929 and 1932 manufacturing production in the US had fallen by 48 percent, and unemployment had risen to nearly 24 percent of the American labor force. Under such circumstances it was unrealistic to suppose that the US would willingly increase its imports from Britain. It was equally difficult for the UK to increase exports since, in contrast with commercial debts incurred for productive purposes – what the British called "self-liquidating" loans – it had not been possible to invest the war loans productively. Given that the option of increasing exports was not available, the UK could service its debts only by shipping gold. British gold exports would add to the concentration of reserves in the US, forcing monetary contraction on the rest of the world.[24] The balance-of-payments difficulties caused by such transfers encouraged exchange control, bilateral clearing and the further disintegration of the international monetary system, the reconstruction of which the British viewed as essential to recovery from the slump. As a result of US war debt policy, the British argued, "the international monetary mechanism without which the modern world cannot effectively conduct its daily life is being broken into pieces with all the manifold forms of privation and distress which this involves" (UK Government, 1932, p. 5). Even the US would benefit from wiping the slate clean of debts if this permitted reconstruction of the international financial system.

British observers did not overlook the irony of American inability to see the logic of their position, especially when exceptional measures like farm foreclosure moratoria were being adopted domestically. Sir Frederick Leith-Ross, chief economic adviser to the British government, submitted the following satire to the editor of Punch.[25]

A Tip to our Statesmen

"You cannot expect," said my American friend, "the farmer of Iowa to understand the advantages of debt cancellation. It is no good preaching economics to him: he is a hard-boiled fellow who considers that a debt is a debt and a debtor is a dog. What you have got to do is to follow his methods".

Now, in Iowa, debt cancellation is unknown. Debt repudiation is unheard of. Debts must be honoured. How are they honoured? A farmer can't pay debts out of deficits. His Bank forecloses. A salesman comes down to collect. How does he collect? He advertises the property. The neighbours attend. They stand around, and to make sure that the proceedings are all correct and above board and that the salesman does not quit betimes they put a halter around his neck. Then the bidding opens. It is not brisk. Prospective purchasers find a gun firmly planted in their ribs. It discourages them. Finally, the farmer concerned, or a friend, bids a dollar, and the debt is settled.

This procedure is simple, practical and perfectly effective: and there seems no reason why it should not be given a wider application. The World Conference is to meet in London. As its first proceedings, the Chairman will no doubt emphasise the need for getting together. He will quote amid resounding cheers the encouraging references to good neighbouring relations uttered by Mr. Franklin D. Roosevelt. He will then call upon the American representatives to deal with the question of debts. The representatives of the United States will place on the table the Bonds of the Allied Governments and will express the unanimous conviction of Senate and Congress that these debts must be encashed.

"Well," says the Chairman, "let's see what we can get for them. Any bids?"

No bids forthcoming from the United Kingdom? From France? No: Italy? No: Belgium? No: Holland? No: Germany? at this point Hitler raises his arm with a gesture that commands attention, "Ein Mark". From the opposite end of the Conference room the representative of the Soviet Union shouts "Ein rouble". He is hastily ejected. Hitler has it. He collects the bonds and from henceforward the world is his debtor. Heil Hitler!

After all, it might not be a bad way out.   (Leith–Ross, 1968, pp. 155–6)

As the Depression deepened, US officials hesitantly began to entertain alternatives. Hoover's Secretary of State, Henry Stimson, while opposing unilateral cancellation, suggested in 1932 trading debt concessions for access to British and Commonwealth markets (Stimson, 1932, p. 3).[26] Progress slowed and rhetoric escalated with the approach of the 1932 presidential election. The Hoover Moratorium having expired in the autumn of 1932, immediately following the election France and Britain requested a suspension of the December 1932 installment, which the Americans refused. France then defaulted on her payment, and Britain took the symbolic step of paying the entire installment in gold to protest US accumulation of gold and hesitancy to reflate. When the next installment came due six months later, Britain made only token payment and six other debtors defaulted. In June 1934, Congress condemned token payments, in response to which the British, like the others, paid nothing at all. War debts and reparations sputtered out like a candle in the rain.

What do these negotiations reveal about governments' attitudes towards the renegotiation of foreign debts? Three points emerge. First, to a greater degree than many private lenders, public officials acknowledged the relevance of ability to pay. Had governments participated more actively in the renegotiation of commercial debts in the 1930s, commercial creditors might have been forced to more quickly accept ability-to-pay criteria. Second, although governments should have been best able to appreciate the impact of default on the world economy as a whole, US attitudes toward war debts reveal that some major governments appreciated these impacts incompletely. Third, because of the existence of interlocking debtor–creditor relationships, governments found it impossible to reschedule one form of foreign debt without at the same time considering the others.

Bilateral negotiations

The alternative to global approaches to the debt crisis was to deal with defaults on a case-by-case basis. The difficulty with initiating negotiations between borrowers and bondholders was determining who represented the latter. Typically, representative committees of bondholders were organized. It is tempting to view these committees as an efficient solution to the bargaining game between creditors and debtors. All parties could gain if through negotiations they moved toward the core of co-operative solutions. The bondholders would gain if at least token interest payments were restarted. The debtors would gain if, through the payment of some interest, sanctions prohibiting the flotation of new issues on behalf of foreign borrowers in default, like those regularly imposed by the London market, were removed. By facilitating negotiation, a bondholders' representative committee might improve the position of all those involved and still keep a slice of the pie for itself.

In Britain, the mechanism through which negotiations took place was firmly established by the 1930s. The Corporation of Foreign Bondholders (CFBH) was universally acknowledged to speak for the bondholders. Founded in 1868, the CFBH was composed initially of representatives of the issue houses and of individual bondholders (Jenks, 1927, pp. 288–9).[27] In 1898 it was reorganized by an Act of Parliament; henceforth the Council of the Corporation, its governing body, was made up of representatives of the British Bankers' Association, representatives of the London Chamber of Commerce, and miscellaneous members, at least six of whom were substantial bondholders. The removal of representatives of the issue houses was designed to allay fears that the CFBH was a mere organ of the underwriters, thereby permitting the government to delegate to the Council responsibility for all disputes over defaulted debts. By the 1930s, representatives of the British Bankers Association, the London Chamber of Commerce and individual bondholders were joined on the Council by representatives of the Association of Investment Trusts and the British Insurance Association – representing institutions with substantial holdings of foreign bonds – along with the Stock Exchange and the Bank of England.

The official British government position was that default on foreign loans was a private matter. Officials found it convenient to have a reputable bondholders' committee to which disgruntled investors could be referred. To infer from this that the British government did not involve itself in debt negotiations would be incorrect, however. Rather than divorcing itself from negotiations, when bondholders and issue houses attempted to enlist government assistance, they were required to do so via the CFBH. The CFBH's Minutes noted in 1937, for example, "we know that the Treasury expect any request for Government action to be made to them by this Council and Messrs Lazards, have, I understand, been informed of this attitude" (CFBH Minutes, Poland, February 23, 1937).

Government assistance took various forms. Upon learning of developments that improved the prospects for productive negotiations, the government might pass the information to the Council. Information on the political and economic situation might be obtained from the local Embassy. To initiate negotiations, the CFBH might rely on the local Embassy staff and the Ambassador himself. Although communications from the CFBH to foreign officials might be conveyed by the Ambassador, the CFBH did not hesitate to remind Embassy officials that the Council did the negotiating. When the British Ambassador to Brazil hesitated to convey a sharply worded memorandum and recommended specific revisions, the CFBH instructed the Foreign Office that "the Memorandum should be delivered to the Brazilians without further delay . . . we have no reason to modify its terms (CFBH Minutes, Brazil, July 14, 138). The price paid for government assistance was pressure when settlement was desired for diplomatic or military reasons. In July 1939, with the British government anxious to conclude a political treaty with Greece as a bulwark against German expansion, the Chancellor of the Exchequer and the Foreign Secretary pressed the Council to accept Greece's debt offer to facilitate the successful conclusion of treaty negotiations. According to the CFBH, the Chancellor "in so many words. . . . advised us to take whatever was available" (CFBH Minutes, Greece, July 18, 1939). The CFBH refused. Thus, there is no evidence that the price of government assistance was particularly high.

In the United States, the mechanism for negotiations remained incompletely formed when default broke out. As late as 1913, the US had remained a net foreign borrower. Foreign flotations on the scale of those witnessed in the 1920s were a new phenomenon for the American capital market.[28] There had been no occasion to establish a standing committee representing American bondholders. Initially, *ad hoc* committees were established to negotiate resolutions to individual defaults. As default spread, the shortcomings of the approach became evident (Eichengreen and Portes, 1986, p. 622). Committees set up to negotiate over individual bond issues had higher administrative expenses than an ongoing organization. Temporary committees, with little reputation to protect, might be set up by questionable individuals lured by generous commissions into preying on ill-informed bondholders. Rival committees set up by issue houses, disaffected bondholders and independent entrepreneurs might compete for bondholder allegiance. Each wishing to be first to conclude a negotiated settlement, the debtor could play off one committee against another. *Ad hoc* committees lacked established ties with government and, unlike the CFBH, were unable to credibly threaten sanctions prohibiting future flotations.

In response to these problems, the Foreign Bondholders Protective Council (FBPC) was founded in 1933. As Herbert Feis (the State Department official involved) tells the story, government officials were intimately involved (Feis, 1966, pp. 266–78). Having published in 1930 his classic study of prewar lending (Feis, 1930), he explicitly adopted the CFBH as the model for the new American organization, battling both skeptical officials who opposed government support for the new organization and bankers who wished to control it. Because requests for intervention from bondholders were absorbing so much time, the idea of a bondholders' association was favorably received in the Hoover Administration's State Department in 1932. A committee was set up under State Department sponsorship to draw up plans for a private organization. One problem was how to finance the committee without relying on public funds or the banks, either of which might undermine the independence of the new association. The solution was to solicit finance from charitable foundations and the Stock Exchange until commissions rendered the FBPC self-sustaining. Another problem was determining whether the FBPC would conduct negotiations itself or simply discourage the formation of competing committees by conferring its stamp of approval on a particular committee. The 1933 banking crisis did more than Feis's arguments to defeat the proposal that the bankers form the committees and the FBPC play only a facilitating role. A final problem was enlisting the support of both the banks and the Roosevelt Administration, each of whom feared that any new organization would fall under the influence of the other. Here again the spread of default and the drain on the time of both State Department officials and private bankers did much to induce their accession.

Like the CFBH, the FBPC liaised with the government and enlisted the State Department in its negotiations. In turn, the State Department sent visitors (Feis and William O. Douglas) to consult with the FBPC at its New York office. Owing to the predilictions of the Roosevelt Administration, however, relations between the FBPC and the State Department remained more distant than those between the CFBH and the Foreign Office. The Administration remained suspicious that the FBPC was little more than a mouthpiece for the banks. Compared to sterling bonds, defaults on dollar bonds were both numerous and geographically widespread; active support for the bondholders would have required modifications in US foreign policy not just in Central Europe, as was the case for Britain, but globally. Still more influential was the priority the Roosevelt Administration attached to trade liberalization. Cordell Hull in particular viewed trade warfare as both an economic evil and a source of diplomatic tension. With the passage of the Reciprocal Trade Agreements Act in 1934, the US began to move back toward freer trade, in part to strengthen its international alliances. Effective US pressure on governments in default had to involve, at least implicitly, the threat of trade sanctions, which Hull viewed as incompatible with broader American objectives.

A telling example of government involvement took place in connection with the 1933 German standstill.[29] That summer the German government declared a moratorium on the foreign transfer of interest payments on national, municipal and corporate bonds. The Dutch and Swiss threatened to impose trade sanctions against Germany, with whom they ran balance of trade deficits. The Germans then settled with both countries, whose nationals were to receive full interest on their Dawes and Young Plan bonds and 3.5–4.5 percent on most other German bonds. Sweden, France and Belgium followed suit. The British government no sooner prepared to ask Parliament for power to establish a clearing arrangement than a German financial delegation traveled to London. Following negotiation, an agreement was reached under which Britain would impose no sanctions against Germany, in return for which Germany would continue to service Dawes and Young Plan bonds held by British citizens (Leith Ross, 1968, pp. 186–7). That arrangement survived until the outbreak of World War II.

The contrast with the American response is striking. US officials had been warned by Schacht that a moratorium was imminent. Although the Roosevelt Administration expressed its "shock" at Germany's decision, in response to Schacht's request for help in opening channels of communication with the bondholders, the Secretary of State responded, according to Herbert Feis, that "the American government could not get involved in these private debts . . ." (Feis, 1966, p. 141).[30] Despite official protests, American bondholders received nothing. The contrast with the experience of Germany's European creditors drove home the influence governments exercised over negotiations between debtors and bondholders.

It was through such negotiations that the debt crisis of the 1930s was ultimately resolved. The process was far from efficient and painless, requiring up to a quarter of a century to complete. Bolivia, which had been the first country to default in 1931, was the last to settle in 1955. The expectations of the bondholders and foreign governments differed widely, and considerable time could be required for their convergence.

Each negotiation between bondholders and foreign governments is a story unto itself. Both sides offered concessions as time dragged on: after having received nothing for years the bondholders grew increasingly willing to accept any reasonable offer, while foreign governments grew increasingly anxious to settle in anticipation of the prospect of renewed international lending. The compromises accepted by the bondholders' representatives were significant. Using Eichengreen and Werley's (1988) sample of foreign dollar bonds issued in the United States in the 1920s, the spread between the *ex-ante* yield and the internal rate of return (IRR) realized on these loans can be regressed on the years elapsed between default and settlement, yielding:

$$\text{\textit{Ex-ante} yield} - \text{IRR} = 0.006 + 0.00245 \text{ years elapsed} \qquad R^2 = 0.68$$
$$\qquad\qquad\qquad (3.22) \qquad (20.65) \quad \text{\textit{t}-statistics in parentheses}$$

The return realized by the bondholders relative to the contracted rate declines significantly with the length of the period between the early 1930s and the time of settlement, indicating how the bondholders moderated their demands as the period progressed.[31]

Often a negotiated solution required many years to achieve. That the bond market never recovered fully from the defaults of the 1930s and that large-scale foreign lending through other channels reappeared only 40 years after the interwar defaults must be attributed in part to the difficulty of negotiating co-operative solutions to those defaults. It is not obvious that creditor-government intervention could have expedited the process. As described above, the British and American governments were not adept in their use of moral suasion to influence the stance of bondholders' committees. Had they been more effective arm twisters, it is not clear that it would have been feasible to induce the bondholders to accept the same terms at an earlier date. The bondholders' committees were engaged in a bargaining game with the foreign governments. If creditor governments had somehow compelled the bondholders to settle earlier without altering the behavior of the debtors at the same time, this would have weakened the bargaining position of the creditors and forced them to settle for less. Achieving the same outcome at an earlier date through pressure on the creditors would have required matching pressure on the debtors. The obvious way of accomplishing this was by increasing the cost to the debtors of remaining in default, which accrued in the form of inability to borrow.[32] Only by promoting the reactivation of the international market could the creditor-country governments have brought this about. In a sense, their inability to agree on global plans for restarting lending also impeded the ability of creditor-country governments to expedite privately negotiated solutions to the crisis.

4 Conclusion

Comparing current proposals for achieving a global solution to the LDC debt crisis with their interwar antecedents reveals how little is novel or unprecedented in recent plans. Interwar proposals for dealing globally with the problem of defaulted foreign loans included schemes to swap one liability for another, to encourage creditor-country banks and bondholders to engage collectively in additional lending, to lengthen the maturity structure of the debt, to service the debt in local currency, and to establish an international fund to lend to indebted countries which private markets would not touch. Each of these suggestions has its counterpart in recent discussions of the debt crisis.

Individuals currently advocating global solutions will not be heartened by the failure of the interwar schemes. At the same time, there are lessons to be derived from these earlier failtures. First, bankers will actively resist any plan that limits their control over negotiations or commits them to a specific course of action. Governments will need to be exceptionally adept in their exercise of moral suasion to elicit co-operation. Second, governments must be exceptionally enlightened to recognize the benefits of global plans. As in tariff negotiations, the benefits of debt relief or new money at concessional terms, which accrue to the creditor countries largely in the form of a more stable world economy, are diffuse relative to the costs, be they capital losses on existing loans or the budgetary cost of new ones. Government officials are more inclined to pursue other issues, the payoff of which is more apparent.

NOTES

The research reported here is part of a project on sovereign debt and default in the 1930s, conducted jointly with Richard Portes of Birkbeck College, London, and the Centre for Economic Policy Research and partially funded by a research grant from the World Bank. I thank the Council of Foreign Bondholders for permission to cite from their minutes and correspondence, Harold James for advice, Richard Grossman and Tony Humm for help with the archives, and Alison Clayton for assistance with the statistics. Charles Kindleberger and Peter Lindert provided helpful comments. Opinions expressed are the author's alone and should not be attributed to any above-mentioned organizations or individuals.

1 See Cline (1987) and Fischer (1988) for reviews and critiques of the alternative proposals.
2 The standard work on the subject is Moulton and Pasvolsky (1932). Recent revisionist accounts have offered a more nuanced view of the American position, influencing the interpretation I offer here. See Parrini (1969), Murray

(1969) and Wilson (1971). An account which emphasizes French rather than American intransigence is Rhodes (1969).

3 The debate resembles current discussions in which even those with sympathy for the principle of debt relief find it difficult to agree who is deserving and to know where to stop once the process of extending relief has begun.

4 Total external central government public debt is taken from United Nations (1953), exports from League of Nations (various years). A problem in constructing these ratios was created by the fact that, in aggregating total foreign-currency debt and expressing it in domestic currency, the UN attempted to remove the impact on domestic-currency values of short-run exchange-rate fluctuations, therefore using artificial exchange rates (often the official rate where it differed from the market rate) for the conversion into domestic currency. I used these same artificial rates to convert the debt back into dollars. Market rates were used to express exports in dollars. Because only sovereign debt is included, these figures differ from total-foreign-debt-to-export ratios like those in Cardoso and Dornbusch (this volume).

5 Establishing an international bank to replace the Dawes Plan agencies was not universally supported (see Dulles, 1932).

6 Henderson seems to have been concerned more with the global reserve shortage constraining monetary reflation than with the foreign debt crisis (see Henderson, 1932).

7 There was disagreement between US and European officials about the scope of the new bank. The Europeans, notably Schacht, urged the creation of an institution with ample resources for use in stimulating long-term credit flows and promoting international trade. The Americans, George L. Harrison of the Federal Reserve Bank of New York prominent among them, preferred a modest institution that would concentrate on stabilizing exchange rates (see Costigliola, 1972).

8 In one variant of the plan, however, the BIS would be responsible for appointing its president and the majority of its directors.

9 Cited by Kunz (1987), p. 37. This passage was struck from the memorandum following an icy reception at the BIS. For the original memo, see National Archives RG39, Box 104, M. H. Cochran to J. Cotton, February 11, 1931. The revised memo can be found in this same source and in the Lamont Papers (Baker Library, Harvard University), 181–19, copy of proposals, February 2, 1931.

10 Lamont Papers (Baker Library, Harvard University), 181–19, Copy of proposals, February 2, 1931.

11 I am aware of no conversations to this effect.

12 Lamont Papers (Baker Library, Harvard University), 181–19, N. W. Jay to Thomas W. Lamont, February 14, 1931.

13 National Archives RG39, Box 104, M.H. Cochran to J. Cotton, February 11, 1931.

14 Norman letter to Harrison, March 3, 1931, quoted in Clarke (1967), p. 179. The remainder of this paragraph draws on Clarke, pp. 179–80.

15 NA RG39, Box 104, M. H. Cotton to W. R. Castle, Jr., March 11, 1931.

16 NA RG39, Box 104, M. H. Cochran to J. Cotton, February 26, 1931.

17 A proposal to establish a holding company, or investment trust, to handle foreign bonds, to be made up of the three or four largest international banking houses in New York, had been circulated in December 1930 by Max Winkler of Griscom and Company. National Archives RG39, Box 104, M. H. Cochran to J. Cotton, February 11, 1931.

18 What follows is from Beyen (1951). Harold James informs me that more information can be found in the records of the Reichsbank's Committee on External Debts.

19 The difficulties created by short-term credits in 1931 are recounted by Eichengreen and Portes (1987).

20 James (1986) describes this situation in detail. Forbes (1987, p. 574) reports that in the summer of 1931 as much as £50 million of credit was extended to German banks and to German enterprise by British banks and acceptance houses.

21 It is conceivable that the Bank of England could have bent or broken its rules, as it had done on a number of prior occasions (see Kindleberger, 1978, pp. 174 ff). But there was the counterargument that doing so would itself serve to undermine confidence in sterling.

22 Standstill Agreements were also arranged with Austria and Hungary, the Austrian Agreement serving as a model for the German Standstill (see Forbes, 1987).

23 In an intriguing departure from the borrowing-country line, the Chilean representative, Benjamin Cohen, suggested that the initiative fell on Chile to take measures to restart debt service. Too much of Chile's borrowing had been squandered on "trivial" expenditures such as sending military missions abroad and holding a 100 percent gold cover on central bank liabilities purely for reasons of national pride. Although raising taxes or reducing government expenditures to fund debt service threatened to provoke civil unrest and naval mutiny, Chile had recently reorganized the Nitrate Sales Corporation, which marketed one of its principal exports, permitting 25 percent of its profits to go toward rehabilitating Chilean credit. If the Chilean delegate to the London Conference dramatically announced the measures that had been taken, as Cohen proposed, perhaps other countries might be provoked to similarly resume some service on their foreign debts. Why the Chilean approach differed is unclear. A hint may lie in the fact that Cohen's discussions in Washington proceeded from debt to commercial policy. It could be that the Chileans' ultimate concern was market access and that they viewed concessions on debt as a way to secure favorable treatment for their exports (see United States, 1933, pp. 518–19).

24 The assumption was that the US would not expand its money supply in response to gold inflows, thereby failing to "recycle" its gold imports to the rest of the world.

25 For obvious reasons the satire never made its way into print.

26 The occasion for these suggestions was Britain's decision to extend preferential tariff treatment to the Dominions as part of the 1932 Ottawa Agreement. On the Ottawa Agreement, see Cairncross and Eichengreen (1983), ch. 3.

27 For details, see Eichengreen, Humm and Portes (1987), upon which the present discussion draws.

28 The shifts in America's external position described here are elaborated upon in Eichengreen (1987).

29 This discussion is taken from Eichengreen and Portes (1986), pp. 619–20.

30 The sentence continues, ". . . but that perhaps the Treasury or the Federal Reserve System might be able to suggest a procedure for arranging consultation with the bond holders."

31 A problem with interpreting this equation as evidence of how creditors' demands for compensation declined with time is the possibility of heterogeneity, or "sorting," on the side of the debtors. The alternative interpretation is that the creditors' demands for compensation on each type of loan were inelastic with respect to time, that they demanded less of countries perceived to have less ability to pay, and that the countries with the least ability to pay were the least inclined to settle. In reality, it is likely that both effects were operative.

32 There is little evidence that an individual country's ability to borrow in the 1940s and 1950s depended on its debt service record in the 1930s. But default in the thirties and delays in settling thereafter interfered with the ability of all developing countries to borrow subsequently. In other words, much of the impact on creditworthiness of inter-war default took the form of an externality (see Eichengreen, 1988).

REFERENCES

Bennett, Edward W. (1962), *Germany and the Diplomacy of the Financial Crisis, 1931*, Cambridge: Harvard University Press.

Beyen, J. W. (1951), *Money in a Maelstrom*, London: Macmillan.

Cairncross, Alec and Barry Eichengreen (1983), *Sterling in Decline*, Oxford: Blackwell.

Clarke, S. V. O. (1967), *Central Bank Cooperation, 1924–31*, New York: Federal Reserve Bank of New York.

Cline, William (1987), "Mobilizing Bank Lending to Debtor Countries," *Institute for International Economics, Policy Analyses in International Economics*, 18, June.

Costigliola, Frank (1972), "The Other Side of Isolationism: The Establishment of the First World Bank, 1929–1930," *Journal of American History* LIX, pp. 602–20.

Dulles, Eleanor Lansing (1932), *The Bank for International Settlements at Work*, New York: Macmillan.

Eichengreen, Barry (1988), "The U.S. Capital Market and Foreign Lending, 1920–1955," in Jeffrey Sachs (ed.), *Developing Country Debt and Economic Performance*, Vol. I, Chicago: University of Chicago Press, pp. 107–55.

Eichengreen, Barry (1989), "The Political Economy of the Smoot–Hawley Tariff," *Research in Economic History* (forthcoming).

Eichengreen, Barry and Portes, Richard (1986), "Debt and Default in the 1930s: Causes and Consequences," *European Economic Review* 30, pp. 599–640.

Eichengreen, Barry and Portes, Richard (1987), "The Anatomy of Financial

Crises," in Richard Portes and Alexander Swoboda (eds), *Threats to International Financial Stability*, Cambridge: Cambridge University Press, pp. 10–58.

Eichengreen, Barry and Werley, Carolyn (1988), "How Foreign Bondholders Fared: Realized Rates of Return on Foreign Dollar Bonds Floated in the 1920s," Institute of Business and Economic Research Working Paper, Berkeley: University of California.

Eichengreen, Barry, Humm, Tony and Portes, Richard (1987), "Sovereign Default in the 1930s and the Council of Foreign Bondholders," unpublished manuscript.

Feis, Herbert (1930), *Europe: The World's Banker, 1870–1914*, New Haven: Yale University Press.

Feis, Herbert (1966), *1933: Characters in Crisis*, Boston: Little, Brown.

Feldstein, Martin (1987), "Latin America's Debt: Muddling Through Can Be Just Fine," *Economist*, June 27, 1987.

Fischer, Stanley (1988), "Resolving the International Debt Crisis," in Jeffrey Sachs (ed.) *Developing Country Debt and Economic Performance*, Chicago: University of Chicago Press, pp. 359–85.

Fleisig, Heywood (1970), "Long Term Capital Flows and the Great Depression: The Role of the United States, 1927–1933," unpublished PhD dissertation, Yale University.

Forbes, Neil (1987), "London Banks, the German Standstill Agreements, and 'Economic Appeasement' in the 1930s," *Economic History Review*, 2nd Series, XL, pp. 571–87.

Henderson, Hubert (1932), "A Monetary Proposal for Lausanne," Memorandum written while Secretary of the Economic Advisory Council, May 17, 1932, in Henderson (1955), *The Inter-War Years and Other Papers*, Henry Clay (ed.), Oxford: Clarendon Press, pp. 103–6.

James, Harold (1986), *The German Slump*, Oxford: Clarendon Press.

Jenks, Leland (1927), *The Migration of British Capital*, London: Allen & Unwin.

Kindleberger, Charles (1973), *The World in Depression*, 1929–1939, Berkeley: University of California Press.

Kindleberger, Charles (1978), *Manias, Panics and Crashes*, New York: Basic Books.

Kunz, Diane B. (1987), *The Battle for Britain's Gold Standard in 1931*, Beckenham, Kent: Croom Helm.

League of Nations (various years), *Balance of Payments and Foreign Trade Balances*, Geneva: League of Nations.

Leffler, Melvyn (1972), "The Origins of Republican War Debt Policy, 1921–1923: A Study in the Applicability of the Open Door Interpretation," *Journal of American History* LIX, pp. 585–601.

Leith-Ross, Sir Frederick (1968), *Money Talks*, London: Hutchinson.

Moulton, Harold G. and Leo Pasvolsky (1932), *War Debts and World Prosperity*, Washington, DC: Brookings.

Murray, Robert K. (1969), *The Harding Era*, Minneapolis: University of Minnesota Press.

Parrini, Carl P. (1969), *Heir to Empire: United States Economic Diplomacy, 1916–1923*, Pittsburgh: University of Pittsburgh Press.

Rhodes, Benjamin D. (1969), "Reassessing 'Uncle Shylock': The United States and the French War Debt, 1917–1929," *American Historical Review* LV, pp. 787–803.

Skidelsky, Robert (1967), *Politicians and the Slump*, London: Macmillan.

Stimson, Henry (1932), "Further Note Addressed by the United States Government to His Majesty's Government in the United Kingdom Relating to the British War Debt," Washington, December 7, 1932, Cmd. 4211, London: HMSO.

United Kingdom Government (1932), "Further Note Addressed by His Majesty's Government in the United Kingdom to the United States Government Relating to the British War Debt," Washington, December 1, Cmd. 4210, London: HMSO.

United Nations (1953), *Public Debt*, Lake Placid, NY: United Nations.

United States, Department of State (1933), "Monetary and Economic Conference, London, June 12–July 27, 1933," *Foreign Relations of the United States*, vol. I, Washington, DC: GPO, pp. 452–762.

Wilson, Joan Hoff, (1971), *American Business and Foreign Policy, 1920–1933*, Lexington, Ky.: University Press of Kentucky.

Comment

Jorge Marshall S.

Barry Eichengreen has presented a very clear and instructive paper on experiences of the debt crises of the 1930s and the 1980s. I found it very illuminating as we economists are prone to entirely forget the teachings of history and concentrate on general analysis and policy implications. I must confess that I learned a great deal and enjoyed reading it.

In my comments I confine myself to some remarks which may qualify some of Eichengreen's statements, and explain my position in relation to the essence or main direction of the chapter. Let me first refer to what is said to have been Chile's position on external debt as presented by Ambassador Benjamín Cohen in 1933. It seems strange to hear that such a distinguished diplomat, well acquainted with events in Chile, stated that proceeds of the loans contracted during the twenties were "squandered" on trivial things and on maintaining the gold standard "for reasons of national pride." In fact much of the borrowing was used in public works, in modernizing the main cities, and in setting up modern nitrate plants that allow Chile to operate in that industry and export that product for a long period at a time when most of the obsolete plants had to close down in the face of competition from synthetics. Nor is it true that the gold standard (which required 40 percent and not 100 percent of gold backing on central bank issues), was established by "national pride," but rather on the advice of an American mission which conformed only to overwhelmingly accepted doctrine at the time (1925) in academic and central bank circles. Furthermore to establish the gold standard, Chile had no need to borrow, as the government had already accumulated a large enough stock of the metal to make the conversion.

What is more plausible is Eichengreen's interpretation of Chile's position on debt. With no possibility of resuming debt servicing, the government of Chile offered to its bondholders an ingenious scheme of linking debt service (at near 10 percent of its face value) to profits of the reorganized nitrate industry, in an attempt to give an incentive to exports of nitrates. It should be remembered that, at the time, nitrates had been and still were the most important Chilean export.

On p. 89 Eichengreeen states that the process of negotiation took up to 25 years to complete, and he cites the case of Bolivia. This is undoubtedly a very extreme case. In most other instances the period of negotiation was much shorter. In Chile, the law enabling resumption of foreign debt services was enacted in 1935, and acceptance of most bondholders (US, UK, and Switzerland) was almost finished by 1940. Each country in this respect followed its own timetable, but by the time the World Bank began operation in 1946, practically all Latin American foreign debt had been renegotiated.

Eichengreen feels that the cost to the debtors of remaining in default was their inability to borrow, and that large-scale foreign lending through other channels reappeared only 40 years after the interwar defaults (p. 90). This assertion, in my view, needs some qualification. US official lending to Latin America started in 1939 before it entered the war; for example, Chile and Brazil built their iron and steel industries with Eximbank loans. Other industrial countries set up institutions with the same purpose immediately after the war. Suppliers' credits to the underdeveloped world (in most cases with official insurance) started to increase on a very large scale by the fifties.

The main objective of the World Bank was and still is to channel funds from the capital markets of the developed world to the developing countries. Capitalist countries need to sell and have to compete for markets which, in the case of large equipment and other commodities, can only be sold on credit. Default is therefore a crime easily forgotten or not recognized by potential creditors who are not direct victims of the default.

Eichengreen thinks that the debt problem has not been taken as a threat comparable to protectionism by the creditor countries. This may be so, but as long as the Baker Plan aims to promote adjustment with growth in the main debtor nations, it is implicitly considering the export possibilities of industrial countries, among them its own, and it therefore appears to be an exception to that rule.

The gist of Eichengreen's chapter is that general or political solutions to the debt problem do not appear feasible. I am not sure whether these would be favorable to debtor countries, but I agree that *they will not take place* in the present circumstances, because they are opposed by governments of industrial countries, international institutions and especially by banks and other organizations which have complete control of the financial world (institutions) with which debtor countries have to deal. Indeed creditors are organized (within the IMF, the World Bank, and in the bank steering committees), and it is them who lay down the strategy to be followed by debtors requesting renegotiations.

What is really lacking is better co-ordination and institutional control by debtor countries to try to reach common view-points and reasonable conditions in their individual negotiations with creditors. Division is the certain path to poor settlement and the acceptance of burdensome agreements.

4

After the Debt Crisis: Modes of Development for the Longer Run in Latin America

Deepak Lal

1 Introduction

My brief in this chapter is to consider alternative modes of development for the longer run after the debt crisis has been solved. In discussing this issue, it is clearly of some importance to know whether the solution will involve confrontation between lenders and borrowers, and the long-run disruption of international trade and investment flows, or whether some middle way will be found which allows Latin America to adjust and grow out of its debt burden without severance of its international ties. Being an optimist by nature, I shall assume the latter more hopeful outcome of the debt crisis.

Moreover, there is also an emerging professional consensus that in the face of similar external shocks, the severity of the Latin American debt crisis (as compared with that in East Asia for example) was primarily due to its mistakes (often long-standing) concerning trade and exchange rate (macroeconomic) policies. As Sachs (1985), Balassa (1985), Mitra (1986) have shown, the external shocks faced by Latin America in the 1979–83 period were no greater than those faced by various East Asian countries. Yet the latter (with the exception of the Philippines) managed to adjust fairly smoothly to the global interest rate and terms of trade shocks, without impairment of their medium- and long-term growth processes. The decisive difference was that, for similar debt to GDP ratios in the two regions, Latin America had much higher debt to export and, *ipso facto*, debt service ratios. It is now conventional wisdom that this was due to Latin America's failure to use its foreign borrowing to expand its output of tradables sufficiently to meet future debt-servicing needs.

The question about future modes of development, at least at a techno-cratic level, can be answered fairly simply. The major lesson of the debt crisis, which I believe most professional observers would accept, is the need

Table 4.1 Openness index in selected Latin American countries, 1965–1985*

	1965	1970	1975	1980	1985
Argentina	–	–	33.8	12.8	18.4[a]
Bolivia	40.2	33.6	41.4	30.9	14.6[b]
Brazil	12.5	13.7	19.3	21.0	20.2[b]
Chile	18.6	29.2	61.1	35.5	38.0
Colombia	22.0	22.5	23.8	27.2	21.0
Costa Rica	48.9	55.6	60.5	52.6	56.8
Dom. Republic	23.3	37.2	49.5	39.2	47.7
Ecuador	28.6	33.1	45.5	40.3	33.4[b]
Guatemala	31.3	30.6	37.1	40.0	25.6[b]
Mexico	13.0	10.9	10.8	18.9	13.3
Panama	43.6	45.7	64.0	50.8	37.4
Peru	33.0	26.6	31.4	41.9	31.6[b]
Uruguay	34.8	19.3	29.3	29.0	34.8[b]
Venezuela	45.2	38.3	53.7	52.4	51.6[b]

*This index was constructed as the ratio of total trade (imports plus exports) to GDP.
[a] 1983
[b] 1984
Source: Edwards (1987), constructed from data from the IMF

to improve Latin America's "capacity to transform." As defined by Kindleberger, "capacity to transform is capacity to react to change, originating at home or abroad, by adapting the structure of foreign trade to the new situation in an economic fashion" (Kindleberger, 1967, p. 99). Trade and exchange rate policies are important determinants of this capacity to transform. Latin American experience, as well as that of other developing countries, attests to this fact. An important indicator of Latin America's failure to create this "capacity to transform" – as compared to the so-called Gang of Four (South Korea, Taiwan, Singapore and Hong Kong) – is provided by their different responses to the "transfer problem" associated with the debt crisis. A good measure is provided by an openness index constructed by Edwards (1987) and reproduced in table 4.1. This shows that, during the 1970s, Latin America had been moving away from the "inward orientation," which had been seen since the mid-1960s to be inimical to its growth prospects. This is shown by the rise in the openness index between 1965 and 1980 in most Latin American countries seen in table 4.1. This in turn was due to various measures of trade liberalization undertaken by many countries, partly as a response to the first oil crisis. But this liberalization was half-hearted and (except in Chile) incomplete (see Edwards and Teitel, 1986; Corbo and de Melo (1985) for an overview of the Southern Cone liberalization programs during this period). Hence, when the debt crisis hit, the required adjustment was made by a reversal of these liberal policies, through import contraction rather than export expansion. The openness index then fell for most Latin American countries.

This in turn, as is now commonly accepted, is due to the "inward oriented" development strategy that Latin American countries have by and large followed during the post-war years. It has been recognized (at least since the 1960s), that Latin America needed to move away from import-substituting towards export-promoting industrialization.[1] This has either not been done, or done only belatedly in many cases. At the same time, in large part because of this failure to develop in line with its changing comparative advantage, Latin American countries have relied on various fantastic "macroeconomic fixes" to reconcile the irreconcilable, with dire consequences for the stability of income growth over the long run.

As numerous observers have emphasized, this failure to create the "capacity to transform" is not due to ignorance of the policies required, or because of a lack of professional consensus on the desirable policies. These have been successfuly summed up by Harberger (1984) in a set of policy rules which development professionals would endorse (even though they might disagree about the precise sequence and timing of the requisite policy reforms). Those which are uncontroversial are:

1 avoid false technicism in economic policy-making;
2 keep budgets under adequate control
3 keep inflationary pressures under reasonable control;
4 take advantage of international trade;
5 some types and patterns of trade restriction are far worse than others . . . only a given uniform rate of tariff can automatically avoid capricious and distorting variations in the effective rates of protection actually achieved;
6 if import restrictions become excessive, and reducing them directly is politically impossible, mount an indirect attack on the problem by increasing incentives to export;
7 Make tax systems simple, easy to administer, and (as far as possible) neutral and non-distorting.   (Harberger, 1984, pp. 428–32)[2]

The continuing failure to apply known remedies requires an explanation. Increasingly, many observers realize that these explanations must lie in the realm of political economy. Thus Sachs, in his 1985 survey of responses of Latin America and East Asian countries, rightly notes, "the foundations for export promotion policies in Asia and for import-substitution policies in Latin America are political. It is essential to understand the political economy of export promotion in order to understand the continuing paralysis of Latin American economies" (Sachs, 1985, pp. 525–6). I agree – though, as we shall see, not with Sachs's political economy! The rest of this chapter, therefore is concerned with considering various answers to the question, what, if any, are the impediments, in terms of its political economy which would prevent Latin America from adopting the mode of development – outward orientation – which is generally agreed to be necessary for equitable and stable growth in the long run?

In the next section, I survey various answers to this question, and, not surprisingly, find them wanting. The following section presents a simple trade–theoretic political economy model of that brave abstraction – a "typical Latin American country", which provides some explanations for what I have elsewhere (Lal, 1986) labelled a continent with "a political economy in conflict with its comparative advantage."

2 The Political Economy of Latin America's Trade Regime

Sachs (1985) argues that it is the relative weight of rural versus urban interests in Latin America compared with East Asia, which explains why an export-led strategy has been possible in the latter but not the former region. For "trade restrictions tend to shift income from the agricultural and mineral producing sectors toward the industrial and service sectors." Hence if, as he argues, the weight of rural interests (as judged by the inverse of the degree of urbanization) is decisive in the polity, the country will be successful in developing exports. But, as Williamson and others noted in commenting on Sachs's paper, the political power of rural interests is not necessarily correlated with their relative share in the total population. As Olson (1982) has argued, because of the "free rider" problem, the larger the potential beneficiaries from the activities of a pressure group, the more difficult it is to organize such a group. This partly explains why more developed countries, with a low share of their population in agriculture tend to subsidize, whilst developing countries with a larger share of their population in rural areas, tend to tax agriculture (see Lipton, 1977, for a documentation of the urban bias in most developing countries). Hence Sachs's argument is unconvincing.

Hirschman, as the doyen of Latin American political economists, can be expected to have a view on the factors which have inhibited an outward-oriented development policy in Latin America, though over the years he seems to have changed his mind. In Hirschman (1968) he argues that, because of the power of dominant rural interest groups, it was not possible for the export sector directly to subsidize the industrial sector – the "optimal" policy if the noneconomic objective (presumably) of promoting industry is accepted. Instead, inadvertently and unnoticed, Latin American governments discovered the expedient of maintaining inflationary regimes with an overvalued currency, as an indirect method of achieving the same end.

However, when it was no longer in the interest of industrialists to maintain overvaluation, they were not able to reverse the bias against exporting; they were not influential partly because they did not export. Hence Hirschman's vicious circle: "industrialists are not influential because they do not export, and they do not export because they are not influential" (p. 30). But as with most "vicious circle" type arguments, this is unconvincing.

For underlying these Hirschman Mark 1 arguments is a very peculiar view of the typical Latin American state.[3] It is an aloof and whimsical despotism.

But this view is surely implausible. First, as political scientists have emphasized (see the excellent survey of this literature by Wynia, 1984), though appearing strong, Latin American states are weak – in large part because of the lack of any agreement on the rules of the political game. This leads to a diversity of political rules within many Latin American countries and "is primarily the product of a failure to solve the fundamental problem of political legitimacy that arises in all political systems" (Wynia, 1984, p. 30). This lack of consensus on a legitimate set of political rules means that "groups and individuals who discover that the prevailing rules favour others more than themselves may prefer to undermine the rules rather than obey them" (p. 36).

It also means that every incumbent of the national monopoly, i.e. the state (providing rents for the incumbent and the public goods – hopefully – of law and order for its citizens), will find his monopoly contestable[4] (in the sense of Baumol et al., 1982).[5] The typical Latin American president "plagued by a lack of agreement on the rules of the game . . . may claim as much legal authority as do his more secure neighbours, but in practice he often finds himself constrained by the uncertainties created by the lack of political consensus and his vulnerability to the use of political resources by his opponents" (Wynia, 1984, p. 37). This is a vision of a *harried* ruler "pinned and wriggling on the wall"[6], whose thrashings for survival impart that unpredictability to Latin American economic policy that Hirschman rightly laments.

By 1981, Hirschman views that Latin American state's autonomy as being relatively limited. He distinguishes between an "autonomous state": "the state is endowed with a will of its own . . . [it] has an *interest*, a *raison d'état* which it pursues single-mindedly" (Hirschman, 1981, p. 147), and a "coping state": which for him is "a state which does not act but reacts".

The autonomous state is a "maximizer" whilst the coping state is a "satisficer".

I do not find Hirschman's distinctions between a maximizing "autonomous" and a satisficing "coping" state altogether cogent. It would take me too far afield to explain my doubts about his typology of the state in any detail. Instead, let me present my own typology, which I have found particularly useful in the context of a multi-country comparative study of the political economy of poverty and growth, which I am co-directing with Hla Myint (Lal, 1984, 1986).

The *first* of the types of state, rarely observed but implicitly assumed by much of the technocratic economic policy literature, is the "benevolent state", run by selfless Platonic guardians or a benevolent dictator, maximizing the social welfare of its citizens. The *second*, I label the "predatory state". This is a state run by a self-serving absolute ruler, such as a monarch, dictator or charismatic leader. This sovereign, too, is autonomous, insofar as the constellation of domestic interest groups has little direct effect on his/her policies. For analytical purposes the selfish predatory sovereign is assumed to maximize either net revenue (treasure) or courtiers (bureaucrats).

The *third* type of state I call "factional." This is a state which subserves the interests of the coalition of pressure groups which succeeds in its capture. The interests served are narrowly defined (again for analytical simplicity) to be the economic self-interests of the constituents of government. The method of capturing the state need not be majoritarian democracy, even though such a form of government would be compatible with this type of state.[7]

I would contend that the Latin American state is typically a factional state, though the other types are also observed. Thus, controversially, it can be argued that Pinochet's Chile fits the model of the "benevolent state". It has set itself above the hurly-burly of pressure group activity and seeks to subserve the commonweal – as it sees it. From the scanty evidence available and summarized in the recent World Bank report *Poverty in Latin America*, Chile stands apart, as the one state which has met the adjustment needs of the debt crisis by preserving targetted social welfare programs, whilst cutting back on other inefficient public expenditure and in liberalizing the economy, much as mainstream economic policy advisers would recommend.[8]

Of our second "ideal" type, Mexico under the Partido Revolucionario Institucional (PRI), I contend, provides an example of the "bureaucratic maximizing" variety of "predatory state". But most of the other Latin American states are factional. In a few of these, where there is a political consensus, as in Costa Rica, a relatively stable majoritarian democracy is the form of the factional state. In most of the others, the lack of political consensus has meant a constant shuffling of different coalitions of interest groups capturing the state by fair means or foul.

In all these models the controllers of the state are maximizers – though the maximand clearly differs from one type of state to the other. There is no place for "satisficing" which, as Hahn (1985) for instance has recently noted, is not a well-defined notion.[9] But to delineate the lack of political consensus as a "characteristic trait" of Latin American polities still does not explain it, nor tell us if, and how, it can be changed.

Here Hirschman (1979) is more useful. He now finds a major source of the failure of Latin America to adopt the necessary outward oriented policies to be the fickleness of its intellectuals, and the ideological polarization of proponents of what he calls the "entrepreneurial" and "reform functions" in the course of economic development.[10]

He argues that Latin American intellectuals have been wedded to the "structuralist" school's desire to "search for the deep problems – such as certain land tenure conditions – that were believed to underlie the surface problems of inflation and balance of payments disequilibrium". But they have probably gone too far. The resulting barrage of fundamental remedies proposed to cure Latin American ills by this school – planning in the 1950s, economic integration in the early 1960s, domestic redistribution of income and wealth, and restructuring international economic relations to reduce *dependencia* (in the late 1960s) – has sapped the will of Latin American states. For "now, more difficult tasks were continuously presented to the state and society *whether or not* the previous task had been succesfully disposed of. . . This strange process of ideological escalation may well have contributed to that pervasive sense of being in a desperate predicament which is a precondition for radical regime change" (p. 86).

But this will not do. For surely, apart from any frustration arising from the overloading of the state's agenda, created by this structuralist factory of panaceas, there is the more important question, were the proposed remedies sound? One has only to read Ian Little's (1982) devastating critique of structuralism to recognize that, at least, it is arguable whether Latin American countries would have been better served if the structuralist program had been presented at a measured sequential pace, and been adopted.[11]

I would, however, agree with Hirschman that ideas and ideology do matter, if for no other reason than *my* obvious self-interest in believing this to be the case! But I think the role of ideas and ideology in determining policies can be overdone. Ideas to be fruitful must fall on fertile ground. An important task of social science must, in my view, be to explain why certain ideas, in certain places and at certain times, seem to command attention by delineating the factors which lead to changes in the climate of opinion. For though we may all be persuaded by Keynes's argument about the hysteresis in the process whereby new ideas are accepted by "madmen in authority", nevertheless, the important turning-points in human history have (at least) been correlated with changes in the climate of opinion.

It is in this context that the implicit explanation provided by Veliz (1980) for the failure of Latin America to adopt the required outwardly-oriented industrialization policies is of some interest. Veliz contrasts the centralist Iberian tradition – which, he argues, has moulded the actions of all the incumbents of Latin American states – with the more decentralized tradition based on Lockean rights and the ideas of the Scottish enlightenment, which provided the ideological ballast for the states of Anglo-Saxon extraction during their period of industrialization.[12]

Veliz considers the liberalization of trade in the nineteenth century open economies of Latin America as merely "a liberal pause" in the deep-seated centralizing tendencies inherited by Latin America from its Iberian conquerors. The Great Depression and its aftermath greatly enhanced the role of the central state, which became the main financier of private industrial ventures, the "arbiter in the process of income redistribution through the implementation of a variety of social policies; and it assigned a dynamic role to the public sector" (Veliz, 1980, p. 259).

The role of the intellegentsia in the subsequent decades, however, was to aid and abet the centralizing state because of the "redistributive bent of [the] populism and social democracy" many of them supported. "By the early sixties, the populist and social democratic cornucopia had consolidated huge pressure groups that regarded their better interests as identical with those of a prosperous central State" (ibid, p. 290).

As the means of funding these growing entitlements declined, "the social democratic regimes had to face growing discontent, especially among the middle sectors whose expectations had risen highest during the decades of largess and were consequently more vulnerable to rising inflation and declining economic fortunes. Their appeals, however, were not for a revolutionary change of the social and economic system, but for more state intervention along the same lines as before" (ibid, p. 292). Meanwhile the intellegentsia, Veliz contends, adopted the fashionable view of the Cuban Revolution current amongst the radical intellegentsia in the West at the time, namely that "Latin America [had] become the revolutionary frontier" (p. 295). The terrorist campaigns they launched changed the attitudes "of the urban middle sectors . . . and opened the door to the current process of authoritarian recentralization", (p. 293). It is particularly pertinent in this context that "in Latin America the military have traditionally been drawn not from the upper strata of society, but from the middle and, increasingly, from the lower middle sectors. . . . To the violent revolutionary actions of the extreme left wing terrorists, the middle sectors responded first with legal repressive measures administered by social

democratic regimes. When these appeared insufficient to stem the tide of
violence or when the parallel economic deterioration threatened general
institutional collapse, the middle sectors appealed to the military for help"
(p. 297).

But Veliz notes two paradoxes in the economic policies of economic
liberalization that the subsequent military governments have espoused
(though not always followed).[13] The first is that "it was precisely those
[failed] policies that greatly enlarged and consolidated the vast urban
clientele that called them to power, to dismantle the public sector built
over the past three or four decades would risk their disaffection" (ibid, p.
299). The second paradox is that "absolute central power is exercised
absolutely in the name of liberal economic theories and schemes whose
obvious pre-requisites are diversity and freedom of choice" (ibid, p. 301).

Veliz seems to me to provide a more cogent picture of the intellectual
and social forces underlying the continuing Latin American crisis than that
presented, for instance, by Hirschman. It is these forces which I seek to
examine more analytically in the next section, to show why even though
the technocratic remedies for long-term growth in Latin America are by
now uncontroversial, it may be difficult for Latin American governments to
follow these policies consistently.[14]

3   The Political Economy of the Factional State

The starting point for any political economy of the factional state in Latin
America has to recognize an important but paradoxical difference between
Latin America and East Asia (for instance), This is the former's relative
"embarrassment of riches". An excellent picture of this is provided in
figure 4.1, which reproduces Leamer's (1987) depiction of the factor
endowments of a sample of countries in a triangular endowment simplex
which has three factors of production – land, labor and capital as its three
vortices.[15]

One striking fact is that, whereas most of the East Asian "Gang of Four"
are on, or close to, the labor–capital axis, most Latin American countries –
being relatively land and natural resource abundant, both with respect to
labor and capital – are positioned towards the land vortex. This is their
"embarrassment of riches" which in a 3-factor–n good model can lead to
some surprising and, from the viewpoint of political economy, difficult
development paths, as compared with the land-scarce East Asian countries. In her Graham lecture, Krueger (1977) emphasized the importance
of explicitly accounting for land as a separate factor of production in
models of trade and growth. Leamer's work (1984, 1987) has provided
further empirical and analytical support for her insights.[16]

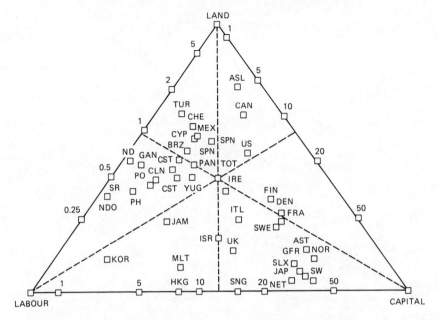

Figure 4.1 Endowment ratios displayed in an endowment triangle

Source: Edward Leamer (1987)

It is the political economy of industrialization that we consider in this 3-factor–n good model, and show how natural resource riches can turn out to be "a precious bane".[17] We follow Leamer (1987) and assume for simplicity that all goods are produced through fixed proportions techniques, so that there is a single input vector corresponding to each commodity. The production functions are the same all over the world, in keeping with the Hecksher–Ohlin tradition. Free trade is assumed. For simplicity we also assume that all goods are traded.[18]

Let us assume that in the world economy, there are five manufactured goods indexed from 1–5, produced with only labor and capital. They are of increasing capital intensity and their input vectors are shown as $M_1 \ldots M_5$ along the labor–capital edge of the Leamer endowment triangle in figure 4.2. In addition there are two agricultural goods. The first A_1 is produced with only labor and land, and lies on the labor (L) and land (T) edge of the endowment triangle. The second A_2 uses all three factors of production, but it is more land-intensive than the agricultural good A_1.

The seven points representing the input vectors and the three axis co-ordinates are connected by line segments to divide the endowment triangle into seven "regions of diversification",[19] for a given set of com-

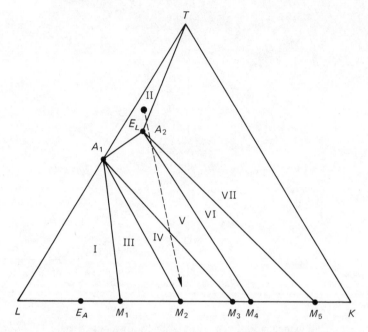

Figure 4.2 Regions of diversification in the Leamer endowment triangle

	Outputs produced	*Wage rate*
Region I	A_1, M_1	W_1
Region II	A_1, A_2	$W_2 > W_1$
Region III	A_1, M_1, M_2	$W_3 > W_1$
Region IV	A_1, M_2, M_3	$W_4 > W_3$
Region V	A_1, A_2, M_3, M_4	$W_5 > W_4$
Region VI	A_2, M_4, M_5	$W_6 > W_5$
Region VII	A_2, M_5	$W_7 > W_6 > W_2$

modity prices for the seven commodities. The factor endowment vectors of different countries can also be represented by points in land–labor–capital space in the endowment triangle. Then it can be shown that countries with endowment points in the same region of diversification will have the same factor prices and produce the same commodities with the vector inputs given by the vertices of the regions of diversification. The commodities produced in the seven regions are listed in the notes to figure 4.2. Given commodity prices, relative factor intensities determine factor prices in each of these regions.

Now consider two possible paths of development in this model. The first is that of the typical East Asian "Gang of Four", whose endowment point E_A is on, or close to, the labor–capital axis. With capital accumulating faster than the growth of the labor force, the country moves from region I, to III to IV. In this process it moves up the ladder of comparative advantage with respect to manufactured goods, with rising capital intensity. Hence, on this development path the wage rises and the rental on capital falls.

The second path is for a land abundant Latin American country whose endowment point E_L lies in the region of diversification II, where it produces both the relatively labor-intensive agricultural good A_1 and the land-cum-capital intensive good A_2. We concentrate on one possible path of development, which seems plausible for a number of Latin American countries. We assume that, as in the previous case, both capital and labor are growing. Over time the economy's land–labor ratio will be falling, and its capital–labor ratio rising. Suppose this path of the economy's changing endowments is given by the dashed line from E_L. Over time, the economy will then move from region II to VII to VI to IV. In this process it will begin to industrialize as soon as it moves into region VII, *but in the most capital-intensive* manufacture. Over time it will move into regions of specialization in which *specialization in increasingly more labor-intensive* goods is required. The factor price consequence of this development path, in line with the emerging and changing comparative advantage of the economy, is that the wage rate will fall, and from the time the economy moves into region VII, the rental rates on capital and land will keep rising. Clearly, as compared with the stylized East Asian case (with rising wages), the distributional implications of this stylized Latin American development path (with a falling or constant wage) for an open economy would seem to be politically hazardous. But note that even though the wage might be falling on the Latin American development path, it will still be higher than on the East Asian path till they converge on the region of specialization in region IV.[20, 21]

It is time to introduce the political features of the factional state. I do this following Lal (1986), using certain ideas developed by Mayer (1984) in endogenizing tariff formation for the political economy of trade policy in developed countries.

Suppose, initially, that there are only two factors of production, capital (K) and labor (L). All individuals in the economy can be described by their respective capital – labor ($k_1 = K_1/L_1$) endowments. The *mean* of the individual k_1 endowments will be the aggregate capital–labor endowment $K = k$ of the economy.

Next we define the set of individuals who are *decisive*, in the sense that they can compete for the capture of the state and thus the determinants of economic policies subserving their interests. Suppose, initially, that *all* economic agents in the population form part of the decisive set of the polity, and the political mechanism is democratic – with "one man one vote" – and the majority capturing the state. All voters vote according to their economic interests. Then from the well-known median voter theorem, the median voter's capital–labor endowment (k_m) will determine the interests that will be served by the coalition of majoritarian interest groups who capture the state. If the distribution of individual factor endowments is symmetric, so that its median and the mean are the same, the median endowment will be identical to the average for the economy as a whole ($k = k_m$). Then, from the law of comparative advantage, we know that the income of the median individual will be maximized by free trade. If, however, the median individual endowment is more (less) capital-intensive than the average, the median voter's income-generating interests will be in a tariff (subsidy) on capital-intensive imports or a subsidy (tariff) on labor-intensive imports. Thus, in this form of the pressure group model, what we need to know is the mean of the national factor endowment, and median of the distribution of the income-generating factor endowments of the set of decisive individuals.

Initially, in our typical Latin American polity with factor endowments given by E_L in figure 4.2 the "decisive" individuals are the landlords. This is the oligarchic phase of Latin American development. The oligarchs' median endowment of land to labor is likely to be greater than the average endowment for the economy as a whole (in region II). This implies that (as in the nineteenth century), the interest of the median "decisive" individual in the oligarchic polity will be served by free trade. As the economy grows, with capital accumulating and population expanding, but without any expansion of the "polity", the median endowment of the land and capital of the landed oligarchy will still be higher than the average of the economy, and so the oligarchy will still wish to maintain free trade.

However, suppose that over time, with the introduction of manufacturing and the growth of the labor-force, pressures grow for enlarging the polity, and a coalition (populist) dominated by individuals with more labor, relative to capital or land, comes to capture the factional state. Suppose this happens during the transition of the economy from region VI (where the wage was higher than in region II) to region V. During this phase, as relatively more labor-intensive manufacturing comes into the "region of specialization", there will be inexorable downward pressures on the real wage. It is in the interest of the median member of the enlarged polity (whose endowments are dominated by labor) to *prevent* this outcome. This end may be achieved by placing a tariff on the more labor-intensive of the two goods produced in region VI, namely M_4. This will, *ceteris paribus*, raise the equilibrium capital-labor ratio in M_5, lower that in M_4, and raise the land-labor ratio in the production of the agricultural good A_2.[22] Thus the A_2 point will shift north-eastwards the K vortex, and M_4 towards the L vortex. This will enlarge the region of specialization VI, and allow the new endowment point which would otherwise have fallen in region V to remain in region VI, with a higher wage and lower rental rates on capital and land (Deardoff, 1984, p. 740).

Over time, however, for well-known reasons, the inefficiencies associated with protection will lower the efficiency of the economy. If this also leads to a lowering of the rate of capital formation relative to the labor supply, then the future transition to a lower real wage economy will be accelerated.

Similar pressures for protection can be expected to arise in a factional state, where the median individual in the ruling coalition of interests controlling the state has an endowment dominated by labor relative to capital or land, when there is a terms-of-trade improvement. For in a country whose exports are more capital-intensive than its imports, the rise in relative export price will put downward pressure on the real wage, as the expanding capital-intensive sector creates incipient excess supply of labor, and excess demand for capital and land (see Lal, 1986a, for the details).[23] It is not surprising therefore that the populist phase in Latin America, by and large, coincided with the terms-of-trade improvements for primary product producers associated with the Korean War boom of the early 1950s. *Mutatis mutandis*, periods of terms-of-trade losses would also be periods where the interest of the median member of the enlarged polity is no longer at odds with a reduction in protection. For the terms-of-trade decline would mean that the relative profitability of the more labor-intensive goods would rise, and this would enlarge the region of specialization in figure 4.2, where the more labor-intensive good would be viable at the continuing high wage (previously validated by protection) without protection. Apart, therefore, from the swings in Latin American politics based on conjunctural factors (primarily of a macroeconomic nature),[24] these considerations based on our model of the long-run development of the Latin American factional state, provide some further reasons why periods of marked terms-of-trade improvements should be associated with pressures for protection and those with terms-of-trade losses with moves towards liberalization.

There are a number of other features of Latin American political economy (touched upon briefly in the preceding section) which I hope the model of the Latin American factional state can illumine. First, as we have noted, the development path charted by the dashed arrow in figure 4.2 can be deflected towards the (K) vortex, the higher the rate of capital accumulation relative to the economy's rate of population growth. The greater this deflection, the more likely it is that the development path will follow the normal course (as in East Asia) with wages rising with capital accumulation and growth. One way to raise the rate of capital accumulation is to supplement domestic savings (which in any case are low in Latin America

by East Asian standards, see Lal and Wolf, 1986) through foreign borrowing. Most Latin American countries have attempted to do so. However
imprudent this course may seem, with hindsight its temptations for the
harried factional states of Latin American are obvious, as are the consequences of the closing of these borrowing opportunities. The worsening in
the terms of borrowing are partly due to the development policies which
were part and parcel of the same imperatives which compelled over-
borrowing.

A second illustration of the uses of the model concerns the political
economy of Latin American inflation. Even if it is true, as Hirschman
argues, that the "inflation cum overvalued exchange rate" policies were
initially adopted as an expedient for taxing the agricultural sector, it is less
implausible that the wild inflationary component of these policies still
serves the same purpose. For many developing countries have maintained
overvalued exchange rates, and a host of other microeconomic distortions
have the net effect of indirectly taxing the agricultural sector. But these
policies have not been accompanied by Latin American rates of inflation.
Thus the inflation tax is not likely to be an integral part of the arsenal to tax
the agricultural sector. In an environment of high inflation, the inflation tax
will ultimately be borne by those who cannot take pre-emptive action.
These are invariably the poorest, who rely purely on their labor and do not
have sufficient financial assets to use the various ingenious devices that are
increasingly available to richer citizens, to allow them to substitute some
indirect or direct form of foreign currency-based assets for domestic money
as a store of value (including, of course, capital flight!). The inflation tax is
therefore better viewed as an indirect method of legislating the cut in the
real wage that may be periodically required on some of the land and
natural resource abundant economy's paths of development.

In this context it is interesting to consider the consequences for our Latin
American factional state if it could not periodically – and at least for a brief
moment – reconcile the dynamic distributional conflict it has inherited
from factor endowments increasingly at odds with the polity.[25] There is one
example where the country's geography in effect imposes a constraint on
the levying of the inflationary tax – Mexico. This case is also of interest
because it provides an example of an exception to the story of the typical
Latin American factional state we have been trying to develop in this
section. Because of its contiguous border with the US – a country with a
strong currency and no exchange controls – it is virtually impossible for
Mexico to levy the inflation tax for any considerable period, for currency
smuggling across contiguous borders is likely to be easier than smuggling
goods and people (if for no other reason than bulk). High inflation in
Mexico sustained over a number of years would lead to the virtual dollari-
zation of the economy. The non-inflationary policies of postwar Mexico,

the absence of exchange control and the relative stability of the peso, are not therefore completely inexplicable in the Latin American context.

The Mexicans, however, like all the other land and natural resource rich Latin American polities, have to face the incipient and actual social conflict which is inherent in the efficient and growth promoting development path charted in figure 4.2. The Mexicans have succeeded, partly because of historical accident, in bucking the Latin American trend by establishing and maintaining what I like to call a "bureaucrat maximizing" predatory state. The PRI provides an elaborate spoils system to buy out, co-opt, and coerce those who might seek to undermine its hegemony. The secret lies in the public sector's use of various direct (through the expansion of government enterprises) and indirect methods (though creating microeconomic distortions), to garner a large share of the rents which accrue in a land and natural resource rich economy. These are then used to buy off discontent and create a political consensus legitimizing PRI hegemony, whose disruption might lead to the conversion of the polity into, perhaps, a populist factional state.

The recent reduction of the resources available to the state to finance the enhanced entitlements created by President Lopez-Portillo following the oil boom, has put this method of mediating the possibly inherent conflict between "growth and equity" present in most land rich economies, under considerable strain. Thus it remains an open question whether the Mexican predatory states' method of suppressing this conflict is viable in the longer run.

4 Concluding Remarks

I hope I have shown why in many Latin American countries there is likely to be a *tendency* towards a conflict between their comparative advantage and politics. It is based essentially on the discordance between the economy's factor endowments, and those of the set of median individuals comprising the possibly changing polity. Radicals have been right (though for the wrong reasons) in sensing the consensual benefits that might follow from land reform. But, if the polity is to be democratic, such a reform would need to give entitlements to rents from land to *the whole population*. By thus bringing the median individual factor endowments closer to the economy's, such a land reform might mitigate the pressures for policies which go against the region's comparative advantage. But the production losses of such a reform could be considerable. It is also difficult to see how the urban "middle sectors" of Latin America could be provided with an incentive for the productive use of any land entitlements they may receive. Thus, this is not likely to be a fruitful line of attack. With population growth, however, the economy's land–labor ratio is likely to fall, and it is of greater importance that in the future the median individual in the democratic polity has an increasing share in the manufacturing capital in the economy. For, then, even if the "outward oriented" development path – so essential for Latin America's long-term progress – implies lower capital–labor ratios and *ipso facto* lower or constant wages in industry during the growth process, this income effect on the labor endowment of the median individual will be counterbalanced by the rising earnings on his industrial capital endowment. It is in this context that the liberalization of domestic financial markets and the widespread dispersal of share-ownership could become an important means of creating and sustaining the political underpinning for the liberal economic policies that Latin America needs for sustained long-run development.[26]

NOTES

The research on which this chapter is based forms part of a multi-country comparative study of "The Political Economy of Poverty, Equity and Growth", financed by the World Bank. The views expressed are personal and should not be identified in any way with the World Bank.

1 See Lal and Rajapatirana (1987) for a survey of the links between foreign trade regimes and economic growth.

2 There is also the need to roll back inefficient and loss-making public sectors, but some may still consider this to be controversial. So I have not included the final set of Harberger's rules concerning the control of the public sector in the above list.

3 Thus he states: "policymakers positively cultivate unpredictability and distance from interest groups" and at the same time they are highly manipulative. These are the socio-political traits that account, perhaps more fundamentally than the cost price structure of the new industries, for their poor export performance".

4 See Lal (1984, 1986) for this interpretation of the constraints, facing the "predatory state".

5 The big exception to these generalizations of course is Mexico. But see section 2.

6 T. S. Eliot: "The Love Song of J. Alfred Prufrock".

7 But note that, because of Arrow's impossibility theorem, even the majoritarian democratic version of the factional state will not become a benevolent state, because of the lack of a majoritarian social welfare function!

8 It *has* made various technical errors in its economic policy. An excellent and balanced account of the Chilean economy, post-Allende, is in Edwards and Edwards (1987).

9 For instance Hahn notes that the new economics of information have emphasized that the "time and effort spent in discovering the set of possible choices . . . [will itself be] an element of [the] domain [of preferences]" (Hahn

(1985). Hence apparently "satisficing" behavior need not contradict the assumption of rational maximizing behavior.

10 He rightly in my view discounts O'Donnell's (1973) thesis as being empirically invalid. O'Donnell argues that the emergence of Latin America authoritarianism in the 1960s was due to the difficulties of "deepening the industrialization process. Deepening is defined as the putting into place through backward linkage of the intermediate input and capital goods industry once the 'last-stage' industries making consumption or final demand goods are established" (Hirschman 1979, p. 69).

11 See also Lal (1983, 1984) for a critique of these views.

12 This contrast is also noted by some authors and used with the formation of dependency systems to explain the different outcomes in the Northern and Southern parts of the land abundant Americas.

13 Veliz argues that the rhetorical espousal of economic liberalization by the military is the result of their desire to curry favor with their social superiors – the upper class business and land-owning groups – "their new upper-class friends who hold the key to their social advancement (their wives and families as well as their own)" (p. 299). He finds the upper classes in Latin America "culturally dependent" on the West. The constituents of these upper classes are the intellectual and old "oligarchs". He writes, "the bastions of Latin American cultural dependence are well manned by the radical intellegentsia and the upper-class business and land-owning groups. The loyalty that the former have demonstrated to the doctrines of violent revolutionary action, the latter have shown to the tenets of free-trading liberalism their forefathers embraced during the prosperous days of the liberal pause" (Veliz, n22. p. 299).

In Lal (1987) I have also argued (in explaining the North–South confrontation of the 1970s) that the similarities between Latin American and other Third World elites in seeking self respect, lie in the continuing sense of inferiority felt by "white" Latin American elites towards the dominant power and life-styles of white Anglo-Saxons.

14 On the political economy of liberalization see Lal (1987).

15 The endowment triangle "represents graphically the relative endowments of three factors (physical capital, labor and arable land). In the three-dimensional factor space, straight lines emanating from the origin contain all endowment vectors with the same ratio of factors. These lines in three dimensions can be represented by points in two dimensions intersecting the positive orthant with a plane to form the endowment triangle. The three co-ordinates in the three-dimensional factor space are represented by the corners of an endowment triangle, and the endowment vectors of each of the countries are represented by points. . . . The main point to keep in mind is that *every endowment point on a straight line emanating from one corner of the triangle has the same ratio of the other two factors*. For this reason the scales of the three factor ratios can be placed on the edges of the triangle" (Leamer, 1987, pp. 963–4).

16 See also Deardoff (1984) for a geometric presentation of Krueger's model.

17 This evocative phrase is due to Hla Myint.

18 For a model that includes non-traded goods see Lal (1986a).

19 These regions of specialization will depend upon commodity prices, and will alter as commodity prices change.

20 It might seem paradoxical that, whilst the *economy's* capital-labor ratio is rising it is falling in manufacturing. But remember that the rate of growth of labor for the *economy* is not the same as that in *manufacturing*. There it is possible for the agricultural labor force to grow more slowly (because of fixed land) than for the economy as a whole, thereby allowing and requiring the labor force in the manufacturing sector to grow more rapidly than for the economy as a whole. Thus a rising capital–labor ratio for the economy as a whole can be associated with a falling capital–labor ratio in manufacturing. Of course there will be some rate of capital growth at which the capital–labor ratio for manufacturing will also be rising along with that for the economy as a whole, and this paradoxical development path would not occur.

21 This is the basis for Krueger's statement that: "first, the distinction between poor and underdeveloped countries emerges clearly from the model, A poor country is one with an unfavorable land–man endowment. An underdeveloped country is one with a relatively small endowment of capital per person. An underdeveloped country, however, could conceivably have a higher per capita income and real wage than a 'more developed' but poor country. Second, a country abundantly endowed with land and therefore with a relatively high wage would not necessarily have a comparative advantage in labor-intensive manufactures, even in its early stages of capital accumulation: the real wage at which persons would leave agriculture might too high. In such an instance, the capital–labor ratio in manufacturing would be higher in the early stages of development in a poorer country, whilst the output per unit of capital and the rate of return on capital would be lower than in the low-wage country" (Krueger, 1977, p. 15).

22 This follows from the simple observation that, with the tariff on M_4 producers will attempt to expand the output of M_4. As it is the most labor-intensive good being produced, an expansion in its output will create excess demand for labor, and excess supply of the land and capital used in producing the other two goods. Full employment of the three factors will be maintained only as producers switch to using more land and capital-intensive techniques, which save on labor producing the other two goods M_5 and M.

23 This can also be seen in terms of figure 4.2, but this exercise is left to the reader! In an earlier paper (Lal, 1986b) I have used a similar model to explain the long-term decline in real wages in the Philippines – another land abundant country, whose political economy is closer to that of Latin America than its East Asian neighbors.

24 A model of these the factional state is provided in Lal (1986a).

25 This dynamic distributional conflict is modelled more explicitly in Lal (1986a), which provides an explicit role for the real exchange rate, and the non-traded goods sector – an aspect I have ignored in this article.

26 I take it that various dirigiste alternatives such as the creation of welfare states based on taxing the rising rents on land and capital are not likely to be efficient, in part because of their incentive effects on both the rulers and the ruled! For

anyone who doubts this, Uruguay would provide the appropriate cautionary tale.

REFERENCES

Balassa, B. (1985), *Change and Challenge in the World Economy*. London: Macmillan.

Baumol, W. Panzar, J. C., and Willig, R. D. (1982) *Contestable Markets and the Theory of Industry Structure*. San Diego: Harcourt Brace Jovanovich.

Collier, D. (ed.) (1979), *The New Authoritarianism in Latin America*. Princeton, New Jersey: Princeton University Press.

Corbo, V. and de Melo, J. (1985), "Overview and Summary: Liberalization and Stabilization in the Southern Cone of Latin America", *World Development*. Vol. 13, no. 8.

Deardoff, A. (1984), "An Exposition and Exploration of Krueger's Trade Model", *Canadian Journal of Economics*. Vol. 17, November.

Edwards, S. (1987), "The United States and Foreign Competition in Latin America". Dept of Economics, Discussion Paper No. 431, UCLA, February.

Edwards, S. and Edwards A. C. (1987), *Monetarism and Liberalization – The Chilean Experiment*. Cambridge, Mass.: Ballinger.

Edwards, S. and Teitel, S. (1986), "Introduction to Growth, Reform and Adjustment: Latin America's Trade and Macroeconomic Policies in the 1970s and 1980s, *Economic Development and Cultural Change*. Vol, 34, No. 3, April.

Hahn, F. (1985), "*In Praise of Economic Theory*". Oxford: Oxford University Press.

Harberger, A. (1984), "Economic Policy and Economic Growth" in Harberger (ed.) *World Economic Growth*. San Francisco: Institute for Contemporary Studies.

Hirschman, A. (1968), "The Political Economy of Import-Substituting Industrialization in Latin America", *Quarterly Journal of Economics*. Vol. LXXXII, No.1, February.

Hirschman, A. (1979), "The Turn to Authoritarianism in Latin America and the Search for Its Economic Determinants", in D. Collier (ed.)

Hirschman, A. (1981), "Policy making in Latin America", in A. Hirschman (ed.) *Essays in Trespassing*. Cambridge: Cambridge University Press.

Kindleberger, C. (1967), *Foreign Trade and the National Economy*. Yale, New Haven: Yale University Press.

Krueger, A. (1977), "Growth, Distortions, and Patterns of Trade among Many Countries", *Princeton Studies in International Finance*. No. 40, Princeton, New Jersey: International Finance Section, Department of Economics, Princeton University.

Lal, D. (1983), "*The Poverty of Development Economics*" Hobart Paperback No. 16. London: Institute of Economic Affairs.

Lal, D. (1984), "The Political Economy of the Predatory State". Development

120   *Global Issues*

Research Department, Discussion Paper 105, Washington D.C., mimeo. (Revised April 1988, University College London).

Lal, D. (1986a) "The Political Economy of Industrialization in Primary Product Export Economies". Paper for the IEA Conference in Delhi, to be published in the conference volume by Macmillan.

Lal, D. (1986b): "Stolper–Samuelson–Rybczynski in the Pacific Real – Wages and Real Exchange Rates in the Philippines, 1956–1978", *Journal of Development Economics*. Vol. 21, April.

Lal, D. (1987), "The Political Economy of Economic Liberalisation", *World Bank Economic Review*. Vol. 1, No. 2, January.

Lal, D. and Rajapatirana, S. (1987) "Foreign Trade Regimes and Economic Growth in Developing Countries", *World Bank Research Observer*, Vol. 2, July.

Lal, D. and Wolf, M. (eds) (1986), *Stagflation Savings and the State – Perspectives on the Global Economy*. New York: Oxford University Press.

Leamer, E. (1984), *Sources of International Comparative Advantage*. Cambridge, Mass.: MIT Press.

Leamer, E. (1987), "Paths of Development in the Three-Factor, *n*-Good General Equilibrium Model", *Journal of Political Economy*. Vol. 95, No. 5, October.

Lipton, M. (1977), *Why Poor People Stay Poor*. London: Temple Smith.

Little, I. (1982), *Economic Development*. New York: Basic Books.

Mayer, W. (1984), "Endogeneous Tarrif Formation", *American Economic Review*. December.

Mitra, P. (1986), "A Description of Adjustment to External Shocks: Country Groups", in D. Lal and M. Wolf (eds).

O'Donnell, G. (1973), *Modernization and Bureaucratic-Authoritarianism: Studies in South American Politics*. Politics of Modernization Series No. 9, University of California, Berkeley: Institute of International Studies.

Olson, M. (1971), *The Logic of Collective Action*. Cambridge, MA: Harvard University Press.

Olson, M. (1982), *The Rise and Decline of Nations*. Yale; New Haven: Yale University Press.

Sachs, J. (1985), "External debt and Macroeconomic Performance in Latin America and East Asia", *Brookings Papers on Economic Activity*. No. 2

Veliz, C. (1980), *The Centralist Tradition of Latin America*, Princeton, New Jersey: Princeton University Press.

Wynia, G. (1984), *The Politics of Latin American Development*. 2nd edn, Cambridge: Cambridge University Press.

Comment

Roberto Zahler

The opinions expressed in this commentary are the sole responsibility of the author and do not necessarily reflect those of the institutions to which he is affiliated. References mentioned in this comment refer to Lal's bibliography.

Deepak Lal's chapter deals with the long-run development strategy for Latin America, under the assumption that the debt crisis will be solved without confrontation between lenders and borrowers. He asserts that the major lesson of the debt crisis, especially when comparing Latin America's response to that of the countries in East Asia, is the need to improve the region's "capacity to transform". He further sustains that the failure to create that capacity is not due to ignorance of, nor the lack of professional consensus on the desirable policies, and that this failure requires an explanation which must lie in the realm of political economy. More specifically, Lal attempts to investigate the impediments that have prevented Latin America from adopting the mode of development – outward oriented – which, according to the author, is generally agreed to be necessary for equitable and stable growth in the long run. To deal with this issue, reference is made to special characteristics attributed to the Latin America state. Lal emphasizes that the typical case is that of the "factional state", which serves the economic self-interests of the coalition of pressure groups which succeed in capturing the state. According to the author, political consensus in Latin America has meant a constant shuffling of different coalitions of these interest groups, with important consequences for development policies.

The region's development policies are then analyzed by using Leamer's (1987) model, assuming three production factors; land, labor and physical capital; five manufactured goods and two agricultural goods. Given the model's and Lal's assumptions, and due to the fact that the "typical" Latin American country would be land-intensive, the development path of the economy, and in particular its industrialization process, would lean – at least some time – towards the more labor-intensive manufactured goods, with a consequent fall in the wage rate. The political economy linked to this stylized Latin American development path for an open economy would be a crucial determinant in the region's weakness to improve its capacity to transform. Considering the political features of the "factional state" which, according to the author, depend on the mean of the national factor endowments and on the median of the distribution of the income-generating factor endowments of the set of "decisive individuals", the introduction of manufacturing and the growth of the labor force would create pressures to enlarge the original polity, formed by the landlords favoring free trade, and coalitions dominated by individuals owning more labor relative to land or capital would capture the state. To prevent the outcome of lower wages linked to the labor-intensive phase of specialization with free trade, the interests of the median member of the enlarged polity would develop strong protectionist pressures with long-run negative implications on resource allocation and welfare. The author argues that similar pressures for protection would arise in a country with a relatively capital-intensive exportable sector, when terms of trade improve and, consequently, in periods of terms of trade losses there should be movements towards trade liberalization. Lal then states two implications of this feature of the model. One relates to the implicit rationale of the policy of accelerating capital accumulation by adding to the low domestic savings rate through foreign borrowing, increasing investment and therefore attempting to reduce or reverse the fall in the wage rate derived from the peculiarities of the region's factor endowments; the other relates to the chronic inflation which has persisted in many countries of the region, and which is interpreted as a method to cut real wages in the way required by the "land and natural resource abundant" economy's path of development.

The author finally highlights the fact that the conflict between the region's comparative advantage and its politics could be mitigated if the median individual in the polity had an increasing share in the economy's land or capital. Lal rules out land reform on the ground that production losses would be formidable and supports increased industrial capital ownership by reforms – such as financial market liberalization and widespread dispersal of share-ownership – which would sustain and strengthen the political underpinning for the liberal economic policies that, according to the author, Latin America needs for sustained long-run development.

I tend to agree with Lal's attempt to try to understand a very "relevant" issue with an enriching approach which tends to differ from those considered generally acceptable by "professional" economists. I also agree with the interesting conclusions derived from the application of Leamer's model regarding the evolution of factor prices in certain stages of the development process in "land-abundant" countries. However, I would like to emphasize some aspects of the problem of "the conflict between Latin America's comparative advantage and its politics" which I consider to be missing or only partially incorporated in Lal's chapter.

The long-run perspectives of the region's growth are not independent of the "solution" to the debt crisis. Lal assumes some means will be found which will allow Latin America to adjust and grow simultaneously. The fact is that, since 1982, the region's investment rate is 30 percent less than its savings rate, the difference being explained by the outward net transfer – due to foreign debt service, terms-of-trade deterioration and capital flight – equivalent to more than 4 percent of GDP, a figure that exceeds even the burden of German war reparations after World War I. With gross investment rates of less than 18 percent it is extremely difficult, even with outward-looking market-oriented and "prices right" policies, for the region to grow at a reasonable pace. In the absence of a dramatic turnaround in the world economy (higher growth rates in the industrial countries, lesser protectionism, lower international interest rates and a recovery of net international financial flows to debtor countries), a scenario which seems highly implausible, the only way out of this situation is for the creditor countries to share a substantial part of the debt burden, an outcome that may imply some sort of "confrontation" between lenders and borrowers. As the evidence indicates, in spite of the dramatic improvement in the region's trade balance during the last six years (in 1982–7 the average annual trade balance surplus was over US$ 25 billion, compared with a deficit of US$ 1.5 billion per year in 1980–1), private banking foreign financing has almost dried up, falling from around US$ 30 billion in 1980–1 to less than US$ 5 billion in 1982–7, where the bulk of the latter consisted of non-voluntary credits. The region's capacity to transform requires much more net foreign financing than is currently available or projected in the foreseeable future, and it appears that it will crucially depend on some type of debt relief which, until now, has been rejected by the creditors.

The author explicitly compares Latin America with the experience in East Asia, considering that the basic distinction between the two regions lies in their different factor endowments, with the postulated implications for trade policies. No reference is made to different historical realities, such as the agrarian reform imposed on some of the Asian NICs and its political economy consequences. Similarly, from this chapter it would appear that those countries engaged in unrestricted free trade policies, with no mention of government intervention in the fields of export financing and/or promotion nor its role in promoting technological development. Furthermore, no mention is made of the cultural differences reflecting deep-rooted austerity and investment behavior, as well as an export tradition in East Asia, as compared to the tendency towards consumption, speculation and "import promotion" in many Latin American countries.

On the other hand, it is surprising that even though the author considers that in many countries "the lack of political consensus has meant a constant shuffling of different coalitions of interest groups capturing the state", he nevertheless ends up with all these *different* power coalitions generating the *same* trade policies. This issue, which is crucial in the author's thesis, deserves much more analysis. It is presented within a framework which makes no reference to time or place, and it would be much more appealing if it were put in a more concrete historical and geographical context, since a time-series analysis of, and a cross-section comparison among countries would surely show significant heterogeneity regarding important aspects such as the relative openness of political systems, socio-economic characteristics of groups and sectors that accede to government, importance and size of the welfare state, economic size, degree of trade and financial opening-up, etc. If this is not done, it would appear that either the interests pursued are not (only) the economic ones or that the "different" coalition groups boil down to one and the same group, a situation which would question the core of Lal's thesis.

The free trade solution – which, according to the author would be the technically appropriate approach for the region's development – is based, among others, on the small country assumption. However, what under certain circumstances may be valid for one country, may be questionable for the region as a whole, especially if one considers that in 1987 primary products represented nearly 80 percent of Latin American exports. It has also been observed that for some exports which have increased substantially in recent years, either their terms of trade have deteriorated and/or their markets are being affected by protectionist measures in other countries. For the region as a whole, while the quantum of goods exported increased by 22 percent in 1982–7, the (nominal dollar) value of those exports decreased by 8 percent and the accumulated fall in the unit value of exports amounted to 25 percent during those years. In brief, if there is evidence that, with increased exports, a country ceases to be a price taker in the market for certain products, the optimal policy would not be unrestricted free trade but rather the implementation of an export tax.

Regarding Lal's argument with respect to the relationship between movements in the terms of trade and the political economy of protectionism, no empirical evidence is given to support his point. In my view, the years of greater trade liberalization in the region during the second half of the seventies, were basically motivated by the extraordinarily high affluence of international financial inflows linked to petrodollar recycling, rather than to the effect of a change in the terms of trade. Also, movements in recent years towards lowering tariff barriers appear to be highly correlated to World Bank structural adjustment loans (SALs) conditionality, rather than to movements on the terms of trade. In relation to the "speeding up" of capital accumulation by complementing domestic with foreign saving, so as to reduce the required fall in the wage rate linked to freer trade policies, the scanty evidence available in Latin America points first, to the fact that foreign saving in many countries and during long periods of time substitutes rather than complements domestic saving, thus financing higher consumption levels; and, second, that the main rationale for this borrowing appears to be the public sector efforts to complement domestic taxation in the years prior to the first oil shock and, later, to sustain high levels of public and private spending, and to profit from the wedge between domestic and foreign interest rates. On the other hand, I agree with the view that the incidence of the inflationary tax falls mainly on those groups or sectors which are not able to "evade" it by substituting indexed or interest-bearing documents and/or hard currency for money. However, I see no relationship between the depreciation of real money balances and the required fall in the *relative price* of labor vis-a-vis that of the other production factors required by the "land and natural resource abundant" economy's path of development.

I agree with Lal's final conclusion regarding the potential benefits derived from policies oriented to alleviate the discrepancy between the economy's factor endowments and those of the set of median individuals comprising the polity. However, based on the concrete experience of reforms in the Southern Cone countries of Latin America during the seventies, I have serious doubts about the consequences of two measures proposed by Lal; financial liberalization and widespread dispersal of share ownership, which had no correlation with the redistribution of factor endowments in the proposed direction. Financial liberalization, in the way it was implemented, stimulated huge interest rate distortions, linked to the creation or consolidation of a few economic conglomerates around financial institutions so as to profit from their *de facto* privileged access to foreign financing, while small- and medium-sized enterprises and consumers bore the bulk of the burden of the outrageously high costs on domestic loans. Finally, privatization of public enterprises, depending on the prices of shares and on the concrete mechanisms such as tax deductions and credit facilities linked to the selling of shares employed in the privatization process, in many cases ended up being more of a counterexample rather than the appropriate policy towards dispersal of share ownership.

5

The Global Economic Environment and Prospects for Recovery in Latin America

John Williamson

1 Introduction

This chapter reviews recent trends in two areas of the global economy and discusses their implications for the prospects of Latin America emerging from the debt crisis. The first subject area is the international capital market. The chapter reviews the size of the market and the direction of capital flows, appraises the significance of recent trends such as securitization and globalization, and outlines the growth of equity finance and debt swapping. The second subject area explored is international monetary arrangements. This section examines some proposals for changes in those arrangements and asks what implications such changes would be likely to have for the ability of Latin America to resolve its debt problem. A concluding section offers an appraisal of the prospects.

2 The International Capital Market

For much of the nineteenth century, Latin America was a major net borrower from the international capital market, primarily in the form of long-term bonds issued in London. It resumed borrowing, though mainly in New York, in the 1920s. The wave of defaults of the 1930s was one of the factors that resulted in postwar reconstruction being planned on the assumption that significant private capital flows would not revive. In fact, direct investment had already resumed by the early 1950s, while the offshore (Eurodollar) bank market emerged at the end of the decade. With the relaxation of exchange controls in the 1970s, external lending by onshore banks and by bond issues has also exploded in recent years. As is

Table 5.1 Measures of the size of the international capital market, 1964–86 ($b)

	Net size of Eurodollar market	Total external bank liabilities[a]	Net international bank lending	Net international bank and bond lending
1964	8			
1965	10			
1966	15			
1967.	18			
1968	25			
1969	44			
1970	57	106[b]		
1971	71	138[b]		
1972	92	174[b]		
1973	132	251[b]		
1974	177	295[b]		
1975	205	447		
1976	247	545		
1977	300	672	405	
1978	375	856	490	
1979	475	1120	615	
1980	575	1334	775	
1981		1531	940	
1982		1620	1020	
1983			1175	
1984			1265	1590
1985			1480	1900
1986			1770	2280

[a] External liabilities of banks in the BIS reporting area and most branches of US banks in offshore centers
[b] Excludes offshore branches of US banks
Source: Bank for International Settlements, *Annual Reports*, various issues

well known, Latin America became a major borrower in the 1970s and a problem debtor in the 1980s.

The present section reviews a number of recent developments in the international capital market that are of relevance in appraising Latin America's likely future relations with it.

Size of the market

The size of the international capital market is perhaps most naturally measured by the stock of lending outstanding. Statistics of the size of the Eurodollar market, one of the major elements of the international capital market, are available as from 1964, and are shown in the first column of table 5.1. The second column shows total (gross) external liabilities of banks in the BIS reporting area (and, as of 1975, of certain offshore branches of US banks). The third column nets out interbank transactions. The fourth column includes (net) bond lending. This gives the best available measure of the size of international lending. The explosive growth of the market is evident. Of the $2.28 trillion outstanding at the end of 1986, some $365 billion was loaned to developing countries.

Another measure of the size of the international capital market is provided by the volume of net new lending. Estimates of new lending through the two main financial instruments, bank credits and bonds, are shown in table 5.2 for the period since the market matured in the mid-1970s. (Comparable statistics are not available for earlier periods.) The expansion of lending is somewhat less dramatic if a crude allowance is made for inflation (column 2), but it is still impressive.

Between 1981 (or 1980 if one measures in real terms) and 1983 the flow of net lending fell precipitously, but in the past three years it seems to have resumed its upward trend. The decline in lending to developing countries accounted for about half that fall. The other major factor responsible for the reduction was financial deregulation in a number of major countries, which reduced the artificial incentives to channel lending through the international markets. The renewed rise in capital flows among the OECD countries since 1983 is presumably attributable to their increasingly close financial integration, which is tending over time to diminish the presumption that a borrower seeking credit will look to lenders in his domestic market rather than abroad. However, this process of increasing financial integration has excluded virtually all developing countries (the exceptions being only Hong Kong and Singapore) since 1982.

The geographical direction of capital flows

The bulk of the deposits placed in the BIS reporting banks has always originated from within the reporting area (essentially the developed countries), just as the bulk of the loans made by those banks has always been made to borrowers within the area. This is especially true in terms of gross deposits and loans, before netting out interbank transactions. In the early 1970s, however, the banks also started making medium-term loans on

Table 5.2 Net lending in international markets (bank credits and bonds), 1975–86

	Net lending (billions of current dollars)	Net lending (billions of 1986 dollars[a])
1975	57	110
1976	97	171
1977	100	169
1978	113	180
1979	145	214
1980	180	236
1981	190	218
1982	145	153
1983	130	134
1984	145	148
1985	175	175
1986	240	240

All flows exclude revaluation effects caused by exchange rate changes
[a] Deflated by US WPI
Source: Bank for International Settlements *Annual Report*, 1978, 1982, 1987

a significant scale to borrowers outside the reporting area – a trend that was accentuated after another group of nonindustrial countries, namely the oil exporters, became major depositors from 1974 on.

Table 5.3 shows flows of bank lending and deposits since 1979 with six areas outside the BIS reporting area: four groups of nonoil developing countries, OPEC, and Eastern Europe. The final rows of table 5.3 show the net flow of bank finance to these areas. The first two years show the "traditional" mid-1970s pattern of the commercial banks intermediating the OPEC surplus back to the developing countries, especially in Latin America, and Eastern Europe. Thereafter OPEC ceased to supply significant sums, and indeed withdrew funds on a major scale in several years. Bank lending to developing countries collapsed from 1982 on, in net as well as gross terms: only the Asian region has maintained a significant level of new borrowing. The desire of the commercial banks to continue lending to developing countries evaporated with the Mexican moratorium of August 1982. All the countries of Latin America, including prudent Colombia, as well as the whole of sub-Saharan Africa, suffered by contagion. For a while it looked as though Asia might also become a no-go area for the banks – even Korea was suspect; but in the event only the Philippines had to reschedule. Bank lending to Latin America has since then taken place almost exclusively through concerted packages of involuntary lending

Table 5.3 Net commercial bank transactions with nonindustrial countries, 1979–86 ($b)

	1979	1980	1981	1982	1983	1984	1985	1986
Bank lending to:								
Latin America	23.2	27.4	30.5	12.1	8.3	5.3	1.7	−1.6
Middle East								
(nonOPEC)	1.2	2.1	2.3	1.7	0.3	−0.4	0.2	−0.6
Africa	2.7	2.0	2.0	1.7	0.6	0.1	0.9	−0.4
Asia	8.2	7.4	5.1	4.3	3.4	4.8	8.3	2.7
OPEC	7.2	7.0	4.2	8.2	9.8	−1.9	0.2	−0.2
E. Europe	7.1	6.8	4.8	−4.6	−1.1	−0.1	5.7	4.4
Bank deposits made by:								
Latin America	4.9	−0.9	4.7	−1.9	5.8	10.1	0.4	0.4
Middle East								
(nonOPEC)	1.7	2.7	1.5	1.8	−0.9	−1.6	1.5	−0.5
Africa	1.8	0.7	0.5	−0.8	0.2	1.0	1.4	−0.2
Asia	3.9	1.5	2.8	5.5	5.3	9.8	2.4	11.7
OPEC	37.0	41.9	3.2	−18.2	−13.0	2.1	7.6	−22.1
E. Europe	4.6	0.9	0.1	2.0	2.7	4.3	2.8	0.1
Net bank lending to:								
Latin America	18.3	28.3	25.8	14.0	2.5	−4.8	1.3	−2.0
Middle East								
(nonOPEC)	−0.5	−0.6	0.8	−0.1	1.2	1.2	−1.3	−0.1
Africa	0.9	1.3	1.5	2.5	0.4	−0.9	−0.5	−0.2
Asia	4.3	5.9	2.3	−1.2	−1.9	−5.0	5.9	−9.0
OPEC	−29.8	−34.9	1.0	26.4	22.8	−4.0	−7.4	21.9
E. Europe	2.5	5.9	4.7	−6.6	−3.8	−4.4	2.9	4.5

Flows are estimated at constant end-of-period exchange rates
Source: BIS *Annual Reports*

negotiated case-by-case between the debtor country, the IMF, and the commercial bank advisory committee. Until 1987, when the "menu" approach incorporated in the Argentinian package gave banks a choice as to the form in which they would fulfill their obligation to recycle some of the interest, all banks were expected to participate in each new money package by making new loans in proportion to their outstanding exposure at the start of the debt crisis in 1982.

The near cessation of bank lending has been the principal cause of the reversal of the net flow of real resources to Latin America, from an inflow of $10–20 billion at the turn of the decade to an outflow of $20–30 billion in recent years (table 5.4).

Securitization

Table 5.5 shows the breakdown of net new lending in international markets between bank lending and bond finance. The figures add to more than the sums shown in the first column of table 5.2 to the extent that banks buy international bonds. Columns 3 and 4 show the gross and net totals respectively.

The story told by table 5.5 is that of the rise and subsequent fall in the pre-eminence of bank lending. In the mid-1970s bond finance still accounted for around a third of international lending, but this declined to under 15 percent in 1980. The invention of the floating rate note in the early 1980s led to a revival of bond finance, which has in recent years rivalled (or, according to other sources, surpassed) bank lending. Indeed, by 1986 almost one-half of bank lending took the form of bank purchase of international bonds.

"Securitization," which in this case involves the issue of bonds that can be passed around from one lender to another in place of securing a credit from a bank that is expected to remain on its books until maturity, seems to have arisen because creditworthy borrowers discovered that they could borrow more cheaply by going directly to the capital market.[1] In effect, this means that the borrowers and the ultimate lenders can divide between them the banks' traditional spread between their borrowing and lending rates. In order to retain a part of the business of lending to the more creditworthy borrowers, the banks are obliged to content themselves with that part of the former spread that remains with the lenders. They are encouraged to find this acceptable by the belief that they will be able to pass the bonds on should the need arise – a belief that is correct where a need for liquidity arises from the lender's difficulties, though it involves a fallacy of composition when the bonds become unattractive because of financial problems encountered by the borrower.

Securitization may also have been encouraged by the practice that arose during the debt crisis of exempting bonds from the process of rescheduling applied to bank credits. The growth of the secondary market in bank credits, where banks dispose of unwanted sovereign debt, has doubtless reinforced the trend as well.

Despite the growth of securitization, bank lending must be expected to remain dominant where creditworthiness is in question. Only large-scale lenders will find it worthwhile to make investments in assessing – and nursing – a borrower's creditworthiness. Loans to such borrowers are unlikely to become marketable, except under the distress terms typical of the secondary market for bank credits.

Table 5.4 Composition of the net flow of external finance to Latin America and the Caribbean, 1979–86 ($b)

	1979	1980	1981	1982	1983	1984	1985	1986
Nondebt-creating flows:								
Official transfers	0.6	0.8	0.8	1.0	1.0	1.3	1.5	1.5
Direct investment	5.1	5.6	7.6	5.9	3.2	3.2	3.7	2.8
SDR allocations, etc.	1.3	0.9	–0.1	0.5	0.1	0.4	0.5	0.2
External borrowing:								
Official creditors, long-term	3.1	4.1	5.1	5.5	8.6	8.8	2.8	5.3
Private markets[a]	27.1	38.0	55.9	24.7	1.9	5.0	2.6	–3.8
Change in reserves (increase = –)	–11.4	–3.7	1.4	19.1	–2.0	–11.4	–1.6	8.7
Reserve-related liabilities	0.3	1.7	1.2	10.9	9.3	3.0	1.2	2.1
Asset transactions[b]	–2.1	–2.6	–9.5	–9.2	–4.9	–6.9	–1.3	–0.4
Errors and omissions	–2.2	–13.8	–19.0	–15.1	–5.4	0.6	–3.2	1.1
Current account deficit	21.8	30.9	43.4	43.3	12.0	3.8	6.2	17.7
Memorandum items:								
Interest payments[c]	16.4	26.0	37.7	45.5	40.5	44.1	41.3	35.6
Net payments of investment income[d]	10.8	15.7	24.3	34.3	32.6	34.7	33.0	28.5
Net resource transfer[e]	8.5	12.6	15.2	4.7	–23.3	–33.4	n.a.	n.a.

[a] Derived as a residual, described as "other borrowing" by IMF. Includes errors resulting from discrepancies in coverage
[b] Primarily changes in export credit extended by Latin American countries (increase = –)
[c] Includes dividends
[d] Excludes payments on foreign direct investment
[e] Current account deficit less net payments of investment income, including profit remittances on direct investment
Source: IMF *World Economic Outlook*, April 1987

Off-balance-sheet financing

Another trend in the financial markets that has attracted much comment is the growth of what is known as "off-balance-sheet financing," involving in particular the growth of "note issuance facilities" (NIFs) and "revolving

Table 5.5 Composition of net international lending, 1975–86 ($b)

	Bank lending	Bonds	Total	Net
1975	40	20	60	57
1976	70	30	100	97
1977	75	30	105	100
1978	90	29	119	113
1979	125	28	153	145
1980	160	28	188	180
1981	165	32	197	190
1982	95	59	154	145
1983	85	58	143	130
1984	90	83	173	145
1985	105	125	230	175
1986	160	156	316	240

Source: BIS *Annual Reports*, 1978, 1982, 1987

underwriting facilities" (RUFs). A note issuance facility involves the sale of short-term notes backed with a guarantee by a group of underwriting commercial banks to take up any unsold notes at each rollover date. The effect is therefore that of a medium-term loan commitment. A few of the most creditworthy developing countries (like Korea) have already exploited such facilities, which are significantly cheaper than standard Eurocurrency loans.

However, since the underwriters have a strong interest in not being left with unsaleable notes on their hands, they are bound to limit the availability of such facilities to the most creditworthy borrowers. Indeed, the regulators are starting to show concern for the risk that the underwriters may have to take on high-risk loans should the creditworthiness of the borrower be eroded during the life of the facility. Since April 1985 the Bank of England has required NIFs to be subject to capital adequacy requirements (to the extent of 50 percent of the face value of the facility). This will certainly reduce and might even eliminate the attraction of these instruments, whose purpose was precisely that of reducing reserve needs for a given level of credit provided to customers and thus for a given level of fee income generated.

It is a mistake to imagine that every innovation in the financial markets has significant potential relevance to developing countries. Off-balance-sheet financing seems to be a case in point.

Globalization

Much has been said and written in recent years about the globalization of financial markets. The process encompassed by this term seems to involve an increase in the number of securities traded in more than one market, an increased willingness to commit funds for investment in several markets, an increase in the number of financial institutions that are present as active traders in more than one market, and improved communications between different financial markets. This process has two results. One is an ability to trade, at least in a limited range of standard assets (primarily foreign exchange and government securities of the major financial powers), at very short notice and at any hour of the day or night. The other is a widening in the range of assets that are considered to be potential candidates for investment.

It is difficult to see that 24-hour trading, giving the ability to react to new developments instantaneously and at any time, serves any important social function. Of course, it is vital for any individual trader to be in position to react as fast as anyone else, and any lead-time he can gain will give him an enormous advantage. But this is a negative-sum game: everyone being able to react faster is like everyone standing up at the proverbial football game – it leaves investors in general worse off.

An extension in the range of instruments that investors are able and willing to consider buying, in contrast, offers real possibilities for social gain. It means that more projects have the chance to attract finance from a wider range of investors. The development is one that is particularly likely to benefit potential borrowers outside the major financial centers, notably those in developing countries.

Risk management

In recent years financial markets have developed novel techniques to allow agents to hedge some of the risks to which they are exposed, and the use of these techniques has been growing at an explosive pace.

The longest established markets of this nature are futures markets for commodities and forward markets for currencies. Futures markets can be used to lock in prices currently quoted as soon as reasonable estimates of crop size are available, thus permitting somewhat greater certainty that expenditures being planned for a few months ahead could be financed without drawing on reserves. Similarly, the currency forward markets could be used to ensure that a known stream of export earnings denominated in one currency can be spent on goods whose price is denominated in another currency without a risk that subsequent exchange rate movements would force an unplanned drawdown of reserves. In both cases, however, the opportunities for risk reduction are very limited, because the longest maturities traded in these markets are modest.

The new markets for interest and currency swaps appear to offer greater potential since the maturities offered are greater. An interest swap involves two parties, one of which typically has a fixed-interest obligation and the other a floating-interest obligation of similar size, agreeing to service each other's debt. The arrangement can be attractive to both parties where their preferences as to the form of debt they service do not match their comparative advantage in borrowing. For example, the World Bank is much better known in the bond markets than are most commercial banks, while both are about equally well placed to raise floating-rate debt. Hence both the World Bank and a commercial bank can gain, if the latter wishes to make a fixed-rate loan, by the World Bank borrowing at a fixed rate and the two entering into a swap. The risk involved in entering a swap is limited but still significant, since a default by the partner can oblige a borrower to service the original loan standing in its own name (while relieving it of the obligation to service the partner's loan).

Similarly, a currency swap typically involves two parties that have raised similar-sized loans denominated in different currencies agreeing to service each other's debts. This can be attractive to both parties where their projected foreign-exchange receipts arise in a currency that does not match their comparative advantage in borrowing different currencies. This could arise, for example, where a German corporation exports to the United Kingdom and thus has a net surplus of sterling earnings that can be used to service its borrowings, but is unknown to the UK capital market, while a British corporation is in the reverse situation (earning a Deutschmark surplus but unfamiliar in Frankfurt). The risk involved in entering a currency swap is somewhat larger than that involved in an interest swap, given how sharply currencies can move and the fact that principal as well as interest obligations are swapped, although this is to some extent offset by the tendency of interest rates and exchange rates to move in opposite directions.

So far developing countries have made little use of the exploding swap markets. This may in part be due to a lack of interest on their part, arising from a failure to realize that currency swaps, in particular, offer the potential for a useful reduction in risk exposure. In fact, a significant contributory cause to the debt crisis was the reduction in the dollar value of developing-country exports induced by the dollar appreciation, which eroded the ability to service debts that were predominantly dollar-denominated. One way of avoiding this risk would have been to contract debts in a bundle of currencies that matched the destination of exports. A simpler technique now potentially available is to swap dollar debt-service liabilities for liabilities in a bundle of currencies that matches the currencies of price determination of the country's net exports.

Banks have so far been reluctant to enter into swaps with developing countries. They resist taking on a counterparty whose underlying liability could be rescheduled, and tend to demand prohibitive fees for such transactions.

Another potential future development that might permit developing countries to improve their risk management would be further expansion of the options markets. Unlike a futures contract or a swap, an options contract does not *oblige* its purchaser to effect a future transaction at a price specified now, but simply gives the purchaser the right (i.e., option) of making such a purchase (or sale). Clearly the option buyer will decide to exercise his option and make that purchase (sale) only if the price specified in the option is lower (higher) than that prevailing when the option matures. The great potential advantage of options relative to forwards or swaps from the standpoint of developing-country borrowers is that the issuer accepts no exposure to the credit risk of the purchaser, since the option is paid for in advance in cash. Thus, the existence of transfer risk should pose no barrier to use of this market. At present both interest and currency options markets are too short term to provide any very useful protection to developing countries, but they are beginning to lengthen.

Equity investment

International portfolio investment (i.e., excluding direct investment, where the foreign investor exerts effective control over the local enterprise) has in the past consisted overwhelmingly of loan capital – bank credits or bonds, whose debt-servicing cost is independent of the success of the enterprise being financed. The main alternative form of portfolio investment involves the purchase of foreign equities, i.e., claims to a share in the profits of foreign private enterprises.

There has in recent years been a sharp increase in cross-border equity investment, mainly among the OECD countries. In the 6-year period 1974–9, the average aggregate outflow of equity investment by five of the six principal countries involved[2] was SDR 0.60 billion, while the inflow averaged SDR 1.65 billion. In the 6-year period 1980–5, these figures jumped to SDR 7.36 billion and SDR 8.56 billion respectively (according to the statistics in the IMF *Balance of Payments Yearbook*, lines 59 and 61).

Nowadays the principal source of demand for foreign equity holdings comes from pension funds. This demand has been growing particularly rapidly, due both to the rapid growth in the size of the portfolios commanded by pension funds and the proportion of those portfolios invested in foreign assets. Foreign commitments of US pension funds reached $16 billion at the end of 1984, more than double their level only two years earlier. By the end of 1982 British pension funds had placed some 15 percent of their assets abroad, a proportion that had risen from only 6 percent three years earlier when exchange controls were abolished. The proportion has risen further since. Similarly, the liberalization of capital outflows by Japan allowed Japanese pension funds to use up to 20 percent of the monthly increase in their portfolios to acquire foreign assets of up to 10 percent of their portfolios; by March 1985 they had placed about 8.3 percent of their total assets abroad. Nowakowski (1983) estimated that at the end of 1982 some 4 percent of the worldwide assets of private pension funds, or $43 billion out of a world total of $1,175 billion, was invested outside the home market.

The reasons for the increase in international equity investment are not hard to find. The most important is the rapid acceptance of the theory of risk diversification that emerged out of academic work in the 1960s: it is now well understood that the overall risk of a portfolio can be reduced, and its expected return increased, by holding a widely diversified portfolio, even if some of the securities in it are individually quite risky. Not only has this been accepted intellectually by the financial community, but in 1974 it was embodied in the Employee Retirement and Income Security Act (ERISA). This legislation provides the basis for regulation of US pension funds; it explicitly accepted that pension fund managers could satisfy their fiduciary responsibility for prudent management of the sums entrusted to them by appropriate diversification, provided that they undertake the research needed to satisfy themselves that securities offer an expected return commensurate with their risk characteristics. Moreover, the theory has been confirmed by experience; for example, American investors who had already diversified internationally before the late 1970s found that their foreign holdings provided valuable support to overall returns during the period of a weak dollar. A second factor supporting increased international equity investment is the marked improvement in information on foreign companies – a product of the information revolution. And of course a third factor is that the sums available – particularly in pension funds – have been growing rapidly, in most cases faster than the capitalization of the domestic equity market.

Lessard and Williamson (1985) reported that up until that time:

> the vast majority of international equity investment [had] taken place among the developed countries. Well over 90 percent of the foreign investments of US pension funds are placed in other OECD countries. In fact, foreign equity investment in what the IMF classifies as developing countries has been of significant size in only five countries (Hong Kong, Israel, Malaysia,

Singapore, and South Africa), of which only Malaysia would be classified unambiguously as a developing country. Hong Kong, Singapore, and South Africa probably account for over 90 percent of such foreign investments as US pension funds have made outside the OECD. Total foreign equity investment in "core" developing countries . . . has been estimated at $700 million, with a further $50 million invested by institutions and the general public in a few developing-country stocks listed on developed country stock exchanges.

The bulk of such investments as have been made by foreign investors in developing-country equities has taken place through the medium of investment funds. Thus, $150 million has been invested in Mexico through the Mexico Fund, $120 million in Korea through two funds, some $50 million each through several funds in Taiwan and Brazil, and $50 million in India (in a fund accessible only to Indian expatriates). A Thai Fund has just been set up . . . Perhaps another $100 million has been invested through regional funds in Southeast Asia.

We went on to urge the virtues of increased investment in the equity markets of developing countries by institutional and other Northern investors. We argued that this would be mutually beneficial. To Northern investors, the emerging equity markets offer good possibilities of very attractive yields. Although the risks involved are also high, for these small equity markets tend to be extremely volatile and both political risk and the danger of insider trading are greater than in most industrial countries, they can be diversified away to some extent (returns have been negatively correlated with those in the large industrial countries in the past). Such risks should certainly be acceptable on a small proportion of the portfolio.

As far as developing countries were concerned, they would gain access to an additional source of external finance, with relatively attractive characteristics in terms of cash flow required for debt servicing. It would also have beneficial effects on the internal economy in terms of a reduction of the cost of capital to private enterprise, a stimulus to the growth of domestic financial intermediation, and in the long run a less inegalitarian income distribution as the rents from being a capitalist are bid down.

At the time our study was published, a good deal of skepticism was expressed regarding the prospects for all of the innovative sources of finance that we suggested trying to tap. So far that skepticism seems to have been justified with regard to our proposals on quasi-equities, standalone finance, commodity-linked bonds, and index-linked bonds. The one area where there have been real signs of change is with regard to equity investment. Seventeen new mutual funds that specialize in securities issued on one or more of the "emerging markets" have been created since mid-1985. The primary investment region is the East Asian NICs, but India, Malaysia, the Philippines and Thailand are also covered, as are

Brazil and Mexico in Latin America. The total invested in emerging markets increased by over $1 billion (which represents more than a doubling) in just over two years.

The sum involved is still modest in comparison to bank finance. Nonetheless, it is growing sufficiently quickly to give rise to real hope for the future.

Debt swaps

The emergence since the debt crisis of a secondary market in sovereign debt has given rise to several innovations involving the swapping of debt.

Originally, most participants in the secondary market entered with the intention of making *debt–debt swaps*. The main objective of banks was to eliminate their exposure in some countries, so as to save costs or to withdraw from countries where they had no confidence in the longer-term outlook. Presumably some of these sales were made to investors for cash, but in most cases it seems that banks accepted the debt of another country in which they were planning to maintain a presence in the long run. In some cases banks from developing countries swapped the debt of another LDC in return for that of their own country, presumably with the intention of receiving interest in local currency.

More recently, *debt–equity swaps* have involved the purchase of debt in the secondary market in order to take advantage of government programs in the debtor countries that allow the use of foreign debt in order to make local equity purchases. (Of course, a creditor bank can use its own debt to make such purchases if it so desires.) The attraction to a foreign investor is that it can invest more cheaply than if it simply bought local currency in the foreign exchange market. If, for example, sovereign debt were selling at a 50 percent discount in the secondary market and the central bank were prepared to redeem the country's debt at par in local currency, then the foreign investor would be able to get twice as much local currency for each dollar as through the exchange market. In practice the authorities redeem their debt at less than par, thus splitting the proceeds of the secondary-market discount between themselves and the foreign investors.

Table 5.6 shows debt–equity swaps authorized up to April 1987. The sums are larger than those involved in new equity investment in developing countries, but still modest relative to the total of bank debt.

Bankers like the idea of debt–equity swaps. It is, indeed, the only form of business with Latin America that has fired them with enthusiasm since the debt crisis broke. It gives them the opportunity either of obtaining some return on assets that they wish to dispose of, or else of exchanging their risky loans for assets that, while still risky, have a good upside potential. Nor should one neglect the fact that debt–equity swaps are

Table 5.6 Debt–equity conversions ($m in face value, up to April 1987)

Country	Total authorized[a]	Period of program
Argentina	500	Feb. to Aug. 1985
Brazil	2,300	Since 1982[b]
Chile	420[c]	Since June 1985
Mexico	950	Since May 1986
Philippines	60	Since April 1986[d]

[a] Note that authorized conversions may differ from amounts of debt actually cancelled; in Mexico, for example, of $953m authorized as of April 1987, $722m in face value of debt had been cancelled
[b] Since November 1984, only direct swaps by original creditors may be registered for purposes of future capital repatriation or dividend remittances
[c] Chapter 19 only. In addition, about $750m more has been reduced through debt–peso swaps (Chapter 18)
[d] Program formally launched only in August 1986, but the figure includes swaps accomplished between April and August
Source: Roberts and Remolona (1987, table 2)

usually extremely complex deals, which carry fees to match.

Evaluation of the benefits and costs to the debtor country is far more difficult. The benefits seem to be as follows:

1 The time-stream of debt-service payments is typically improved, inasmuch as (i) countries usually impose grace periods before profits and/or capital may be remitted; (ii) the demand to remit tends to be high when the economy is prospering; and (iii) a substantial proportion of earnings are usually reinvested.
2 The resources are usually used for productive investment, sometimes helping to achieve objectives of privatization or enlarged investment in priority sectors.
3 The country's external liabilities are reduced to the extent that the central bank redeems the debt at less than par.

But debt–equity swaps also impose a number of costs on the debtor country:

1 To the extent that the investment financed by a debt–equity swap would have been made anyway, the country loses an inflow of foreign exchange. Instead of obtaining cash with which it can increase its imports, it merely retires some of its debt.

2 Unless the proceeds of the swaps are used to buy newly privatized concerns from the government, the payments to foreign investors will increase the money supply. This may threaten to increase inflation or, if the increased money supply is sterilized, to raise interest rates and crowd out domestic investment.
3 Equity capital tends to be more expensive to service than debt. Admittedly a good part of the return may take the form of capital gains (resulting from reinvested earnings), so the medium-run cash flow implications may not be adverse (see benefit 1 above), but in the long run the country's net worth will be less. (This may, however, be offset by a higher value of the domestic capital stock if the quantity and/or quality of investment benefits.)
4 Debt–equity swaps permit *de facto* a preferential exchange rate for some foreign investors. Like all economic "distortions," this raises questions of both efficiency and equity. Will the investments approved for inclusion in the program be those with the highest social yield? Do foreign investors merit a subsidy that their domestic competitors are denied?

It would be foolish to claim that a definitive answer could be given as to whether the benefits exceed the costs, or vice versa. Nevertheless, Roberts and Remolona (1987) have argued that the critical issue is usually the degree of *additionality* involved. If a debt–equity swap is used to finance an investment that would not otherwise have been made, there is no lost inflow of foreign exchange, which was the first and perhaps the major cost. But if it finances an investment that would have been made anyway, the second benefit is absent. The country simply loses free foreign exchange and retires an equivalent amount of its debt.

The third form of debt swap is what Roberts and Remolona term a *debt–peso swap*. This involves the government offering to buy back its sovereign debt from its own citizens, who use their dollar holdings to buy bank debt on the secondary market. It is a method of attracting back flight capital, which has so far been used principally by Chile. The issues that arise in appraising the desirability of debt–peso swaps are almost identical to those that arise with regard to debt–equity swaps, except that instead of asking whether one can tolerate subsidizing foreign capitalists *vis-à-vis* domestic capitalists one has to bring oneself to subsidize those who placed their funds abroad *vis-à-vis* those who patriotically kept them at home. Debt–peso swaps also have the additional danger of stimulating renewed attempts to get money out through under-invoicing exports and over-invoicing imports, so as to be able to arbitrage it back at the preferential exchange rate.

The newest addition to the family of debt swaps is the *debt-for-nature swap*, pioneered by Bolivia and Conservation International in July 1987.

Conservation International bought Bolivian debt on the secondary market and retired it in return for Bolivian establishment of a national park plus endowment of a (local currency) fund to maintain it. Debt-for-nature swaps involve some striking differences to debt–equity swaps: (i) the stream of future debt-service obligations is extinguished, rather than improved; (ii) external liabilities are reduced by the full amount of the transaction; (iii) the swap creates no short-run monetary pressures, although future maintenance expenditures from the endowed fund will do so. Views may differ on the productivity of the investment undertaken. Those of us who believe that developing countries typically underinvest in conservation can hardly help welcoming debt-for-nature swaps.

Another potential addition to the swap family is a debt-for-dollar swap, better known as a *buyback*. A debtor country with free foreign exchange that it wished to use to reduce its outstanding debt would enter the secondary market in order to purchase its own debt at the discounted price. If its debt were selling at a 50 percent discount, every dollar so spent would enable it to extinguish $2 of debt. This practice has up to now been precluded by the sharing clause included in bank syndication agreements, but two recent developments suggest that in certain circumstances the banks may be prepared to renegotiate or suspend those clauses. One of these developments is the agreement that allows Bolivia to buy back its bank debt at a price of around 10 cents on the dollar by using funds that it is hoped will be provided by donor countries for this purpose. The other is the agreement that allows Mexico to offer a special issue of bonds, whose principal will be collateralized by zero-coupon US Treasury securities, to be swapped with willing banks at a fraction of the face value of outstanding debt. Whether this mechanism will allow Mexico to buy more debt relief per dollar (in this case the dollars will be used to buy zero-coupon bonds from the US Treasury) than would a straight buyback program is not yet clear. Having let Mexico try, however, it would be parodoxical if the banks were to refuse to renegotiate the sharing clause in cases where countries sought to buy back a part of their debt.

3   International Monetary Arrangements

It is not only the international capital market that has, arguably, sabotaged Latin American economic performance in recent years. Complaints have also been directed at the international monetary system. Edwards (1987) has provided the firmest evidence to date that increased variability of the real exchange rate of developing countries has had detrimental effects on their economic performance. In cross-section regressions explaining GDP growth in total and per capita in 1965–71 and 1978–85, he found that exchange rate instability had a statistically significant effect in reducing growth in the period of floating rates. A similar investigation of investment ratios established that, under floating, real exchange rate variability had discouraged investment. (However, he failed to establish a similar relationship between exchange rate instability and export growth – the channel through which it had generally been hypothesized that exchange rate volatility would operate, and where past failure to find strong relationships had often been cited to justify dismissal of criticism of the international monetary system.)

The other major criticism of international monetary arrangements is that a lack of effective policy co-ordination has resulted in almost a decade of anemic world growth. Slow world growth would seem to be disadvantageous to Latin America on almost every count. It depresses the prices of the primary product exports that still constitute a major part of the foreign sales of Latin America. It reduces the size of the markets for non-traditional exports, and may also provoke protectionist pressures that reduce access to such markets as remain. It reduces inflation, which tends to increase the real burden of debt service (Dornbursh 1986, pp. 190–2). Even the benefit of lower nominal interest rates that is normally associated with weak demand has been conspicuously absent in the 1980s.

A dilemma: macroeconomic stabilization versus microeconomic efficiency

The question may be posed, why should misalignments among the major world currencies create instability in the real exchange rates of developing countries? Cannot these countries peg to a basket of currencies chosen to stabilize their effective exchange rate, and thus avoid real exchange rate instability? If they choose to continue pegging to the dollar, do they have anyone to blame but themselves?

Matters are not so simple. In the first place, a constant peg to a basket of currencies[3] implies constantly changing bilateral exchange rates against each specific trading partner. A basket peg stabilizes the incentive to export and import in *general*, but it does not stabilize it with respect to any country in particular. The lack of predictability in bilateral real exchange rates may well be what discourages investment and/or leads to its inefficient allocation, thus impeding growth.

In the second place, a policy of pegging to a basket of currencies that represents the country's trade pattern[4] does have a serious (though not seriously documented) disadvantage. It deprives business firms of any secure link to a major international currency that they can use as a vehicle currency in which to invoice, cover forward their transactions in other currencies, borrow, and lend. It is true that even if a currency is pegged to the dollar there is some risk that it will change *vis-à-vis* the dollar, but such changes are likely to be less frequent and certainly be more predictable than the random changes between a trade-weighted basket and any single vehicle currency. Traders will know that changes against a dollar peg will be motivated by the needs of the domestic economy, either to offset differential inflation or to promote payments adjustment, and that will give them a basis on which to predict changes against the dollar. In contrast, if their currency is pegged to a basket, the changes between the basket (and thus their currency) and a vehicle currency are essentially random.

Thus developing countries face a dilemma in choosing whether to peg to a trade-weighted basket to stabilize their macroeconomic performance or to a single currency in order to provide their businessmen with the microeconomic benefits of stability in terms of a vehicle currency. What can be done to ease or resolve this dilemma?

A possibility open to an individual country is to retain a dollar peg but modify it when it becomes evident that significant macroeconomic distortions are developing. For example, the country could devalue against the dollar when the dollar appreciates to a degree that threatens the country with overvaluation. There are two snags with this compromise approach. One is that it jeopardizes the microeconomic benefits that provide the rationale for pegging to a single currency in the first place. The other is that market operators will be able to guess when the rate might be changed relative to the dollar (since one would wish to move the rate against the dollar only after the dollar had made a sizable and apparently semi-permanent move against other currencies, for otherwise the policy would effectively amount to pegging to a basket). This would raise the problem of speculative anticipation of changes in the peg. Thus, while countries that peg to a single currency should be prepared to change their rate against the peg currency when necessary, this compromise does not provide a very satisfactory solution.

The SDR as vehicle currency

Another possibility would be to peg to the SDR. Work by Brodsky and Sampson (1984) and Helleiner (1980) suggests that a constant peg to the 16-currency basket SDR would in the 1970s have led to less instability in the effective exchange rates of most developing countries than any other obvious peg (see tables 5.7 and 5.8). The major exceptions to this rule are the Caribbean countries, for most of which the US dollar remains a better peg, and some of the francophone African countries, for which the French franc remains preferable. Even there the disadvantage of the SDR is in most cases fairly minor. Admittedly the SDR has since then been redefined as a basket of only 5 currencies, but a study of Jordan confirmed that this

Table 5.7 Optimal peg for 65 developing countries, 1973–79

US Dollar
Bahamas, Dominican Republic, Haiti, Honduras, Panama, Trinidad and Tobago, Venezuela

French Franc
Central African Republic, Chad, Comoros, Gabon, Mali, Niger, Senegal, Burkina Faso

Pound Sterling
Paraguay

SDR (16-currency basket)
Afghanistan, Barbados, Botswana, Burma, Burundi, Congo, Ecuador, Egypt, El Salvador, Ethiopia, Guatemala, Guinea, Guinea-Bissau, Guyana, Iraq, Ivory Coast, Jamaica, Jordan, Kenya, Korea, Liberia, Libya, Madagascar, Maldives, Nepal, Nicaragua, Oman, Pakistan, Romania, Rwanda, Sao Tome and Principe, Sierra Leone, Somalia, Sudan, Suriname, Syria, Uganda, Yemen A.R., Yemen P.D.R., Zambia

ECU
Benin, Bolivia, Cameroon, Costa Rica, Grenada, Malawi, Mauritius, Seychelles, Togo

The optimal peg is defined as whichever one of the five above currencies and currency baskets would have minimised instability of the effective rate for the country concerned over the period 1973–79 if the value of the peg had been maintained constant.
Source: Brodsky and Sampson (1984)

did not destroy the attractiveness of an SDR peg (Takagi, 1984). Hence from a macroeconomic standpoint the SDR would be a reasonably attractive peg. If only the SDR were a vehicle currency with active markets in which traders could invoice, cover, borrow and lend, a policy of pegging to the SDR could then resolve the dilemma of choosing between macroeconomic and microeconomic stability. Moreover, if all (or most) developing countries were to peg to the same unit, such as the SDR, South–South trade would become free of the microeconomic risks that traders face when their respective currencies fluctuate randomly against each other.

That obviously raises the question as to how the SDR could be converted into a vehicle currency. The first and crucial step would in my view be to create an SDR clearinghouse that would permit SDRs to be traded between the official and private sectors, as proposed by Peter Kenen (1983). Once that were done it would be possible for countries to peg

Table 5.8   Optimal peg for 130 developing countries, 1973–79

US Dollar
Bahamas, Costa Rica, Dominican Republic, Haiti, Honduras, Mexico, Neth. Antilles, Panama, Sao Tome and Principe, St. Pierre and Miquelon, Trinidad and Tobago, US Virgin Islands, Venezuela

French Franc
Central African Republic, Chad, Comoros, French Guiana, Guadeloupe, Mali, Martinique, Niger, Reunion, Senegal, Burkina Faso

Pound Sterling
Bolivia, Paraguay, St. Helena, Tonga

SDR
79 countries, not listed elsewhere

ECU
Benin, Brunei, Cameroon, Cyprus, Gambia, Malawi, Malta, Mauritania, Mauritius, Seychelles, Sierra Leone, Swaziland, Togo

Actual practice (e.g. basket, if other than above)
Fiji, Guinea-Bissau, Grenada, Kiribati, Morocco, Nauru

The optimal peg is defined as in table 5.7
Source: Helleiner (1980)

directly to the SDR by intervening in SDRs. Since the private sector would need to hold SDRs in order to transact with central banks that wished to intervene, there would be strong pressures for private agents as well as central banks to build up SDR transactions balances. A full range of the financial markets that characterize a vehicle currency would not be long in following.

Target zones

For better or for worse, proposals to turn the SDR into a vehicle currency are not at present on the international agenda. But proposals to stabilize exchange rates among the major currencies are. Successful implementation of the target zone proposal could indeed be expected to ease the dilemma confronting non-Caribbean Latin American countries in deciding whether to replace a dollar peg by a basket peg. (Given the size of the fluctuations that target zones would still permit, of ± 10 percent in effective rates and thus more than ± 20 percent on bilateral cross rates among the major currencies, the dilemma would not be totally resolved and accordingly the case for converting the SDR into a vehicle currency would remain.)

Successful implementation of target zones would offer a second benefit to developing countries. By reducing the size of payments swings among the industrial countries, it would reduce the need for periodic redirection of the trade flows of the developing countries. For example, increased exports from Latin America have in recent years been directed overwhelmingly at the US market. Now that the United States is in the process of seeking an adjustment of the order of $150 billion in its nonoil trade balance, its imports from all sources, including Latin America, are likely to decline (at least relative to trend). This need not result in a decline in total Latin American exports, provided that demand in the rest of the OECD expands by enough to prevent a world recession, since Latin America has gained competitiveness in Europe and Japan with the decline of the dollar and is thus well-positioned to increase its exports to those markets. But there will inevitably be frictional costs in making the adjustment, which would have been avoided by less extreme payments imbalances among the industrial countries.

A third benefit of greater exchange rate stability among the major currencies is that it would avoid a repeat of the increased burden of debt service payments that arose from the dollar's appreciation in the early 1980s. Since most debt is denominated in dollars while export revenue is earned in a basket of currencies, and since the dollar price of primary commodity exports tends to be reduced by dollar appreciation, debt servicing capacity is eroded by a rise in the value of the dollar. This risk – but also, of course, the chance of a windfall benefit from downward overshooting of the dollar – would be reduced by a successful target zone system.

Policy co-ordination

The other current proposal for improving international monetary arrangements involves greater policy co-ordination among the major countries. At the moment it is not at all clear what this may eventually mean. The IMF is beavering away to produce a series of indicators that will hopefully allow the "Group of Seven" (G-7) to establish that their several policy intentions are collectively consistent with a satisfactory evolution of the world economy. Dornbusch and Frankel (1987) interpret it as an attempt to "fine tune" the world economy, presumably with the G-7 making discretionary policy changes that they believe will maximize some collective welfare function. Williamson and Miller (1987) proposed a system of policy co-ordination that uses exchange rates and endogenous formula-determined growth rates of nominal domestic demand as intermediate targets to guide monetary and fiscal policies, thus absorbing the target zone proposal within a more comprehensive framework.

If any of these proposals were to be successfully implemented, they would tend to limit the business cycle as well as currency misalignments and payments disequilibria. This would presumably be beneficial to developing countries, but once again the benefit of limiting recessions would have to be offset against the cost of curbing inflationary booms, which ought to offer debtors a good chance to work down their debts. However, in view of the way that most Latin American countries seem to have borrowed procyclically in the past, the loss of unsustainably strong upswings may actually be a blessing, since it would remove the temptation to overborrow at a time when debt repayment would be more appropriate.

The general verdict in the literature seems at the moment to be that, while policy co-ordination could in principle yield net benefits, these would at best be small (Oudiz and Sachs, 1984, Fischer, 1987). One study, however, concluded that the main beneficiaries would in fact have been the developing countries (Sachs and McKibbin, 1985). This is quite plausible: inasmuch as better co-ordinated policies permitted the world economy to be operated at a higher percentage of capacity, the inflation costs might come close to offsetting the output gains for the industrial countries, while still leaving substantial terms-of-trade gains for the developing countries with no offsetting cost.

My own view is that the verdict that policy co-ordination offers only marginal benefits is unproven even for the industrial countries. The Oudiz and Sachs paper that pioneered this conclusion was based on the premise that policy-makers revealed their preferences as between competing objectives by the outcomes they achieved, which were assumed to be the best attainable given the policies pursued by the other countries (i.e., history was interpreted as the Nash equilibrium). But should we really conclude that the balance of payments is unimportant for US welfare just because the first Reagan administration pursued policies that resulted in a big deficit? Why do we assume in this exercise that those German policies that have resulted in high unemployment are optimal when we spend much of the rest of our time arguing that they are not? I at least will need to be shown that a welfare function that I judge reasonable would show no major difference between the historical outcome and a co-operative equilibrium or the Williamson–Miller "blueprint" before I would dismiss the potential of co-ordination. The only study I know of that has yet addressed this question has reached the opposite conclusion (Currie and Wren-Lewis, 1988).

4 Concluding Appraisal

The continued vitality of the international capital market implies that the difficulties of Latin America since 1982 cannot be ascribed to a general failure of the market. Latin America has not been crowded out by a shortage of loanable funds: it has been cut off because it was judged uncreditworthy. It will be able to return to the market when both its ability and willingness to service debt make it once again creditworthy.

Unfortunately there is as yet scant sign of a return of creditworthiness; even Colombia's situation remains delicate. At least for a time there was some reversal of capital flight in Argentina, Chile and Mexico, but the bankers remain as reluctant as ever to increase their exposure.

A more hopeful element is the renewed role of equity finance. Increasing sums of new money are being invested in the stock markets of those developing countries that have well-functioning markets (including, but not just, the Gang of Four). The market in debt–equity swaps has thrived whenever a debtor country has permitted it to. Suggestions are now afoot to allow the use of a part of interest payments for reinvestment in equities as a permissible form of recycling. While the creditors are more enthusiastic about most of these developments than the debtors, there seems also to be an increasing recognition on their part that equity finance is consistent with the more capitalistic style of development that, with greater or lesser degrees of conviction, they are in the process of embracing.

Despite the encouraging progress of equity finance, it remains unrealistic to expect that this will be able to take the place of debt finance in the near term (meaning before perhaps the mid-1990s). Debt–equity swaps even tend to reduce cash flow in the short run; at best, with 100 percent additionality, they leave it unchanged, otherwise they use some of what would otherwise have been a cash inflow to retire debt. These swaps may nonetheless be worthwhile because of their other characteristics, including their possible role in paving the way for net inflows of equity capital. But they do not relieve the immediate foreign exchange shortage that confronts most Latin American countries.

Given the past dominance of bank creditors in the external borrowing of Latin America, it is inevitable that the main burden of providing finance in the next few years will fall on the banks. There is a continuing danger that if they do not find ways of recycling a substantial part of their interest receipts, e.g., through the menu approach of Cline (1987), then the debtor countries will develop alternative mechanisms that are less likely to preserve the value of the banks' claims. These mechanisms are unlikely to include outright repudiation, which would be an act of economic warfare that would not bring any advantages (other than possible political sex appeal) to compensate the risks involved. But that is small comfort to the banks. If free rider problems prevent them doing enough recycling to keep the risk of creeping moratoria at bay, perhaps the main question is whether the unfortunate experience of the banks will prevent equity investors providing a renewed flow of real resources with better risk characteristics in the 1990s.

Unlike the international capital market, only an extreme optimist could describe the international monetary system as enjoying continued vitality. Its ills have contributed to the difficulties of Latin America. Exchange rate variability among the industrial countries has presented South American countries with a dilemma in choosing between the macroeconomic stability offered by a basket peg and the microeconomic convenience of a dollar peg. US payments adjustment is going to involve a significant redirection of Latin American exports. Dollar overvaluation added to the burden of debt service. And the lack of effective policy co-ordination contributed to the weak world economy of the 1980s.

Although there is now discussion of international monetary reform and increased policy co-ordination that might remedy these weaknesses, it would be unwise for Latin America to rely on being bailed out by policy changes in the industrial world. Not only are the spillovers of insufficient magnitude, but it must be judged unlikely that very much progress will be made in these areas by the industrial countries in the next year or two. The failure of the White House–Congressional summit to achieve a meaningful cut in the US budget deficit, even under the spur of the stock market collapse, means that the "hard landing" (i.e., recession) envisaged by Stephen Marris (1987) remains all too likely to precede any real international reform. The international environment is unlikely to offer Latin America much early help in overcoming the debt crisis. That will have to remain dependent primarily on its own endeavors. Fortunately the history of the post-war world suggests strongly that in the long run the dominant determinant of a country's economic progress is its own policy choices rather than its international environment.

NOTES

1 In national markets securitization has also been promoted by the packaging of standardized securities by intermediaries who saw in this a way of earning a part of the banks' traditional spread.
2 United States, United Kingdom, Japan, West Germany, and the Netherlands. Swiss statistics are available only since 1984.
3 Or, in a high-inflation country, a peg that depreciates to neutralize the excess of

its inflation rate over that in the average of its trading partners as represented in the basket.

4 There is a literature on the choice of trade weights: imports versus exports versus both; elasticity-weighted or volume-weighted; whether exports should be weighted by individual country exports or by total world exports of a given product; and so on. See Williamson (1982) for a survey. Fortunately it seems that the gain from pursuing added degrees of sophistication is modest.

REFERENCES

Bergsten, C. Fred, Cline, William R. and Williamson, John (1985), *Bank Lending to Developing Countries: The Policy Alternatives*. Washington: Institute for International Economics.

Brodsky, David A. and Sampson, Gary P. (1984), "The Sources of Exchange Rate Instability in Developing Countries: Dollar, French Franc and SDR Pegging Countries", *Weltwirtschaftliches Archiv*. no.1.

Cline, William R. (1987), *Mobilizing Bank Lending to Debtor Countries*, Washington: Institute for International Economics.

Currie, David and Wren-Lewis, Simon (1988), "Evaluating the Extended Target Zone Proposal". CEPR Discussion Paper No. 221.

Dornbusch, Rudiger (1986), *Dollars, Debts, and Deficits*. Cambridge, MA: MIT Press.

Dornbusch, R. and J. Frankel (1987), "Macroeconomics and Protection," in R. Stern (ed) *U.S. Trade Policies in a Changing World Economy*. Cambridge, MA: MIT Press.

Edwards, Sebastian (1987), "Implications of Alternative Exchange Rate Arrangements for the Developing Countries". Mimeo.

Fischer, Stanley (1987), *International Macroeconomic Policy Coordination*. NBER Working Paper No. 2244, May.

Helleiner, Gerald K. (1980), *The Impact of the Exchange Rate System on the Developing Countries: A Report to the Group of Twenty-four*. UNDP/UNCTAD Project INT/75/015.

Kenen, Peter B. (1983), "Use of the SDR to Supplement or Substitute for Other Means of Finance," in George M. von Furstenberg (ed) *International Money and Credit: The Policy Roles*. Washington: International Monetary Fund.

Lessard, Donald R. and Williamson, John (1985), *Financial Intermediation Beyond the Debt Crisis*. Washington: Institute for International Economics.

Marris, Stephen (1987) , *Deficits and the Dollar*. Washington: Institute for International Economics, revised edn.

Nowakowski, C. A. (1983), "Charting a Course for the Decade Ahead: Go Global or Go Aground." Stamford, Conn: Intersec Research Corporation.

Oudis, Gilles, and Sachs, Jeffrey (1984), "Macroeconomic Policy Coordination Among the Industrial Economies", *Brookings Papers on Economic Activity*. 1.

Roberts, David L. and Remolona, Eli M. (1987), "Debt Swaps: A Technique in Developing Country Finance," in R. A. Debs, D. L. Roberts and E .M.

Remolona, *Finance for Developing Countries*. New York: Group of Thirty.

Sachs, Jeffrey and McKibbin, Warwick J. (1985), *Macroeconomic Policies in the OECD and LDC External Adjustment*. NBER Working Paper No. 1534, January.

Takagi, Shinji (1984), "Testing the Performance of the SDR Peg in Jordan, 1975–83". Mimeo.

Williamson, John (1982), "A Survey of the Literature on the Optimal Peg," *Journal of Development Economics*. Vol. 11.

Williamson, John and Miller, Marcus (1987), *Targets and Indicators: A Blueprint for the International Coordination of Economic Policy*. Washington: Institute for International Economics.

Comment

Mario I. Blejer[1]

This is a very interesting and informative chapter which provides important insights into the external constraints faced by developing countries in their process of adjustment. Williamson discusses separately two broad subjects– developments in the international capital market and the current international monetary arrangements. However, the linkages between these two subjects are much stronger than they appear from the discussion in his chapter. Indeed, many of the recent developments in the capital markets are very strongly related to the same sources that gave rise to the disarray, as discussed by Williamson, in the international monetary system. The large swings and fluctuations in the value of major currencies and in interest rates, and the magnitude of the payments imbalances of the large industrial countries could be seen as the reason behind the growth and diversification of the international capital market and the motivation for the creation of new instruments and new mechanisms which are so well described in this chapter. This is similar to what is observed in individual countries, that is, when instability and inflation become entrenched in the system, there is a tendency for the financial markets to grow and become much more sophisticated.

What constitutes the central link in this context is the large imbalance in the US economy. The driving force behind both the problems with the international monetary system and the development of the international capital market is the large US fiscal deficit and the emergence of the United States as the largest debtor country in the world. This is a central variable to be observed by the debtor countries in the developing world because, in one way or another, fiscal imbalances in the United States affect real interest rates, creating instability in the value of the dollar and give rise to protectionist trends.

In addition, and this is particularly important for highly indebted developing countries, the persistence of US fiscal imbalances may lead to some type of international crowding out. It is clear from Williamson's analysis that the size of the international capital market has largely expanded. However, the demand for credit in this market has also grown and will continue to grow given the deficit financing needs of the US. Despite the deterioration in the international position of the US, the market still considers it a creditworthy debtor and a better risk choice than the debt-ridden developing countries. If the *stock* of debt of less developed countries stands at approximately $365 billion, clearly, a yearly flow of financing for the United States of about half of that amount could largely reduce the ability of developing countries to obtain voluntary credit from the international capital market.

The balance of payments of the United States is a reflection of the fundamental imbalance in its economy, and a serious consideration for developing countries is how these imbalances will be corrected. If the trade balance disequilibrium results in protectionist policies, the outcome will, indeed, differ from the one that could emerge from US internal adjustments, and this type of developments should be the core of the concern of developing countries when the international environment is to be considered.

Regarding international co-operation, the discussion by Williamson is quite exhaustive. Two aspects which bear heavily on the debt problem could be added. They are the need for co-ordination in bank regulations and in the tax area. Such co-ordination should create an environment of understanding between the creditors, which could help in the process of negotiation.

Turning to Williamson's discussion of debt–equity swaps and equity investments, my impression is that the normative appraisal of these schemes hangs on the attitude toward foreign investment in general. The claim that swaps discriminate between domestic and foreign investors, for example, cannot be distinguished from similar claims regarding foreign investment incentives in general. Regarding the cost profile of servicing debt versus servicing equity (interest payments versus dividends and remittances), I would think that a country would be better off to service foreign equity than foreign debt. A negative correlation between the ability to pay and the actual need to pay may exist with debt but not with equity. Dividends are to be paid only if the investments are profitable while interests arise from all loans regardless of their application. Assume that foreign interest rates increase, causing some global contraction. Servicing the debt becomes more expensive while, on the other hand, a contraction reduces profitability and, with it, the need to transfer dividends and remittances.

Debt–equity swaps become more of a problem at the systemic level – when a foreign investor considers an investment opportunity, it seems that countries with debt problems but which are implementing a debt-equity-swap scheme will have an unfair, although artificial, edge over those without a debt overhang.

As for the probability that swaps and other investment schemes would help to ease the debt crisis, it all depends on the perception of foreign investors that stability will prevail in the debtor countries. A negative attitude toward foreign ownership will give rise to fears of nationalization, interference in the decision-making process, regulations, limitations on repatriation, and so on, and even the more ingenious of schemes will probably not have any impact.

In conclusion, I find it extremely important to consider the interaction between the international conditions and the debt problem. In this context the need for both the international monetary system and the international capital market to generate credibility and certainty should be stressed, since this would generate the mechanisms leading to flexibility and to the attainment of a negotiated solution. Unilateral measures have a negative impact on international markets and reduce credibility and certainty. In addition, the promotion of certainty requires that accurate and timely information be available, and the international financial institutions have an important role to play here. The current involvement of the IMF in the process of policy co-ordination, surveillance, and the elaboration of macro-economic indicators is as important as its role in the adjustment and financing processes of developing countries, if not more so. However, particularly in discussions within highly indebted countries, this role of the Fund has not been stressed enough and it is in the context of Williamson's chapter that this could probably be highlighted.

NOTE

1 The views expressed are the sole responsibility of the author and do not reflect those of the IMF.

6

Controlling Inflation: the Problem of Nonindexed Debt

Guillermo Calvo

1 Introduction

It is probably fair to say that monetary theory has reached a stage where the case of "passive" money (Olivera, 1971) commands the same level of intellectual respect as the standard textbook closed-economy case of active money. Passive money, one should perhaps be reminded, is a situation where the supply of money (or its rate of growth) is an endogenous variable, being, therefore, a function of some of the other variables in the system. The importance of distinguishing between active and passive money systems was sharply brought home by the Mundell–Fleming model (Dornbusch, 1980), in terms of which one can show that the effects of fiscal and monetary policies with perfect capital mobility depend crucially on whether the economy is under fixed or flexible exchange rates (the former corresponding to passive, and the latter to active money).

The identification of a passive money regime may not be as obvious as the Mundell–Fleming paradigm might suggest. Money, for example, could be active in the short run, but passive in the long run. This would probably be the case in a closed-economy context (where, for simplicity, we assume that population and technical knowledge are constant) if it were not possible to reduce the fiscal deficit below a certain positive fraction of GNP, and the authorities insisted on trying to stop inflation by refusing to monetize the deficit. In the short run the supply of money would be exogenous, but eventually the accumulation of bonds would tend to make the situation unsustainable and lead to a possibly explosive expansion of the money supply.[1]

The above delayed-passivity of the supply of money is a fascinating subject as it reveals the possibility that politicians implement "bad" but short-run popular policies (a big fiscal deficit with low inflation, for example) without having to suffer the consequences, since inflation may not return until they are out of office.[2] But there are also circumstances in which the future upsurge of inflation has little to do with any kind of "fundamental" mismanagement of the operational part of the fiscal budget; instead, in these cases future inflation arises from the need to pay for the services of the public debt, or to eliminate a generalized bankruptcy situation that would occur if inflation were to be kept relatively low. This slightly unfamiliar theme will be the subject matter of the present chapter.

I became interested in this subject after noticing the serious straits that economies like Argentina, Chile and Bolivia have been put into as a consequence of not being able to induce a nominal interest rate level compatible with their long-run inflationary targets (see, e.g., Calvo, 1986); Corbo, de Melo and Tybout (1986), Edwards and Cox-Edwards (1987), Sachs (1986)). In all of these experiences, the *ex-post* real rate of interest remained at an alarmingly high level that, with the possible exception of the on-going stabilization program in Bolivia, may have been responsible for the eventual liquefactions and/or socializations of the public and private debt.

A brief account of the above-mentioned experiences, however, may not generate any need to develop new economic theory, since the relatively high nominal interest rates were eventually followed by also relatively high inflation rates (once again, with the temporary exception of Bolivia). Thus, those events would seem to be compatible with the following straightforward explanation: "the nominal interest was high, because people realized that inflation was going to flare up in the future due to (say) an unduly large fiscal deficit." I am not going to quarrel with this point of view. Instead, I will attempt to go a little further into the economics of the fiscal deficit itself, and explore the possibility that "people expected a relatively high inflation, which brought about relatively high nominal interest rates, which swelled the public debt service, which increased fiscal deficit . . . ". In other words, I am going to study the possibility that the nominal interest rate *causes* inflation, instead of the other way around.[3] Notice that the above reasoning would not hold if the public debt was fully indexed to the price level, because in that case the nominal interest rate is determined by the *actual*, not the *expected*, rate of inflation. Thus, a central ingredient of my analysis is the existence of nonindexed debt.

This chapter aims to explore the above-mentioned relatively novel relationship between the nominal interest rate and inflation. It should be noted from the outset, however, that although the "threat" of high real rates plays an important role for generating "high-inflation" equilibria, my examples are not capable of rationalizing a "transition period" in which the *ex-post* real rate of interest is relatively high due to inflationary expectations (as it appears to be in the above-mentioned country experiences).[4]

The chapter is organized as follows. Section 2 presents the central argument in the simplest, almost purely graphical form. It is shown that in a world where taxation is distorting and the public debt is not indexed to the price level, a benevolent government may choose the level of inflation as a function of the nominal interest rate, which may lead to the existence of multiple self-fulfilling expectations equilibria; each of these equilibria will be chosen depending on the interest rate which is, in turn, determined by the expectations of the private sector. Section 3 goes into more specific two-period reduced-form examples to get some further insight on the assumptions that could be made to generate these examples, and to make sure that one has not forgotten some obvious "second-order" condition. This is further pursued in section 4, where the analysis begins at a more micro level with some assumptions on the role of money in production. Section 5 discusses extensions to more than two periods, and to set ups where there is only private nonindexed debt. Conclusions and more general implications of the analysis are contained in section 6.

2   A Simple Model

Consider a world of two periods, $t = 0, 1$; in period 0 people form (point) expectations about the rate of inflation between period 0 and period 1, which we denote π^e. I assume that individuals can invest in a risk-free asset with an exogenous one-period real rate of return equal to $r > 0$. Therefore, the coexistence of the latter with nonindexed debt yielding a nominal interest rate i, requires:

$$1 + i = (1 + r)(1 + \pi^e) \tag{1}$$

Let the real stock of public debt at the end of the period 0 be denoted by b; if the debt is not indexed, nominal amortization plus interest in period 1 will be

$$b(1 + i)$$

Thus, letting π stand for the actual rate of inflation between periods 0 and 1, total *real* debt service in period 1 would be

$$b \, \frac{1 + i}{1 + \pi} \tag{2}$$

In period 1 the nominal interest rate, i, is a predetermined variable, so if taxation were socially costly and π could be manipulated by the fiscal or monetary authorities, they may be tempted to set π as large as possible. Notice that changes of π at time 1 do not affect π^e at time 1 because, like i,

π^e is a variable which is determined in period 0; thus, increasing π at time 1 would not lead to a reduction in the demand for money if, as we usually do, it is assumed that the latter depends only on expected inflation. Clearly, therefore, if the costs of inflation are related to π^e alone, then a government attempting to minimize the social costs of servicing the debt would set $\pi = \infty$, or, alternatively, it would eliminate the present currency (the Burmese solution). In all other cases, however, the optimal response of the government will call for setting π at a finite level, and, in view of (2), it is reasonable to expect that π will be an increasing function of i; more formally, we assume that the government's optimal response is summarized by the relationship shown in figure 6.1:

$$\pi = \phi(i), \quad \phi' > 0 \tag{3}$$

We will concentrate on situations where, in period 0, the public knows that the government in period 1 is going to behave according to (3). Therefore, since we are abstracting from uncertainty, expectations are accurate (perfect foresight), which means

$$\pi^e = \pi \tag{4}$$

Combining (1) and (3), we get

$$1 + i = (1 + r)(1 + \pi) \tag{5}$$

Curves (3) and (5) are depicted in figure 6.1. Both curves are upward sloping and can, therefore, cross each other more than once. Each crossing depicts an equilibrium; for example, if the public expects that inflation will be π^0, then the simultaneous existence of nominal and real assets requires that the nominal interest rate be set at i^0 at time 0; when time 1 arrives, and it is the turn for the government to "move," the economy has inherited i^0 and the government will find it optimal to respond by choosing $\pi = \pi^0$, validating expectations. Unfortunately, however, unless we are able to impose further equilibrium conditions, equilibrium will in general not be unique (see figure 6.1).

To put some realistic color into the above framework, imagine that after a period of relatively high inflation, the government (at time 0) "puts its house in order" to ensure the existence of a low-inflation equilibrium (π^0, say): if the public believes that inflation will be lowered to π^0 (recall figure 6.1), the other "fundamentals" have been arranged to yield an inflation equal to π^0; the stabilization policy is, from that standpoint, "credible." The public knows, however, that if the nominal interest rate settles at i^2 the government will be induced to give up the stabilization program, at least

Global Issues

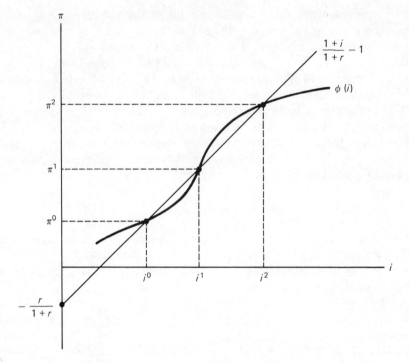

Figure 6.1 Equilibrium interest and inflation rates

partially. The reason for the latter is that everybody knows that if the nominal interest rate is i^2 it will be unduly costly for the government to keep inflation at π^0; in fact, the government will actually be induced to raise it to π^2 which was the reason why investors required $i = i^2$.

The situation would be quite different if the interest rate was fully indexed to the rate of inflation. Thus, if the real interest rate on bonds is denoted by r_b, then the nominal *ex-post* debt service (including amortization) will be

$$b(1 + r_b)(1 + \pi)$$

Consequently, the real debt service in period 1 would be

$$b(1 + r_b) \tag{6}$$

Moreover the Fisher equation with perfect foresight – the equivalent of equation (5) above – now reads

$$r_b = r \qquad (7)$$

implying that the real debt service is simply

$$b(1 + r) \qquad (8)$$

which is independent of both the expected and the actual rate of inflation. Consequently, the optimal government's response would be independent of the expected rate of inflation and the nominal interest rate. To be sure, there may still exist other channels through which expected inflation finds its way into the money-printing machines, but indexation of the debt would have removed one of its tentacles.

An important observation is that in our story the government is not pushed to higher inflation because of its "inability to pay." Here the government chooses to generate a higher rate of inflation because it is too costly not to do so. Another observation is that at equilibrium the government has no incentive to surprise the public by departing from the expected policy. It would be wrong, however, to conclude that the role of policy surprises is not important just because unanticipated or surprise inflation is not an attractive option at equilibrium; in the present model equilibrium points *themselves* are determined by the public taking into account the potential for policy surprises.[5]

In addition to the burden of the debt in period 1, the government would normally face other fiscal obligations, which we denote by g. Since the presence of g makes total government obligations in period 1 equal to

$$g + b\,\frac{1 + i}{1 + \pi} \qquad (9)$$

one would normally expect the optimal inflation response to be an increasing function of g, thus,

$$\pi = \phi(i,g) \quad \phi_i > 0,\ \phi_g > 0 \qquad (10)$$

Therefore, recalling figure 6.1, an increase in government expenditure would shift the set of equilibrium inflation rates. At equilibria like (i^0, π^0) and (i^2, π^2), the rate of inflation would tend to rise (locally), while at equilibria like (i^1, π^1) inflation would tend to fall. Despite the ambiguity, we see that according to this model, government expenditure (not its deficit) affects the rate of inflation.

The predictive power of the model could be improved by dropping some of the above equilibria. One way to do this would be to superimpose a pseudo-dynamics as follows: we will say that a given equilibrium is stable if (locally) a higher (lower) than equilibrium expected inflation, leads the monetary authorities to set $\pi < \pi^e (\pi > \pi^e)$. In other words, an equilibrium is stable if the government's response to wrong inflationary expectations is to set the rate of inflation towards the equilibrium one. According to this criterion, therefore, equilibria (i^0, π^0) and (i^2, π^2) would be stable, while (i^1, π^1) would not. Thus, at a stable equilibrium, a higher government expenditure is always (locally) inflationary.

Similar conclusions could be reached in relation to the stock of bonds; one could, for instance, show that at stable equilibria the higher the outstanding debt, the higher will also be (locally) the rate of inflation. There is also the interesting possibility of "losing" some of the equilibria as curve ϕ in figure 6.1 shifts up or down; but at this stage our discussion will benefit from further parameterization.

3   An *Ad Hoc* Model of the Inflation/Taxation Costs

In this section we will examine more detailed specifications of the social costs involved in taxation and inflation. If total government expenditure is given by (9), then required taxes, x, must satisfy[6]

$$x = g + b \, \frac{1 + i}{1 + \pi} \tag{11}$$

We denote the deadweight loss of taxation by $z(x)$, and we assume

$$z(x) \geq 0 \text{ for all } x \tag{12a}$$
$$z''(x) > 0 \tag{12b}$$

Condition (12a) requires no discussion, while (12b) – strict convexity – is made to ensure the existence of a global optimum.

More controversial and less obvious are the costs of actual (as against expected inflation), $f(\pi)$. We will examine the following formulation:

$$f(\pi) \;=\; \frac{\alpha}{2} \, (\frac{\pi}{1+\pi})^2 \;+\; \frac{\beta}{2} \, \pi^2, \; \alpha > 0, \; \beta > 0 \tag{13}$$

for $\pi > -1$. Most of the work in this area has assumed a form akin to the second term in (13) (see Barro and Gordon, 1983; Bohn (1988), by which the marginal cost of inflation increases as the economy moves away from some (unconstrained) optimal level ($\pi = 0$ in the present case). The first term is, on the other hand, somewhat unusual (see, however, Calvo, 1988);

it shares the above-mentioned property of π^2 for $\pi \leq 0.5$, but the implied marginal cost of inflation declines monotonically for $\pi \geq 0.5$. In fact the first term of (13) converges to $(\alpha/2)$ as $\pi \rightarrow \infty$. The two terms together, therefore, allow us to capture a situation where the cost of inflation rises steeply for relatively low inflation, reaches some kind of a plateau, and eventually rises without bound for large inflation. What I have in mind is a situation in which going, say, from zero to 20 percent annual inflation raises costs considerably, the marginal cost of going from 20 percent to 80 percent is positive but relatively small, but marginal cost rises sharply, once again, when inflation exceeds 2000 percent per annum.

Taking (11) and (13) into account total cost, v, satisfies:

$$v = z(g + b\frac{1 + i}{1 + \pi}) + \frac{\alpha}{2}(\frac{\pi}{1+\pi})^2 + \frac{\beta}{2}\pi^2 \qquad (14)$$

Consider now the cost-minimization problem faced by the government in period 1. Recalling our previous discussion, we take as given the nominal interest rate, i, and minimize (14) with respect to π. The first-order condition for this problem is

$$\partial v/\partial \pi = 0 = -z'(x)b\frac{1 + i}{(1 + \pi)^2} + \alpha\frac{\pi}{(1 + \pi)^3} + \beta\pi \qquad (15)$$

Without loss of generality, we will constrain our attention to the case where $i > -1$; furthermore, we will assume throughout that $g \geq 0$ and $b > 0$. Thus, under these conditions, it follows, by (11), that $x > 0$ which, by (12) and (15), implies that $\partial v/\partial \pi < 0$ for $\pi \leq 0$. Hence, the minimum of v is attained at $\pi > 0$, positive inflation. Moreover, at a point where (15) is satisfied, one can check (recalling that π is necessarily positive for $\partial v/\partial \pi = 0$) that the second-order condition for a minimum also holds (i.e. $\partial^2 v/\partial \pi^2 > 0$). This can readily be used – noticing that $v \rightarrow \infty$ as $\pi \rightarrow \infty$ – to argue that, given i, there exists a unique value of π that minimizes total cost, v. Thus, we have just proved the existence of an optimum response function like $\phi(\cdot)$ in the previous section.

As in the previous section, we define equilibrium as a point where curve $\phi(\cdot)$ crosses the one corresponding to the Fisher equation under perfect foresight (equation (5)). Thus, the set of equilibrium solutions can be formally found by using (5) into (15), which, recalling (11), is

$$-z'(g+(1+r)b)b\frac{1 + r}{1 + \pi} + \alpha\frac{\pi}{(1 + \pi)^3} + \beta\pi = 0 \qquad (16)$$

or, equivalently,

$$\Omega(\pi) \equiv \alpha \frac{\pi}{(1 + \pi)^2} + \beta\pi(1 + \pi) = z'(\overline{x})b(1+r) \qquad (17)$$

where,

$$\overline{x} = g + (1+r)b \qquad (18)$$

Notice that equilibrium taxes, $\overline{x}$, are independent of monetary factors. Condition (17) is depicted in figure 6.2.

Looking at figure 6.2 it immediately follows that it is possible to have (at most) three equilibrium solutions, confirming the findings of the previous section. Furthermore, we can use figure 6.1 to depict the $\phi(\cdot)$ function associated with (15) in the three-solutions case. Clearly, the low-and the high-inflation solutions are stable; stability, however, cannot rule out the existence of multiple solutions. Finally, as can be easily checked by looking at Figure 6.2, there is a value of equilibrium taxes, $\overline{x}$, above (below) which the economy displays a unique equilibrium; the important point is, however, that as equilibrium taxes go up (down), we tend to loose the low-inflation (high-inflation) equilibria. Thus, a sudden rise (fall) in government expenditure, g, or the stock of debt, or the real interest rate, r, may result in moving catastrophically (in the technical sense of the word) from the low- (high-) to the high-inflation (low-inflation) equilibrium.

In order to understand the simple economics behind the existence of multiple equilibria, it is useful to go back to our discussion of equation (13). In the first place, notice that when there are three equilibrium solutions, (16) implies a ϕ function like the one in figure 6.1. We see in figure 6.1 that (coming from the left) the first section of the ϕ-curve is relatively flat; thus, there is a sluggish response of π to a change in the nominal interest rate, i; this is so, because the policy-maker is conscious of the fact that the cost of inflation is a relatively steep function of inflation when inflation is relatively low. As we walk past the first equilibrium (i^0,π^0), the marginal cost of inflation rises but less steeply, so the optimal response of government becomes more sensitive to the rate of interest (i.e. ϕ becomes steeper); after the second equilibrium (i^1,π^1), however, the marginal cost becomes, once again, a steeper and steeper function of the rate of inflation, which leads the government to be less responsive to changes in the nominal interest rate – thus, curve ϕ becomes flatter once again, and a new equilibrium comes to life.

The main contribution of this section was to show that multiple equilibria arise even though the government is always reacting in a *globally* optimal manner, and that there may be a sudden outburst or slowdown of inflation in response to relatively small changes in equilibrium taxes and government expenditure; the latter was shown to be the case even if the

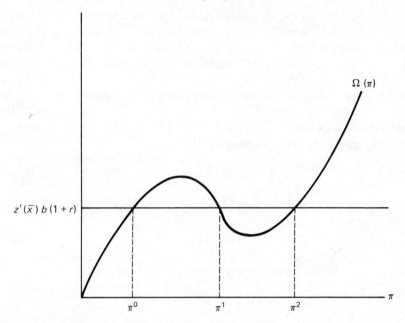

Figure 6.2 Equilibrium rates of inflation

economy has a tendency to move to neighboring equilibria in response to shocks, and it is related to the catastrophic loss of low-inflation (high-inflation) equilibria as $\bar{x}$ rises (falls).

4 Some Microfoundations

In this section we will look a little more closely into the foundations of the above type of argument in order to provide a more solid and intuitive justification for multiple equilibria.

Most of our time here will be spent on justifying the first term in (13) since it is essential to generate multiplicity of equilibria (recall (17)). We will assume that output is a function of real monetary balances, m, and satisfies the following functional form:

$$F(m) = y - \frac{\gamma}{2}(m - \bar{m})^2 \qquad (19)$$

where y, γ and $\bar{m}$ are positive constants; y is, obviously, the maximum attainable output, and $\bar{m}$ is the unconstrained or Friedman's optimum quantity of money. The assumption that liquidity shortages (i.e., $m < \bar{m}$) cause lower output has an intuitive appeal which is probably not shared by the assumption that excess liquidity (i.e., $m > \bar{m}$) interferes with production. Fortunately, however, for the relevant case in which the equilibrium nominal interest rate is positive, the economy operates in the liquidity-shortage region, so the possible objection is of no concern to us. The quadratic form is adopted for simplicity.

We assume that in period 0 (competitive) firms choose the level of nominal monetary balances that they are going to use in period 1, M_1, taking into account the expected price level in period 1, P_1^e. Thus nominal expected profits in period 1 are given by

$$P_1^e F(M_1/P_1^e) - (1 + i)M_1 \tag{20}$$

Thus, at optimum

$$F'(m^e) = 1 + i \tag{21}$$

where $m^e = M_1/P_1^e$. Hence, by (19) and (21), we get

$$m^e = \bar{m} - \frac{1}{\gamma}(1 + i) \tag{22}$$

This defines the demand for money.[7]

The stock of real monetary balances in period 1,

$$m = M_1/P_1 \tag{23}$$

may differ from m^e to the extent that $P_1 \neq P_1^e$. Let us define

$$1 + \pi^e = P_1^e/P_0 \tag{24}$$

where P_0 is the price level in period 0. Then, Fisher equations (1) and (24) imply

$$P_1^e/P_0 = \frac{1 + i}{1 + r} \tag{25}$$

Thus, denoting, once again,

$$1 + \pi = P_1/P_0 \tag{26}$$

we have, recalling (23) and (24),

$$m = (M_1/P_1^e)(P_1^e/P_0)(P_0/P_1)$$

$$= m^e \frac{1 + i}{1 + r} \frac{1}{1 + \pi} \tag{27}$$

Consequently, by (22) and (27),

$$m - \bar{m} = [\bar{m} - \frac{1}{\gamma}(1 + i)] \frac{1 + i}{(1 + r)(1 + \pi)} - \bar{m} \qquad (28)$$

The term in square brackets equals $m^e > 0$ (by assumption). Thus, given i, an increase in actual inflation, π, unambiguously lowers real monetary balances, m; furthermore, since at equilibrium $(1+i)=(1+r)(1+\pi)$ and, by (22), $m < \bar{m}$, an increase in π depresses output. This represents the "cost side" of inflation in the present model.

Net output, which will be our measure of social welfare, W, is the difference between total output and the deadweight loss from taxation; thus, recalling (11) and (12), net output is given by

$$W = F(m) - z(x) \qquad (29)$$

In line with our previous analysis, we assume that the government in period 1 tries to maximize W, taking the nominal interest i as given. This will allow us to derive the corresponding optimal response function, ϕ. The first-order condition for this problem is, recalling (28),

$$\partial W/\partial \pi = -\gamma \left\{ \bar{m} - [\bar{m}-(1+i)/\gamma]\frac{1 + i}{(1+r)(1+\pi)} \right\} \qquad (30)$$

$$[\bar{m}-(1+i)/\gamma]\frac{1 + i}{(1+r)(1+\pi)^2} + z'(x)b\frac{1+i}{(1+\pi)^2} = 0$$

The last term is unambiguously positive and, as in the model of section 3, captures the tax-collection costs which are saved by the inflation-provoked reduction in total debt.

Notice that if $(1 + i) > 0$ and the associated $m^e > 0$ (recall (22)) – the relevant region – then $\partial^2 W/\partial \pi^2 < 0$ at points where (30) holds. This shows that if (30) holds for a given π and i, then π is the optimal response to i, it corresponds to the unique global maximum given i; hence, the associated $\pi = \phi(i)$.

For a full characterization of the equilibrium solutions all that we have to do now is to use the Fisher equation with perfect foresight (5) in (30), which yields, recalling (18):

$$(1+i)[\bar{m} - (1+i)/\gamma] = z'(\bar{x})b(1+r) \qquad (31)$$

Except in a borderline case, (31) has either two distinct solutions in $i > -1$, or no solution at all. The no-solution case is the relevant one when $\bar{x}$ is larger than a well-defined critical level. Recalling (17), we see that this configuration of solutions is exactly what we would get in the *ad hoc* model of previous section if $\beta = 0$, i.e. if the second term in (13) was eliminated.

In sum, the previous microeconomic story shows that the change in the curvature of the cost of unanticipated inflation function ($f(\pi)$ in (13)) can be obtained in a context where the underlying production and utility functions have the standard curvatures.

Finally, by the analysis of section 3, three or more roots can be obtained if the cost of inflation becomes unbounded as $\pi \to \infty$. This would be relatively easy to engineer in the present context by, for example, assuming a nonlinear utility function (not a linear one like the one above) such that marginal utility becomes infinitely large as output (or net output) hits a critical low level.

5　Extensions: Several Periods, Private Credit Markets

Several periods

Thus far, our models assume that the government has to raise taxes to finance its fiscal expenditures at time 1. It is interesting to examine, however, the more realistic situation in which it is possible to finance the deficit via bonds; in order to consider that case, however, one needs to allow for at least one more period.

We assume that there are three periods: 0, 1 and 2. In period 0, b_0 is predetermined as in the previous models; however, now at the end of period 1, the stock of bonds, b_1, can be nonzero, but it must satisfy the budget constraint:

$$b_1 = g_1 + b_0 \, (1+i_0)/(1+\pi_1) - x_1 \tag{32}$$

where

$$1 + \pi_t = P_t/P_{t-1}, \, t = 1,2 \tag{33}$$

and the subindexes in the other familiar variables indicate the period to which they corresponds, or at which they are determined. Period 2 is the last one, and thus taxes, x_2, must be raised to cover all the expenses; hence,

$$x_2 = g_2 + b_1(1+i_1)/(1+\pi_2) \tag{34}$$

We assume that the government attempts to minimize social cost as before; however, in the present context we have to be more careful, because what is optimal to announce from the perspective of period 1, it may not be optimal to implement in period 2 (i.e., "time inconsistency" may arise). We are going to be interested mostly in time-consistent paths in which the government at time 1 takes into account its own optimal actions from the perspective of period 2.

The (present discounted) cost as seen from period 1, V_1, is

$$V_1 = z(x_1)+f(\pi_1)+\frac{1}{1+\delta}[z(x_2)+f(\pi_2)] \tag{35}$$

where $\delta \geq 0$ is the planner's rate of discount, whereas the cost in period 2, V_2, is simply

$$V_2 = z(x_2)+f(\pi_2) \tag{36}$$

The minimization of V_2 with respect to π_2 given i_1 – which is the problem faced by the government in period 2 – is identical to the one we examined in the previous sections. The minimization of V_1, however, offers some new vistas.

In order to get a better appreciation of the problem of minimizing V_1, let us use (32) and (34) in (35), so

$$V_1 = z(g_1-b_1 +\frac{1+i_o}{1+\pi_1}b_o)+f(\pi_1) +\frac{1}{1+\delta}[z(g_2 +\frac{1+i_1}{1+\pi_2}b_1)+f(\pi_2)] \tag{37}$$

The government in period 1 is assumed to minimize V_2 given i_o, b_o and the exogenous path of g, by choosing x_1, b_1 and π_1 (the variables under its direct control) subject to (32), and taking into account that the next period it will attempt to minimize V_2 taking b_1 as given (which is a direct consequence of actions taken in period 1), and i_1 which is, in equilibrium, determined in the same manner as in the previous sections.

One can achieve an even better understanding of the maximization problem in period 1 by splitting it into partial ones at each point in time. Let us define $C(g_t-b_t;i_{t-1},b_{t-1})$ as the minimum with respect to π_t of

$$z(x_t) + f(\pi_t) \tag{38}$$

subject to

$$x_t = g_t - b_t +\frac{1 + i_{t-1}}{1 + \pi_t}b_{t-1} \tag{39}$$

taking as given (g_t-b_t), b_{t-1}, and i_{t-1}. This is essentially the minimum cost problem studied in previous sections.

It is thus clear that the minimum of V_2 is $C(g_2;i_1,\acute{b}_1)$. By our previous analysis there may be several values of i_1 which are consistent with perfect foresight. Let us define the following set:

$$I(g_1-b_1) = \{i_1: \ (1+i_1)=(1+r)(1+\pi), \text{ and } \pi \text{ solves}$$
$$(38), (39) \text{ at } t=2, \text{ given } b_o \text{ and } i_1\} \qquad (40)$$

Clearly, this is the set of nominal interest rates between periods 1 and 2 for which the perfect-foresight Fisher equation (5) would hold. Therefore, the present discounted cost of choosing b_1 in period 1, given g_1, i_o and b_o is

$$C(g_1-b_1;i_o,b_o) + \frac{1}{1+\delta}\, C(g_2;i_1,b_1) \qquad (41)$$

where $i_1 \ \varepsilon \ I(g_1-b_1)$.

The first interesting problem that we encounter in trying to minimize (41) with respect to b_1 is that, due to the multiplicity of equilibria discussed in the previous sections, (41) is, in general, a *correspondence*, not just a regular function. Consequently, the last-period multiplicity of equilibria faces the government with the serious dilemma of deciding which one of the various equilibria will be expected by the public. The public, in turn, needs to know the government's policy about b_1 before being able to figure out the set of equilibrium interest rates – i.e., the set $I(\cdot)$. Therefore, we now see that by extending the horizon we have compounded the problem from being one of multiplicity of equilibria, to one where, in addition, there exists a fundamental uncertainty about the optimal response and behavior.

A formal solution to the above problem would be to assume, for example, that the government is "optimistic" and expects the public to expect the lowest equilibrium inflation. This is equivalent to saying that in (41) i_1 is the minimum of the set $I(g_1-b_1)$; under normal circumstances there will be a well-defined minimum of (41) with respect to b_1 and, quite possibly, such an attitude on the part of the government will lead to higher values of b_1 (i.e., more debt in the second period) than if a higher $i_1 \ \varepsilon \ I(g_1-b_1)$ were expected.

The point of the matter is, however, that the government would not be optimizing if the public's expectations differed from the government's forecast, and it is not clear what is optimal for the government to do in the absence of some prior distribution over the set of equilibrium i_1s.

In sum, the inclusion of more periods in the previous story not only does it not help in reducing the number of equilibria, but it reveals the fundamental uncertainty that a policy-maker must face when the result of his present actions depends on people's expectations about the future, in a world with more than one equilibrium future path.

Private credit markets

The existence of nominal contracts may be problematic even in the absence of government's debt, or in a world where all the public debt is indexed to the price level. For example, Argentina during 1977–82 appears to be an instance in which the government took measures to reduce the real value of *private* debt by provoking a significant increase in the rate of inflation (see, e.g., Fernandez, 1983; Balino, 1987). Leaving aside the specifics of this episode, it appears that, for an extended period of time, the private sector expected a sudden devaluation of the currency which turned out not to happen (the "peso" problem); as a consequence, during that period the *ex-post* real rate of interest tended to be substantially high, a situation that induced a sizable and unplanned (and apparently undesirable) redistribution of wealth within the private sector. The simple solution to the problem was to provoke a maxi-devaluation.

Some aspects of the above-mentioned scenario are covered by the model of section 2, because there is nothing there that really requires the existence of government debt. We referred to it in that section in order to motivate the existence of an upward-sloping optimal response function on the part of the government, $\phi(\cdot)$. However, if the government were concerned about wealth distribution between lenders and borrowers, it would also pay close attention to variable

$$\frac{1 + i}{1 + \pi} \tag{42}$$

and, hence, optimal π would be, once again, related to i, and a similar multiple-equilibrium story could be told without assuming the existence of public debt. Thus, with this interpretation in mind, the model can readily be used to explain the inflationary explosion that followed the peso-problem period in Argentina, for example, as a consequence of prior high nominal interest rates.[8]

The main reason why in the main sections of the present chapter we chose not to make the nonindexation of private credit transactions the focus of the discussion was only that we do not seem to have a very good explanation for the lack of indexation of private contracts (Fischer, 1983) and, consequently, we have a very poor idea of how sensitive nominal contracts are to policy changes. Of course, we also do not have a complete theory of why governments fail to index their debt, but there are at least nationalistic and other kind of atavistic considerations that could help to explain it.

6   Summary and Conclusions

The central point of this chapter is that a policy aimed at controlling the price level may encounter serious difficulties if credit contracts are not fully indexed to the price level. To make this point, we focused on the realistic case in which the government issues nonindexed debt, and showed that there is a strong theoretical argument supporting the view that the economy may exhibit more than one equilibrium solution.

In our story, the government tries at all times to maximize social welfare; since taxes induce deadweight losses, the existence of nominal debt is a constant temptation to shrink it by means of inflation. When the expected inflation is relatively low, the nominal interest will also be low and, thus, the attractiveness of inflation for reducing the size of public debt will be relatively small. This shows the possibility of a low-inflation equilibrium. On the other hand, if inflation was expected to be relatively high, the nominal interest rate will tend to reflect it point by point, and hence the temptation to liquefy the debt will be enhanced, which, in our examples, gives rise to the high-inflation equilibrium.

An obvious implication of the analysis is that, contrary to the view expressed in connection with the recent Austral and Cruzado Plans, deindexation of the public debt may jeopardize, not help, the success of a stabilization program.

It would be too premature, however, to conclude that full indexation is optimal for a "real world" situation in which there are a variety of random shocks, and fully contingent contracts are prohibitively costly. In fact, history teaches us that inflation/devaluation processes have provided handy and, perhaps, relatively cheap ways of reducing the public debt,[9] given that they did not require approval by Congress and the government could not be sued for breach of contract.[10] On the other hand, if the public debt had been fully indexed to the price level, countries may have been forced to engage in open default, possibly a very costly solution as testified by our present experience with international debt.

An interesting alternative to debt indexation is to attempt to put bounds on the nominal interest rate. The government, for example, may refuse to sell Treasury bills below a certain price. In the context of the models studied in this chapter, for instance, the government could lock the economy into the low-inflation equilibrium by, for example, refusing to sell bonds at (implicit) interest rates higher than the smallest (equilibrium) one. In practice, however, this policy may run into two types of difficulties:

(a) it is hard to have an accurate estimate of the relevant parameters (particularly in the short run); and (b) the private sector may also be engaging in nonindexed credit transactions, giving rise to an independent source of multiplicity of equilibrium (recall the section on 'Private Credit Markets'). Problem (a) can be partially resolved by enlarging the band of interest rates acceptable to government, but still ruling out the ones that would obviously be unsustainable in equilibrium without an eventual inflationary surge. Problem (b) is more difficult, because I suspect that it is normally very hard for the government to regulate private credit. At best what the monetary authorities could do is to regulate the interest rate at financial institutions, but my feeling is that large borrowers and lenders have no major difficulty in bypassing that kind of regulation, and in the final analysis such a policy may end up just hurting the "small guy." An alternative, which should be more thoroughly analyzed, would be to use differential taxes favoring indexed over nominal credit contracts.

The existence of multiple equilibrium solutions which could be Pareto ranked (like in our examples) implies that the government could bring about a Pareto improvement if it just had the means to change expectations from one equilibrium solution to another. The policy-maker that succeeds in such a task will assure himself a place in history and in the hearts of his people as the architect of price stability with no perceivable social cost. I feel, however, that to bring about such a wholesale change of expectations is not a trivial problem unless it involves some kind of precommitment on the part of the government.

It is interesting to note that the imposition of price controls – like in the recent "heterodox" stabilization programs of Argentina and Israel – would not necessarily solve the indeterminacy problem in the present context, because the controls themselves would not be credible. Unless there exists some way to control the controllers, the public would know that if today's rates of interest correspond to the high-inflation equilibrium, then price controls will be relaxed in the future to generate the *then* optimal rate of inflation.

In closing, I would like to emphasize, once again, that our examples still miss an interesting transition period in which the *ex-post* real interest rate exceeds the *ex-ante* one (as it appears to be the case in the above-mentioned experiences of Bolivia, Chile, and Argentina). This is, however, relatively straigthforward to remedy by introducing uncertainty about some taste parameter or government expenditure, for example, and it looks like a promising line for future research.

NOTES

I would like to thank Felipe Morande, and Salvador Valdes for their extremely perceptive comments. Research on this paper was done while the author was a Visiting Scholar at the International Monetary Fund.

1 Recent analyses of this case are Sargent and Wallace (1981), McCallum (1984), Liviatan (1984), Drazen (1985), Calvo (1985).

2 Of course, the new administration will make every effort to put the blame onto the previous one, but this is always difficult in our macro reality in which random shocks play such an important role that true causal relationships are hidden by a host of spurious correlations.

3 It is worth mentioning here, however, that other than the reversion of the conventional causal relationship between inflation and the nominal interest rate, our analysis will be perfectly consistent with Fisher's equation and the other tenets of orthodox monetary theory.

4 See, however, section 6 for a possible extension to cases in which *ex-post* and *ex-ante* real rates of interest are not equal.

5 For example, it would be incorrect to assert that the phenomenon discussed in this chapter is not quantitatively important on the basis of a calculation showing that the potential gain from surprise inflation, say, is a relatively small number. According to this analysis, the potential for advantageous policy surprises may actually be small *because* the public realize that otherwise the government would be tempted to surprise them!

6 For the sake of simplicity, and without loss of generality, we will hereafter abstract from the inflation tax on noninterest-bearing money. Notice, incidentally, that its inclusion would amount to just adding some function of π to the right-hand side of (11).

7 We will constrain our attention to regions in which $m^e > 0$.

8 It should be noted, however, that the perfect-foresight assumption rules out the existence of equilibria with real rates of interest higher than r. Hence, the model is not capable of explaining the incredibly high real interest rates that prevailed during the peso-problem period, unless one is prepared to argue that the latter reflected an exogenous increase in r.

9 Keynes (1971) has an interesting discussion of these issues in the aftermath of World War I.

10 This does not mean, of course, that there were no costs for the politicians in charge of the operation.

REFERENCES

Balino, Tomas J. T. (1987), "The Argentine Banking Crisis of 1980." IMF Working Paper, November.

Barro, Robert J. and Gordon, David B. (1983), "A Positive Theory of Monetary

Policy in a Natural-Rate Model," *Journal of Political Economy*. Vol. 91, No. 4, August, pp. 589–610.

Bohn, Henning (1988), "Why Do We Have Nominal Government Debt?," *Journal of Monetary Economics*, January, pp. 127–40.

Calvo, Guillermo A. (1985), "Macroeconomic Implications of the Government Budget: Some Basic Considerations," *Journal of Monetary Economics*. Vol. 15, January, pp. 95–112.

Calvo, Guillermo A. (1986), "Fractured Liberalism: Argentina Under Martinez de Hoz," *Economic Development and Cultural Change*. Vol. 34, April, pp. 511–34.

Calvo, Guillermo A. (1988), "Servicing the Public Debt: The Role of Expectations," *American Economic Review*, September, pp. 647–61.

Corbo, Vittorio, Melo, Jaime de and Tybout James (1986), "What Went Wrong With the Recent Reforms in the Southern Cone," *Economic Development and Cultural Change*, Vol. 34, April, pp. 607–40.

Dornbusch, Rudiger (1980), *Open Economy Macroeconomics*. New York: Basic Books.

Drazen, Allan (1985), "Tight Money and Inflation: Further Results," *Journal of Monetary Economics*. Vol. 15, January, pp. 113–20.

Edwards, Sebastian and Cox-Edwards, Alejandra (1987), *Monetarism and Liberalization*. Cambridge, MA: Ballinger.

Fernandez, Roque (1983), "La Crisis Financiera Argentina: 1980–1982," *Desarrollo Económico*. April–June, pp. 79–97.

Fischer, Stanley (1983), "On the Nonexistence of Privately Issued Indexed Bonds," in *Inflation, Debt and Indexation*, edited by Rudiger Dornbusch and Mario Henrique Simonsen; MIT Press, Cambridge, Massachusetts, 1983.

Keynes, John M. (1971), *A Tract on Monetary Reform*. London: Macmillan St Martin's Press for the Royal Economic Society.

Liviatan, Nissan (1984), "Tight Money and Inflation," *Journal of Monetary Economics*. Vol. 13, pp. 5–15.

McCallum, Bennett T. (1984), "Are Bond-Financed Deficits Inflationary?," *Journal of Political Economy*. Vol. 92, pp. 123–35.

Olivera, Julio H. G. (1971), "A Note on Passive Money, Inflation, and Economic Growth," *Journal of Money, Credit and Banking*. Vol. 3, February, pp. 805–14.

Sachs, Jeffrey (1986), "The Bolivian Hyperinflation and Stabilization." NBER Working Paper No. 2073, November.

Sargent, Thomas J. and Neil Wallace (1981), "Some Unpleasant Monetarist Arithmetic," *Quarterly Review of the Federal Reserve Bank of Minneapolis*. Fall, pp. 1–17.

Comment

Felipe Morandé

Guillermo Calvo's paper is a lucid analysis of the problem of controlling inflation in a context of nonindexed debt. In my view, the chapter has two main contributions, one related to its main subject, the other a formal one. The former has to do with the chapter's emphasis on how difficult it could be to manage (and reduce) inflation when debt contracts are not (explicitly at least) linked to price level changes. I will come back to this topic later in my comment.

The formal contribution is essentially the style used for presenting the idea. Such a style, after motivating the problem, looks first for a very simple and *ad hoc* explanation as to why that problem exists. Then, it starts a process of providing increasingly sophisticated microfoundations to such an *ad hoc* explanation. This growing process of being explicit about optimizing agents makes progressively clear what type of issues concerning the general subject can be addressed and what other issues cannot be addressed with the model assumptions and specifications. Thus few flanks are left open for criticism as to what the model is not able to explain, and the commentator is almost forced to end up criticizing the assumptions themselves – something that not many economists like.

I point to what I have called the "formal contribution" of Calvo's paper in order to place my comments on the main subject in the right perspective. Indeed, my first two comments could be blamed for doing exactly what they are not supposed to do: asking the model to address as issue which it cannot do. I formulate them anyway because any new research in the direction of understanding the inflationary process should take into account what previous research was not able to explain.

First, the article blames the incidence on public debt of high interest payments for the comovement between the nominal interest rate and the rate of inflation. The causality chain goes from a higher expected inflation rate forcing a higher nominal interest rate in financial markets and thus higher interest payments by the government on floating rate bonds. And this, *ceteris paribus*, causes a higher fiscal deficit and then more inflation. So, eventually, causality runs from higher nominal interest rates to higher inflation rates, contrary to what is normally assumed in macroeconomics.

For this "reversed causality" (in Calvo's words) to be true, it is *required* that public debt be nonindexed (with respect to inflation). Although this is a plausible – and novel – idea, one can argue that the same stylized fact can occur in a completely different context. In fact, a similar inflation–nominal interest rate comovement took place in Chile between 1976 and 1980 at a time when peso-denominated public debt was low and totally indexed, while a significant portion of private debt (also in peso terms) was also indexed. Therefore, many competing ideas are plausible and Calvo's one must be seen in this perspective.

Second, accepting the author's claim that indexing public debt avoids the "reversed causality" problem, does not imply that controlling inflation in a context of indexed debt is a simpler task. Apart from the likely real cost of indexation – loss of flexibility – that Calvo mentions, one can state two other reasons as to why debt indexation could possibly make things even worse. First, public awareness of inflation and of the need to control it, as well as the pressure on the government to act against it, tends to decrease if many contracts become indexed. In Calvo's notation, this might imply a lower $f(\pi)$ and eventually an indeterminate (π). And second, indexation is probably the result of rich inflationary experiences that also cause other contracts (wage contracts, for example) to be indexed. Since indexation rules are normally defined in terms of past or lagged inflation, this will imply a sort of inflationary inertia in the economy, that generally implies a greater real cost of stopping inflation when compared to a situation without indexation. This, in turn, will make governments more reluctant to pursue price stabilization programs.

But, as I said earlier, Calvo's construction should not be criticized for not being able to predict how complicated it would be to control inflation when contracts are indexed, because that was not its purpose. The model as a simplified representation of reality does not address such a possibility. However, what one is entitled to do is to look at that theoretical construction and investigate how sensitive it is to alternative micro assumptions. The author does so in his "extensions". In this respect, I have the following questions:

1   What is the assumed relationship between monetary and fiscal authorities? The possibility of financing a fiscal deficit by printing money is apparently ruled out. So the question arises as to what would happen to the general equilibrium price level and inflation rate if money management is also part of the story. This would imply a choice with respect to which authority dominates, fiscal or monetary. Such an assumption is somehow made in the introduction to the chapter with the allusion to "passive money", which in turns also justifies why money enters only in the production function. This implicit treatment of money would benefit from more discussion of the literature on fiscal deficit financing and its relation

to monetary policy (see Sargent and Wallace, 1981, for example).

2   Is it necessary to have a more explicit framework for putting money in the production function in the specific way Calvo does? What type of transactions technology will make firms consider the loss function in the paper?

3   Related to the previous paragraph, a social welfare function $W = F(m) - z(x)$ belongs to the family of monetary models with money in the utility function. Does this imply that more money is preferred to less? One cannot say without knowing the explicit framework mentioned in (2) or if there is no explicit treatment of the passive nature of the money supply.

Finally other possible extensions could be, on one side, the study of the relation between the real rate of interest and inflation and its link to the abundant literature in the US about the interest rate effects of fiscal deficits; and, on other side, the consideration of an open economy in which public debt could be, say, dollar-denominated – a different type of indexation.

REFERENCE

Sargent, T. and Wallace, N. (1981) "Some Unpleasant Monetarist Arithmetic", Federal Reserve Bank of Minneapolis *Quarterly Review*, Fall.

Part II
Country Studies

7

Argentina's Foreign Debt: Origins and Alternatives

Carlos A. Rodriguez

1 Introduction

In a period of only ten years, 1976–86, Argentina's gross foreign debt increased by $43,805 million, equivalent to 57 percent of 1986 GDP, or more than six times the value exported in that year. The estimated value of the gross foreign debt at the end of 1986 was in the neighborhood of $51,704 million, whereas at the end of 1976 it was just short of $8,000 million.

The possibility of amortizing such a debt is remote, as is that of paying the total amount of interest accrued each year. In 1986 the interest payment alone represented the equivalent of 62 percent of exports for the entire year. This implies that the gross debt continues to grow due to the refinancing of the interest, as has been the case in the last four years (1983–6) when, according to our estimates, only 60 percent of the accrued interest was paid. As a result, the gross debt increased during that period at the annual rate of 4.5 percent. During the same four years, the dollar index of Argentina's exports and import prices fell at the annual rate of 5.07 percent. Similar figures of decline or stagnation are shown by export values (dropping nearly 18 percent in 1986) or by the gross income per capita, standing in 1986 below the level reached in 1970.

Table 7.1 shows the evolution of the international reserves, the gross debt and the net debt, the latter being the difference between the first two.

A distinction must be made between two markedly different periods as to the process of generation of the foreign debt. The first is that of acquiring the debt and the second that of its growth due to the refinancing of interest charges. The first period covers the years 1978–82, during which the debt increased by nearly $34,000 million. From 1983 onwards the chances of obtaining fresh money were scant and the debt continued to increase due almost exclusively to the refinancing of interest.

In the second period, (1983–6) the gross debt increased by $11,757

Table 7.1 Evolution of external debt in Argentina, (1970–1986)

	Reserves ($m current)	Gross debt ($m current)	Net debt ($m current)	Services ($m current)
1970	725	3,259	2,534	289
1971	317	3,762	3,445	341
1972	529	4,694	4,165	387
1973	1,412	5,210	3,798	479
1974	1,341	6,274	4,933	421
1975	618	7,495	6,877	487
1976	1,772	7,899	6,128	492
1977	3,862	9,307	5,445	578
1978	5,829	12,496	6,667	681
1979	10,137	19,034	8,897	920
1980	7,288	27,162	19,874	1,531
1981	3,719	35,671	31,952	3,700
1982	3,013	43,243	40,230	4,718
1983	3,205	45,079	41,874	5,408
1984	3,499	46,171	42,672	5,712
1985	6,153	49,326	43,173	4,882
1986	5,580	51,704	46,124	3,970

Sources: Reserves 1970–85: FIEL
1986: Merrill Lynch
Gross debt 1977: Fundacion Mediterranea
1978–86: Banco Central de la Republica Argentina
Financial services 1979–85: FIEL
1986: estimated

million, 3,392 of which were allotted to the accumulation of reserves. The remaining $8,865 million were used for refinancing unpaid interest.

Figure 7.1 shows the historical evolution of the gross debt–exports ratio starting from the year 1938. The relative stability shown by this ratio for 40 years is evident when compared with the increase experienced in the 10 years to 1986. All would seem to indicate that in this latter period a significant change occurred in the structure of the financing of Argentina's economy and in the motivation of international banks which suddenly decided to increase the historical debt–exports ratio by more than fivefold.

A change of this magnitude could be justified only by a very important innovation in the real economy, such as the discovery of new investment opportunities which would require a substantial contribution of foreign

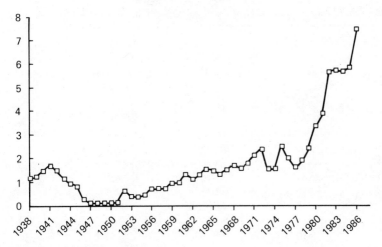

Figure 7.1   Gross debt–exports ratio

capital. We know, however, that this did not happen, since there was no transfer of real funds from the rest of the world in any significant amount (the only substantial deficit in the trade account in the period in question was in 1980 and that was in the neighborhood of $2,500 million). If the Argentinians did not get into debt so as to import, then for what purpose did they do it? And why did the international banks, traditionally so conservative in this respect, agree to quintuplicate credit to a country that had remained relatively constant for more than 60 years? These are some of the unknowns which arise from the study of the origin of Argentina's foreign debt and which I will discuss in this work.

The adjustment undergone by the Argentinian economy has been very severe. Declared imports dropped from the 1980 level of $10,000 million to only $4,300 million in 1986. In real terms, this level of imports was only 70 percent of the historical average for the preceding 15-year period, which amounted to $6,113 million, expressed in constant 1986 dollars. At the same time the fiscal deficit, that reached a high point of 18.1 percent of GDP in 1982, was reduced to only 6 percent of GDP by 1986.

The drop in imports encouraged the expansion of the imports-substitution sector and therefore resources were not released for the exporting sector, a situation which was made worse by the significant deterioration in the terms of trade as from 1985. Both these causes led to the country's exports in 1986 being, in constant dollars, only 77 percent of what was exported in 1980. The country entered into a vicious circle in which the cutting of imports to improve the short-term ability to pay soon led to a corresponding decline in the level of activity as well as of exports.

Trade 7.2 Trade and current account in Argentina: 1970–1986

	Exports ($m current)	Imports ($m current)	Trade account ($m current)	Current account ($m current)
1970	1,773	1,694	79	−159
1971	1,740	1,612	128	−389
1972	1,941	1,905	36	−223
1973	3,266	2,235	1,031	715
1974	3,931	3,635	296	127
1975	2,961	3,946	−985	−1,285
1976	3,916	3,033	883	650
1977	5,652	4,162	1,490	1,290
1978	6,400	3,834	2,566	1,834
1979	7,810	6,712	1,098	−550
1980	8,021	10,540	−2,519	−4,768
1981	9,143	9,430	−287	−4,714
1982	7,625	5,338	2,287	−2,358
1983	7,836	4,505	3,331	−2,461
1984	8,107	4,584	3,523	−2,391
1985	8,400	3,818	4,582	−953
1986	6,900	4,300	2,600	−2,640

Declared imports according to IMF international financial statistics
Sources: Up to 1985: Data bank of FIEL and BCRA
1986: Merrill Lynch (est.) and own estimates

So, with the strategy adopted, the obtaining of resources for servicing the debt lessens the possibility of generating these resources in a sustainable manner, from which it can be concluded that the servicing of the debt is not achievable in the medium term.

Having set out the problem, the analyst faces two challenges. The first is obviously that of discussing alternative solutions since there is no clear-cut way out of the present situation. As long as it is allowed to continue, not only does the problem remain unsolved, but the economy is also kept in a state of recession, entailing an additional cost that is unnecessary if the problem is not going to be solved anyway.

The second challenge is to find out the causes of this enormous level of indebtedness, since it is not realistic to think that it is caused by a simple error in calculation on the part of a multitude of debtors and creditors. Rather, the evidence suggests that there were major agents in this process and that they were the ones who blundered. When an important participant in a market makes a mistake, losses tend to be significant.

We believe that there were two principal agents in Argentina's foreign debt problem. The first was the Argentinian government which encouraged the indebtedness of its state enterprises in foreign currency. This may have been in order to acquire assets in local currency, with successive devaluations only diluting these assets but not the debts. This was made worse by endorsements, either real or potential, which were granted to private debtors. The end result was the nationalization of the debt in 1981 when the government took on practically the entire private debt in exchange for loans in pesos which were quickly diluted. The implication of this sequence of events is that the great debtor is the Argentinian government and not the private sector which, in contrast, saw its foreign asset holdings increase by a figure which could be equivalent to more than half the increase of the country's gross debt.

The other important agent was the international financial community that, on the basis of the real or potential endorsements by the state, proceeded to loan to the country unprecedented amounts which went way beyond the country's ability to repay, let alone that of the state which was providing the endorsements.

In my interpretation, the phenomenon analyzed is similar in its consequences to the draining of a business enterprise. Basically, the insolvent state became indebted in dollars, and the greater part of those dollars was sold in exchange for assets in pesos to many local investors whose strategy was exactly the opposite of that of the government. Thereupon the state itself diluted the real value of the peso assets through successive devaluations, which led to the state ending up with the debt and the local investors with the dollars.

The foreign banks allowed this to happen by overestimating the government's ability to pay, and they apparently continue to overestimate it, since the succeeding negotiations not only contain no exoneration in the agreed rates, but rather fines and extra charges for nonfulfillment. This appears unreasonable for a debtor who, were it not a sovereign state, should have convened a meeting of its creditors long ago.

To close this introduction I will give details of the flow of funds of the external sector for the periods 1971–82 (the long period of generation of the debt) and 1983–6 (the period following the generation of the debt). There the reader will be able to appreciate not only the magnitude of the problem, but also the factors related to the origin of this debt, which will be discussed in detail in the rest of this work.

The flow of funds for the periods 1971–82 and 1983–6 are shown in table 7.3. I have classified the sources of funds into three groups: increase of the gross foreign debt, direct foreign investment, and exports. On the other hand, there are four possible uses for those funds: imports, payments for real services and transfers, financial services (interest on the debt minus interest gained on reserves), and accumulation of international reserves.

Table 7.3 External sector's flow of funds ($m)

	1971–82	1983–6
Sources		
Gross debt increase	39,984	8,461
Direct investment	2,712	2,001
exports	62,406	31,243
Total supply of funds	105,102	41,705
Uses		
Reserves accumulation	2,288	2,567
Imports	56,382	17,207
Real services and transfers	960	2,489
Net interest	14,735	19,992
Nondeclared imports	6,695	2,201
Not explained	24,042	–2,751
Total demand of funds	105,102	41,705

In the period 1971–82 the sources of funds exceed the identifiable uses by $24,042 million, the equivalent of 60 percent of the gross debt increase of the period. The figures clearly indicate that the debt was not spent on declared imports since nearly half its increase remains unexplained even when imports are subtracted.

Apparently a substantial figure for nondeclared imports was not included in the official statistics put together by the government. There is no official proof that these imports existed, which does not imply that they are not an open secret. Not to include at least an approximate estimate of these non-declared imports would deprive the numerical estimates contained in this work of any realism. For this reason I have attempted to do this by means of an estimate based on the scant information available emanating from other sources not connected with the Argentinian government. These sources are the exports to Argentina declared by other countries, figures which have been compiled by the IMF. For the period 1971–82, my estimated figure for nondeclared imports is $6,695 million.

In the period 1983–6, the unexplainable amount is reduced significantly (in fact it becomes negative). In the following section I will give several explanations for the origin of these nonidentified uses, which in my interpretation really correspond to the nondeclared holding of external assets brought on by the flight of capital.

Anticipating the conclusions arrived at in this work, we can establish four premises:

1   The debt would not have existed at significant levels if the state had not generated it, either directly or by endorsing it. Furthermore, the inconsistency of the economic policies followed from 1981 led to the redistribution of the burden of the debt, to the point that not many of those who incurred it finally ended up paying it.

In spite of the debt (nearly all of it public) of $51.7 billion dollars, my estimates based on the scant data available indicate that the capitalized value of the flight of capital which took place during this process, as of the end of 1986, was approximately $34.4 billion.

2   The official figures indicate that the Argentinian foreign debt was not allocated entirely to finance imports as seems to be the general belief. During the period of greater increase in the debt, 1978–81, the accumulated trade account surplus was $858 million, which implies that the country exported more than it imported and, therefore, imports can hardly have contributed to the foreign debt. Obviously, if there had been no imports, the debt would have been lower. There were apparently, nondeclared imports about which I am unable to express an opinion, since I do not know what they consisted of. It is generally believed, however, that these imports were associated with the purchase of armaments, in which case they would have nothing to do with the process of freeing the economy and currency convertibility. It is also possible that spending on tourism could be significantly higher than official estimates indicate, particularly with respect to the purchase of durable goods by tourists travelling abroad. I am not of the opinion, however, that this belief, which has become quite generalized, has any firm basis. Suffice it to say that the debits for travel, transport and passenger services increased from a level of $470 million in 1977 to $2,700 million in 1980. Remember that the cost of one million television sets was approximately $400 million, less than one fifth of the increase in tourism spending in 1980 alone.

My results suggest that the destination of a large part of the foreign debt must be sought in the financial system and not in the real sector.

3   Under the conditions in which it is being renegotiated, Argentina's foreign debt, both the capital and part of the interest, cannot be serviced. Strategies such as the debt–equity swaps, which have lately been under discussion, are not a realistic solution to the problem.

4   The results are consistent with the theoretical analysis. In recent work, Auernheimer (1986) analyzes the effects upon foreign indebtedness in a world with capital mobility in which the government pursues inconsistent economic policies. Among other things, Auernheimer concludes that "the possibility of possessing and trading foreign assets with the rest of the

world allows domestic residents to behave in a manner that to some extent 'compensates', at least partially, [for] the adoption of incorrect measures", arriving at a final situation in which all that happens is "a mere redistribution of external assets from the government to the public".

If the fiction that the debt will be serviced completely is kept up, the present recessive situation will be maintained and the problem will increase at the exponential rate implied by the refinancing of interest, plus the fines and extra charges for nonfulfillment. The distrust generated by the burden of the foreign debt means that, in order to keep national currency in force, an interest rate must prevail which is incompatible with the survival of the real economy at a politically acceptable level of activity (this does not imply that part of the very high real interest rate is not due to the general design of the internal economic policy).

Section 2 analyzes the phenomenon of the origin of the foreign debt, placing emphasis on the causes that led to the creation of a debt for the purchase of foreign assets rather than for financing imports. Section 3 discusses the possibility of the debt being paid, as well as some ways this could be achieved.

2   The Origin of the Foreign Debt

The conceptual framework

The balance of payments of a country endeavors to reflect the transactions between that country and the rest of the world. Unfortunately, the difficulties inherent in the related statistical compilation mean that in many cases only the net results of those transactions can be reflected. Such is the case of the transactions related to movements of capital, tourism or, more general, to the sale of foreign currency through money exchange offices in periods of currency convertibility.

Leaving the nondeclared illegal transactions on one side, the sum of the sale of goods abroad plus the net earnings through foreign investments in the country should be equal to the change in the country's net financial position *vis-à-vis* the rest of the world. The country can acquire (net) assets from the rest of the world, whether it be by exporting more than it imports (and receiving external assets in return) or by charging higher interest payments on its investments abroad than it pays for what foreigners have invested in the country. The net balance of these transactions is the balance of payments current account, which consequently is also the country's (net) rate of purchase of external assets. If the current account is negative, the (net) rate of acquisition of external assets is negative and the net foreign debt increases.

It is important to differentiate between net and gross rate of acquisition of assets. A country can have large (gross) debts abroad but may have invested those funds in external assets; in this case there would not be a net debt, although there could be a financial problem if the gross debt had to be serviced and the external assets did not yield the appropriate interest.

From an accounting viewpoint, a positive balance in the current account can be broken down into three categories:

1 accumulation of central bank reserves;
2 increase in the country's gross external assets (excluding reserves);
3 decrease in the gross foreign debt.

In analyzing external indebtedness, it is important to distinguish not only the net position of the country, but also the identity of the holders both of the gross debt and of the external assets, the difference in which gives rise to the net debt. If within a given country an individual has a large debt in foreign currency and another has a similar amount in external assets, the country as a whole does not have a problem of indebtedness. It could, however, face payment difficulties if it is not possible to transfer the external resources between the creditor and the debtor.

In the case of Argentina, the principal debtor is the state, which also owns the Central Bank's international reserves. In this case it is perfectly correct to subtract these reserves from the gross debt in order to obtain a preliminary estimate of the net debt which is shown in the third column of table 7.1. We can see that the subtraction of the reserves does not significantly alter the magnitudes under discussion, since the increase in the net debt thus calculated for the 1976–86 decade is $39,997 million, somewhat less than the increase in the gross debt because of the increase in the reserves of $3,808 million over the 10-year period.

Unfortunately, it is not possible to carry out a similar operation by subtracting from the gross debt the external assets possessed by Argentinians as well as the international reserves. Argentinians do not usually declare their holdings in external assets. It is possible to make a close estimate of these assets if we know the amount of the gross debt, since we only have to subtract from it the international reserves and the accumulated amount of the current account results. This estimate is only approximate since it ignores any kind of capital gains or losses which could have taken place between the time of acquisition and the present.

Assuming that the said assets were equal to zero in 1970, the estimate of the external assets possessed by Argentinians is shown in table 7.4 in the "Assets*" column. This series is the difference between the net debt from table 7.1 and the "Debt*" series, the latter being equal to the 1970 net debt plus the accumulated current account deficits and direct investment in the

Table 7.4 Preliminary estimate of the level of external assets ($m)

	Net debt	Debt*	Current account	Assets*
1970	2,534	2,534	−159	0
1971	3,445	2,912	−389	533
1972	4,165	3,125	−223	1,040
1973	3,978	2,401	715	1,397
1974	4,933	2,264	127	2,669
1975	6,877	3,549	−1,285	3,328
1976	6,128	2,899	650	3,228
1977	5,445	1,837	917	3,608
1978	6,667	579	985	6,088
1979	8,897	3,260	−2,946	5,637
1980	19,874	9,079	−6,607	10,795
1981	31,952	13,599	−5,464	18,353
1982	40,230	16,188	−2,846	24,042
1983	41,874	19,739	−3,734	22,135
1984	42,672	22,790	−3,319	19,882
1985	43,173	22,766	− 953	20,407
1986	46,124	24,833	−2,640	21,291

In the years 1977 to 1984 the current account includes our estimate for nondeclared
Imports
* = estimates

subsequent years. The assumption is that any increase in the gross debt
that was not used to increase reserves or to finance current account deficits
(after adding direct investment, since this is not considered as part of the
foreign debt being discussed) should have been accumulated in the form of
external assets. The current account used in making this calculation includes the estimate of nondeclared imports, since otherwise they would be
incorporated into the estimate of external assets.

By construction, the 'Debt*' variable in table 7.4 would be a preliminary
estimate of Argentina's net indebtedness position or, in other words, the
gross debt minus the international reserves and the sum of the outflow of
capital ('Assets*').

The estimate shown in table 7.4 probably understates the true holding of
external assets. The reason is that the return on these assets is very
probably not declared in the current account, as is also the case with their
holding.

In order to estimate a reasonable yield rate for external assets, I have
proceeded as follows. For each year I calculated the average interest rate

Table 7.5 Average interest rate accrued on the foreign debt

1970	11.4	1979	10.2
1971	12.1	1980	11.8
1972	10.8	1981	16.2
1973	10.9	1982	14.1
1974	9.6	1983	13.1
1975	8.9	1984	13.2
1976	6.9	1985	11.1
1977	8.5	1986	8.7
1978	9.6		

Estimated interest rate on the foreign debt is calculated on the assumption that reserves gain an interest equal to 60 percent of the interest on the debt. The formula used is the following:

i percent $=$ net financial services/(debt(-1)$-0.6\times$reserves(-1))

on the foreign debt using the information on financial services from the balance of payments. This rate is shown in table 7.5.

I make the assumption that the average return on nondeclared external assets is equivalent to 60 percent of the rate paid on the gross debt. This allows the possibility of one part of the external assets being in the form of cash, or of a fraction of them having been consumed. The choice of 60 percent is arbitrary and readers can work out their own alternative calculations since they know both the rates as well as the calculation methodology used.

In some cases the return on the external assets could be identical to the rate paid on the debt if the supposed external creditor should turn out to be Argentinian. It is possible that a large part of Argentina's gross debt may really be to Argentinian creditors operating through foreign representatives; this theory would suggest that the country has no foreign debt problem, but this is inapplicable for all practical purposes since the Argentinian state, which is the debtor, has no way of distinguishing the nationality of the true holders of its foreign debt securities. And even if it could, that would not change the problem since those assets may well have been purchased legally.

The third column in table 7.6 shows the final estimate of the Argentinian external assets (in the 'Ext assets#' column) assuming that these obtain a rate of return (not declared in the current account) equal to 60 percent of the rate accrued for the gross debt.

The column 'Net debt#' shows the true net debt as estimated by substracting from the net-of-reserves debt the estimated holdings of nondeclared external assets.

Table 7.6 Final estimate of net debt and external assets ($m)

	Gross debt	Reserves	Ext. assets#	Net debt#
1970	3,259	725	0	2,534
1971	3,762	317	533	2,912
1972	4,694	529	1,074	3,091
1973	5,210	1,412	1,503	2,295
1974	6,274	1,341	2,861	2,072
1975	7,495	618	3,673	3,204
1976	7,899	1,772	3,725	2,402
1977	9,307	3,862	4,294	1,151
1978	12,496	5,829	7,025	−358
1979	19,034	10,137	7,005	1,892
1980	27,162	7,288	12,660	7,214
1981	35,671	3,719	21,451	10,501
1982	43,243	3,013	28,956	11,274
1983	45,079	3,205	29,317	12,557
1984	46,171	3,499	29,392	13,280
1985	49,326	6,153	31,870	11,303
1986	51,704	5,580	34,418	11,706

\# = aggregate of estimates
$\text{EA\#}(t) = (1+i \times 0.6) \times \text{EA\#}(t-1) + \text{EA}^*(t) - \text{EA}^*(t-1)$
i = interest rate in dollars on the gross foreign debt; this rate is shown in table 7.5

With this last correction we see that the estimate for external assets is in the neighborhood of $34,418 million. This, added to the reserves amounting to $5,580 million, leaves a true net debt ('Net debt#') estimate of $11,706 million, a figure still considerably higher than that observed during the average of the 1970s.

With this information in hand, the interpretation of the phenomenon of the foreign debt takes on an interesting aspect. The numbers show that the increase in the gross debt was not totally utilized to finance or increase in imports or drops in exports, since the estimated true net debt of the Argentinians increased by an amount approximately equivalent to only one quarter of the increase in the gross debt.

What really happened was that one sector of the country became indebted in foreign currency while another sector took to accumulating that currency. One sector believed that external credit was cheap and the other that the situation was not sustainable and that the price of the dollar would rise.

We can now imagine the typical situation which led to the present state of affairs. As of 1976, and especially in 1978–80, the country experienced very high rates of return in dollars on peso investments. The rates were high precisely because the market expected a change in the value of foreign currency (on the economic situation of Argentina in this period of foreign debt generation, see, for example, Calvo, 1985; Dornbusch, 1984; Fernandez, 1986; Fernandez and Rodriguez, 1980; Rodriguez, 1982, 1983). However, that opinion does not seem to have been similarly shared by all the agents, or at least some of them do not appear to have paid much attention to it (particularly the state enterprises which resorted extensively to external credit). So, an individual (or company) A, who believes that domestic rates are attractive, takes an external credit, deposits the foreign currency in the Central Bank while declaring the debt, obtains pesos in return and places them on a time deposit. Individual B, who believes that the dollar will go up in price, takes a credit in pesos for the same amount as that deposited by A and buys dollars at a money exchange office. With free convertibility, B does not have to declare that he possesses dollars (in fact, there was actually a limit on the amount of dollars that could be bought each time at a money exchange office, but office boys made the tedious queues, and this limit, ineffective). So the gross debt increases, the external assets do also, but nobody knows who has them. All the operations that have been carried out are perfectly legal and could take place in any country with convertible currency.

What do not take place in most countries are the tremendous oscillations in relative prices which occur in Argentina. The year 1981 brought unexpected successive macro devaluations that diluted peso assets and liabilities. Individual A ends up with a debt in dollars and assets in pesos which are worthless, while B's peso debt disappears and he ends up with the dollars.

Several alternatives to this simple explanation come forward. In the first place, A and B could well be the same person. In effect, A, on leaving the Central Bank with his pesos, could have rebought the dollars at a money exchange office and repaid his debt without advising the Central Bank of this payment (this requires that the foreign bank help him out by continuing to demand the service of the debt even though it has already been paid). This operation is quite common in the financial world and is known as 'back to back lending' (self-loan). Obviously, A (or B) has gone to a great deal of trouble and paid commission just to have a debt recorded at the Central Bank. This would not be of any use if there continued to be only one exchange rate and the currency remained convertible. But A (or B) expected that this would not happen, and in fact he proved to be right. Starting in 1981 and through successive measures, the government took it upon itself to absorb A's (or B's) debt at prices much lower than those of the market, which means that the visionary investor managed to buy dollars at a much lower price than the rest of his countrymen. In fact, he did not buy dollars but foreign debt securities from the government, which is what was given to the supposedly creditor foreign bank. He is now receiving the dollars through the servicing of the debt.

In this last stage, individual *A* (or *B*) transfers a non-existent dollar debt to the Argentinian state in exchange for making payments in pesos which are rapidly diluted by successive devaluations and low interest rates. *A* (or *B*), for very few pesos, has bought the possibility of eventually collecting the dollars of the debt that has been transferred to the state. The state, which owed nothing, now owes *A*'s (or *B*'s) dollars and has assets in pesos which rapidly lose their value. The cycle is complete and we arrive at the present situation in which *A* (or *B*) gained and the state lost. It should be said that everything that has taken place is either quite legal, or impossible to prove, so the state has no way out but to pay.

Another alternative is that individual *A* takes on an external credit, declares the debt and buys machinery. Individual *B* sells him the machinery and, instead of replacing stock, buys dollars. Once devaluation occurs, the state buys the debt from *A* on terms that are advantageous to the latter. The state ends up with the debt in dollars, *A* has the machinery, and *B* has the dollars. Once again the real external assets have remained unchanged but the state has ended up with the foreign debt.

Since the government generated approximately one half the foreign debt, it is clear that it took over *A*'s role in the previous interpretations. The state enterprises became indebted in unprecedented amounts, very probably acting on the suggestion of the authorities who needed foreign currency to sustain the exchange rate. We know that this indebtedness did not give rise to an equivalent transfer of real funds from abroad. This means that if the state enterprises invested the product of these loans in real resources, whoever received the pesos in payment must have refrained from replacing part of the goods and has bought dollars. This is the most favorable case for the government since, although it now has the foreign debt, its ability to pay also increases thanks to the investment effected.

It is also possible that the authorities may have induced the state enterprises to become indebted in order to contribute foreign currency to the Central Bank. Having no need to invest, the state enterprise could have taken the pesos it received in exchange and deposited them in the financial market, where they were then lent to individual *B*, who bought dollars. When the devaluations came, the state enterprise ended up with the dollar debt and with assets in worthless pesos, while *B* had a debt in worthless pesos and assets in dollars.

There are probably many more operations, in addition to those I have described, that could help explain the origin of the foreign debt. All of them will probably agree on the final result: somebody in the private sector ended up with the dollars and the state ended up with the debt.

In general, all the operations described are legal, marginally legal (or not very ethical), or impossible to detect. If a culprit is sought, the case described clearly shows that it lies with the state for having voluntarily taken over the external debts either directly or by endorsing or acquiring the private debt.

We can conclude that Argentina, as a result of these financial transfers connected with the external debt, ended up being a country with a poor public sector and some rich residents, although the possibility should not be disregarded that some of those who acquired the credits in pesos to buy dollars (individuals *B*) may have been nonresidents.

Is this of any help to the government from the viewpoint that there could be a potential taxable base, the product of which could be applied to servicing the debt? The answer is probably no since, as we have seen, there are no records of who are the holders of these supposed nondeclared external assets. What is more, the government repeatedly attempted to offer opportunities for foreign currency held abroad to be brought back into the country.

So far, these attempts have not met with success. And if, one day they should, it is highly probable that a large portion of these foreign currency funds would come back in no other shape than self-loans. And even if this were so, the problem of the debt exists, and it is not going to be solved by getting further into debt. It is known that financiers place capital in a country that has a high degree of uncertainty such as Argentina only if they are going to obtain a profitable rate of return. That was the case of the Austral Plan which, in its first year, obtained some capital inflow at the cost of an interest rate in dollars of over 60 percent per annum. Obviously, the country is not going to solve its debt problem by refinancing it internally at a cost 6 times higher than the original debt itself.

In short, the foregoing reasoning implies that one should not hope for a significant solution to the debt problem through any type of operation with Argentinian capital held abroad. If efforts to attract this capital were to succeed, it would most probably be at a cost far higher than that of servicing the current debt, whereby the problem would only become greater.

3 Possible Solutions to the Foreign Debt Problem

In 1986 it was estimated that the interest accrued on the foreign debt was $4,291 million, a figure similar to the country's estimated imports for that same year, or equivalent to 62 percent of its exports. It was estimated that the current account surplus left for paying interest on the debt was $1,651 million (calculated as the difference between the contractual interest on the debt and the current account balance). In addition the country used up $573 million of reserves and received direct investments also for $573 million. The sum of those three items gave $2,797 million as the country's available cash for either service interest or finance capital outflows. The capital outflow, in my methodology, is measured by the increase in the value of 'assets*' in table 7.4, i.e. $884 million. The amount of interest paid was therefore $1,913 million. The difference between the contractual interest of $4,291m and the interest paid of $1,913m is exactly the $2,378m of increase in the debt. The ratio of interest paid to interest due was 44.5 percent in 1986.

The estimated figures indicate that the interest on the debt is not being fully paid, not even in real terms. The roll-over of the interest causes the debt to increase at an exponential rate equal to the unpaid component of the interest rate. Since the resulting rate of increase of the debt (averaging 4.57 percent per annum over four years) is higher than the dollar inflation rate (that in fact was negative for those four years), the debt continues to increase in real terms.

The possibility of the situation improving internally and of a sufficiently large trade surplus being achieved to pay at least the real portion of the interest does not appear possible. Even granting that such a trade surplus were attainable, the question remains if the corresponding fiscal surplus could be generated for the government to acquire those dollars without resorting to inflationary means.

One may well ask what developing country could manage to pay interest charges in an amount equivalent to that of its imports. In fact, they are not being paid and the international financial market acknowledges this. Argentina's foreign debt securities were negotiated, at the end of 1986, at approximately 65 percent of their par value. This market value would seem to reflect the expectancy that the country would service only an average of 65 percent of its debt. This is more than my calculations indicate was actually being paid in 1986.

A similar calculation to the preceding one (table 7.7) indicates that, in the period 1983–6, interest payments amounted to $12,555m on a total accrued amount of $21,016m, the gross debt increasing thus by the difference, or by $8,461m. For this period 1983–6, the estimated fulfillment ratio was 59.7 percent, much higher than that for 1986 alone. This fall in the fulfillment ratio in 1986, and the much larger fall in 1987, when the trade surplus is expected to be only about $600m, may be the explanation for the subsequent fall in the market price of Argentine debt in 1987 to levels of about 30 percent of par value.

Table 7.7 Estimate of the servicing of the foreign debt in 1983–1986 ($m)

Source of funds	
Current account before	
contractual interest	10,370
Decrease in reserves	–2,567
Direct investment	2,001
Total	9,804
Use of funds	
Capital outflow	–2,751
Interest paid on debt	12,555
Total	9,804
Interest accrued on gross debt	21,016
(minus) interest paid on gross debt	12,555
(equals) gross debt increase	8,461

Both in the creditor countries and in Argentina, a business enterprise forced into the situation of refinancing half the servicing of its debt would convene a meeting of its creditors in order to discuss a refinancing structure and an exoneration of interest charges. This is not possible in the international market, since there is no appropriate judicial forum.

Some of the creditor banks have already chosen to sell their Argentinian debt on the secondary market, accepting the 35 percent loss (as of 1986). Other banks did not divest themselves of the debt since, if they did, their books would reflect the 35 percent loss of capital. However, the capital of these banks is an accounting fiction, the shareholders being well aware that part of their assets have a lower market value than that shown in the books. There are, however, important issues regarding the opportunity for the banks to take the losses involved in the writing down of a significant fraction of their loans. For it to be convenient for them to do so, it is necessary that they have other profits against which to balance the losses involved in the loans written off.

The denominated "debt capitalization" strategies have recently appeared on the scene. These are designed to allow creditor banks to divest themselves of these securities at par in exchange for other securities or assets of the same nominal value (which they would keep on their books) but of a lower-than-par real value. In the case of Argentina, the simpler version would be that the government buy from the creditor bank, paying in Australes, the foreign debt securities at par on condition that the bank buy a certain amount of Australes, paying in dollars at the official exchange rate (lower than the free market rate). All the Australes thus obtained should be invested in the purchase of Argentinian real assets.

From the interaction between the exchange gap and the additional amount of dollars that the bank must exchange at the official exchange rate, the result of the operation is that the central bank buys the debt at somewhat more than 65 percent and the foreign bank sells its debt at somewhat less than 100 percent. In actual fact, both banks share the 35 percent.

Let us assume that the operation is carried out and the foreign bank finds some attractive real assets. To be attractive, they must have a higher expected rate of return than that implied by the Argentinian debt at the market value of 65 percent. If the rate is the same, I do not see why the banks would take the trouble to enter into this operation if they could sell their debt on the secondary market.

In fact, the creditors would now have their capital invested in Argentina and they would be subject to the country's tax laws. They would no longer be creditors of foreign debt securities but rather they would be on the same footing as domestic investors. It is known that the high degree of instability of Argentina's economy makes it not too attractive to investors and that is why, were a creditor to accept the operation, he would demand a rate of return even greater than that offered by the original debt. And if the investment is profitable, as was expected, the country does not resolve the problem of the payment of the debt since now the interest charges are transformed into even larger dividends. Obviously, some type of more favourable restructuring of maturities will have been obtained, but that is all.

I must make it clear that the plan I have referred to for capitalizing the debt is the one that is discussed just in the case of Argentina. There are alternative systems proposed for other countries, such as Chile, that incorporate the "privatization" of public enterprises as part of the process. This is an interesting alternative but it is not a part of the plan discussed in Argentina, for which reason I will not discuss it here.

Assuming that the capitalization were carried out, the problem would remain of what the central bank could do with the thousands of millions of Australes it issued in order to buy the foreign debt securities. If it left them in the market, the operation would simply not exist because the resulting hyperinflation would simply destroy the financial system. It would therefore have to redeem those Australes with some kind of bond in Austral denomination which would appear attractive to entrepreneurs who have sold their factories. We know that in the present circumstances, for a bond in Australes to be attractive, it must offer a rate of return with an equivalent in dollars considerably higher than the international rate (as of the end of 1987 the marginal cost to the government of obtaining additional funds through dollar denominated internal debt was in the order of 40 percent per year). This means that the state would continue reducing its patrimony, at a higher rate than before capitalization and, unless a dilution soon occurred, through the application of inflationary measures.

If the latter did occur, the effect would be that the state would end up without the foreign debt, the entrepreneurs without their factories, and the foreign banks would have exchanged the foreign debt for the factories. The problem of servicing the debt would not have been totally solved since dividends would still have to be paid, although now the problem of generating enough fiscal surplus to acquire the dollars to pay for the debt will not exist.

Finally, I do not believe that capitalization is a viable solution for the global debt problem, unless the government decides to give some capital assets of its own in exchange for the foreign debt securities. Otherwise the capitalization will be exhausted in a process of substitution of foreign debt by more expensive internal debt. Besides, the problem remains of whether the country has sufficient assets to be able to capitalize a significant part of the debt. The province of Buenos Aires has 30 million hectares of arable land. At an average price of 800 dollars per hectare, that would mean a total of $24,000 million, less than half the value of the foreign debt!

Authorities seem to have recognized the limited scope offered by the capitalization scheme for Argentina, as the debt–equity swap agreement signed with the bank syndicate in 1987 calls for 5-year plan with a total amount of $1.9 billion of debt at par value being converted into equity, giving an average of $380 million per year. Obviously, as instrumented, this scheme does not call for any great effort to be made in the area of debt–equity swaps.

The solution of the problem of the foreign debt will not be reached through its capitalization or by its refinancing with more appropriate maturity dates. It will rather be reached through acknowledging that the country is not in a viable position to undertake the total payment of the foreign debt. The market has already acknowledged this by trading the debt with a discount that, at the end of 1986, reached 35 percent of its par value. The deterioration of the fiscal and trade accounts during 1987 increased the discount to about 70 percent of par value, but those abnormal conditions should be considered temporary. With some effort in structural adjustment, Argentina should be able to improve on the fiscal deficit and generate a trade surplus similar to that prevailing during the average of 1982–6 and therefore the discount of 35 percent on the debt seems a realistic estimate of the country's ability to pay.

The record for 1982–6 shows that the country generated trade surpluses of an annual average of $3,264m. At the same time, for each year the fiscal deficit exceeded the amount of interest to be paid by the public sector. This means that the main debtor, the public sector, did not generate by genuine fiscal means, a single Austral with which to acquire the dollars generated by the trade surpluses. We must conclude that any interest that was paid by the public sector must have been so by funds acquired through the inflation tax or new issues of internal debt (Rodriguez, 1987). Such possibilities seem to have ended by 1988 with inflation rapidly rising and internal interest rates on new government paper annually in the order of 40 percent in dollar terms. Therefore, an important element in a future solution to the debt problem lies not in the ability of the country to generate trade surpluses but in the inability of the government to generate the required fiscal surpluses.

We will therefore assume that in any solution to be implemented, Argentina will improve in its fiscal deficit so that some Australes will be freed by the government in order to acquire dollars generated through the trade surplus. This also means that the public sector will be freeing resources for them to move into the traded sector and generate the required trade surplus. Under present circumstances, trade surpluses similar to those observed during 1982–6, averaging $3,264m, are not impossible to produce. All that is necessary is for the government to generate fiscal surpluses of a similar magnitude in order to acquire those dollars without having to resort to the inflation tax or excessive increases in internal debt.

The market option would be therefore that the international creditors accept a reasonable reduction on the book value of Argentina's debt in exchange for the conditions being established whereby the remaining balance be serviced with complete and unquestionable regularity. This requires, in the first place, that the final amount of the debt be structured over a very long period of time and that the interest rate be the most attractive (the lowest) on the international market.

With a 35 percent exoneration, Argentina's debt at the end of 1986 would have decreased to $33,607 m. At that time the LIBOR was at 6.24 percent and therefore the service would have meant an annual interest of $2,097m. Since then the LIBOR has increased and at the end of 1987 it was about 8 percent, meaning that the service would have risen to $2,688m. This amount is slightly smaller than the average surplus in the current account during 1982–6 before paying interest of $2,740m. With improving terms of trade (as appears to be the case since 1987) and the unavoidable fiscal adjustment, Argentina should be again able to generate a surplus of this magnitude.

The amount of amortization to pay off each year would depend on the refinancing period, but it should not pose a problem. To the extent that the international inflation rate is positive (as appears to be the case after 1987), the payment of nominal interest would already include a measure of real amortization. In any case, the refinancing of the amortization would be almost automatic if Argentina were to show that it services its debt regularly over 1 or 2 years. With 50-year maturity, a nominal amortization of 2 percent per annum means an additional $672m which, in principle, could be taken care of with the reserves in hand. After 1 or 2 years the banking community will start lending again, at least to cover the amortization.

This solution involves a realistic exoneration on the current debt and the condition that, since payments will be made regularly, the rate established will not exceed the LIBOR rate. Both are exceedingly reasonable conditions. After all, the payment being made would be what the market expected to collect.

In order to make the transaction attractive to the creditors, a clause could be established indicating that non-fulfillment of the servicing of these new securities would mean that the debt would revert to the original securities and even that a parity of more than 65 percent could be agreed upon, to the extent that conditions can jointly be set up to allow a sustainable improvement in the trade balance. It is highly probable that some creditor banks may not accept this solution until they are forced to do so, and this is quite logical since every creditor must try to collect until the very last moment. That is the reason for the existence of a legal form such as the convocation of creditors. In this case, if all the alternative options leading to a stable solution should fail, Argentina could execute its own convocation by producing a new type of foreign debt security, in the terms that have been described, offering to exchange them for the present securities over a fixed period of time. It should be made clear in the announcement of the tender offer that all available foreign exchange will be primarily allotted to the payment of these new securities. This announcement is fundamental. In the case of the BONEX, which carry an implicit promise of this type, we can see that they are quoted at values approximately 20 points higher than the rest of the foreign debt.

In case it should be argued that the 35 percent exoneration on the book value presents a legal problem, the securities could be issued at par on condition that the exoneration be applied on the interest rate which in this case would be set at 65 percent of the LIBOR rate. This alternative implies that the new debt issues should trade below par to the extent that they carry an interest rate below the market rate.

In any event, a unilateral action on the part of Argentina should be used only as the last resort as it would have certain costs in terms of the future reinsertion of the country in the international capital markets. As far as possible, such a solution should be carried out by the mutual agreement of all parties involved. Needless to say, for this type of solution to have any chance of being accepted by the creditors, Argentina should offer guarantee that the reduced debt will be normally serviced. For this, the best way is for the country to accept the instrumentation of a serious adjustment effort of its economy, probably under the supervision of international institutions. From a practical standpoint, it would be possible to gradually transfer the old debt into the new (smaller) debt, pending the fulfillment of the different stages of the adjustment program.

4   The Problem of Incentives

Most of Argentina's foreign debt is documented as interest-bearing obligations based on a floating rate (LIBOR), plus a spread. As shown in the previous sections, full service of interest cannot be paid and the unpaid component is rolled over. Since there is no expectation that full service will ever be paid, Argentinian debt sells at substantial discounts. To the extent that all foreign exchange available must go to pay interest, debtors have no incentive to improve on their trade surpluses as all of the improvement would go to decrease the amount of interest being rolled over. Creditors are forced to accept any trade surplus results the debtor countries wish to generate. Perhaps the best proof of this presumption is the observed trade surplus experimented during the first 26 months of the Austral stabilization Plan, from June 1985 through September 1987, which gradually but persistently converged to almost zero.

A viable debt relief proposal must incorporate three aspects: (1) give incentives to debtor countries to generate foreign exchange, (2) allow creditors to share in the extra foreign exchange being produced; and (3) offer the proper guarantees that the agreement will be carried out.

From the above perspective, the solution of simply writing down a fraction of the debt will work only to the extent that unforeseen circumstances do not again force the situation of contractual interest not being fully serviced. Preventing this happenning would require a write-off substantially larger than one that creditors are likely to accept.

Another alternative would be to convert all interest-bearing debt into equity, entitling the holder to a share of the debtor's production of foreign exchange. Contrary to the case of a partial write-off discussed above, in this case there would be no need to assign priority in the use of foreign exchange to the service of the new security, as nontendered debt will most probably fall in price or, at least, there is no reason why its price should rise.

If return of the new equity were to be stipulated as a fraction of the trade surplus, debtors will have the incentive to expand exports and imports while keeping the trade surplus at zero. This solution would violate condition (2) above and would not be acceptable to creditors.

A more viable alternative is to link the return on equities to actual exports. Debtors may have now an incentive to expand exports as they keep a fraction of the extra proceeds. They will not have an incentive to cut exports as this would also mean cutting imports. Creditor countries will have an incentive to favor the export promotion policies of debtor countries as this will increase their dividend receipts. Since most probably there will be an adjustment program for debtors as a condition for the arrangement, this program, under multilateral supervision, should be based on export promotion for debtors and lower import restriction for those exports on the part of creditor countries. As part of the adjustment program, governments of debtor countries should be prevented from collecting the required fraction of exports through the use of additional export taxes as this would be to the detriment of trade expansion and economic efficiency.

A fundamental condition for this solution to work is that provision must be included in the adjustment program for the public sector to generate the fiscal surpluses required to purchase the stipulated fraction of exports to be paid as dividends.

If successful, this strategy would not only offer the debt relief and the correct incentives but can be used as a concerted multilateral effort to expand trade.

Tying debt service to export proceeds has the attraction of giving the debtor the right incentives for the production of foreign exchange, while the straight write-off of a fraction of the debt has the advantage that no new instruments are required and the methodology is familiar to accepted banking practices.

Perhaps these alternatives are idealistic in view of the conditions in which the debt is currently documented, and the fact that some creditors collect higher interest than others. In particular, there seems to be a tendency to pay interest to private creditors with new money provided by international institutions. It is also the case that many smaller banks are not contributing funds towards the roll-over of the unpaid interest and are therefore collecting full service on their loans thanks to the funds provided by the larger banks. If that is the case, perhaps this may not be the appropriate moment to attempt this consolidation and exoneration, because of lack of interest on the part of the private creditors. I have no doubt, however, that this point will come once the flow of new funds from new creditors ceases. At that point the global nonviability of the system of refinancing interest with positive real rates, which already exists, will become equally evident to all, except that the longer that point takes to arrive, the larger the real amount of the debt will be and, consequently, the larger the problem to be solved.

NOTE

The final revision of this paper was done while the author was a consultant at the Research Department of the IMF. The views expressed here are those of the author and do not necessarily represent those of the IMF.

REFERENCES

Auernheimer, Leonardo (1986), "Allowing Markets to Compensate for Government Mistakes", *Journal of Monetary Economics*, Vol. 19.

Calvo, Guillermo A. (1985), "Fractured Liberalism: Argentina Under Martinez de Hoz", New York: Colombia University Discussion Paper No. 275, May.

Dornbusch, Rudiger (1984), "Argentina Since Martinez de Hoz", unpublished manuscript, Massachussets Institute of Technology, June.

Fernandez, Roque (1986), "Los Costos de Intermediacion Financiera en el Sistema Bancario Privado de Argentina", *LIBERTAS* (ESEADE) October.

Fernandez, Roque and Rodriguez, Carlos A. (1982), *Inflacion y Estabilidad*, Buenos Aires: Ediciones Macchi.

Rodriguez, Carlos A. (1982), "The Argentine Stabilization Plan of December 20th", *World Development*, Vol. 10, No. 9.

Rodriguez, Carlos A. (1983), "Politicas de Estabilizacion en la Economia Argentina: 1978–82", *Cuadernos de Economia*. Universidad Catolica de Chile, April.

Rodriguez, Carlos A. (1987), "Por que no se paga la deuda externa?", *Ambito Financiero*, Buenos Aires, September 28.

Comment

Andrés Solimano

My discussion of Carlos Rodriguez's chapter will focus on three issues:

1 the origins of debt accumulation in Argentina;
2 the distributive patterns implicit in debt servicing;
3 debt reform proposals.

1   Origin of the Debt

Rodríguez states that most of debt accumulation in Argentina between 1978 and 1982, the period of the more rapid build-up of debt, was neither the counterpart of current account deficit nor accumulation of reserves, but mainly a reflection of the acquisition of foreign assets by Argentinians (and perhaps some foreign agents). Thus, an important part of the Argentinian debt financed capital flight during those years.

Once this fact is established the next question is, why did that happen? On that matter the chapter is not very explicit.

Was the capital flight a private-sector response to an unsustainable exchange rate policy, namely the *tablita*? Why did the public not turn to importable goods in anticipation of future devaluation, like Chile? Did the liberalization of the capital account encourage capital flight in Argentina? Did foreign creditors carry out screening on the destination of the funds they were lending to Argentina?

These and others are important questions that I think should be addressed when studying such a neat case of the use of debt financing for capital flight.

Among the lessons one could draw from the Argentinian experience I would like to point to three: (1) to what extent is the use of the exchange rate for anti-inflationary purposes a sound policy in economies with inflationary inertia, fiscal imbalance and weak operation of the law of one price at an aggregate level? (2) what is the desirability of liberalizing the capital account of the balance of payments before domestic economic and political stability is achieved? (3) a consistent foreign debt strategy must pay close attention to the domestic relative price structure – in particular to the real exchange rate – in order to assure that resources will be allocated to activities which generate foreign exchange needed for debt repayment in future periods.

2   Distributive Issues

Servicing the debt which to a large extent financed the acquisition of foreign assets, as in Argentina, involves a perverse redistribution of income from wage earners to domestic assets holders.

On the one hand, the generation of trade surpluses required to pay at least a part of the debt interest, will require a depreciated real exchange rate which has its counterpart in depressed real wages, hence squeezing labor's real income. On the other hand, a sizable part of the interest payments represents the return to assets that Argentinian wealth owners hold abroad. The problem is that the government cannot tax the domestic holders of foreign assets since it does not know who are they.

In addition, the "true" net debt of Argentina (total debt minus net international reserves minus foreign assets held by Argentinians) is obviously less than the official record of the external debt. However, servicing this "foreign" debt involves domestic income transfer and a lack of government command on these resources which poses serious economic and distributive problems.

3   Debt Reform Proposals

Rodríguez's calculations of sustainable trade surpluses show (and he explicitly acknowledges this) that it is very unlikely that Argentina will be able to service all its debt in the future.

The problem is, then what is to be done? Debt relief schemes are implicitly disregarded by the author even though he is in favor of a market solution in which Argentina's foreign creditors would accept a loss in their claims on the country (given by the discount of the Argentinian debt in the secondary market), in exchange for a commitment made by Argentina to service the rest of its debt punctually. According to Rodríguez, with a LIBOR interest rate of 6 percent per year and a discount of 35 percent, interest payments would come down to some $2,500 million per year, an amount Argentina could (supposedly) service without severe hardships.

The author is certainly right in asserting that debt–equity swaps may not be a permanent solution to the debt problem, since the scheme merely changes the composition of the country's total liabilities from debt to equity, hence reducing interest payments and increasing dividends and profit remittances.

It is clear that the level of Argentina's foreign liabilities would not change, and the main benefit from the scheme would come from the postponement of the flow payments because of regulations on profit and dividend remittances embodied in the debt–equity operation. With a weak trade surplus and severe domestic macroeconomic instability, it does help to postpone payments on debt. However, in the medium run, the "solvency issue" of the country still remains an open question.

8

The Chilean Economy in the Eighties: Adjustment and Recovery

Juan A. Fontaine

1 Introduction

The Chilean economic experience of the early eighties has been the subject of intense controversy, both in Chile and abroad. Like many other countries in Latin America, Chile suffered severe recession in 1982–3. What seems to give the Chilean case added interest is the fact that the crisis was preceded by the implementation of a fairly consistent set of economic reforms, aimed at establishing in Chile a free market, outward-looking economic system.[1] Probably as interesting as the connection between the free market experiment and the following economic crisis is that Chile has faced the crisis, and to a large extent overcome it, keeping unchanged the basic elements of that model and applying policies that can be termed as orthodox. This chapter summarizes the strategy of adjustment and recovery applied since the crisis and its (still incipient) results.

The chapter is organized as follows. The second section describes the origin of the disequilibrium between expenditure and income that gave rise to the 1981–2 crisis. The third section describes the policies and results of the 1984–6 period of adjustment and recovery, while the fourth section refers to the foreign debt strategy adopted, including Chile's "best-seller," debt–equity swaps. The fifth and final section summarizes the three main lessons that, in my opinion, can be drawn from the previous analysis.

Before continuing the exposition, I owe the reader an explanation. This chapter intends to sketch the basic features of Chile's recent experience of economic adjustment and recovery. But I am afraid that, as my personal views on the subject may have been influenced by my own participation in some of the events covered, I may have inadvertently introduced a bias in the presentation that follows. I only hope readers will make allowances for this.

2 The Genesis of the Imbalance

One of the most striking (and often overlooked; exceptions are Silva, 1983 and Gutiérrez, 1987) features of Chile's recent economic history is the dramatic deterioration experienced in its terms of trade.[2] From an average value of 100 for 1965–74, terms of trade fell to 50 in 1975–79 (see table 8.1). This drop was mainly caused by the fall in copper prices and the increase in oil prices of 1975. Between 1976 and 1979, there was a moderate recovery in the terms of trade. Later, a new drop occurred, and the index fell to 42 in 1984–6, the lowest level since the Great Depression.

The 1975 terms-of-trade shock was faced with a severe adjustment program and with the implementation of a wide set of structural reforms aimed at establishing a free market, outward-oriented economic system in Chile. Following the severe recession of 1975, Chile's economy underwent a healthy export-led expansion between 1976 and 1979, with GDP growing at an average rate of 7 percent per year (3.4 percent including the year 1975) and exports of goods and services growing at an average rate of 13 percent a year in volume terms (see table 8.1). Inflation rates that reached 370 percent in 1975 gradually decreased to 33 percent in 1979, as a consequence of the fiscal and monetary discipline applied. Net foreign debt gradually declined relative to exports, from 3.1 times in 1975 to 1.6 in 1979. In fact, in 1979, there were good reasons to think that the structural adjustment policies had been able to overcome the effects of the terms-of-trade decline. Only unemployment and investment rates, the former stubbornly high and equally low the latter, remained as witnesses of the hardships inherent in the adjustment to such a dramatic terms-of-trade deterioration.

With the benefit of hindsight, it seems clear that both of these problems were the reflection of an inadequate relative price structure. In fact, interest rates averaging 16 percent and 14 percent in 1978–9 in real terms for indexed and non-indexed deposits, respectively, constituted an un-equivocal sign of an imbalance between aggregate expenditures and income. In order to adjust internal expenditures to the prevailing income level (depressed as it was by the fall in the terms of trade) without having to rely on interest rate levels that seriously damaged investment and employment growth, a higher real rate of exchange to the peso[3] and a lower real wage level were called for. Both of these prices were essentially fixed through policies and regulations.

The international outlook, however, was by then misleading. As stated earlier, the terms of trade showed a rising trend. Also, interest rates in world capital markets were negative in real terms. It seemed only natural that Chile would yield to the offers of the foreign banks, aggressively

Table 8.1 Chile: main economic indicators

Year	GDP (% real var.)	Unemployment rate[a] (%)	Real wages (% real var.)[b]	Consumer price index[c] (% var.)	Exports (goods and services) (% real var.)	Imports (goods and services) (% real var.)	Terms of trade (index, average 1965-74 = 100)	Net foreign debt over exports of goods
1975	-12.9	14.9	-2.7	374.7	2.4	-38.7	47.9	3.13
1976	3.5	12.7	10.8	211.9	24.4	4.3	52.3	2.17
1977	9.9	11.8	21.5	92.0	11.9	35.5	48.2	2.25
1978	8.2	14.2	14.3	40.1	11.2	17.6	47.7	2.27
1979	8.3	13.6	10.9	33.4	14.1	22.7	53.1	1.60
1980	7.8	10.4	8.6	35.1	14.3	18.7	52.3	1.48
1981	5.5	11.3	9.0	19.7	-9.0	15.7	49.4	3.06
1982	-14.1	19.6	0.3	9.9	4.7	-36.3	39.5	3.93
1983	-0.7	14.6	-10.9	27.3	0.6	-15.1	45.9	4.02
1984	6.3	14.0	0.2	19.9	6.8	16.5	42.6	4.60
1985	2.4	11.9	-4.5	30.7	6.9	-11.0	41.1	4.58
1986	5.7	8.8	2.0	19.5	10.6	9.2	44.8	4.18
1987*	5.4	–	–	21.1	6.9	16.2	–	3.45
1965-74 average	2.67	4.50[c]	1.86	72.97	3.96	5.22	100.0	2.48
1975-79 average	3.03	13.44	10.67	121.33	12.58	4.56	49.8	2.28
1980-83 average	-0.76	13.98	1.41	22.65	2.31	-7.17	46.8	3.12
1984-86 average	4.78	11.57	-0.80	23.26	8.08	4.23	42.8	4.45
1984-87* average	4.94	–	–	22.72	7.79	7.10	–	4.20

* Provisional figures

[a] Nationwide, for October-December of each year: *Instituto Nacional de Estadísticas*

[b] Yearly average nominal wages deflated by CPI: *Instituto Nacional de Estadísticas*

[c] 1965-72

[d] Twelve months ended December

Source: Banco Central de Chile

Table 8.2   Chile: key prices 1979–1987*

	1979	1980	1981	1982	1983	1984	1985	1986	1987
Real exchange rate[a] (index 1980=100)	115.3	100.0	87.2	97.2	116.2	121.5	149.7	164.7	170.4* (Sep)
Real interest rate (%)[b]	11.7	6.3	7.4	5.9	6.1	14.7	6.2	3.5	4.8* (Nov)
Real wage index[c] (index 1980=100)	92.0	100.0	108.9	108.6	97.1	97.2	93.0	94.9	94.6* (Sep)

[a] Average real effective exchange rate for each year, computed as the weighted average (import weights) of the wholesale price indexes of Chile's 12 major trading partners, converted into pesos at the official exchange rate and deflated by the Chilean CPI.

[b] Average annual rate paid by banks on 3–12 months UF-indexed (CPI indexed) deposits in December of each year.

[c] Instituto Nacional de Estadísticas nominal index of wages and salaries deflated by CPI, average for each year

Source: Banco Central de Chile

generous at that time, and seek through debt to alleviate some of the effects of the expenditure adjustment over investment and employment.

Between 1979 and 1981, perhaps inadvertently, macroeconomic policies turned expansionary. While restrictions on the inflow of medium-term foreign credits were lowered, the nominal rate of exchange of the peso was fixed to the dollar, establishing a powerful incentive for the private sector to go into foreign debt.[4] This resulted in an acute real appreciation of the peso (see table 8.2). A considerable expansion of the quantity of money and credit was allowed as well, through both the "monetization" of the influx of foreign credits and also by a substantial reduction in reserve requirements.[5] Monetary expansion was accompanied, as usually happens, by a quick appreciation in asset prices, a process that came to an abrupt halt in 1982 with the consequent explosion of a major financial crisis. A mechanism of mandatory full cost-of-living adjustments for wages, subject to collective bargaining, was also instituted, and the minimum wage and public sector salaries were considerably increased, giving an expansionary tilt to a previously distinctively conservative fiscal policy.

It would go beyond the scope of this chapter to detail the causes and effects of these policy changes. The matter has been the subject of intense controversy. According to some authors, the root of the problem lies in the opening of the capital market which was too fast or too intense.[6] Others believe that the cause of the imbalance has to be found in the (lack of) regulations prevailing in the banking sector that may have stimulated an excessive credit expansion. Yet for others (myself included) the disequilibrium had its main origin in an inadequate mix of exchange rate, fiscal, and monetary policies.

Whatever the origin of the problem may be, by 1980–1 an important excess of expenditure over income had taken place. By 1979, the goods and services trade balance – measured at current prices – showed a deficit of 3 percent of GDP, a net transfer from abroad of reasonable dimensions for a capital-importing country. Two years later, the trade deficit had increased to 10 percent of GDP, showing a transfer of an unsustainable size (table 8.3). Behind the worsening of the trade balance, there was a dramatic loss of competitiveness of exports – their growth was only 2 percent a year in volume during 1980–1 – and a steep increase in imports that grew in volume terms at a rate of 17 percent per year (table 8.1).

In contrast to other Latin American experiences, there was no consumption boom in Chile. In fact, domestic savings (the portion of GDP that is not devoted to consumption) remained relatively constant or increased, depending upon whether they are measured at current or at constant prices respectively (table 8.3).[7] The growth of expenditure in 1980–1 was concentrated in investment. Gross domestic investment increased from 18 percent of GDP in 1979 to 23 percent in 1981 if measured at current prices, or from 20 percent to 28 percent, if constant prices are used. Given that the rate of public investment did not experience significant variations during the period, the excess of expenditure was, specifically, the result of an increase in private investment.

It is important to emphasize this fact. On the one hand the private nature of the investments that took place during the period suggests a rational evaluation of them, and thus a higher future productive capacity. It cannot be denied that these figures include the accumulation of stocks of imported goods, and some construction projects that can only be explained in the context of the inadequate relative prices prevailing at that time. But leaving these investments aside, an important contribution to the formation of productive capital seems to have taken place during this period. Otherwise, the substantial increase in exports and employment observed during the latest years could not have occurred.

On the other hand, the private investment nature of the excess of expenditure that took place in 1980–1 somehow rendered the ensuing adjustment more complex and painful. Because they seem to be less credit-intensive, adjustments of consumption excesses are simpler, once the authorities have the will to carry them through. The curtailment of

Table 8.3 Chile: aggregate demand composition

	1975	1976	1977	1978	1979	1980	1981	1982	1983	1984	1985	1986	1987*	Averages			
														1965–74	1975–79	1980–83	1984–87
A. At Constant 1977 Prices																	
Consumption/GDP	0.87	0.84	0.87	0.87	0.86	0.83	0.85	0.89	0.87	0.83	0.80	0.78	0.77	0.917	0.858	0.847	0.795
Gross investment/GDP	0.14	0.14	0.14	0.16	0.20	0.24	0.28	0.11	0.09	0.15	0.14	0.15	0.18	0.203	0.165	0.162	0.155
Exports/GDP	0.17	0.20	0.21	0.21	0.22	0.24	0.20	0.25	0.25	0.25	0.26	0.28	0.28	0.113	0.220	0.228	0.268
Imports/GDP	-0.18	-0.18	-0.22	-0.24	-0.28	-0.30	-0.33	-0.25	-0.21	-0.23	-0.20	-0.21	-0.23	-0.234	-0.242	-0.236	-0.218
Resource balance/GDP	-0.01	0.02	-0.02	-0.03	-0.05	-0.07	-0.13	0.002	0.04	0.02	0.06	0.07	0.05	-0.120	-0.023	0.008	0.050
Domestic savings/GDP	0.13	0.16	0.13	0.13	0.14	0.17	0.15	0.11	0.13	0.17	0.20	0.22	0.23	0.083	0.142	0.153	0.205
B. At Current Prices																	
Consumption/GDP	0.89	0.83	0.87	0.86	0.85	0.83	0.88	0.91	0.87	0.87	0.84	0.82	0.80	0.849	0.866	0.860	0.833
Gross investment/GDP	0.13	0.13	0.14	0.18	0.18	0.21	0.23	0.11	0.10	0.14	0.14	0.15	0.17	0.149	0.155	0.153	0.150
Exports/GDP	0.25	0.25	0.21	0.21	0.23	0.23	0.16	0.19	0.24	0.24	0.29	0.31	0.33	0.145	0.221	0.234	0.293
Imports/GDP	-0.27	-0.21	-0.22	-0.24	-0.26	-0.27	-0.27	-0.21	-0.21	-0.25	-0.26	-0.27	-0.30	-0.145	-0.241	-0.245	-0.270
Resource balance/GDP	-0.02	-0.04	-0.02	-0.03	-0.03	-0.04	-0.10	-0.02	0.03	-0.01	0.03	0.04	0.03	0.001	-0.028	-0.018	0.023
Domestic savings/GDP	0.11	0.17	0.13	0.14	0.15	0.17	0.12	0.09	0.13	0.13	0.16	0.18	0.20	0.151	0.134	0.140	0.167

* provisional figures
Source: Banco Central de Chile

private investment, besides needing such willpower, requires the undoing
of the complex credit network on which such private investment projects
usually lean. That is one of the reasons why the 1982–3 adjustment in Chile
detonated a severe financial crisis that probably intensified the real effects
of the adjustment.

The fate of any excess of expenditure is more or less the same: a balance
of payments crisis followed by a recession. In 1981 the adjustment was
precipitated and seriously aggravated by the fall in the terms of trade and
the rise in international interest rates. Faced with the imminence of a
significant macroeconomic adjustment, the influx of foreign loans rapidly
decreased during the second half of that year and domestic private capital
probably started to flow out of the country. In late 1982, after the Latin
American foreign debt crisis exploded, the flow of international capital
turned negative. Both residents and nonresidents hastily started to seek
ways to reduce their peso exposure. Internal economic activity underwent
a severe contraction starting in the fourth quarter of 1981, and ending
eighteen months later. Unemployment climbed above 20 percent of the
labor force in 1982 (table 8.1). Real wages, that continued to rise up until
mid-1982, fell abruptly during the second half of that year, in the midst of
successive devaluations and a quick resurgence of inflation. In the meantime, the adjustment gave way to a severe financial crisis the culminating
point of which was government intervention in the main private financial
institutions at the beginning of 1983. This gave way to the formal renegotiation of Chile's foreign debt with international banks. In 1983, GDP was
15 percent below 1981 and net foreign debt was 4.0 times the value of
exports of goods and services (table 8.1).

3   Adjustment with Growth

From 1984 on, the Chilean economy has experienced a mixture of adjustment and growth. The central objective of the macroeconomic program
has been to form the basis of the ground for a sustained recovery in
economic activity and for a progressive reduction of foreign debt requirements (see Büchi, 1985, 1986, for an official presentation of the program
and its results). This program has been part of a global strategy of
structural reform that – following essentially the line of the economic
reforms of the previous decade – seeks to foster exports and domestic
savings. Since 1983 the macroeconomic program has been supported by the
IMF (through a stand-by program initially, and then through an extended
fund facility (EFF)) and since 1985 by the World Bank (through three
structural adjustment loans (SAL) programs).

In 1984–6 GDP growth showed an average of 4.8 percent per year (see table 8.1). In 1987, with an estimated growth of 5.4 percent, GDP will be 3.6 percent above its previous peak. Growth has been led by the tradable goods sectors – agriculture, fishing, mining, and industry – that represented in 1986 39 percent of GDP, some three points above 1981.

The composition of agregate demand has also varied, with exports and gross investment increasing at average annual rates of 8 percent and 10 percent respectively in volume terms. The increasing diversification of exports is shown by the growth of noncopper exports of goods that have increased at an average rate of 13 percent per year in volume terms. Just as important is the recovery of gross private investment, averaging 11 percent per year during 1985–6.[8] This time investment seems to have definitely been concentrated in tradable sectors. In the course of 1987, noncopper exports and private investment are estimated to have grown 12 percent and 28 percent respectively in volume terms.

GDP growth has been accompanied by a considerable reduction in unemployment rates. Between 1982 and 1986 unemployment rates decreased from 19.6 percent to 8.8 percent, notwithstanding the fact that special fiscal programs of employment (PEM and POJH) declined to 4.5 percent of the labor force from 9.5 percent during the same period. The growth of employment averaged 5.9 percent per year, revealing an unexpectedly rapid response of the demand for labor to output growth in tradable sectors and to labor cost reductions. The flexibility shown by the labor market in recent years seems to be a consequence of the fundamental reforms of labor legislation implemented in 1979–81.

Real wages did not increase in the 1984–6 period. As shown in table 8.1 real wages increased sharply between 1980 and 1982, only to drop dramatically in 1983. By 1986 they averaged a level 5.1 percent below that of 1980. The sustained reduction in real wages has certainly been a source of widespread hardship among lower income groups. However, it is interesting to note that the rapid growth in employment from 1983 onwards has made total labor income grow approximately at the same pace as GDP.

The adjustment can be seen clearly in the evolution of the trade balance. Between 1981 and 1983 the trade balance in goods and services went from a deficit of 13 percent of GDP to a surplus of 4 percent, measured at constant prices (table 8.3). Since then, the trade balance has continued to increase, climbing to 7 percent of GDP in 1986. The total 1981–6 change, equivalent to 20 points of GDP, was the consequence of an 8 points increase in exports and a 12 point decrease in imports. If the measurements are made at current prices, the results are less noteworthy because of the deterioration in the terms of trade. The figures at constant prices reflect the adjustment *efforts*. Those at current prices indicate the *results* of such efforts.[9] Nevertheless, the trade balance went from a deficit of 10 percent of GDP in 1981 to a 4 percent surplus in 1983, and since then has stayed somewhat below that level.

The counterpart to the adjustment of the balance of payments accounts is, of course, the adjustment in expenditure patterns. Using constant prices once again, gross investment, after falling from 28 percent of GDP to 9 percent between 1981 and 1983 as a consequence of the crisis, averaged 15 percent in 1984–6 and it is estimated to have reached about 17 percent in 1987 (table 8.3). The other component of expenditure – consumption – after falling dramatically in 1982–3, has shown an extraordinarily moderate pattern, thus allowing domestic savings (the portion of GDP that is not devoted to consumption) to rise from 13 percent of GDP in 1983 to 22 percent in 1986.

The observed combination of adjustment and growth has been the result of the application of a fairly orthodox set of macroeconomic policies. Even though the image of orthodoxy in Chile's economic policy may have been somewhat exaggerated, there is no doubt that its basic elements obey, in a quite predictable manner, the teachings of conventional macroeconomic theory. In my opinion, Chile's experience suggests that, after all, conventional macroeconomic theory provides the policy-maker with quite a useful tool.

If one had to choose from the policies implemented just *one* as deserving credit for obtaining the results mentioned above, that would undoubtedly be the exchange rate policy. Since the end of 1982, the Central Bank has applied a policy of daily mini devaluations of the peso aimed at preserving a given real exchange rate level.[10] This level has been altered from time to time in order to set a real exchange rate deemed to be consistent with the medium-term outlook for terms of trade, interest rates and the availability of foreign financing. This policy has resulted in an 89 percent increase in the effective real rate of exchange between 1981 and 1986 (table 8.2).

The adjustment of relative prices induced by the devaluation of the peso has worked wonders in the promotion of exports and the substitution of imports. The structural transformation of certain sectors, such as agriculture, forestry and fishing, is visible (see Ceron, 1987; Staplefield, 1987; and Velis, 1987). It obeys, to a large extent, a devaluation-induced utilization of investments that took place in the seventies and beginning of the eighties, a process that is now being reinforced by substantial investments in these sectors. In addition to these supply-side effects, the devaluation has helped to curtail domestic expenditure, keeping real wages significantly below precrisis levels. Low real wages have stimulated employment and corporate savings.[11]

But, in my opinion, the effects of the devaluation have not been limited solely to the current account of the balance of payments. An often overlooked effect of a right exchange rate is its impact on capital flows. Despite the existence of the so-called "debt crisis", private capital flows seem to have continued flowing out or into the countries affected, responding to risk-adjusted interest rate and asset price differentials. These differentials are, of course, very much affected by (expected) exchange rates. In Chile, as will be explained in the next section, the massive devaluation of the peso that took place between 1981 and 1985 seems to have helped to reverse the capital outflow that had previously triggered the crisis.

The merits of the exchange policy should not overshadow the effects of other complementary measures in the areas of export promotion and import substitution. Thus it is fair to point out the role played by a series of tax initiatives concerning exports,[12] the increase from 10 percent to 20 percent of the basic tariff rate for imports, and the application of a special adjustable tariff system to three important agricultural crops.[13]

The real devaluation of the peso could not have been sustained unless accompanied by an appropriate combination of fiscal and monetary policies.

Fiscal policy has achieved remarkable results. These results stem essentially from the strong fiscal adjustment (the fiscal shock) of 1975, which was able to eliminate chronic fiscal deficits. One difference between Chile and some of its neighbors is surely that Chile applied corrections in public expenditures and the tax system 10 years before the debt crisis. Consequently, the fiscal problem lately faced has been much milder than in other countries. Nevertheless, it is remarkable that during 1984–6 fiscal policy has been able to keep public investment at a sizable 7.0 percent of GDP per year, and at the same time reduce the public sector deficit from 4.4 percent in 1984 to 1.9 percent in 1986. This is, of course, the consequence of a dramatic increase in public saving to 4.8 percent of GDP in 1986 from 0.5 percent in 1984. This increase in public savings has been consistent also with a reduction from 46 percent to 10 percent in the corporate income tax rate, thus fostering corporate savings and investment.[14] The tax reform was carried out despite the negative impact of low copper prices on fiscal revenues. The fiscal adjustment has proceeded essentially by cutting current expenditures – both real wages and other outlays – and increasing the operating surplus of public firms (most of them favored by the real exchange devaluation).

In the evolution of fiscal policy during this period there are two additional considerations to bear in mind. One is that the 1981 social security reform had a large negative acounting effect on the public sector budget.[15] This makes it hard to make meaningful comparisons of fiscal accounts before and after the reform. One way of getting round the problem is to consolidate the fiscal deficit with the "surplus" registered by the new private system. This consolidation shows an increase of over 7 percentage points of GDP in adjusted public savings between 1982 and 1986.

The other consideration to keep in mind is an increase in the kind of public debt that does not show up in the deficit of the nonfinancial public sector. As a result of the renegotiation of Chile's foreign debt with banks, the government had to underwrite the private financial system's foreign debt. In addition, when the financial crisis of 1982–3 was threatening the stability of the financial system, the Central Bank had to establish a series of subsidized loan programs and exchange rate insurance schemes for the banking sector and its debtors.[16] The financing for such programs stemmed mainly from foreign loans (the so-called "new monies") contracted by the Central Bank with the same foreign banks that were creditors of domestic banks. Thus by guaranteeing old external debts and contracting new debts through the Central Bank the government has come to accumulate a sizable volume of foreign contingent liabilities (table 8.4).

Since 1985 no new Central Bank subsidized programs have been established, and those then available were phased out as soon as contractually possible. Meanwhile, the widespread improvement in the financial health of both the banking and the corporate sectors and the mechanisms of debt conversion refered to later on are reducing the value of this contingent public debt. Assuming this process continues (thus ruling out any severe world recession) and with a little help from a mild inflation tax (of say 10–15 percent) this form of public debt should gradually be reduced over time.

The administration of the monetary policy constitutes a relatively new experience in Chile. Up until 1975, monetary policy was generally subordinated to the requirements posed by fiscal financing. After a short interlude, it became captive to the exchange rate policy, and especially so after the nominal rate of exchange was pegged to the dollar in 1979. Later, when the financial crisis began, monetary policy was subordinated to the urgent needs of a banking system that was on the edge of bankruptcy. Only since the beginning of 1985 has it been possible to develop an autonomous monetary policy, within the context of a free and competitive capital market, in which both the private and the public sectors raise the funding they need.

Monetary policy since the beginning of 1985 has targetted real interest rates, leading market rates to levels that are deemed compatible with the exchange rate and fiscal adjustments previously described (table 8.2). Interest rate targeting is not fashionable nowadays and real interest rate targeting sounds distinctively heterodox. But in Chile market real rates are easily identifiable due to the extensive use of indexed financial instruments.[17] In my view, real interest rate targeting has played a crucial role in regulating the level of aggregate demand, in stimulating investment,

Table 8.4 Chile: total foreign debt ($m)[a]

	1982	1983	1984	1985	1986	1987[b]
1. Medium- and long-term	13815	14832	16963	17650	17768	17352
Public Sector	5157	6689	10601	12161	12942	14725
(of which private debt with an official guarantee)	(62)	(61)	(1781)	(1647)	(1540)	(3044)
Private sector	8658	8143	6362	5479	4826	2627
2. Short-term	3338	2599	1914	1668	1574	1955
Public sector	1503	1705	1742	1564	1384	1576
Private sector	1835	894	172	104	190	379
3. Total (1+2)	17153	17431	18877	19318	19342	19307
Public	6660	8394	12343	13725	14326	16301
Private	10493	9037	6534	5593	5016	3006

[a] Excludes debts with IMF, certain trade related nonbank debts and foreign debt payable in domestic currency
[b] As of September 1987

in ensuring that domestic savings do not flow out of the country and in inducing – through a reduction in debt service costs – a gradual improvement in the financial health of the (previously severely sick) domestic debtors. Monetary policy has been carried out through open market operations and Central Bank lending and borrowing at pre-established rates. These domestic credit operations have been conducted within the limits set for the Central Bank net domestic assets in the IMF program. Fortunately these limits have not been binding since 1985 due to the use of appropriate estimations of the demand for money and some overperformance in the net international reserves target.[18]

Of course, the key to the success of the monetary policy implemented has been the consistency of the real interest rate target with the other macroeconomic targets. All through 1985, for example, it was possible to induce an important reduction in real interest rates because a strong fiscal adjustment was being implemented at the same time (table 8.2). Similarly, in 1986, a new reduction in interest rates was made possible because increasing confidence in the peso would otherwise have called for an appreciation of the exchange rate. Finally, at the beginning of 1987, in view of a vigorous increase in aggregate demand, the Central Bank had to induce a moderate increase in interest rates. In each of these instances, the Central Bank has attempted to keep real interest rates positive and above comparable international rates, so as to retain domestic savings inside the country.

In sum, macroeconomic policies have played a crucial role in the adjustment process. They have by no means been passive. On the contrary, a great deal of "fine-tuning" has been exercised on the exchange rate and the real interest rates. Despite all that has been written about the failures of activist macroeconomic policies, the Chilean case suggests that under some circumstances they do work. In my view, in the current situation the influence of macroeconomic policies stems from their capacity to convey to the private sector, in a credible manner, the authorities' views on the availability of foreign financing to sustain a given rate of economic growth. But this message is taken seriously if the authorities have credibility, something that results only from realistic policies. Activist macroeconomic policies can be efficient only to the extent that they are strictly realistic.

4   Foreign Debt Strategy

Among the main debtor countries in Latin America, Chile stands out as being able to maintain the net transfer paid abroad within tolerable dimensions. In 1983–6 Chile was not only able to reschedule or refinance 100 percent of amortization payments, but has refinanced 76 percent of the net (nominal) interest payments on its net foreign obligations as well. The remaining 24 percent interest essentially constitutes the net transfer Chile made in favor of all its creditors. Note that this transfer amounts to only 2 percent of total external debt, so that Chile has in effect paid in cash an interest rate of that size, indirectly capitalizing the remainder of its contractual debt service.[19]

Among the solutions typically voiced for the debt problem is the capping of interest payments. But my computation above leads to a striking conclusion: the first order effect of applying an interest cap of, say, 2 percent over Chile's total foreign debt would have been to leave unchanged the real net cash transfer Chile made to all its creditors during 1983–6. One cannot help concluding that the Chilean economy would have been no better off in 1983–6 with a "debt-relief" of such dimensions than it was under the strategy applied. There are some significant second order effects, however, between the two strategies. On the one hand, even if the global transfers were the same, there may be significant differences between those carried out by the diverse types of debtors and received by the different classes of creditors under both strategies. On the other hand, as is obvious, the (indirect) capitalization of interests causes an increase (nominal, at least) in future obligations. More of this later.

Allow me first to dispel an apparent paradox. If the Chilean economy has been able to attract foreign financing of such dimensions, what then were its adjustment efforts for? The answer is twofold. On the one hand, the main problem faced by the Chilean economy, not only since 1982 but since 1975, is the depression in its terms of trade. The role of the foreign debt crisis has been to (seriously) exacerbate the effects of this phenomenon, insofar as it has prevented Chile from incurring even more debt in order to smooth out or postpone the expenditure and structural adjustments called for by a sustained deterioration in terms of trade.

Such an impact can be seen when comparing Chile's real net transfer abroad measured in current prices and in constant prices. The former measures the transfer effectively *received* by the country's creditors and averaged 2 percent of GDP during 1983–6. The latter represents the *effort* of adjusting expenditure and averaged 5 percent of GDP (table 8.2).[20] The difference is explained by the deterioration in the terms of trade, a transfer involuntarily effected by Chile in favor of the purchasers of its exports and the producers of its imports. This last transfer is the one that, were it not for the debt crisis, one would have expected the international capital market to smooth out.

But there is an additional factor to consider concerning the relation between adjustment and financing. As mentioned in the previous section, even in a situation of foreign debt crisis, international capital responds in a predictable manner. Sound macroeconomic policies attract it as much as the not so sound ones repel it. A widely used analysis of the debt problem assumes that the capital account of the balance of payments is exogenous to macroeconomic policy, being essentially determined in the course of the official bank debt negotiations. However, Chile's experience is that the net flows controlled in such negotiations represent only about half of the net requirements of foreign financing (see table 8.6). The remaining portion still responds, to some extent, to conventional incentives. In my view, the adjustment policies have been instrumental in attracting this portion of the required foreign financing.

In its external bank debt renegotiations, Chile has followed the familiar pattern: rescheduling of amortizations (first, bi-annually, later, multi-annually), obtaining "new monies", successive "repricings".[21] Through these mechanisms Chile was able to refinance about half the interest payments on its debt with international banks, in addition to rescheduling all the amortizations. Because 67 percent of the debt with international banks was privately owed, however, some additional complexities had to be faced. As said before, the government guaranteed the rescheduled debt of the domestic financial system.[22] The debt of the corporate private system, however, did not receive such guarantee and – in case it were not directly rescheduled by the creditors – it was assumed by the Central Bank once paid in pesos by the original debtor. Concerning interest payments, as we saw, the country as a whole partially refinanced them thanks to

Table 8.5 Chile: balance of payments 1984–1987[a] ($m)

	1984	1985	1986	1987
Current Account	−2060.0	−1328.5	−1090.7	−892.2
1. Trade balance	293.0	849.6	1099.7	1078.5
Exports	3650.3	3804.1	4198.9	5045.8
Copper	1603.8	1788.7	1757.1	2145.3
Others	2046.5	2015.4	2441.7	2900.5
Imports	−3357.3	−2954.5	−3099.1	−3967.3
2. Nonfinancial services	−434.0	−337.8	−387.6	−473.1
3. Financial services	−2017.7	−1901.0	−1877.3	−1600.6
4. Transfers	98.7	60.7	84.5	103.0
Capital Account	1978.7	1348.1	912.6	1161.6
1. Foreign investment[b]	67.0	62.4	57.4	105.8
2. Amortization payments[c]	−487.5	−419.5	−431.3	−289.3
3. Medium- and long-term disbursements	1620.2	1470.6	1218.7	1028.1
(Commercial banks)	(780.0)	(714.0)	(370.3)	(0.0)
(Official organizations)	(90.4)	(61.0)	(24.2)	(17.4)
(Multilateral organizations)[d]	(358.4)	(488.4)	(483.0)	(502.1)
(Suppliers and project-financing)	(391.4)	(207.2)	(341.2)	(508.6)
4. Net use of short-term trade lines	292.3	−29.3	241.9	103.0
5. Other short-term trade related-flows	−6.4	48.7	119.9	73.5
6. Net change in foreign assets	313.1	370.2	31.0	−84.4
7. Net short-term credits to Central Bank	180.0	−155.0	−325.0	225.0
Errors and Omissions	98.6	−118.2	−49.4	−223.9
Balance of payments Surplus (+) Deficit (−)	17.3	−98.6	−227.5	45.5

[a] 1984–6: provisional figures
   1987: projections
[b] Excluding investment through debt–equity swaps
[c] Excluding repayment of loans arising from debt–equity swaps and other debt conversion mechanisms
[d] Including SALs from the World Bank.

Source: Banco Central de Chile

"new-money" loans and other funds that were channelled mainly to the Central Bank. Domestic debtors, in the meantime, paid in general the full amount of interest owed. The Central Bank, through a series of loan programs, recycled the foreign credits helping domestic debtors to meet their interest payments. Therefore, even though the net global real re-

Table 8.6 Sources of net external financing ($m)

	1984	1985	1986	1987*
Capital Account Surplus[a]	1798.7	1673.1	1237.6	1161.6
Commercial banks[b]	1041.3	828.3	584.6	328.0[e]
(as % of capital account)	57.9	49.5	47.2	28.2
Official sources[c]	244.4	379.4	265.2	352.5
(as % of capital account)	13.6	22.7	21.4	30.3
Private sources[d]	513.0	465.3	387.8	481.1
(as % of capital account)	28.5	27.8	31.3	41.4

* Projection
[a] Differs from table 8.5 in that Short-term credits to the Central Bank are excluded, except for 1987 (see footnote[e], below) and the effects of the 1985 retiming ($170 millions) are added
[b] Includes medium- and long-term net flows plus net variation of short-term credit lines and the effects of the 1985 retiming. Interest repricings are *not* included as a source of financing
[c] Includes net credits from IDB, World Bank (SAL included) and government agencies. Amortizations include bank credits with official guarantee. Excludes IMF credits
[d] Includes net foreign investments, project-financing by banks and suppliers, intercompany credits, trade related flows and identified changes in foreign assets
[e] Includes the $225 million disbursements of short-term credits to cover the 1987 gap. These will be paid in 1988 with part of the proceeds from the "retiming" of interest payments negotiated with bank creditors as part of the 1987–8 financial package. Since they imply an increase in short-term debt of the Central Bank, strictly speaking they *should not* be included in net international reserves. However, I do not follow this procedure here to facilitate comparisons with previous years

Source: Banco Central de Chile

source transfer from Chile to its creditors has been relatively small, it has created a complex network of internal transfers between the Central Bank and the original domestic debtors, most of them private. The fact that the internal transfer problem has been managed without creating the inflationary strains seen in other Latin American economies, speaks well of the efficiency of the Chilean capital market after 1983. One of the crucial reforms of the seventies was the creation of a formal private capital market in Chile.[23] After some serious setbacks during 1982–3, these efforts proved succesful.

That half of net foreign financing not provided by international banks, comprises (1) credits from official and multilateral agencies; (2) supplier credits and project-financing; and (3) trade-related flows and changes in international assets that essentially reflect the movement of capital by residents. Sources (2) and (3) are clearly a form of the so-called "voluntary" financing.

As can be seen in table 8.5, credits from multilateral agencies provided a large share (about 23 percent on average) of net financing.[24] Sources (2) and (3) are shown in table 8.6 under the "Private Sources" heading. As shown, net private *voluntary* financing increased from 28 percent of the capital account surplus in 1984 to an estimated 41 percent in 1987. Private project-financing was initially negatively affected by the reduction in domestic investment. It has been recovering lately, however, and it is estimated to have constituted an important source of financing in 1987. This is partially due to the fact that Chile, deliberately, excluded from restructuring those loans that were associated with foreign investment projects. The effort made to meet these obligations is now starting to bear fruit.

Movement of capital by residents has been favorable from 1984 onwards. Despite the lack of adequate information regarding this flows, balance of payment figures clearly suggest a positive sign. The main mechanisms for attracting these resources in 1984–5 were dollar deposits with domestic banks and currency swap operations with the Central Bank. During 1986 and 1987, some of the foreign debt conversion mechanisms provided an extremely efficient channel for the repatriation of a surprisingly large amount of capital. As indicated in the previous section, these capital movements have been shown to respond in a highly predictable manner to interest rate differentials and exchange rate expectations. Chile's experience suggests that an appropriate combination of interest and exchange rates allows, not only the halt of capital flight, but its reversion as well.

As explained above, during 1983–6 Chile has been able to refinance not only amortizations, but also a major portion of interest payments. Naturally, the consequence of this is an increase in the nominal stock of foreign debt (table 8.4). An obvious solution to this problem would be to expect that, through successful structural adjustment, GDP and export growth will be high enough to induce a gradual reduction in the relative debt burden. The problem with this approach is that it demands an unrealistically large dose of patience, particularly when applied to an economy like Chile's that held, at the end of 1984, a foreign debt equivalent to 120 percent of its GDP and 4.6 times as large as its exports.[25]

By reducing the flow transfer to its creditors, the Chilean strategy clearly ran the risk of aggravating the excess stock of debt problem. In my view, this problem has two dimensions. One, that given the size of the stock of debt relative to GDP or exports it implies too large a variance for the consumption stream of the country's residents. This is uncomfortable not only to them but to their creditors as well. The other dimension of the problem is that the debt is too concentrated in a particular class of creditors. Both aspects of the debt problem call for a change in the structure of the debt, a financial restructuring process. The object of such a financial restructuring would be to move from a situation in which the debt is maintained only by almost a unique class of creditors (commercial banks) and through a specific type of contract ("sovereign debt" subject to floating rates) to a situation in which a plurality of creditors are involved and diverse contractual risk-sharing provisions are used. The idea is to reduce the risks associated to a high debt/GDP ratio through risk diversification.

It is beyond the scope of this chapter to develop a full analysis of this viewpoint. For the purpose of this exposition, an example of its application will suffice:[26] debt conversion mechanisms are exactly such a means of restructuring net foreign liabilities of a country. In Chile these mechanisms were established essentially at the request of the market. Central Bank intervention was called for to authorize (with some restrictions) these operations within the framework of the (tight) foreign exchange regulations prevailing in Chile, and because they required certain amendments to the rescheduling agreements with international banks.[27] From 1985 to date, these mechanisms have cut $2.9 billion of Chile's measured foreign debt, (table 8.7), some 20 percent of the medium- and long-term debt with international banks in 1985.[28] These mechanisms have offset the increases in the foreign debt accruing from current account deficits and the depreciation of the dollar (15 percent of Chile's debt is denominated in nondollar currencies), thus rendering the *nominal* stock of debt roughly constant.

The two most popular mechanisms are: (1) chapter XVIII of the Foreign Exchange Regulations, allowing Chilean residents to buy Chilean debt abroad and collect its value in pesos from the original debtors; and (2) chapter XIX of the same regulations, allowing foreign investors to subject the pesos obtained through an operation similar to the one described above to foreign investment treatment. In essence, the first mechanism allows for the use of nonofficial assets held abroad to prepay, at a discount, official foreign debts. The second allows for the conversion of publicly-owned or publicly guaranteed foreign debts into equity held by foreign investors, i.e., claims over domestic real assets. Foreign investors are given remittance rights over the dividends and capital value of these investments after four and ten years, respectively.

Naturally, a scheme such as this implies benefits as well as costs. Its most obvious benefit, the discount, is relevant only to the extent that there is a positive difference between the value the debtor assigns to its obligation and the value at which it is prepaid through debt conversions. In Chile, debtors (most of them private banks) freely negotiate the price at which

Table 8.7 Debt conversions ($m)

	1985	1986	1987 Q1	Q2	Q3	Q4[a]	Total
1. Capitalizations[b]							
DL 600 and others	101.1	51.3	2.4	1.7	–	35.0	189.1
2. Chapter XVIII[c]	115.2	410.6	133.5	94.6	160.0	205.3	1119.2
3. Chapter XIX[c]	25.8	203.4	225.6	49.9	71.5	258.3	834.5
4. Portfolio swaps[d]	41.0	27.2	–	–	–	–	68.2
5. Other[e]	88.3	275.9	65.1	64.5	95.4	102.2	691.4
Total	371.4	968.4	426.6	210.7	326.9	600.8	2902.4

[a] Only through end November
[b] Debt–equity swaps on original debtor companies by using the foreign investment law (DL600).
[c] Compendio de Normas de Cambios Internacionales, Banco Central
[d] Portfolio swaps among Latin American banks
[e] Includes write-offs of corporate debts and direct payments by private nonfinancial sector debtors without access to the official exchange rate market

Source: Banco Central de Chile

the conversion or prepayment of the debts is set. Thus, unless externalities are involved, the presumption is that the transaction is beneficial for the country as a whole. In fact, it can be argued that given: (1) the terms of the debts being converted (enjoying government guarantees and exchange risks hedged with the Central Bank); (2) the price paid to the Central Bank for the chapter XVIII's *cupos* (to be explained below); (3) the heavy taxation of remittances of profits on foreign investments (a flat rate of 40 percent); and (4) the restrictions imposed on profit and capital remittances, debt conversions in Chile are fewer than what would be seen in an unregulated situation.

Anyway there is a more subtle benefit associated with debt conversion mechanisms – that of facilitating a restructuring of net international liabilities in the sense explained above. Even if the discounts are not all that favorable to the debtor country, it may well be good to allow debt conversion if it is able to reduce the risk class of the stream of consumption that its inhabitants are entitled to. My contention is that a country with a foreign debt roughly equal in size to its GDP faces very high risks, and that by the use of unofficial assets held abroad (chapter XVIII) or debt–equity swaps (chapter XIX) it can significantly reduce its risk class. This is so because both are ways to reduce public foreign debt, in the former case by running down an asset that is only loosely tied to the country, and in the latter case by replacing debt with equity, a form of liability with residual payments that does not enjoy either commercial or exchange rate guarantees. The two alternative ways to achieve this same end, namely, to reduce debt ratios through higher trade surpluses (a higher real resource transfer in flow terms) or through debt forgiveness are too costly. They reduce the risk class at the cost of also reducing the expected rate of economic growth.[29]

The costs of debt conversion mechanisms are generally associated with the alternative uses of the foreign exchange devoted to the purchase of the debts[30] and to the destabilizing effects on exchange markets, fiscal or monetary policies that they allegedly may create. The experience in Chile demonstrates that there are ways to mitigate the negative side-effects of debt conversions. Chapter XVIII operations are rationed by an auction system by which banks bid for the right to use portions of a quota (the *cupo*) set twice a month by the Central Bank. The *cupo* (and its scarcity price) takes care of the effects of these operations on the (parallel) exchange market. Chapter XIX operations are approved on a case-by-case basis, seeking to ensure that they do not encourage foreign exchange outflows. Although this is impossible to achieve with certainty, Chile's balance of payments' results do not suggest any unexplained increase in outflows. In addition, the cash inflow of foreign investment has increased, not decreased. The fiscal impact of debt conversion has been managed by allowing public entities to behave as private ones: they may enter into a conversion only if they make a profit, that is, if the discount they get more than offsets the interest rate differential between domestic loans (used to fund the prepayment) and the external credits to be prepaid. Finally, the monetary effects have been controlled by a device just as simple as the previous one: by sterilizing the peso creation in the only case in which it happens, i.e., when the converted debt is owed by the Central Bank. Given the depth and sophistication of the Chilean domestic capital market this has not proved difficult. It is ironic that debt conversions are accused of creating all kind of unpleasant macroeconomic effects, after having been in place for two years in just the country better known in Latin America for its devotion to macroeconomic stability.

5   Conclusion

In my opinion, the case of Chile shows that a gradual "solution" to the foreign debt problem can be found, combining structural adjustment and economic growth. This requires, however, that it overcome great difficulties and challenges. Let me summarize what I think are the three lessons that can be drawn from this experience.

The first one is that structural adjustment takes time – much longer time than typically envisaged in the planning horizon of policy-makers. In Chile the structural adjustment efforts were initiated in the mid-1970s and the fruits are only lately (and slowly) starting to emerge. The current growth in exports, for example, would not have been possible without the private investment made in the past, some of them financed with the much criticized foreign loans of the late seventies and early eighties. This can be proved with "biological certainty": the fruit and timber being exported now come from trees that were planted years ago. Other examples of structural reforms implemented long ago that are only recently sharing their benefit are: (1) the fiscal adjustment; (2) the creation of a formal private capital market; and (3) the reforms of labor legislation.

The second lesson is that relative prices work. As has been said in previous sections, the Chilean evidence suggests that an adequate combination of key prices – exchange rate, interest rates, wage level – operates efficiently in bringing about the required adjustments on the demand side (consumption and investment) as well as on the supply side (exports, import substitution, employment). Also, relative prices are instrumental in securing the amount of foreign financing required for growth. The Chilean experience definitely does not lend support to any "elasticity pessimism". However, again, time is required to appreciate the full impact of relative price changes.

Finally, a substantial amount of foreign financing is required for economic growth. This results not only from the lags in the adjustment process, but from the obvious observation that developing countries are typically capital importers. Once this proposition is accepted, it follows that net real transfers from debtor countries to creditors should be small and/or last for only short periods. This means that the current emphasis on current account deficits and debt ratios – an approach shared by too many economists and bankers, both from debtor countries and creditor institutions – as the targets of macroeconomic programs should be replaced by a more balanced view. This view should not seek to reduce the (relative) stock of net foreign liabilities, but to reduce the risks associated with a given level of foreign debt.

In 1987 Chile witnessed the fourth consecutive year of adjustment and growth of its economy. 1988 was generally expected to be similar to 1987, in terms of economic growth, inflation and balance of payments results, unless a severe world recession or some other factor were seriously to undermine the current climate of stability. Few countries in the region can count on even one year of macroeconomic tranquility ahead. Starting in 1989, the foreign financing outlook appears less clear but again, ruling out a severe world recession, the challenges seem to be considerably smaller than those overcome in previous years. Also, lately, the fates seem to have decided to reward good behavior: terms of trade have finally started to improve, led by copper prices, although nobody knows how long this recovery is going to last. Keeping up the structural adjustment effort could be harder once the emergency posed by depressed terms of trade no longer exists. The true test of the structural adjustment could be its ability to survive a period of terms-of-trade bonanza.

NOTES

This chapter summarizes the Chilean experience as viewed from my position at the Central Bank of Chile. The opinions presented here are, however, strictly personal and therefore do not necessarily represent those of that institution. I thank Mariela Iturriaga for her efficient collaboration, and all my collegues at the Central Bank for many useful discussions on these topics. As usual, all remaining inaccuracies are my own responsibility.

1 For an analysis of the causes of the 1982–3 crisis in Chile, see Edwards and Edwards (1987), and their extensive list of references. My own views of some of the issues they cover are in Fontaine (1983).

2 The account in this section has some resemblance to that of Balassa (1984). See also Fontaine (1983).

3 Throughout this chapter, as typically done in Chile, exchange rates are defined as the dollar price of the peso. Thus a *high* exchange rate means in fact a *low* peso value.

4 Ironically, the fixed exchange rate policy was (initially) proposed and (later) criticized as being an anti-inflationary tool. In my view, it served the opposite purpose: essentially, it was to get the domestic private sector to support expansionary domestic policies through external credits.

5 Between December 1979 and December 1980 reserve requirements were reduced for demand deposits from 42 percent to 10 percent and for time deposits from 8 percent to 4 percent. In addition, some public sector deposits (Cuenta Unica Fiscal) also saw their reserve requirements substantially reduced.

6 Some of the accounts of the period give the impression that in 1980–1 the capital account was dramatically liberalized. In fact, many restrictions were lifted (Edwards and Edwards, 1987), but significant restriction on inflows remained up until 1982, and were always present on outflows except for a brief interlude in 1982. An important and often overlooked restriction was the obligation to convert the proceeds of foreign loans into pesos at the official exchange rate, simultaneously obtaining from the Central Bank permission to buy in the future the foreign exchange needed to service the loans. In my view,

this restriction unavoidably involved the Central Bank in external debt renegotiations when its foreign exchange reserves were not large enough to meet the
external debt service of the private sector.

7 Given the size of the terms-of-trade changes of the period, extreme caution is
required to make meaningful comparisons between national accounts aggre-
gates of different years. Table 8.3 follows the (eclectic) solution of showing both
the current-price and constant-price ratios (using 1977, the national accounts
base year, as the base for relative prices). See Cerón and Staplefield (1987) for a
rigorous analysis of this subject.

8 No consistent breakdown of investment figures between private and public
investment has yet been produced for the period. The estimate given in the text
comes from the subtraction of the nonfinancial public investment (from total
investment figures (Table 8.2).

9 Constant price measurements use 1977 relative prices. They show the adjustment effort in volume terms for exports and imports, consumption and
investment. To the extent that utility functions depend on physical quantities, it
is fair to say that constant-price figures are a correct measurement of the
adjustment efforts. I am aware that the opposite view can also be held: relative
prices (hopefully) should be equivalent to marginal utilities, thus rendering
current-price measurements an adequate proxy of the marginal efforts of
adjustment. The fact that, intuitively, constant-price measurements sound a
better proxy for the adjustment efforts, suggests, in my opinion, that these have
by no means been marginal!

10 More specifically, the Central Bank sets a reference peso/dollar exchange rate
which is devalued daily according to the difference between the domestic
inflation in the previous month and an estimation of the average (dollar)
inflation of Chile's main trading partners. The Central Bank buys (sells)
whatever quantity is supplied (demanded) by banks for authorized transactions
at a price 2 percent below (above) the reference price. The exchange rate (for
authorized transactions) floats freely within these bands. An extra-legal (parallel) market takes care of unauthorized transactions.

11 For an analysis of the effects of the devaluation of the peso on employment, see
Rosende (1987).

12 Several measures have been taken to expand and to expedite indirect tax
rebates and drawbacks for direct and indirect exporters. Also, small sized
exports are given a flat rebate equivalent to 10 percent of the export value *in
lieu* of these mechanisms.

13 The ostensible aim of this system is to isolate domestic prices of wheat,
sugarbeet and vegetable oil from short-run fluctuations of international prices.

14 Distributed dividends are added to earned incomes to compute the base for the
individual global income tax (*impuesto global complementario*). Thus, the tax
reform is a powerful incentive for reinvesting corporate profits. The tax reform
seems to have helped to increase corporate savings and investment, and to
improve debt–equity ratios in the corporate sector.

15 The 1981 social security reform established as an alternative to the old pay-as-
you-go system a privately administered fully funded pension system (Baeza,
1986). The fiscal impact referred to in the text comes from the fact that during a

(long) transitional phase the old system has to continue honoring its commitments (paying pensions) without counting on the flow of contributions of those (the majority) who chose the new system. Of course, this flow gets accumulated in the new pension funds (the AFPs) and shows up as a massive increase in financial savings. From 1982 to 1986 financial savings (M_7 in Central Bank jargon) increased at an average rate of 6.3 percent per year in real terms.

16 The most important programs were: (1) two rounds of internal debt rescheduling at subsidized (but positive) real rates refinanced at the Central Bank for small-and medium-sized debtors; (2) the establishment of a preferential dollar--foreign exchange debt service (already terminated); (3) the granting of exchange rate insurance (initially with a subsidy involved) for the rescheduled foreign debts of the domestic banks; (4) the purchase by the Central Bank of the bad portfolio of domestic banks with a repurchase agreement on the part of the share-holders at a 5 percent real interest rate, to be paid out of banks' profits; (5) the granting of subsidized credits to buyers of shares in privatized banks (*capitalismo popular*) and (6) the assumption by the Central Bank of losses by the financial institutions liquidated during the crisis.

17 In fact, most deposits of maturities over 90 days, mortgage bonds and public debt securities are donominated in a unit of accounting called *Unidad de Fomento* (UF). The UF is adjusted daily according to the inflation rate of the previous month. This creates a quasi-instantaneous indexation mechanism. Market rates on UF-denominated deposits and securities are a market indicator of the "real" rate of interest, something not typically available in capital markets.

18 In setting the IMF targets an important role has been played by a quite conventional demand for money equation (M_1-A) that fits remarkably well the data for the period. This same demand equation is used to monitor month-to-month changes in M_1-A. See Matte and Rojas (1986) for an explanation of the demand for money model.

19 Strictly speaking, net factor payments include remittances of dividends on foreign investment and interest earned from international reserves. Its main component, however, is interest payments on foreign debt. Therefore the ratio of net factor payments to total external debt slightly underestimates the rate of interest actually paid.

20 See note 9.

21 An interesting innovation was the introduction in the 1987–8 package of the "retiming" of interest payments. This changed the interest payment period from 6 months to 12 months, thus allowing a one-time relief currently estimated at $470 millions, scheduled to take place in the second half of 1988. A weaker version had already been implemented in 1985, when the interest payment period was augmented from 3 months to 6 months. In the case of the new version an interesting side-effect is that of fixing interest rates one year ahead of payments, a nonneglible feature when (as seems to be happening) interest rates are heading upwards.

22 A small fee was charged to both foreign and domestic credits for the use of the guarantee from 1986 on.

23 Key reforms were: (1) the deregulation of interest rates; (2) the creation of the

Unidad de Fomento as a fully indexed (to CPI) unit of accounting in which most financial instruments of maturities over 90 days are denominated; (3) the creation of large institutional investors, such as the AFPs (see note 15), and (4) some deregulation of insurance companies and commercial banks.

24 The two more active lenders have been the Interamerican Development Bank and the World Bank. The share of Chile's medium- and long-term foreign debt held by multilateral organizations increased from 3.2 percent in 1982 to 10.8 percent in 1986. This increase can be explained by (1) the comparatively low reliance on these credits up till 1982; (2) the SALs granted by the World Bank as part of the debt renegotiation package of 1985–7; and (3) a deliberate policy on the part of the Chilean government of presenting profitable loan projects to these institutions and setting realistic conditions for the disbursement of the funds. This attitude is essentially equivalent to the one required to successfully deal with private sources of financing.

25 This view – the so-called "muddling through" – has forcefully been put forward, for example, by Feldstein (1987). Also it typically lies behind every "medium-term outlook" formulated by debtor countries in order to get additional loans from their creditors. It remains to be seen, however, if the real transfers needed from debtor countries to their creditors, typically of the order of 2–3 percent of GDP, can be sustained for the (long) period needed to make those projections come true. Some of the difficulties were clearly outlined by Selowsky and Van der Tak (1986).

26 Other examples are: (1) the increase in the share of debt held by nonbank creditors (also seen in Chile); (2) "securitization" of part of the debt; (3) project-financing guaranteed by the returns of the projects, and (4) the use of hedging and interest-capping devices.

27 For a description of Chilean debt-conversion mechanisms see Garcés (1987) and Larraín (1987).

28 Note that the word *measured* is used in the text. It refers to the fact that these mechanisms do not in fact alter *net* liabilities in any meaningful economic sense (except for the discount), because they are funded with either unofficial reserves held by Chilean residents abroad or foreign investments, which are just another kind of foreign liability. Debt conversions, however, do reduce debt as conventionally measured. This reduction shows, however, an important economic change: a change in the nature of contractual risk-sharing provisions associated with these foreign assets and liabilities.

29 On this subject, I have benefitted much from interesting discussions with Lester Seigal, from the World Bank.

30 Alternatively this is sometimes put as the "additionality" problem. The underlying assumption is that only "additional" foreign exchange should be used to prepay foreign debts. Of course, using nonadditional resources for buying back debts at a discount may very well be a profitable investment from the country's viewpoint. At current rates, for someone expecting to pay full its interest, the implicit yield of buying back the debt at a 50 percent discount, is about 800 base points above LIBOR.

REFERENCES

Baeza, Sergio (1986) (ed) *Analisis de la Prevision en Chile*. Centro de Estudios Publicos.

Balassa, Bela (1984) "Experimentos de Politica Economica en Chile, 1973–83", *Estudios Publicos*. No. 14, Autumn.

Büchi, Hernán (1985), "Exposicion del Estado de la Hacienda Publica", *Boletín Mensual* del Banco Central de Chile, December.

Büchi, Hernán (1986), "Exposicion del Estado de la Hacienda Publica", *Boletín Mensual* del Banco Central de Chile, December.

Ceron, Irene (1987), "Oferta Exportable de Productos Agricolas: Evolucion y Perspectivas", *Centro de Estudios Publicos*, Documento de Trabajo N°87, September.

Ceron, Irene and Staplefield, Irma (1987), "Esfuerzo Interno de Ahorro y Crecimiento Economico. Evolucion 1960–86 y Perspectivas a 1995". mimeo, September.

Edwards, Sebastian and Edwards, Alejandra (1987), "*Monetarism and Liberalization: The Chilean Experience*". Cambridge, Ballinger. MA.

Feldstein, Martin (1987), "Muddling through can be just fine", *The Economist*. No. 7504, June 27–July, 3.

Fontaine, Juan Andrés (1983) "Que Paso con la Economia Chilena?", *Estudios Publicos*. No. 11, Winter.

Garces, Francisco (1987), "Comentarios sobre las Conversiones de Deuda Externa en Chile", *Boletin Mensual* Banco Central de Chile, April.

Gutierrez, Mario (1987) "Los terminos de Intercambio y la Economia Chilena: un analisis de la influencia de factores externos y efectos sobre la estructura de crecimiento interno", *Banco Central de Chile*, Serie de Estudios Economicos N°30, April.

Larrain, Felipe (1987), "Market-based Debt-reduction Schemes in Chile: A Macroeconomic Perspective," CPD Discussion Paper No 1987–2. World Bank, February.

Matte, Ricardo and Rojas, Patricio (1986), "Evolucion del Mercado Monetario en Chile y una Estimacion de la Demanda por Dinero" Mimeo. Banco Central de Chile, December.

Rosende, Francisco (1987), "Una interpretacion del Desempleo en Chile", *Centro de Estudios Publicos*. Documento de Trabajo No. 89, October.

Selowsky, Marcelo and Van der Tak, Herman (1986), "The Debt Problem and Growth", *World Development*. September.

Silva, Ricardo (1983), "Destino del Ingreso de Capitales", *Odeplan*. March

Staplefield, Irma (1987), "Oferta Exportable de Productos Pesqueros. Evolucion y Perspectivas". *Centro de Estudios Publicos* Documento de Trabajo No. 85, July.

Velis, Hector (1987), "Analisis Quincenal del Sector Silvoagropecuario 1981–85", *Centro de Estudios Publicos*. Documento de Trabajo No. 77, January.

Comment 1

Eduardo Aninat

Juan Andrés Fontaine's chapter is an interesting account and elegant defense of the Chilean official policies for economic adjustment during the period 1980–6. A by-product of the chapter is an active advocacy of the orthodox policy-mix applied in Chile in 1974–80.

Given limited time and space, I shall not proceed to discuss Fontaine's figures and calculations. I prefer instead to concentrate my comments on a few issues concerning the course of Chilean adjustment to the macro crisis of the early eighties.

The first issue is a confession. When Fontaine describes and explains the gradual structural adjustment process to the debt and terms-of-trade crisis in the Chilean case, he argues forcefully that it has proceeded in both an orderly and a successful way. In fact, when one examines the results achieved during the three years from 1985 to 1987 any independent observer has to agree that Chilean macro results have been better than originally expected: they came closer to a reasonable balancing of the foreign trade and savings–investment gaps; they proceeded systematically period after period; and they emanated from a set of more coherent public policies than those used by a host of neighboring countries also struck by the same disease. The degree of "market noise" has been, on average, much lower than that forecasted by a majority of educated economists for the Chilean adjustment process, and private business expectations have finally been rewarded by such a blend of coherent macro policies.

In fairness one should recognize the achievement of such goals. Among the causes for gradual and orderly success, one must list in prime position – as Fontaine does forcefully and eagerly throughout his chapter – the consistent management of the macro policy-makers. But I would add several other explanatory factors: strong co-operation from abroad in a particularly critical period (IMF, IDB, several World Bank loan programs, etc.); and an important degree of luck in respect of the timing of changes in the relevant external scenario for Chile (oil price decline; copper and other export price rises; delay of contractionary domestic policies in the USA, etc.); and last but not least, the very peculiar political regime ruling the country which literally, very strongly and rapidly, forced the economic medicine on the population.

Fontaine's chapter has two notorious flaws: the first is the absence of relevant space to describe and comment on the series of actions leading to the salvage of private business conglomerates and firms (including banks), via the process of emergency loading of financial commitments onto the fiscal accounts as a whole, and onto the Central Bank's balance sheet in particular; the drafting of special financial legislation (on some limited occasions even with the names of benefitting companies); the application of exchange-rate insurance schemes in the context of frequent and significant devaluations of the currency (at the cost of the Central Bank); the indirect replacement of the original private debtor by the Chilean state with regard to notes owing to foreign creditor banks (to the latter's joy and with his active collaboration) through the granting of government guarantees for a large part of the old private sector loans. In sum, the fiscal and Central Bank accounts provide a veritable "black box" for "debt conversion" measures, this time from private sector shoulders to public sector shoulders. Thus, the requirements placed on the Chilean public sector performance in the short run and the very long run, are particularly severe in the Chilean case. Annual fiscal accounting has shown positive results during the last three years; but the public finance space for policy-making has been severely constrained or restricted for decades in the future: an ideological side-benefit?

Nevertheless, the most important flaw in Fontaine's chapter is on different grounds. The old, classic and very relevant topic of the incidence of the macro policies referred to, is conspicuously absent from his work. In this sense, his argumentation has somehow avoided the most important issue when examined from the point of view of welfare economics. After all, the government's nice orderly accounting must have served some purpose in terms of specific population groups, at the very least for those groups who ended up conveniently unloading their old costly debts. . . . One of the most crucial issues concerning the foreign debt and terms-of-trade crisis of the 1980s is precisely the question of who bears the costs of the adjustment process.

Using Fontaine's figures on employment and unemployment, on consumer price index movements, on wage rate trends, and on domestic interest rates charged and paid in the capital market, I contend that there is a strong presumption in favor of the hypothesis that the larger share of the costs arising from the 1981–6 crisis have been paid by wage-earners and the work-force at large, a smaller part of the bill having been picked up by profit-earners, rentiers and capital owners at large.

True, it is very complex to translate changes in functional income distribution to personal income distribution. But the setting and symptoms observed during the adjustment process (at least in the subperiod 1982–6), tend to show rather regressive results in that area as well. Amongst the many instances for such losses accruing to the relatively worse-off groups in the population, is the successive retailoring of the fiscal budget: rising fiscal revenue items which impinge on the real incomes of the middle and poorer classes, and simultaneously reducing in real terms, the public transfers directed to specific target groups (public sector pensioner recipients among others). The evidence on income distribution change is nevertheless not entirely conclusive, mainly because the adjustment process has not been systematically analyzed from this very important perspective.

One must also remember that the adjustment process is far from concluded! There are several more years of private and social costs yet to be paid by various segments of the population on the road ahead to equilibria. This leads me to one last thought on the interesting chapter by Fontaine.

I cannot but agree with the author's statement concerning the fact that "the true test of the structural adjustment could be its ability to survive a period of terms-of-trade bonanza." It is clear from the facts presented by Fontaine that since Chile was able to refinance during 1983–6 not only amortizations but also a major portion of interest payments, the nominal stock of foreign debt has in fact increased. As such, much of the cost associated with the bargaining on real debt repayment has in fact been postponed to a future horizon.

The true final test of the whole strategy will thus come at a later time, that is, once economic conditions become sufficiently secure to permit the possibility of debt reduction, but also once Chilean political conditions become truly democratic so as to allow citizens to confront openly and freely the crucial trade-offs concerning that option *vis-à-vis* the recovery of consumption and welfare standards of the population.

Acknowledging that much progress on the macro balances has been achieved, it is nonetheless true that crucial issues are far from resolved in the case of Chile.

Comment 2

Dominique Hachette

My comments will deal with the genesis of the imbalance, fine tuning, the cost of adjustment, and the foreign debt strategy.

The Genesis of the Imbalance

A good explanation of the genesis of the indebtedness would have been welcome, since it would show the roots of the problems, adjustments and conclusions described later in the chapter. Unfortunately, it is missing. Besides, the author, in his explanation of the crisis, tends to minimize the responsibility of the authorities, leading the reader to think that the essence of the crisis described was foreign: two serious shortcomings in a chapter devoted to debt. The supply side was certainly foreign, but not the demand side of indebtedness. The demand for private capital inflows was the consequence of: (1) a boom in domestic expenditure and in the price of all kind of assets; (2) a significant rise in the accumulated foreign debt costs; (3) limited internal credit availability related to the monetary and credit policies tied to the on-going stabilization policies; (4) the interest differential between the effective rate on loans in domestic currency and the expected (*ex-ante*) rate on loans in foreign currency; and (5) incoherent macroeconomic policies which concluded in distress borrowing and moral hazards. However, the inflows of private capital do not appear to have been influenced, at least to any significant degree, by the fixed exchange rate during the period 1979–82 (this idea goes against current wisdom). In fact, the direction of causality may have been the reverse: the inflows of private capital drove the real exchange rate down by lowering the relative prices of tradables to nontradables. Had Chile at the time chosen a policy of floating exchange rate, it is likely that appreciation of the peso would have occurred anyway. Also, even if the inflows of private debt may have been influenced by their relative cheapening, the main factor behind the demand for foreign funds was an explosive surge of desired domestic expenditure – within the framework of relatively tight stabilization policies – fed by abundant world liquidity.

Finally, moral hazards were important in explaining the observed inflows of private indebtedness and surely more important than any risk reduction brought about by the fixed nominal exchange rate between 1979 and 1982.

Fine-tuning and Monetary Policy

The author indicates that monetary policy since the beginning of 1985 has targetted real interest rates, leading market rates to levels deemed compatible with the exchange rate and fiscal adjustments previously described. "All through 1985, for example, it was possible to induce an important reduction in real interest rates . . ." (p. 219). "A great deal of fine-tuning has been exercised on the exchange rate and the real interest rates" (p. 220) etc.

I am willing to share some of the author's enthusiasm for the beauty of his baby – the fine-tuning of the "real interest rate" – but I do not want to carry it too far. I think an alternative hypothesis can be valid and should be given more attention. In particular, the combination of a modest and declining fiscal deficit, stable rules for the exchange rate after 1983, a slow recovery of GDP and of savings, growing credibility in the macroeconomic management may have been sufficient conditions to set the interest rate trend and level. Of course, the Central Bank by acting prudently, if not passively, did not disturb this behavior. Anyway, the authorities should be congratulated not so much for fine-tuning as for coherent fiscal monetary and exchange rate management.

Finally, I share with the author the view that "activist macroeconomic policies can be efficient only to the extent that they are strictly realistic." However, I would suggest that fine-tuning and realism may sometimes be contradictory.

The Cost of Adjustment

Although the author focuses a significant part of his chapter on "adjustment with growth," the cost of adjustment does not come out clearly. The change in relative prices which generated a reduction in expenditure in absolute terms and relative to income after 1981, was not without the postponement of a major reduction in unemployment until the "medium term." The trend in unemployment is clearly downward after 1983. However, "in the period 1982–5, unemployment was over 15 percent, and over 20 percent if part of the fiscal programs of employment are included." In addition, some indicators suggest that the reduction in consumption, a consequence of the crisis, and further adjustments to this and to the debt problem, was concentrated on the poor. Consequently these developments tended to worsen income distribution.

In these conditions, it is a blessing that the cost of adjustment was partially postponed as foreign debt increased, as rightly pointed out by the author. The balanced view taken in this chapter would be improved if the author could analyze, at least briefly, this important issue considering its socio-political repercussions. Nevertheless, I do recognize that this distributive topic may, along with adjustment, be more related to the fall in terms of trade than to the precipitated accumulation of foreign debt.

The Foreign Debt Strategy

This is quite an interesting story. However, some comments are required. Firstly, relevant international comparisons on the domestic adjustment to foreign debt problems would require a good understanding of the domestic financial network which accompanied these adjustments. It changed the financial structure of firms; it created new obligations among productive firms and among financial ones, and the Central Bank; it prepared the way for changes in property, and in particular in foreign investment, etc. The author recognizes the "complex network of internal transfers between the Central Bank and the original domestic debtors," but does not go beyond the superficial recognition that the transfer problem did not create inflationary strain. This is insufficient especially when the only reasoning behind his analysis is the doubtful assumption of an efficient or well-behaved capital market, which nobody in Chile would take at face value.

Secondly, the author has shown us how the Chilean economy has undergone a major adjustment since 1982. He also has underlined the fact that, despite this significant adjustment, the country is financing only part of the interest on foreign debt and capitalizing the other. Debt is further increasing and so will the debt service in the near future. That is, Chile has not adjusted to debt apparently, only to terms of trade. These developments worry the author as he rightly senses that further adjustments are unlikely. On the other hand, the author concludes that "large" inflows are required for economic growth (his third principle). Unfortunately, he does not reconcile these two considerations which may appear as highly contradictory in the chapter. Rather, he concludes rightly that what "should be reduced are the risks associated with a given level of foreign debt and not with the stock of foreign liabilities." This conclusion is, however, incomplete. The only way out besides manna from heaven in the form of a *perdonazo* or improvements in terms of trade, is the further opening of the economy with a more aggressive export policy, where a tariff reduction should not be fully discounted, but where a generalized drawback should be put in place and where the exchange rate policy should be set for that purpose, and not used for stabilization objectives.

9

Colombia and the Latin American Debt Crisis

Jose Antonio Ocampo

1 Introduction

Colombia has been regarded in the international community as an exception to the disequilibria and mismanagement which led to explosive foreign indebtedness in Latin America. In the late 1970s indeed the country enjoyed exceptionally good debt ratios, which reflected the tradition of "prudent" economic management and the favorable external conditions which it faced in the second half of that decade. Nonetheless, like most countries in the region, Colombia experienced a sharp deterioration in macroeconomic and debt indicators in the early 1980s.

After 1982, the economy went through three different phases. During 1983 and the first half of 1984, a "heterodox" policy package was implemented, aimed at correcting existing disequilibria and generating a domestic recovery. However, due to the drain on foreign exchange reserves which took place during this period, it was followed by a phase of "orthodox" policy management with increasing external conditionality in the second half of 1984 and in 1985. The short but significant coffee boom of 1986 opened a new stage of development, characterized by the resumption of growth at historical rates and moderate fiscal and balance of payments deficits. Rising oil exports guarantee that this expansion will continue to the early 1990s.

Regardless of its good debt ratios and profile, its highly praised adjustment experience and its good export and growth prospects, Colombia has been unable to return to borrowing in private capital markets on a truly voluntary basis. Although the country has borrowed significantly since 1982, the lion's share of new lending has come from multilateral and bilateral institutions. This fact, in the face of record amortization payments in the following few years, and with the deepening world financial crisis, has recently led many analysts – including the major opposition party – to press for a rescheduling of debts with commercial banks. Although the government signed in January 1988 a new $1 billion loan from commercial banks, this was only possible after long and painstaking negotiations and strong political pressure on the banks by the US, other major DC governments and the leading multilateral institutions. The country may thus be placed in the near future in a position in which rescheduling may be the only feasible alternative.

This chapter reviews the evolution of Colombia's foreign debt and macroeconomic policies since the early 1970s and discusses prospects for the next five years. The chapter is divided into three sections. Section 2 considers events from the early 1970s to 1982. The evolution of debt indicators and macroeconomic policies since 1982 are analyzed in section 3. Finally, section 4 summarizes the current debt policy of the Colombian government and considers prospects up to 1992.

2 The Erosion of the Colombian Stereotype

From boom to crisis

The period of fastest growth in postwar Colombian economic history came abruptly to an end in 1974. The boom, which led to GDP growth of 6.5 percent a year since 1967, was based on three favorable conditions: (1) a set of coherent external policies adopted in confrontation with major multilateral institutions and the Agency for International Development (AID) in 1966–7, which included the crawling peg, stable export promotion policies and generalized exchange and import controls; (2) the expansion of public expenditure, financed by increasing taxes and by an ample and regular supply of foreign credits; and (3) the rapid growth in international trade and increasing real commodity prices (Ocampo, 1987b).

The boom came to an end with the contractionary fiscal and monetary policies adopted by the new Lopez administration – inaugurated in August, 1974 – to reduce the relatively high inflation rate which had appeared in 1973 and 1974. Falling coffee prices and the effects of world recession on nontraditional exports initially had an adverse effect on external accounts. However, the Brazilian frost of mid-1975 led to a boost in world coffee prices. The major preoccupation of economic authorities was then how to manage five consecutive years of booming coffee exports and current account surpluses. Since it was decided from the outset that the coffee sector would not play the major role in the stabilization effort (real domestic coffee prices were raised significantly in the early part of the boom, largely to accelerate the renovation of plantations), fiscal austerity was enhanced and a harsh monetary policy was adopted – including 100 percent marginal reserve requirements on checking accounts, increased reserve requirements for savings and term deposits and the partial sterilization of external surpluses by forcing exporters to hold foreign exchange certificates for 3–4 months before they could be sold to the Central Bank. Simultaneously, strong controls on capital flows were adopted and devaluation was temporarily suspended in 1977, leading to a significant appreciation of the currency for the first time since the crawling peg had been adopted (Sarmiento, 1982; Jaramillo, 1979; Ocampo and Reveiz, 1979).

The inauguration of the new Turbay administration, in August 1978, led to a radically different economic strategy: an expansion of public expenditure, accompanied by a contractionary monetary policy and a significant liberalization of import controls. The expansion of public investment was justified on developmental grounds – the need to integrate the domestic market and to face the energy crisis (Departamento Nacional de Planeación, 1979) – and by the urge to reverse the significant reductions in public investment during the Lopez administration, which in some sectors had generated demands which could no longer be ignored. As the expansionary government investment program was combined with rapid increases in public-sector wages – which had experienced a significant reduction from 1972 to 1977 – and, in the central government, with tax benefits granted in 1979 and leniency in tax administration, the consolidated public-sector deficit increased rapidly: from virtual equilibrium in 1978 to 7.1 percent of GDP in 1982, or 6.5 percent if the National Coffee Fund is excluded (see table 9.1).

The basic assumptions of this strategy were that the economy was close to full employment and that, due to imperfections in the domestic capital market, public investment could only be financed by long-term borrowing abroad. Thus, in the government's conception, import liberalization and monetary controls prevented the development of an inflationary spiral. Indeed, given the characteristics of the global strategy, these policies were complementary. While import liberalization redirected real demands created by fiscal expansion, monetary policy compensated the growth of the money supply generated by massive borrowing abroad. In 1980, however, the harsh monetary controls of previous years – which, by then, had generated a complete set of financial innovations to circumvent existing regulations – were replaced by massive open market operations in a free capital market (Jaramillo, 1982).

This set of policies was followed up to 1982, regardless of a radical turnaround in world coffee market conditions. Despite weakening prices, coffee revenues were kept high from 1978 to 1980 by record volume sales in an unregulated market. The collapse of coffee prices in mid-1980, after a period of growing instability led, however, to the reintroduction of the quota agreement in the last quarter of that year. Lower prices and volumes

Table 9.1 Basic macroeconomic indicators, 1970–1987

	Growth rates (%)[a]		Balance of payments ($m)[b]			Consolidated public sector surplus or deficit (% of GDP)[c]			
	GDP	Industrial production	Trade balance	Current account	Gross international reserves	Exclud-ing National Coffee Fund		Including National Coffee Fund	
1970	–	–	–20	–291	258	–1.0		–0.9	
1971	6.0	8.5	–152	–457	265	–2.5		–2.6	
1972	7.7	10.7	116	–201	393	–3.1		–2.4	
1973	6.7	8.5	260	–77	524	–3.0		–3.4	
1974	5.8	8.3	–47	–405	448	–1.3		–0.4	
1975	2.3	1.2	297	–127	553	–0.5		–0.2	
1976	4.7	4.4	560	189	1172	0.6		1.3	
1977	4.2	1.4	705	390	1836	–1.3		–1.5	
1978	8.5	10.0	667	330	2493	0.9		0.4	
1979	5.4	6.1	537	512	4113	–2.4		–0.9	
1980	4.1	1.2	13	104	5420	–3.9		–2.6	
1981	2.3	–2.7	–1333	–1722	5633	–4.3		–5.2	
1982	0.9	–1.4	–2076	–2885	4893	–6.5		–7.1	
1983	1.6	1.1	–1317	–2826	3176	–7.1		–7.9	
1984	3.4	6.0	–404	–2050	1887	–6.5	–6.7	–5.8	–6.7
1985	2.4	2.3	149	–1220	2313		–4.0		–2.7
1986	5.1	7.7	2007	659	3511		–3.6		–0.7
1987	5.1	6.3	1370	–482	3483		–1.9		

Sources: [a] DANE, Cuentas Nacionales, 1987: FEDESARROLLO
      [b] Banco de la Republica, 1987: FEDESARROLLO
      [c] DANE, Cuentas Nacionales, 1984–1987, right-hand column: Departamento Nacional de Planeacion

led to a fall in coffee revenues from an average of $2.1 billion in 1978–80 to $1.5 billion in the following years. This did not lead, however, to a redesign of balance of payments policies. On the contrary, economic policy enhanced the external deficit by increasing import licenses to a peak $6 billion level, both in 1981 and 1982, and by linking the peso to the dollar when the latter was experiencing the first wave of appreciation in international markets. Thus, by 1982 the country was running a $2.9 billion current account deficit (see table 9.1) and the peso was overvalued by some 30 percent with respect to its 1975 level, generally recognized as an adequate reference to determine the "equilibrium" exchange rate.

Economic growth was not fast in the second half of the 1970s, except in 1978, when extraordinary harvests temporarily reduced inflation rates, creating a windfall gain for all wage earners (Londoño, 1985). Slower expansion affected, in particular, manufacturing production – which for the first time in the postwar period grew at a slower rate than aggregate GDP – and commercial agriculture, and led to a significant reversal of efforts to diversify the export structure. These (mild) "Dutch disease" features explain most of the slowdown with respect to the 1967–74 boom. (The "Dutch-disease" hypothesis has been suggested, in particular, by Edwards, 1984, and Thomas, 1985.)

Deterioration of economic conditions was, on the other hand, dramatic in the early part of the 1980s. Indeed, as the country accumulated the highest ever external and fiscal deficits and faced a substantial deterioration of all debt indicators (see the next section), it experienced the worst recession in the postwar period. An orthodox interpretation of these developments would indicate that the expansionary fiscal policy led to the deterioration of the balance of payments. However, this account fails to explain why the economy entered simultaneously into a severe recession. An alternative explanation would argue that trade and fiscal events had independent policy determinants (import liberalization and exchange rate appreciation, on the one hand, and expenditure and tax policies, on the other). Exports were also affected by the evolution of international coffee prices and by the external demand for nontraditional exports. The recession may be seen in this light as a sign that the contractionary effects generated by the deterioration of external accounts swamped fiscal expansion (Ocampo, 1987a; Ocampo and Lora, 1987).

The "Latin Americanization" of prudent Colombia

The early 1970s closed an important chapter in the history of Colombia's foreign debt.[1] Debt and debt service ratios, which had been high since the mid-1960s, increased temporarily in 1971 and then started to fall at a fairly rapid rate. Improvements in the current account and the windfall gains generated by the unexpected acceleration of world inflation explain the favorable evolution of these indicators in the early 1970s. A significant change in the source of funds also took place during these years: AID ceased to be the major source of external funds, as commercial banks became the major financier of the country. As table 9.2 shows, AID – the major source of external financing since 1962 – still represented 27 percent of Colombia's foreign debt in 1970. Its share in net external borrowing fell, however, to 14 percent in 1970–4. Simultaneously, commercial bank lending, which made up slightly over a quarter of the external debt of the country in 1970, became the source of 61 percent of net borrowing in the

Table 9.2 Colombian foreign debt, 1970–1992 ($m)

	Public sector, medium- and long-term[a]					National Coffee fund[b]	Public sector enterprises, short-term[c]	Banco de la Republica, short-term[d]	Private sector	Total foreign debt	
	AID	Other bilateral and multilateral	Bonds and suppliers	Commercial banks	Total					Excluding short-term debt of public enterprises	Including short-term debt of public enterprises
1970	518	616	146	39	1.319	48	n.d.	106	457	1.930	
1974	723	990	220	287	2.220	106	n.d.	18	1.038	3.382	
1978	746	1.354	273	523	2.896	346	n.d.	11	1.164	4.417	
1979	736	1.503	252	965	3.456	379	n.d.	7	1.847	5.689	
1980	722	1.764	247	1.446	4.179	148	200	4	2.278	6.609	6.809
1981	702	2.026	238	2.202	5.168	288	188	3	2.874	8.333	8.521
1982	681	2.449	277	2.671	6.078	360	381	2	3.450	9.890	10.271
1983	662	2.955	278	3.063	6.958	559	295	97	3.596	11.210	11.505
1984	640	3.522	461	3.467	8.090	468	186	92	3.521	12.171	12.357
1985	619	4.632	573	3.608	9.432	391	596	246	3.415	13.484	14.080
1986	597	5.647	645	4.623	11.512	55	173	34	3.249	14.848	15.023
1992*	9.988			4.760	14.748	55	38	33	3.211	18.047	18.085

* Official projection

Sources: [a] and [e] Banco de la Republica (1987)

[b] 1970–80: Balance sheets of the National Coffee Fund; 1981–6: Republica de Colombia (1987b)

[c] Republica de Colombia (1987a), table 4

[d] Revista del Banco de la Republica, several issues

Projections to 1992: Republica de Colombia (1987b)

next four years. This trend was strong despite the fact that the government had since 1971 adopted measures to control private borrowing abroad (Jaramillo and Montes, 1979). Changes in the composition of external funds obviously led to a deterioration in credit conditions, particularly in the term structure of new loans. From 1970–2 to 1975–7, when Colombia ceased to receive new loans from AID, the average maturity of public sector medium- and long-term loans fell from 22.1 to 15.2 years and the average grace period from 5.2 to 4.0 years.[2]

The coffee boom accelerated the fall in the debt ratios in the second half of the 1970s. Five consecutive years of current account surpluses reduced the net debt and the net debt service to a modest 32.3 percent and 9.7 percent of exports in 1980. This trend was compatible, however, with two different phases in the evolution of the debt, which reflect the radically different economic strategies followed by the Lopez and Turbay administrations. Between 1974 and 1978, Colombia's foreign debt and that contracted with commercial banks grew at very moderate rates: 6.9 percent and 9.2 percent. These rates were significantly lower than those typical in the early part of the decade (15.1 percent and 27.4 percent). "Prudence" ceased to be, however, the major feature of Colombia's debt strategy after 1978. On the contrary, the rapid growth of public and private external liabilities, particularly with commercial banks, became the major characteristic of the debt scenario.

The explosion of the foreign debt with commercial banks continued up to 1982, when the Mexican crisis closed this source of funds to the country. As a whole, the debt with commercial banks tripled between 1978 and 1982, representing some 80 percent of net external borrowing. While the country continued to run current account surpluses in 1979 and 1980, and new borrowing was thus reflected in record levels of reserve accumulation, this ceased to be true in the following years. With booming current account deficits in 1981 and 1982, the favorable trend in the debt and debt-service ratios typical of the 1970s was sharply reversed.

Reliance on commercial banks after 1978 also resulted in an additional deterioration in borrowing conditions. Average maturities for new public sector medium- and long term loans fell from 15.2 years in 1975–7 to 13.4 years in 1979–82, as interest rates increased sharply following international trends; average grace periods improved slightly, from 4.0 to 4.3 years. Simultaneously, short-term liabilities increased rapidly. Although a breakdown similar to that presented in table 9.3 is not available for 1978, short-term obligations were some $1.1 billion in that year – i.e., 25 percent of outstanding liabilities.[3] By 1982, these debts had increased to $3 billion, i.e., close to 30 percent of the total debt.

Thus, as the debt crisis hit the region, "prudent" debt management had certainly ceased. The economy had entered the Latin American pattern of

Table 9.3 Term-structure of Colombia's foreign debt ($m)

	1982		1986	
		(%)		(%)
Medium- and long-term	7.270	70.8	13.392	89.1
public	6.078	59.2	11.512	76.6
private	1.192	11.6	1.880	12.5
Short-term	3.001	29.2	1.631	10.9
public	741	7.2	228	1.5
private: financial system	1.637	15.9	861	5.7
other	621	6.0	508	3.4
Banco de la Republica	2	–	34	0.2
Total	10.271	100.0	15.023	100.0

Source: Republica de Colombia (1987a), table 3

rising external liabilities to finance current account disequilibria, currency overvaluation and fiscal imbalances. By 1982 the extremely solid external position of the country had made a radical turnaround. With current account disequilibria of $2.9 billion, record short-term obligations and the closing of international capital markets, the threat of a rapid erosion of the strong reserve position of the country ($5.3 billion in mid-1982 and $4.9 billion in December of that year) was for the first time quite evident.

3 The Impact of the Latin American Debt Crisis

From crisis to (moderate) boom

The evolution of economic activity and debt indicators since 1982 may be seen as the result of a series of interrelated external and internal events. Between 1982 and 1984 the country faced a series of unfavorable external shocks, which compounded the effects of the 1980 collapse of coffee prices: the closing of commercial banks to new lending after the Mexican crisis of August 1982, the Venezuelan devaluation and adoption of exchange controls in February 1983, and hardening attitudes by the international banking community in mid-1984. On the contrary, the Brazilian droughts of 1985 generated in the following year a short but significant coffee boom. High quotations in the international market and increasing volumes permitted by the suspension of the quota agreement in February 1986 led to a rapid increase in coffee revenues in that year.

Internal events were mostly related to changes in government policy.[4] Three major phases in economic policy can be broadly defined: a phase of "heterodox" policy management (1983 and the first half of 1984); a period in which an "orthodox" policy package was superimposed on previous heterodox policy measures (second half of 1984, and 1985); and a final phase of growth with moderate fiscal and external imbalances (1986 and 1987). A final set of internal events was related to the discovery of important oil fields in 1983 onwards. Although partly the result of good fortune, these discoveries should be seen as a handsome return on long-term investments in energy induced by high international prices and by the exploration policy adopted by the Lopez administration in the mid-1970s.

The basic assumptions of the "heterodox" policy package adopted by the Betancur administration in late 1982 and in 1983 was that they had unlimited room for manoeuvre, given the strong reserve position of the country. Thus, it was possible to simultaneously pursue gradual external adjustment and internal policy targets. Balance of payments policies focused on traditional instruments: acceleration in the crawl of the exchange rate, adoption of a restrictive import licensing regime, stronger exchange controls, tariff surcharges, higher export subsidies and prior import deposits. Demand management did not play a major role in external adjustment. However, contrary to what the IMF and later analysts argued, this did not mean that the government adopted expansionary fiscal and monetary policies. On the contrary, significant reforms of the income, sales, departmental and municipal taxes were adopted in 1983 and 1984 and central government investment expenditures were reduced.

As the tax reforms increased government income with a lag, tax proceeds were adversely affected by recession and the government did not adopt policies to control the expenditure programs of public enterprises, the consolidated public sector deficit stagnated at fairly high levels (see table 9.1). On the other hand, monetary targets stabilized the growth of the money supply (M1) at rates consistent with historical or "inertial" inflation of some 20–25 percent. Given the rapid reserve drain which started in 1983, the rate of growth of domestic credit increased to compensate for the contractionary effect of falling foreign assets. This "monetary margin" was used to increase central bank budget financing (from 3.4 percent of GDP in 1982 to 3.9 percent in 1984) and to expand credit to the private sector.

The strategy led to a rapid improvement of the trade and current account balances. The former rose continuously from early 1983 and was in equilibrium by the last quarter of 1984. However, the deterioration in the invisible trade (largely due to reduced border sales and tourism from Venezuela), falling interest income from abroad and mounting interest payments meant that the effect of improving the trade balance was reflected only partially in the current account (see table 9.1). Furthermore, devaluation had been effective by late 1984 in reversing the real appreciation of 1980–2, although it was generally agreed that the peso was still overvalued. Improvements in the current account led to an initial expansion of economic activity.[5] Nonetheless, the recovery was short lived. After falling 0.9 percent in the first half of 1983 with respect to the same period in the previous year, nonagricultural GDP increased at an annual rate of 7.0 percent in the second half of 1983; by the first half of the following year that rate had decreased to 3.0 percent and tended to fall.

The major cost of economic policy in this period was a significant reserve drain. By mid-1984, gross international reserves were $2.1 billion, $3.5 billion less than the peak 1981 level. Reduced supplies of credit from commercial banks (see the next section) together with falling domestic demand for foreign loans[6] in the face of high current account imbalances explain the sharp reduction of international reserves. Given pre-existing disequilibria, it is unclear whether any gradual strategy – indeed any adjustment policy at all – would have avoided a significant reserve drain, or whether this process would have ceased had the "heterodox" economic strategy been pursued for a longer period. In any case, domestic pressure built up for a radical change in economic policy, which was finally adopted in the second half of 1984 by the new Minister of Finance, Roberto Junguito. The change in the attitude of the international financial community was also a significant factor behind this change in policy. Indeed, in the first few months in power, the new minister had to face the effects of an unfavorable report by the IMF regular consulting mission, the temporary suspension of negotiations of the first sectorial loan from the World Bank, and the pressure from commercial banks and multilateral institutions to sign a stand-by agreement with the IMF. The decision by President Betancur to host the meeting of Latin American presidents in Cartagena in May 1984 to adopt common principles in the face of the debt crisis was no doubt instrumental in the financial community's change of attitude.

The basic elements of the new strategy were active demand management and rapid devaluation. The effects of previous tax reforms adopted in 1983 and early 1984 were enhanced by the impact of two new reforms approved by Congress in December 1984 and mid-1985, which included an 8 percent tariff surcharge on most imports, the elimination of several exemptions to the sales tax, a forced subscription of government bonds proportional to income tax, a partial redistribution of earmarked revenues within the government, a significant extension of the withholding mechanism for income tax and the partial elimination of income tax exemptions for Ecopetrol and Carbocol, the government oil and coal companies. These reforms, together with a significant cut in the central government budget in 1985 and the establishment of controls on the expenditure programs and excess liquidity of major public enterprises led to a significant reduction in the consolidated public sector deficit in 1985 (see table 9.1). This policy was accompanied by a 32 percent *real* devaluation between the last quarter of 1984 and the same period in 1985, as measured by the weighted import exchange rate. These policies were superimposed on previous exchange and import controls. In fact, the former were strengthened in late 1984, when minimum payment periods for new imports were established. However, since mid-1985, the severe import controls adopted in previous years were partially liberalized.

Regardless of the radical change in economic policy, negotiations with the international financial community were difficult, as the Colombian government refused to sign a stand-by agreement with the IMF. The government claimed that, for domestical political reasons, this was not an acceptable alternative, that the country had not been subject to economic mismanagement, that it had good export prospects and that, in any case, self-discipline had been adopted. An attempt to use the World Bank as a countervailing force in the negotiations failed, as the private banks did not recognize it as an adequate interlocutor and through the first few months of 1985 insisted on a formal agreement with the IMF. Strong pressure by the Governor of the Federal Reserve, Paul Volcker, and by the US Treasury was crucial in the adoption of an intermediate formula – an IMF monitoring of economic policy – which was finally accepted by the banks in mid-1985. Although this opened the way to negotiations with commercial banks for a "jumbo" $1 billion loan, it did not represent the basis for a return to private capital markets (see the next section).

The orthodox program was mildly contractionary. The growth rate of nonagricultural GDP, which had been falling throughout 1984, reached a minimum of 2.1 percent in the first half of 1985. Annual figures also indicate the deceleration of economic growth in 1985, particularly in the industrial sector (see table 9.1). The country ran a slight trade surplus in 1985, a position which had already been achieved in the last quarter of 1984. The significant improvements in the capital account explain the sharp reversal in the reserve trend. Most of the improvement was not associated, however, with orthodox policies as such or, indeed, to an increasing supply of funds from the international banking community, but rather to specific measures which accompanied the program: controls on short-term capital flows of public enterprises, the establishment of minimum payment periods for new imports and the $229 million loan from the Andean Reserve Fund.

However, it was generally agreed at the end of 1985 that both external and fiscal adjustment had been achieved and that the economy was ready for a new phase of economic growth.

The strength of the recovery in 1986 and 1987 (see table 9.1) was associated, however, with two largely exogenous events: the coffee boom of 1986 and the discovery of new oil fields from 1983 onwards. The latter allowed the country to return to a net surplus position in its oil trade in 1986 and to maintain a substantial overall trade surplus in 1987, regardless of the collapse in coffee prices. Nonetheless, government policy has been successful in the past two years in consolidating the adjustment of external and fiscal accounts and in averting the unfavorable domestic effects of a very sharp coffee cycle. Real devaluation was not reversed in 1986, regardless of improvements in external receipts; rather, additional real gains were achieved, at least as measured by the import exchange rate. The significant inflows of foreign exchange in that year were used to improve the debt profile of the country (see the next section). On the other hand, the noncoffee public sector deficit continued to decrease, both in 1986 and in 1987. Finally, the countercyclical use of National Coffee Fund finances – generation of major surpluses in 1986 to sterilize part of the boom and absorption of the price collapse in 1987 – helped to avert both the inflationary pressures generated by rising coffee incomes and the contractionary effects of falling international prices.

The barrio effect

A brief look at table 9.2 may indicate that Colombia has been able to avoid the financial crunch experienced by most Latin American countries since 1982. Indeed, the country was able to significantly increase its net debt–export ratio from 1982 to 1985 – reaching in the latter year more than three years of exports of goods and nonmonetary gold – before falling during the 1986 coffee boom to some 70 percent of its peak 1985 level. This was not only the result of the collapse of international reserves, but also of the rapid growth of the total debt – 11.1 percent a year from 1982 to 1985. New public sector medium- and long-term debt commitments were highly unstable, but were kept high throughout the period: after increasing from an average of $1539m in 1979–81 to $2352m in 1982, they fell to $1392m in 1983, increased to a new peak of $2726m in 1984 and fell to $2302m in 1985. However, the short-term evolution of this indicator was to a large extent related to domestic demands and policies rather than to international market conditions. In particular, the fall in public sector commitments in 1983 was related to the untimely controls on public indebtedness established by the Minister of Finance in late 1982 to reduce the rapid growth of the debt. Finally, the net financial transfer[7] continued to be positive during the adjustment period ($240 million a year in 1983–5), in contrast to most countries in the region. This result was largely related to the favorable transfer of resources generated by direct private investment ($424 million in the same period), associated with the large coal and oil projects underway.

The impression that the country was not significantly affected by the debt crunch is not confirmed, however, by a closer look at the facts. In particular, Colombia has not been able to make good its historical record or even its most recent and highly praised adjustment experience in terms of access to commercial banks lending and reduced conditionality. As in most countries in the region, net resources from commercial banks have been extremely scarce since 1982, and the country has not been able to resume borrowing in private capital markets on a truly voluntary basis. Moreover, borrowing conditions deteriorated in the early phase of the debt crisis and have lagged behind improvements obtained by other Latin American countries in recent years. Finally, the country has not escaped negotiations with a cartelized banking community – to use the expression of Diaz-Alejandro (1987) – nor the multiple conditionality associated with these negotiations. Thus, the only truly exceptional treatment has been that granted by official lenders, which may be seen as having operated in a concerted way to prevent Colombia from becoming an unnecessary nuisance in the midst of the debt crisis. Also, the country was able to improve its debt profile by transforming its debt with commercial banks from short-term into medium-term liabilities.

Major changes in the composition of the foreign debt of Colombia since 1982 are shown in tables 9.2 and 9.3. The total debt with commercial banks has grown only marginally since 1983. In recent years, the share of these banks in net lending has fallen to 12 percent, compared to about 80 percent during the boom years of foreign indebtness (1979–82). The relative exposure of commercial banks has thus decreased from 64 percent in 1982 to 52 percent in 1986. Thus, the ability of the country to increase its global debt at a fairly rapid rate has depended entirely on official lenders – both multilateral (particularly the World Bank and the IDB) and bilateral – and, less important, on suppliers and moderate bond issues ($40 million in 1986 and $50 million in 1987). Public sector borrowing from these sources (excluding AID, which ceased to be a lender in 1972) increased from 1982 to 1986 at an annual rate of 23.3 percent, compared to 13.8 percent in 1978–82; indeed, net funds thus obtained – $3566 million – were equivalent to three-quarters of the increase in Colombia's foreign debt in 1983–6 (see table 9.2). Moreover, official agencies increased the supply of funds to the country, not only in the traditional form of project-financing, but through disguised balance-of-payments loans under several sectoral headings (export promotion, agricultural development, support for the financial sector, industrial recovery, etc.) and through a rollover mechanism managed by the Central Bank to accelerate disbursements.

Medium- and long-term loans from commercial banks to the public sector have increased by close to $2 billion since 1982 (see table 9.2). As this amount exceeds by a considerable margin the increase in the banks' exposure, it reflects major changes in the composition of the debt. As table 9.3 shows, this is part of a global transformation of short-term into medium- and long-term liabilities, which has also taken place in the private sector and has resulted in significant improvements in the debt profile of the country. Thus, at the end of 1986, Colombia was closer to its "debt stereotype" than what was true at the outset of the crisis. However, as we will see in section 4 of this chapter, the large amortization payments expected in the next few years, associated with debts contracted during the boom period of foreign indebtedness, indicate that the stereotype is not perfectly applicable at present either.

While the reduction of short-term liabilities improved the debt profile, there was a deterioration in the conditions of the new medium- and long-term loans contracted by the public sector. The average maturity fell from 13.4 years in 1979–82 to 13.3 years in 1983–6, while the average grace period fell from 4.3 to 3.7 years. Reductions were particularly sharp for loans contracted with commercial banks in the early part of the crisis (see table 9.4).[8] Simultaneously, the average margin over LIBOR for commercial loans increased from 0.68 percent in 1979–82 to 1.63 percent in 1983 and 1.44 percent in the 1985 $1 billion "Jumbo" loan. The latter spreads were generally better than those obtained by most Latin American countries during the first two rounds of debt reschedulings, though worse than those obtained during the third round; the term structure of both the 1983 and 1985 loans contracted by the national government were substantially worse than those obtained by other countries in the region. In recent years, the country has lagged behind the improvement in credit conditions obtained by Latin American countries. Thus, in the $1 billion "Concorde" loan, conditions (0.94 percent over LIBOR, effective grace period of 5.1 years and 10.1 years for maturity) are considerably worse than those obtained by most countries in recent reschedulings (see also the comparisons included in *La Nota Economica*, No. 23, August 15, 1987). Both in the negotiations of the Jumbo and Concorde loans, the banks have argued that conditions could not match those typical in renegotiations of past debt, as it was necessary to attract the banks into "voluntary" transactions (Junguito (1986); and "Notas Editoriales," *Revista del Banco de la República.* August 1987).

Nonetheless, the history of negotiations of these loans (Junguito, 1986, 1987; Garay and Carrasquilla, 1987; Lora, 1988) clearly dispel the "voluntary" character of the operations. Firstly, long and painstaking nego-

Table 9.4   Borrowing conditions from commercial banks during the debt crisis

	Maturity (years)[a]	Grace period[a] (years)	Margin over LIBOR	Special fees
			(%)	(%)
1. Colombia				
1979–82 (weighted average)	10.1	5.4	0.68	n.a.
1983–$210 million loan for				
the national government	5.1	2.1	1.63	1.00[c]
1985–$1 billion Jumbo loan	8.2	2.7	1.44[b]	0.75[c]
1987/8 – $1 billion Concorde loan	10.1	5.1	0.94	0.63[c]
II. Latin American reschedulings				
1982/3 – first round	7.3	n.a.	2.09	1.18
1983/4 – second round	9.6	n.a.	1.66	0.75
1984/5 – third round	12.9	n.a.	1.20	0.03
1986/7 – fourth round	17.0	n.a.	0.85	0.00

n.a. not available
[a]   From signing date
[b]   Weighted average of 1.50% for four years after signing date and 1.38% thereafter
[c]   Facility and drawing fees. In addition commitments fees of 0.5% on undisbursed amounts

Sources: I. 1979–83: "Notas Editoriales", Revista del Banco de la República, August 1987, table 2; 1985 and 1988: term sheets of the loans
       II. CEPAL, Balance preliminar de la economia latinoamericana, 1985 and 1987; country conditions weighted by amounts renegotiated

tiations with a committee of major lenders and participating banks were necessary in both cases (12 months from first contacts to the contract in the Jumbo loan and 9 months in the Concorde negotiations). Moreover, the negotiations were successful only after strong pressure was exerted on the banks by the US Federal Reserve and Treasury, by other DC governments and by the heads of the two major multilateral institutions. This process created considerable uncertainty in the country, as the government was forced to guarantee that foreign debts were served on a normal basis while negotiations proceeded. Secondly, distribution of the loans among participating banks indicates that both were in fact concealed refinancing operations. The share of the banks in the Jumbo loan was equivalent to 100 percent of amortizations expected in 1985–6 plus 7.5 percent of outstanding credits at the end of 1984, while in the more recent Concorde loan they have been equivalent to 80 percent of amortizations in 1987–8 plus 2 percent of outstanding loans at the end of 1984. Thirdly, some form of surveillance by major multilateral institutions has been forced upon the country in both cases. The Jumbo loan was conditional on an IMF monitoring of economic policy, as we saw in the previous section. The Concorde credit does not include this provision, but the government agreed to deliver to the banks the 1987 and 1988 IMF Article IV consultation reports. Moreover, the $200 million which will be used by the National Electrical Financial Company (FEN) are subject to a $300 million co-financing by the World Bank, drawdowns being subject to fulfillment of sectorial conditions established by the latter institution. Moreover, during the Jumbo negotiations, considerable pressure was exerted by the banks on the Colombian government to recognize the debts of the subsidiaries of Colombian banks in Panama, and to adopt policies favorable to heavily foreign-indebted Colombian private firms, including the redesign of the mechanism approved by the monetary authorities in 1984 to reschedule private debts. During recent negotiations, similar pressures have been exerted in relation to the foreign debt of the new paper company, Papelcol. Finally, the government was also forced in both cases to accept foreign jurisdiction in case of conflict. This led to considerable legal difficulties and delayed disbursements of the Jumbo loan by nine months.

Conditionality has not been limited, however, to the macro and microeconomic provisions just mentioned, but also to sectorial policies. This has been the major cost of the disguised balance-of-payments loans contracted with the World Bank in the past three years. Most important in this regard – given its global effects – were the liberalization clauses included in the 1985 loan for export promotion. Acceptance of this condition ended close to two decades of autonomous trade management. Liberalization proceeded smoothly in 1985–6, as it coincided with increasing supplies of foreign exchange and a rapid depreciation of the currency. On the contrary, it placed considerable burdens on government policy in the face of the speculative demand for import licenses generated by the collapse of coffee prices in 1987. With no major increase in the import budget, the speculative demand for goods under free licensing crowded out imports under prior licensing, leading to record turndowns of requests during the first half of 1987 (*Coyuntura Economica*, September 1987). Moreover, the government has been faced with increasing contradictions between its commitment to further liberalize the import regime – an assertion which has been included in documents presented to the international financial community – and its promise to protect new economic activities. The latter, together with the considerable uncertainty which characterizes the supply of foreign exchange, indicates that the country should not embark upon a liberalization process which it may not be able to sustain in the future.[9]

4 Prospects

The debt strategy

The current debt strategy of the Colombian government[10] is based on four premises: (1) the modest net financial requirements in the next few years, which reflect the absence of basic macroeconomic disequilibria; (2) the considerable amortization payments expected, which require, in any case, substantial new credits; (3) the significant redistribution of public expenditure necessary to implement the current development plan; and (4) the advantage of returning to borrowing in private capital markets on a truly voluntary basis.

Official balance of payments projections for 1987–92 are summarized in table 9.5. These forecasts assume 3 percent OECD growth, 4 percent world inflation, 8 percent LIBOR, high oil prices (close to $18 per barrel in 1988, constant in real terms to 1992), a constant real exchange rate and domestic GDP growth of 4.5 percent in 1987 and 4 percent from 1988 onwards. The table also shows comparable figures for 1981–4, the years of large external disequilibria. The remarkable improvement in the trade and current accounts reflect in part the adjustment policies implemented since 1983. Nonetheless, most of the expected improvement is associated with oil transactions. Indeed, the net change in the oil accounts – from a $336 million annual trade deficit in 1981–4 to a $1758 surplus in 1987–92, or from an annual deficit of $319 million to a $1336 surplus if service transactions are included – is equivalent to 69 percent and 106 percent of the expected improvements in the trade and current accounts. Since, according to the government, direct investment will finance a large proportion of the current account imbalance, net indebtedness is expected to be quite modest – $500 million a year, equivalent to a rate of growth of the gross and net foreign debt of 3 and 4 percent a year and unchanged exposure of commercial banks (see table 9.2). This is consistent with a further fall in the net debt–export ratio, as exports are expected to increase at an annual rate of 6 percent between 1986 and 1992 (see table 9.6).

Nonetheless, gross financial needs are substantial, due to the large amortization payments due in the next few years. Public sector amortizations will be four times higher than those typical in the early 1980s. Moreover, if international reserves are to be kept at present levels, the public sector will have to borrow on a gross basis on a larger scale than was typical in 1981–4. Large amortization payments will be largely associated with debts contracted with commercial banks during the years of booming foreign indebtedness. Amortization payments to commercial banks in 1987–92 will be equivalent to the total amounts contracted with these

Table 9.5   Balance of payments and financial requirements according to official projections ($m)

	1981–84	1987–92
A. Trade and Services		
Exports[a]	3.362	6.599
Imports	4.645	4.865
Trade balance	−1.283	1.731
Nonfinancial services and transfers (net)	−406	−370
Financial services (net)	−682	−2.169
B. Financial Requirements		
Current account deficit	2.371	808
Public debt amortizations	395	1.530
Multilateral	142	440
Bilateral	75	200
Commercial banks	115	770
Others[b]	63	120
Total financial requirements	2.766	2.338
C. Sources of Financing		
Direct foreign investment	410	395
Other private flows (net)	107	−27
Public sector (medium- and long-term)	1.424	2.029
Multilateral	442	792
Bilateral	220	297
Commercial banks	629	752
Others[b]	135	189
Public sector (short-term)	119	−21
Total sources of financing	2.060	2.377

[a] Goods and nonmonetary gold
[b] Suppliers and bonds

Sources: 1981–84: Republica de Colombia (1987a), tables 2 and 10
          1987–92: Republica de Colombia (1987b), appendix tables 17 and 21

agents at the end of 1986. Although this is also true of suppliers' credits, no major difficulties are expected to affect the contraction of new lending of this type in the next few years. Finally, amortization payments to official lenders will be equivalent to only 40 percent of commitments from these institutions at the end of 1986.

The new development plan requires, on the other hand, a substantial redistribution of public expenditure. The plan expects, in particular, that the share of energy, transport and communications in public investment will fall from 75 percent in 1987 to 52 percent in 1990.[11] This will allow the new social programs – agrarian reform, integrated rural development, rehabilitation of regions subject to political violence, basic health and education, day-care centers, water and sewerage, nutrition, etc. – to increase their share in investment. The intergovernmental transfer required will rely in part on domestic mechanisms, such as full income tax payments by Colombia's state-owned oil company, Ecopetrol, transfers from this company to the central national government and use of its surpluses to finance social programs in the oil regions. However, foreign debt service and borrowing play a crucial role in this transfer: heavily indebted public sector companies in the infrastructural sectors are expected to honor their obligations abroad, as part of these payments return to the central national government and other entities through new loans to finance the new social programs.

Rejection of a rescheduling strategy is not based, then, on the reduced amount of resources which could be involved in the process. Rather, when stating that amortizations are the *only* source of difficulties in the next few years, the government implicitly accepts that rescheduling payments to commercial banks would be a viable alternative. However, it has chosen what may be called an "implicit" or "voluntary" refinancing operation, in contrast to the explicit rescheduling strategy defended by the major opposition party. This choice is based, first of all, on the conviction (or, rather, the hope) that the country may return to borrowing in international capital markets on a truly voluntary basis. Secondly, the government has argued that the country has not been subject to rationing or higher costs in trade financing, nor has it paid any other costs associated with rescheduling operations. Thirdly, there is fear that an explicit refinancing strategy will alienate multilateral and bilateral institutions on which the country has depended heavily for new financing since 1982, as Colombia has played the role of a "showcase" for orthodox adjustment and debt strategies. Finally, the government fears that such an alternative strategy would generate financial indiscipline in heavily indebted public sector companies and would become an obstacle to the redistribution of resources necessary to implement the new development plan.

Critics of the official debt strategy have pointed out five major weaknesses of the current financing program (See for example Rodado, 1987; Urdinola and Kertzman, 1987; Marin, 1987; Sarmiento, 1987a, 1987b, ch. x). First, they have emphasized that the growth rates which it assumes – characterized as "vigorous" by the government – are lower than average GDP growth in the postwar period and insufficient to correct labor market disequilibria inherited from the recent recession. Secondly, they also pointed out the fact that the government strategy has worsened borrowing conditions, compared to those obtained by other Latin American countries in recent reschedulings (see section 3: "The Barrio Effect" above). Thirdly, the government program has been criticized for lack of realism, given present conditions in international capital markets. Moreover, some analysts argue that, even if the government is successful, after a series of long and painful negotiations, in getting new loans, this process would generate uncertainty about the availability of foreign exchange, which may become an obstacle to a sustained recovery of economic activity. Finally, the official strategy has also been criticized for the distortions it generates in public expenditure and budgeting, as current laws allow the government to spend only on the basis of new credits when the loans have been contracted.[12]

In the final section of this chapter, we will consider the relation between external financing and economic growth in Colombia in the next five years and the impact of probable developments in the international debt scenario. Problems associated with intergovernmental finances and budget programming will not be considered. This reflects the macroeconomic focus of this chapter, but also the view that, contrary to both the government and some of its critics, this type of consideration should lead to changes in fiscal laws or expenditure programs, rather than in the external financing strategy. It also reflects the fact that, from a global point of view, all external resources in the next few years will be used to refinance debt service payments.

Growth and debt scenarios

Official balance of payments projections should be revised in at least four major ways. First of all, they assume a constant 12.5 percent rate of growth of nontraditional exports. This rate is not consistent with existing econometric estimates and expectations of OECD economic growth. Secondly, the official estimates implicitly assume an unusually low income elasticity of demand for nonfinancial services (0.3). Thirdly, direct foreign investment projected is very high by historical standards. In this respect, a significant decline with respect to the first half of the 1980s can be expected, as large investment in coal has been completed and there may be some reduction in oil investment. Finally, official balance of payments projections do not include the effects of pipeline capacity and oil explorations on petroleum exports in the next few years. They assume that crude oil exports will increase to a peak of 268,000 barrels per day (b/d) in 1989, after which they will stagnate at 250,900 b/d. Alternative estimates by Ecopetrol (1987) indicate, however, that, due to pipeline capacity, exports in 1989 will be limited to 206,600 b/d, but as the result of investments in new pipelines and oil exploration, exports will continue to increase in the early 1990s, reaching 367,500 b/d by 1992. This alternative estimate indicates that oil exports will exceed the official projection by an average of 40,600 b/d in 1988–92.

Alternative scenarios were built on the following assumptions: (1) OECD growth of 2.5 percent, dollar inflation of 4 percent, except for nonfinancial services (3 percent) and coffee (2 percent), and an effective interest rate of 9 percent; (2) historical elasticities for the imports of goods and nonfinancial services, and for minor and nonfinancial service exports are applicable;[13] (3) direct investment is $100 million a year less than assumed by the government; and (4) alternative oil exports calculated by Ecopetrol apply. Under these assumptions, we simulated the effects of: (1) different domestic growth rates; (2) different oil price scenarios (a "high" scenario of $18 *v.* a "low" scenario of $15 per barrel in 1988, both constant in real terms to 1992); and (3) different exchange rate strategies.

Projections of current account deficits and the net debt/export ratio under these alternative scenarios are summarized in table 9.6. As the first two columns indicate, the net effect of assumptions used by the government is actually to underestimate improvements in the current account, particularly in the early 1990s, when additional expansion of oil exports can be expected. Nonetheless, these improvements would not materialize if oil prices remain depressed or if the Colombian economy grows at a faster rate.[14] As the last two columns of the same table show, even in the high growth-low oil prices scenario, a significant reduction in the net debt/ export ratio could be achieved, however, by a moderate real devaluation (3 percent a year), or equivalent trade policies, starting in 1988.

The major conclusion of these simple exercises is that, as long as the country is able to maintain its moderate debt ratios, the availability of foreign exchange would not become a constraint, even if the economy grows at fairly rapid rates. Thus, restrictions on economic growth can only originate in: (1) a very unfavorable evolution of the world economy (low OECD growth, very depressed oil and other commodity prices, or higher interest rates); (2) an extremely low return on oil investments; (3) adverse policy decisions (revaluation of the exchange rate in the face of oil abundance or further liberalization of imports); and (4) an immoderate low supply of foreign credits. In any case, given the uncertainty which characterizes some of the assumptions included in the projections, active exchange rate or trade policies are probably warranted.

Given the official debt strategy, the large amortization payments due in the next few years, and current conditions in the international capital markets, the possibility that the country will face restrictions in the supply of foreign credits is by no means remote. Indeed, the official strategy is equivalent to making *certain* amortization payments in return for *uncertain* loans from commercial banks. Such a scheme did not generate major problems in 1987, but could become a very risky strategy under certain conditions (an unexpected drop in the price of oil, a sharp increase in world interest rates, a world recession, etc.). Indeed, the revealed benefits of the

Table 9.6 Projection of the current account deficit and the net debt–export ratio under different scenarios

	Official projection	4% GDP growth, constant real exchange rate and high oil rates	5% GDP growth and constant real exchange rate		6% GDP growth			
					Constant real exchange rate		Low oil prices and 3% real devaluation	
			High oil prices	Low oil prices	High oil prices	Low oil prices	a	b
A. Current account deficit ($m)								
1988	946	535	590	779	644	833	724	682
1989	723	695	818	1.057	941	1.181	927	831
1990	856	49	257	641	468	852	411	247
1991	858	−7	304	749	624	1.068	390	141
1992	920	−9	428	937	882	1.390	413	58
B. Net debt–export ratio								
1987	2.28							
1988	2.22	2.13	2.14	2.28	2.15	2.29	2.25	2.25
1989	1.95	2.03	2.05	2.23	2.08	2.26	2.16	2.14
1990	1.93	1.66	1.72	1.94	1.77	2.00	1.84	1.79
1991	1.87	1.49	1.58	1.85	1.66	1.94	1.69	1.62
1992	1.81	1.34	1.47	1.79	1.61	1.93	1.56	1.46

Effects of real devaluation
[a] Imports of goods and minor exports sensitive to exchange-rate adjustments
[b] Includes also sensitivity of nonfinancial services to exchange-rate adjustments

official standing were so insufficient in 1987, as manifested in the sluggish negotiations of the Concorde loan, that the Minister of Finance was forced in October to inform the banks, in his speech at the Colombian Bankers' Association meeting, that were they not to collaborate, the country would have no alternative but a concerted rescheduling (Alarcon, 1987). As the government has to start negotiating a new (Challenger?) loan for an estimated $1.6 billion in mid-1988, it would have to consider anew its debt strategy in the face of the recent experience. It may well this time choose a rescheduling strategy, or may be forced by the banks in that direction.

The last but obviously not least important question relates to the response of the government to possible developments in the Latin American scenario. Events in 1987 have shown that "self help" – to use the moderate expression of Sachs (1987) – is an increasingly viable alternative, as demonstrated by the long list of countries which have adopted for extended periods a partial or complete suspension of bank debt servicing, the wider latitude for manoeuvre which these countries have been granted by the international financial community and the recognition of "debt realities" by major US banks. These events have, in turn, increased the likelihood of more aggressive solutions to the debt crisis which were given limited audience for a long time – partial write-offs, securitization of debts with commercial banks, etc. Were any of these "heterodox" solutions to succeed, particularly with (explicit or implicit) support from the major multilateral institutions and the US government, the basic assumptions of the current Colombian strategy would be completely undermined. Under these conditions, the country could hardly choose any but the "heterodox" solutions, as a highly *uncertain* access to new commercial capital on a voluntary basis (the uncertainty of which would clearly increase with the generalized adoption of alternative debt strategies) can hardly be a substitute for a *certain* reduction in debt service obligations. Indeed, only the (unfair) threat of retaliation from multilateral institutions and DC governments could lead the country in a different direction. Regardless of its good record, Colombia has not escaped the "Barrio Effect". It can hardly choose not to experience its more favorable dimensions.

NOTE

This chapter extensively uses results from a larger project on "Monetary and Financial Policies in an Open Economy" financed by the International Development Research Centre of Canada.

 1 For an analysis of foreign debt trends in the 1970s and early 1980s, see Perry *et al.* (1981), Villar (1983), Ocampo (1988) and "Notas Editoriales", *Revista del Banco de la Republica*, November 1986.

2 These and similar estimates in this chapter are calculated from Banco de la Republica (1987) and refer to weighted averages of annual data included in this publication.
3 This estimate is based on the debts of the domestic financial sector, 30 per cent of debts of the obligations of private nonfinancial companies and the external liabilities of the National Coffee Fund.
4 For a detailed analysis of economic policy in this period see Junguito (1986), Garay and Carrasquilla (1987), Ocampo (1987a), Ocampo and Lora (1987) and the several issues of *Coyuntura Económica*. For the sake of brevity, the discussion will refer only to some macroeconomic policies and indicators.
5 An unexpected reduction in food price inflation also generated a windfall gain for wage earners, which reinforced the recovery.
6 Most of the reduction in the domestic demand for foreign loans was associated with changing import trends. Management of the short-term liabilities of public enterprises and the National Coffee Fund was also crucial, while capital flight played a secondary role (see Ocampo, 1987a).
7 The net financial transfer is defined here as the capital account plus the financial service transactions balances. It thus includes short- and long-term debts and direct foreign investment.
8 Only loans contracted by the national government since 1982 are included in the tables. Conditions for commercial loans to other public sector entities have been generally worse.
9 "Notas Editoriales", *Revista del Banco de la República*, April 1987; Departamento Nacional de Planeacion (1987), pp. 282–8; and INCOMEX (1987).
10 See República de Colombia (1987a and 1987b); "Notas Editoriales", *Revista del Banco de la República*, August 1987; and Cabrera (1987). See also a defense of the government strategy in Palacios (1987).
11 Departamento Nacional de Planeacion (1987), Table 6, p. 317.
12 Contraloria General de la Republica, *Informe Financiero Mensual*, August 1987, p. 14.
13 Income and price elasticity of demand for imports of goods are assumed to be 1.0 and −0.5, following Villar (1985). For minor exports, disaggregated elasticities estimated by Villar (1984) are used, weighted by 1985 shares in trade. The overall price elasticity calculated is 0.9, while the income elasticity (assumed to apply to OECD economic growth) is 2.0. For imports of nonfinancial services, income and price elacticities are 1.0 and −0.5. For the exports of nonfinancial services, a price elasticity of 0.5 is superimposed on official projections. Price elasticities for nonfinancial services are derived from Correa (1985).
14 Terrorist attacks on oil pipelines may also reduce export revenues, as has been shown in the first few months of 1988. Nonetheless, coffee prices may be more favorable, as recent events in the world market seem to indicate.

REFERENCES

Alarcon, Luis Fernando (1987), "Discurso de clausura de la XXV Convencion Bancaria". Mimeo, Cartagena, October 29th–30th.

Banco de la Republica (1987), *Deuda Externa de Colombia, 1970–1986*. Mimeo, April.

Cabrera, Mauricio (1987), "Notas sobre la estrategia colombiana de endeudamiento externo en el mercado voluntario de capitales", *Debates de Coyuntura Economica*. No. 6, June.

Correa, Patricia (1985), *Determinantes de la cuenta de servicios no financieros de la balanza cambiaria colombiana, 1974–1983*, MA thesis, Universidad de los Andes.

Departamento Nacional de Planeacion (1979), *Plan de Integracion National*. Bogota.

Departamento Nacional de Planeacion (1987), *Plan de Economia Social*. Bogota.

Díaz-Alejandro, Carlos F. (1987) "Some Aspects of the Development Crisis in Latin America", in Rosemary Thorp and Laurence Whitehead (eds), *Latin American Debt and the Adjustment Crisis*. London: Macmillan.

Ecopetrol (1987), "Plan de Desarrollo Ecopetrol Año 2000". Mimeo, Direccion de Planeacion Corporativa, August.

Edwards, Sebastian (1984), "Coffee, Money and Inflation in Colombia", *World Development*. Vol. 12, No. 11–12.

Garay, Luis Jorge and Alberto Carrasquilla (1987), "Dinamica del desajuste y proceso de saneamiento economico en Colombia en la decada de los ochenta", *Ensayos sobre politica económica*. No. 11, June.

INCOMEX (1987), "Lineamientos de la politica de comercio exterior", *Comercio Exterior*. Vol. 20, No. 1, September.

Jaramillo, Juan Carlos (1979), "Colombia: Sector Externo, 1977", *Revista del Banco de la Republica*. March-April.

Jaramillo, Juan Carlos (1982), "La liberacion del mercado financiero", *Ensayos sobre politica economica*. No. 1, March.

Jaramillo, Juan Carlos and Fernando Montes (1979), "El comportamiento de endeudamiento privado externo para la financiacion de las importaciones, 1971–1977", *Revista del Banco de la Republica*. March.

Junguito, Roberto (1986), *Memoria del Ministro de Hacienda, Julio 1984-Septiembre 1985*. Bogota: Banco de la Republica.

Junguito, Roberto (1987), "El problema de la deuda externa de America Latina y la posicion de Colombia", in Jose Antonio Ocampo and Eduardo Sarmiento (eds), *¿Hacia un nuevo modelo de desarrollo? Un debate*. Bogota: Tercer Mundo-FEDESARROLLO-Universidad de los Andes.

Londoño, Juan Luis (1985), "Ahorro y gasto en una economia heterogenea: el rol macroeconomico del mercado de alimentos, *Coyuntura Economica*. Vol. 15, No. 4, December.

Lora, Eduardo (1988), "Colombia durante la crisis de la deuda externa: Un caso de excepcion?", in Eduardo Lora and Jose Antonio Ocampo, *La deuda externa colombiana: de la moratoria de los treintas a la encrucijada de los ochentas*, Bogota: FEDESARROLLO-Tercer Mundo.

Marin, Rodrigo (1987), "La reprogramacion: una propuesta con fundamento", *Economia Colombiana*. July-August.

Ocampo, Jose Antonio (1987a), "Crisis and Economic Policy in Colombia, 1980–5", in Rosemary Thorp and Laurence Whitehead (eds), *Latin American Debt and the Adjustment Crisis*. London: Macmillan.

Ocampo, Jose Antonio (1987b), "Foreign Assistance and Development in Colombia". Paper presented in the Conference on "Aid, Capital Flows and Development", World Bank: Institute for Contemporary Studies, Tailloires, France, September.

Ocampo, Jose Antonio (1988), "Cuatro decadas de endeudamiento externo colombiano", in Eduardo Lora and Jose Antonio Ocampo, *La deuda externa colombiana: de la moratoria de los treintas a la encrucijada de los ochentas.* Bogota: FEDESARROLLO-Tercer Mundo.

Ocampo, Jose Antonio and Edgar Reveiz (1979), "Bonanza cafetera y economia concertada", in Edgar Reveiz (ed.), *La cuestion cafetera.* Bogota: CEDE, Universidad de los Andes.

Ocampo, Jose Antonio and Eduardo Lora (1987), "Colombia", in *Stabilization and Adjustment Policies and Programmes.* Country Study No. 6, Helsinki: WIDER.

Palacios, Hugo (1987), "El financiamiento externo colombiano entre 1987 y 1990: Negociacion o reprogramacion?", *Debates de Coyuntura Economica.* No. 6, June.

Perry, Guillermo, Roberto Junguito and Nohora de Junguito (1981), "Politica economica y endeudamiento externo en Colombia, 1970–1980", *Desarrollo y Sociedad.* No. 6, July.

Republica de Colombia (1987a) *Programacion Financiera, 1987–1990.* May 4–8.

Republica de Colombia (1987b) *Economic Information Memorandum.* September.

Rodado N. Carlos (1987), *El debate sobre la deuda externa.* Bogota: Camara de Representantes.

Sachs, Jeffrey (1987), "Some Alternatives for Managing the Debt Crisis in Latin America". Mimeo, Inter-American Dialogue, July.

Sarmiento, Eduardo (1982), *Inflacion, produccion y comercio internacional.* Bogota: Procultura-FEDESARROLLO.

Sarmiento, Eduardo (1987a), "Del ajuste a la refinanciacion de la deuda", *El Espectador.* June 14th, p.4-D.

Sarmiento, Eduardo (1987b), *Hacia un modelo de crecimiento equitativo.* Bogota: Universidad de los Andes.

Thomas, Vinod (1985), *Linking Macroeconomic Policies for Adjustment with Growth: The Colombian Experience.* Baltimore: John Hopkins University Press.

Urdinola, Antonio and Fanny Kertzman (1987), "La deuda externa colombiana: ¿La penultima moda?", *Debates de Coyuntura Economica.* No. 6, June.

Villar, Leonardo (1983), "Nuevas tendencias del endeudamiento externo colombiano", *Coyuntura Economica.* Vol. 13, No. 3, September.

Villar, Leonardo (1984), "Determinantes de la evolucion de las exportaciones menores en Colombia, 1960–1981", *Coyuntura Economica.* 14:3, October.

Villar, Leonardo (1985), "Determinantes de las importaciones en Colombia: Un analisis econometrico", *Ensayos sobre politica economica.* No. 8, December.

Comment

Jorge Marshall R.

It is important to emphasize the conclusion drawn from José Ocampo's paper: Colombia's good behavior – even according to the international banking system and the IMF – has not meant a greater access to the voluntary financial market. In other words, the benefits from sound macro-economic management in Latin America are unevenly distributed between creditors and debtors. This is because they do not generate new financing from foreign banks. Thus, the Colombian experience reinforces the dissat-isfaction of Latin America with the current strategy to solve the debt problem. At the same time, it reduces the expected cost of heterodox solutions for the debt crisis, while the orthodox way does not lead to the voluntary resumption of lending for the foreseeable future.

Ocampo's chapter analyzes in detail Colombia's economic evolution from the crisis of 1982 up to the government's economic program for the period 1987–90. The size of the public sector deficit, the exchange rate and monetary policy were all key factors in explaining the stability of Colom-bia's economy, when compared with other experiences in Latin America. But looking at the evolution of the domestic adjustment process, it is worth noting changes in economic policy such as the one produced during Betancur's government. In the first phase, a program of nonrecessive adjustment was implemented based on expenditure-switching policies as well as import substitution and export promotion, all of which CEPAL would term an efficient adjustment program. During this stage, aggregate demand was not used to reduce imports.

In terms of trade balance the result of this package was successful, even in the short run. However, the neglect of macroeconomic management led to a quick loss of reserves during 1984. This new situation demanded a change in the government's economic policy. This time Colombia followed a rather orthodox prescription, based on a strict management of the aggregate demand.

This experience shows, on the one hand, that there is room for im-plementing nonrecessive adjustment policies. The management of the exchange rate is doubtless the most salient variable for this purpose. But, on the other hand, macroeconomic management, – monetary and fiscal policy – is essential during the adjustment process. Before too long, inadequate fiscal and monetary policies may prevent the achievement of recomposition of the demand and aggregate supply.

The chapter under discussion also presents the subject of the conditionality of the World Bank and IMF programs. Before going into a deeper analysis of the subject, it is interesting to take a retrospective view of the diagnosis and conditionality of the supervision programs signed by Colombia and the IMF in 1985. Although Ocampo does not pay much attention to this aspect, the available data make it possible to state that in Colombia the adjustment was more recessive than necessary, even taking foreign financing as given. Again it appears that Colombia has received less financing than other debtors in Latin America.

On the subject of conditionality, Ocampo emphasizes the loss of autonomy over the domestic economic policy as a result of the conditions of World Bank loans. I do not intend to discuss that here; however, it seems necessary to accentuate the benefits obtained by a country that keeps a close relationship of consultation and discussion with international institutions such as the World Bank. For those countries with strong fluctuations in economic policy in the last two or three decades, and there are many in Latin America, it is interesting to note the important role played by the consulting groups and other mechanisms in the internal debate.

The relationship with the World Bank has allowed Colombia to keep high levels of public investment, as well as a stable real exchange rate. Both are significant factors in the stable growth of that country. Thus, the problem seems to be in the renewal of World Bank and IMF conditionality so as to give a greater priority to national interests during critical periods.

Regarding the problem of access to the voluntary financing market, the Colombian experience proves the rigidity of the criteria of the international banking system, and at the same time suggests the need to find new financial strategies. In particular, countries should seek gradual access to foreign financing markets, linking such a process to the structural change of the economy.

Latin America will be able to go back voluntarily to the foreign capital markets as long as it regains credibility in its capacity to repay. But it has to be accepted that repayment capacity related to new exports and efficient import substitution is fundamentally different from that on loans given to the country through the domestic financial system. Here we are confronted by a failure in the foreign capital market, which does not take into account information about profitability and the payment capacity of different domestic activities.

An adequate system of guarantees, in which creditors, the government and the World Bank could participate, would allow partial and selective access to the foreign capital market so as to finance new investments in the tradable goods sector. This is the case with some investment funds which are appearing recently in some countries. A strategy of selective external financing may contribute to the growth of tradable activities, which is an essential component of a more equitable adjustment in Latin America.

10

Mexico's Debt Burden

Francisco Gil-Diaz

1 Introduction

The foreign debt problem is now old enough for several issues which two or three years ago were the subject of heated discussion now to seem to be fairly well settled. Most notably, it is now evident that the combination of economic growth in the developed economies, with its favorable effect on debtor countries' exports, and *ad hoc* packages of structural adjustment and additional financing to the indebted nations have not generated a solution acceptable to all the parties involved. Thus, after several years of painful effort, the resumption of steady growth is still not an imminent prospect – to say the least – for most of the debtor nations, while on the other hand banks have seen the prices of their shares diminish.

This chapter attempts, first, to illustrate how, despite considerable adjustment, the servicing of the external debt remains an exceedingly heavy drain on public resources and foreign exchange.

In the second section of the chapter the Mexican external debt crisis of the late thirties is briefly re-examined. The relatively short period in which the current debt crisis originated and the sources of Mexico's foreign debt are analyzed in sections 3 and 4. Section 5 examines the implications of the external debt for the growth prospects of the Mexican economy and section 6 analyzes the Mexican adjustment strategy of the last few years. The chapter concludes with an assessment of what the future may hold in store.

2 The Suarez–Lamont Agreement

In some recent contributions to the contemporary debt-crisis literature, it has become commonplace to make at least a passing remark on the debt problems and defaults of the thirties. This brief historical incursion shows that Mexico's historical experience of foreign debt contains more lessons and wisdom than is currently realized.

At the end of the 1930s, Mexico faced a foreign debt which had several causes: (1) the unpaid debts of the nineteenth century and those debts acquired up to 1913, when lenders finally realized that the ongoing Mexican Revolution was creating havoc; (2) the debt of the Mexican railways; (3) the amounts owed to foreign proprietors of land expropriated because of land reform; (4) the claims by shareholders of the oil companies which were nationalized; (5) the foreign debt of some Mexican states; and (6) accumulated interest on unpaid amount minus the small payments Mexico was able to make in the 1923–7 period, before President Elias-Calles suspended all payments because of the difficult economic and financial situation of the country.

Throughout all this period, even after defaulting, the Mexican government repeatedly tried to reach an agreement with its creditors. It wished to find a mutually acceptable solution so that Mexico should again receive voluntary capital, because of the urgent need for infrastructure and basic social expenditures which required some inflationary finance. This was quite apart from servicing the foreign debt. Finally, in 1942, thanks in no small part to the brilliant and prolonged efforts of Eduardo Suarez,[1] (Suarez, 1965 and Bazant, 1968) foreigners' claims on Mexico, which had reached $510 million in 1942, were reduced to $43 million. On the same lines, in 1946 the remaining foreign debt related to the railways was reduced from $558 million to only $50 million.

Thus, with two strokes, Mexico's foreign debt was reduced to a little less than one tenth of its former value. As a result, the country was able to gradually re-enter international markets.

After eight years (1946–54) of punctually servicing its restructured foreign obligations, Mexico started slowly and prudently to increase its net indebtedness in foreign capital markets. This source of savings allowed it to continue growing without having recourse to the inflationary tax, as had been the case throughout the forties and early fifties.

3 Recent Trends in Mexico's Foreign Debt

High budget deficits from 1972 to the end of that decade increased Mexico's public foreign debt from $6.7 billion in 1971 to $39.8 billion in 1979. More recently, from the first quarter of 1980 to the first quarter of 1983, Mexico's public foreign debt doubled and its private foreign debt almost tripled in nominal terms. In that same period, Mexico's total foreign debt in real 1978 dollars net of the international reserves of the Central Bank increased 85 percent. Using whichever criteria one may wish to measure Mexico's foreign debt, in two years it acquired breathtaking increases from already high levels.

As is widely known, in August of 1982, as its internal macroeconomic troubles finally led foreign banks to practically curtail lending, Mexico had to suspend payments on the principal due on its public foreign debt as well as on private interest payments abroad. Because of the deep economic problems at the time, accompanied by unprecedented inflation, the sheer magnitude of the debt service precluded an immediate internal adjustment sufficient to allow Mexico to continue to service its debt in normal terms.

The debt was restructured in three stages. The first involved $18.8 billion of public debt which was extended to eight years including four years of grace, and included all principal repayments on the external public debt due between August 1982 and December 1984. The interest rate was 1 7/8 percent above LIBOR. The second stage (August 1985) involved the restructuring of $48.7 billion of maturities falling due between 1985 and 1990. This agreement meant larger repayment periods, lower spreads, no commission and the use of basic interest rates which reflected the cost of funds to creditor banks. Even though the 1985 debt restructuring eased the debt service burden, the sharp reduction in oil prices in 1986 made it necessary to return to the bargaining table. The outcome (March 1987) included the restructuring of $4.7 billion dollars of the external public debt over a 20-year period with seven years of grace; a reduction of the spread over LIBOR from 1.2 to 0.81 percentage points and the provision of new funds ($14 billion). This arrangement contained a creative package which, among other things, included a trigger of additional lending if the oil price fell below a critical level, while lesser amounts would be lent if the average oil price exceeded a certain threshold.

The agreement was indeed path-breaking, although it still was a once-and-for-all kind of deal. It was a sort of automatic refinancing mechanism based on the attainment of certain goals and contingent upon conditions external to the borrowing country, but it was only one shot. Even so it was ingeniously devised and might be a constructive precedent for a long-lasting solution. Another interesting characteristic is that the IMF agreement upon which the new loans were based contained more than one definition of the budget deficit. In the agreement there are the traditional public sector borrowing requirements but also the primary deficit and the operational deficit.

It was not only fresh money for the public sector that was included in the history of Mexico's debt in the past five years. The private sector's debt which reached the unbelievably high figure of $22.5 billion at the beginning of 1983, including commercial bank loans, interfirm credits and suppliers' credits, experienced a remarkable decrease of $9 billion up to the end of 1987. Some large amounts were paid off in the second half of 1987 as banks sold heavily discounted private loans in order to avoid restructuring most of this debt for an additional 20 years at the beginning of 1988. This had been agreed in the 1986 restructuring when the payment term for the public sector's debt was extended further.

In terms of constant US dollars, the trend of Mexico's foreign debt shows a marked reduction (see table 10.1). Total foreign public debt net of the international reserves of the Central Bank (NFD) reached a maximum of $61.4 billion at the beginning of 1983, almost double the amount of the first quarter of 1980. From its maximum value it had fallen 22.2 percent in real terms by the end of 1987.

If third quarter 1987 market values of debt are used, the reduction is much greater. The average discount for private and public debt has fluctuated at around 50 percent. At such a discount the market value of Mexico's foreign debt is $50.5 billion, minus $13.8 billion in reserves, the foreign debt is scaled down to $36.75 billion, which at constant 1978 dollars is worth $21 billion, an undoubtedly manageable figure if market values could be translated into actual figures.

On the subject of debt discounts, it has been argued that the market value of debts is the outcome of an internationally thin market and thus not truly representative of the prices a full participating market would determine. However, it is hard to conceive a thin market when such huge stocks are involved. On the one hand, banks could put more debt into the market but at the going price they prefer to hold on to it. Thus obviously at a 50 percent discount they prefer to hold on to most of their portfolio. Or, on the other hand – and this amounts to the same thing – if the debt is "really" worth more than 50 cents on the dollar, there are enough banks with ample resources who could bid up the so-called "nonrepresentative" price of LDC foreign debt. If the price is too low, many banks could profit from buying such debt and from putting such worthy investments into their portfolio; however, they do not.

Another fruitful way of looking at recent debt trends is to examine the nominal figures. After the debt problem exploded in 1982, NFD reached $92.2 billion at the beginning of 1983. Since then, it has come down nominally $0.4 billion. That is despite the amount of money forthcoming as a result of multiple negotiations with commercial banks, IMF agreements, World Bank support and so on, and despite the popular image that the country has been enjoying several extensions of fresh money, the net use of foreign resources has been negative during the 5-year period from 1983 to 1987 (including a projected figure for 1987).

In 1983, the first year of a tough adjustment program, the availability of foreign resources was $1.1 billion, the second year −$3.4 billion, the third $2.8 billion, the fourth barely $0.1 billion. 1986 was the one year in which Mexico's oil revenues fell short by $8.5 billion. In that year, with $2.5 billion of increased public foreign debt, the country managed to pay $1.4 billion of private debt and to increase its international reserves by $1 billion. Finally, in 1987, the increase in credit to the public sector, $11.1 billion, has almost been offset by additional private debt amortizations ($3.0 billion) and increases in reserves of $6.9 billion.

Table 10.1 Mexico's recent total foreign debt position ($bn)

	Public debt (1)	Private debt (2)	Gross reserves (3)	Net Foreign debt position (1)+(2)−(3)=(4)	Net foreign debt position constant 1978 prices
1980					
I	35.4	8.0	3.2	40.2	33.2
II	37.2	9.0	3.5	42.7	34.0
III	39.1	9.7	3.7	45.1	32.3
IV	41.5	11.0	4.0	48.5	37.0
1981					
I	44.7	11.6	4.3	52.0	38.7
II	48.9	13.5	3.7	58.7	42.6
III	56.1	14.0	4.0	66.1	46.7
IV	67.1	14.9	5.0	77.0	53.6
1982					
I	68.5	17.1	3.3	82.3	56.8
II	72.1	17.5	2.2	87.4	59.5
III	71.0	17.8	2.0	86.8	58.0
IV	71.8	20.1	1.8	90.1	60.0
1983					
I	72.8	22.5	3.1	92.2	61.4
II	71.9	22.3	3.6	90.6	59.6
III	73.2	21.9	4.2	90.9	59.1
IV	75.5	20.6	4.9	91.2	58.8
1984					
I	76.0	19.9	5.8	90.1	57.4
II	76.0	19.5	7.1	88.4	55.7
III	76.7	19.3	8.0	88.0	55.0
IV	77.0	18.9	8.1	87.8	54.4
1985					
I	76.9	18.5	7.7	87.7	54.0
II	76.9	18.1	7.0	88.0	53.6
III	77.8	17.8	5.8	89.8	54.3
IV	78.8	17.6	5.8	90.6	54.3
1986					
I	78.8	17.2	6.0	90.0	53.7
II	79.3	16.9	4.4	91.8	54.9
III	80.5	16.6	4.5	92.6	55.0
IV	81.3	16.1	6.8	90.7	53.6
1987					
I	84.6	15.9	9.0	91.5	53.5
II	88.5	15.5	13.8	90.2	51.9
III	88.8	15.0	14.6	89.2	50.9
IV	92.4	13.1	13.7	91.8	51.8

Source: Balance of Payments Statistics, Banco de Mexico

Table 10.2   Division between floating and fixed interest rates of Mexico's external public debt ($m)

	1980	1981	1982	1983	1984	1985	1986
Total[a]	34336	53482	59733	63358	65342	68008	71249
Variable rate debt	26608	42953	46389	50889	52829	53740	54686
Share in %	77.5	80.3	77.6	80.3	80.8	79.0	76.7
Fixed rate debt[b]	7728	10528	13344	12469	12513	14268	16563
Share in %	22.5	19.7	22.4	19.7	19.2	21.0	23.3

[a]   Balance of payments data, Banco de Mexico
[b]   Fixed rate debt originates in loans from multilateral banks (International Bank for Reconstruction and Development and Interamerican Development Bank); some bilateral loans; private placements and suppliers credits. Information provided by Direccion de Deuda Publica, SHCP (Mexico's Treasury)

As suggested above, the preliminary data for the end of 1987 show a continuation of these trends, i.e., further amortizations of private debt and increases of international reserves which compensate for increased lending to the public sector.

The breakdown between variable and fixed interest rates on Mexico's foreign debt has remained approximately the same from 1980 to 1986 (see table 10.2). Variable rate public foreign debt was 77 percent of the total in 1980. It went up to 81 percent in 1983 as commercial bank debt grew much faster than multilateral loans but, in the crisis years, while commercial bank credit stagnated, growing only 7.3 percent from 1983 to 1986 (barely 2.4 percent per year), credit from multilateral sources increased by 32 percent. Thus, while multilateral credit, mostly from the World Bank and from the Interamerican Development Bank, accounts for less than one quarter of total public foreign debt (one fifth in 1983), it accounted for more than half of the increase in credit to the public sector in this latter period.

4   The Sources or Proximate Causes of Mexico's Foreign Debt

The Net Flow of External Indebtedness (FEI) will be defined as the net acquisition of public and private foreign debt by the country, minus the net flow of direct foreign investment (Dornbusch, 1984). By the accounting definition of the balance of payments, net indebtedness will finance the increase in international reserves , ΔIR, the increase in other official assets and in the international assets of domestic banks, ΔOIA, the current account deficit, CAD, and an errors term whose large swings are usually indicators of the amount of capital flight.

$$FEI = \Delta IR + \Delta OIA + CAD + E \tag{1}$$

For the present purpose I will construct four time aggregations. As a representation of the years of growth with stability, the 1970–2 figures will suffice. In the two decades prior to the seventies, recourse to foreign credit had been moderate, budget deficits reasonable and above all viable, and the resulting current account of the balance of payments did not require foreign debt to grow in relative terms. The policy began to change in 1972, but as the end of an era it still does not show the strains of the new, mainly budgetary, policies. Therefore the 1970–2 averages reflect reasonably well the effects of the budgetary policies of an era that was about to end.

The 1973–6 period encapsulates the first stage of the second era, the one that runs through 1982 and that is characterized by high budget deficits, an active use of foreign credit and the onset of inflation. However, 1973–6 is a pre oil period. With the appearance of oil exports in 1977–82, there are renewed budget deficits, higher levels of public spending, enlarged balance of payments gaps induced by large quantities of foreign lending, and higher inflation than in the previous period. It is also marked by the suspension in 1982 of foreign voluntary lending and the initiation of the protracted crisis that was going to be nurtured by a collapse in the country's terms of trade. In spite of difficulties compounded by a negative availability of foreign resources, the government achieved a considerable adjustment in its finances in the 1983–7 period. However, the later years are also characterized by low growth and high inflation.

The events described above have a sharp reflection in the balance of payments, as table 10.3 shows.

In 1970–2 the deficit on the current account was relatively small, but since the net flow of financial indebtedness, "NFI", was insufficient to finance it, there was a negative residual (column 5) which probably reflects capital inflows.

As the budget deficit increased in relative terms, the current account deteriorated in the 1973–6 period. Figure 10.1 portrays the strong relationship between the primary (noninterest) budget deficit and the primary current account balance, which suggests that private saving and investment are, even over the economic cycle, relatively constant proportions of aggregate income, letting budgetary swings be reflected in the balance of payments.

The large increase in the budget deficit in 1973–5, whether one takes the operational[2] or the primary definition, 4.4 percent and 2.4 percent of GDP respectively, required large inflows of NFI, 7.4 times as much in nominal

Table 10.3 Structure of the net flow of external financial savings ($m)

Net flow of financial savings[a] (1)=(2)+(3)+(4)+(5)	Increase in intl. reserves[b] (2)	Increase in other intl. assets[c] (3)	Deficit on the current account[d] (4)	Residual[e] (5)
1970–72	2503	567	15	3322	−1401
1973–76	18460	−680	39	13637	5463
1977–82	67258	356	2097	46594	18210
1983–87	8769	11882	1047	−6833	2673

[a] Public and private net flow of financial indebtedness plus net flow of foreign direct investment
[b] Change in the gross international reserves of the Central Bank
[c] Up to 1979 it includes only credits to FOMEX (Mexico's Import Export Bank). From 1980 onwards it includes the external assets of domestic banks and PEMEX (Mexico's state-owned oil company)
[d] Net of the interest income imputed on the identified foreign assets of Mexicans (except those accruing on Banco de Mexico's foreign reserves)
[e] Some of its large movements are indicative of capital flight

Source: Balance of Payments Statistics, Indicadores del Sector Externo, Banco de Mexico. See also table A.3

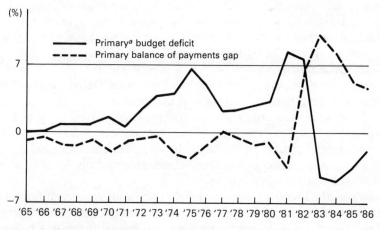

Figure 10.1 Primary public sector deficit/primary balance of payments gap (as a proportion of GDP)

[a] Primary means non-interest
Source: Indicadores economicos, Banco de Mexico

terms as during 1970–2. This inflow of $18.4 billion was not enough to finance the current account deficit plus an important amount of capital flight ($5.4 billion). Therefore, reserves were used to give a total availability of $19.1 billion; of these, 71 percent financed the deficit on the current account and 28 percent capital flight.

Relative magnitudes were similar in the 1977–82 period, where 69 percent of NFI financed the current account deficit while 27 percent went to finance capital flight. Only one half of 1 percent went to increase international reserves.

The last period comprises the first year of adjustment in response to the suspension in foreign voluntary lending, up to 1987. The marked reduction in foreign capital flows is evident. From $86 billion in the former two periods, or $67 billion in the preceding one, the flow falls to $8.7 billion. Moreover, it is also strikingly evident that this amount was not available to finance a public sector deficit nor its mirror image, a deficit in the current account, which showed a surplus of $6.8 billion. Rather, all of the net availability of financial resources went to increase international reserves. But international reserves increased by even more. The difference, $3.1 billion, came from the surplus of $11.8 billion on the current account. The remainder of the current account surplus went to finance the $2.6 billion capital flight item which, in this period, includes a substantial amount of payments of unregistered private foreign debt.

An example of private foreign debt whose service was not in the controlled foreign exchange market and was therefore not registered at the Treasury, were suppliers' credits. There are other instances such as interfirm credits, and so on. As the foreign exchange market returned gradually to normal in 1983, private firms struggled to pay these credits and they succeeded in reducing them by substantial amounts. The most outstanding example for which there is a record are the $4.77 billion of suppliers' credits declared by firms to the Commerce Department in 1982. After a few years there was no trace of these debts.

It is impossible to ascertain how much of the residual item is capital flight or payment of private debt, but the numbers presented above suggest it was a substantial amount of the latter. In any case, whatever capital flight there was in this period it has been financed completely by the current account and not by capital inflows.

Whatever the numbers for capital flight and for its sources of financing, in the nontechnical financial literature and amongst foreign commercial bankers, there is a basic misconception about capital flight; it is believed that the net credit provided by foreign banks has been used, at least partially, to finance capital flight. This can occur only given a very restrictive set of assumptions. To see this, consider the effects on the balance of payments of financing a budget deficit. When net foreign lending finances the government deficit, the inescapable conclusion is that, unless private saving experiences a compensating increase in excess of private investment, net foreign lending will induce a corresponding deficit in the balance of payments. This deficit can be structured in an infinite number of ways. For example, it can come about fully as an excess of imports over exports with no capital flight. Or it may come about solely as capital flight with an balanced current acount. In both cases the capital inflow finances government spending and not capital flight, even if there is capital flight.

If, in the second case, the accounts were balanced through capital flight, society will be better off financially than if the whole amount had been destined to greater imports and/or lower exports, since the money was not spent, and society has an asset upon which it can draw in the future. Only when the Central Bank incurs foreign debt to finance an excess demand for foreign currency created by a portfolio shift of residents who desire to place part of their wealth abroad, will the additional debt truly finance capital flight. In this case, since the Central Bank has to get rid of domestic debt as people sell their domestic assets in exchange for foreign currency, the Central Bank is substituting foreign debt for domestic debt in its effort to sustain the exchange rate, by feeding foreign exchange to those who wish to put their wealth abroad. But this is a very special sort of operation, at least in Mexico, where foreign debt up to 1982 had been contracted, not to feed dollars to those who were making a run against the peso, but instead to finance the government's budget deficit.

As analyzed in this section, the contracting of debt to fortify the Central Bank occurred only during the last period, but the reserves thus acquired were not used to finance speculative attacks on the peso.

In conclusion, in the 1983–September 1987 period, the country had a negative availability of foreign credit. As table 10.3 shows, the net financial flow minus the increase in the international assets of the country was -$3.07 billion, or -$770 million per year, hardly what one might label as outside support to growth.

5 The Implication of Mexico's Foreign Debt for Growth

The more fundamental way to go about an analysis of the economic implications of the foreign debt burden is to relate it to economic growth. The net transfer of resources a country makes abroad has a domestic counterpart in depressed real wages, consumption levels, investment, and growth.

At the same time that Mexico has borne the negative effects on its

Table 10.4 Mexico's terms of trade (adjusted for interest rate movements)

	1960–69	1970–79	1980	1981	1982	1983	1984	1985	1986
Terms of trade	86.5	110.2	123.5	127.4	94.5	77.4	66.5	71.5	54.6

Source: Banco de Mexico, Informe Anual, p. 108

Table 10.5 Primary (noninterest) current account surplus ($b)

	1982	1983	1984	1985	1986	1987
Noninterest current account income	26.7	27.7	30.8	28.9	22.8	29.4
Noninterest current account expenditures	22.0	13.4	16.7	19.4	17.2	18.3
Noninterest current account surplus	4.7	14.3	14.1	9.5	5.6	11.1

Source: Indicadores Economicos, Banco de Mexico

growth rate of a large cumulative transfer of resources abroad over the past five years, its economic performance has been seriously impaired by a drastic fall in its terms of trade.

As tables 10.4 and 10.5 indicate, the country's terms of trade fell 56 percent from 1980 to 1986, while the cumulative primary current account surplus (net transfer of resources) has been a huge $59 billion from 1982 to September of 1987.

This transfer of resources abroad has averaged yearly 6 percent of GDP measured in dollars, clearly an inmense proportion for a country with a low per capita GDP and a labor force which is growing at a number estimated between 800,000 and 1 million workers per year. Such a rapid increase in the working population has been coupled with a fall of output of 2.6 percent in 1987 with respect to 1981. That is, despite a still rapid rate of population growth (2.3 percent per year) and a still faster growth of the work-force (between 2.6 and 3 percent per year), the country has averaged a dismal −0.4 percent yearly rate of growth from 1981 to 1987.

Another figure which illustrates the impact of external shocks on income is the real wage. The average annual real minimum wage has fallen from an index of 92.8 in 1981 to an expected index of 56 in 1987, a fall of 40 percent.

The debt burden can also be looked at through the relation between interest payments abroad and Mexico's GDP measured in dollars.

Table 10.6 Mexico's interest payments abroad and GDP ($b)

	1980	1981	1982	1983	1984	1985	1986	1987
Interest payments abroad	6.1	9.4	12.1	10.2	11.8	10.3	8.4	8.1
Dollar GDP	186.3	239.6	195.1	142.7	171.3	176.8	127.2	164.2
Interest/GDP (percentage)	3.3	3.9	6.2	7.1	6.7	5.8	6.6	4.9

Source: Indicadores Economicos, Banco de Mexico

Table 10.7 The relative size of Mexico's public internal debt (with respect to GDP)

	1981	1982	1983	1984	1985	1986	1987
Total internal debt	15.6	19.1	19.4	17.8	17.9	19.8	17.6
Total in pesos	13.3	15.3	16.8	16.6	16.9	18.3	17.1
Total in dollars	2.3	4.1	2.6	1.2	1.1	1.5	0.5
Financial assets of the public	28.5	29.4	27.2	27.7	27.6	28.0	33.6
Ratio of peso internal debt to M5	46.7	52.0	61.8	59.9	61.2	65.4	50.9

Source: Indicadores Economicos, Banco de Mexico

The average of the post-debt crisis period (1982–7) is clearly extremely high, because not only is it 6.2 percent of GDP on average, but as the preceding sections showed, there has been no net foreign credit available to Mexico to even partially finance this outflow.

Finally, concerning investment, both private and public investment have suffered from the decrease in available funds. The public sector has had to rely on internal funds (M5) out of which it took an estimated 66 percent in 1986, compared to only 45 percent in 1981 (see table 10.7).[3] Such an absorption of financial resources by the public sector has crowded out private spending, since the private sector has also been a net amortizer of its own foreign debt since 1983.

Interestingly, while real total investment fell by 40 percent from 1981 to 1986 (table 10.8), real construction investment fell much less, only 25 percent. This was partly due to a change in relative prices. Of the components of investment, construction is intensive in domestic resources while machinery and equipment depend largely on imported inputs, so that its 55

Table 10.8   Mexico: fixed real capital investment index (1970=100)

	1970	1971	1972	1973	1974	1975	1976	1977	1978
Total	100	98.3	110.3	126.6	136.6	149.2	149.9	139.8	161.1
Construction	100	98.4	110.0	124.4	131.5	141.3	146.3	146.9	161.9
Machinery and									
equipment	100	98.1	110.7	129.5	143.4	159.8	153.9	135.5	159.9

	1979	1980	1981	1982	1983	1984	1985	1986	1987
Total	193.7	222.6	255.4	214.7	154.8	163.3	173.7	153.4	
Construction	183.1	206.0	229.4	217.7	174.5	180.2	186.8	170.3	
Machinery and									
equipment	207.9	244.8	290.2	210.6	128.4	140.8	156.2	130.9	

Source: Sistema de Cuentas Nacionales de Mexico

percent fall reflects a response to the higher relative price of imported goods (the real exchange rate is estimated to be 84 percent higher in 1987 than in 1981). This has helped to retain labor in the very highly labor-intensive construction industry, especially since, within the industry itself, housing is more labor-intensive than the rest, and its share has risen markedly.

The figures shown are obtained from the national accounts and reflect therefore the real fall in the main deflator of investment: wages. The fall in real wages has helped to obtain a much greater reach for a public investment which has shifted from its earlier emphasis on heavy industrial investment into infrastructure and social investments such as housing. However, despite these cheering words, the fact is that total investment, public and private, has been seriously depressed by the acute shortage of funds.

It would have been interesting to perform an investment growth exercise such as the one presented theoretically by Selowsky and Van der Tak (1986), who explore, through an incremental-capital-output ratio (ICOR) based growth model, the impact of curtailed foreign financial flows on growth. However, the applicable ICOR for Mexico would be highly debatable and the conclusions questioned for this reason. But the study quoted is done with reasonable numerical sets of the relevant parameters and reaches a broad conclusion which seems applicable to countries like Mexico subject to such an intense external drain: "Any program of adjustment compatible with a sustained 'minimum' GDP growth in the range of 4 percent a year will require significant net borrowings as a percentage of GDP, particularly in the short run. During the first 3 years of such a program, those annual flows may be around 3–5 percent of GDP, in real terms, for countries with a medium debt overhang (real interest payments around 5 percent of GDP)" (p. 1120).

When it is evident that net financial flows, far from reaching the minimum requirements mentioned above, have been a negative percentage of GDP from the onset of the crisis to the present, the evidence points to the reason why Mexico has had such a hesitant performance.

While the figures for net foreign financial flows speak for themselves, a skeptic might suspect that our difficulties have been compounded by bad economic management. Indeed, while economists may argue over the details, and while the timing and appropriate magnitude of the adjustments may also be subject to discrepancies, the Mexican economy has undergone an unquestionable process of adjustment. This process compares quite favorably with the rather timid fundamental adjustment measures of other countries which have nevertheless used significant amounts of net foreign resources and which have therefore been able to experience some growth. But these Pyrrhic victories have only postponed the moment of truth.

6 The Size of the Adjustment

The magnitude of Mexico's adjustment can be measured in several ways. Some of the changes have been structural in nature: for instance, the opening to foreign trade, the substantial correction in the prices of public sector goods and services, and the sale and liquidation of public enterprises. The other changes involve the size of the government deficit and short-term credit and exchange rate measures. For the purpose of this chapter the more important changes are those related to the budget, so only a summary presentation will be made of the others.

As Mexico entered its recent crisis, it had one of the tightest trade policies in the Western world. Not only was it not a member of GATT, but what is most important, it had quantitative controls on all its imports. The imports of consumer goods were virtually banned, and there were flat prohibitions on the imports of many inputs and capital goods as well. Prohibitions had been the futile instrument used in the vain attempt to contain balance of payments deficits as well as to protect prematurely senile adolescent industries. However, at the end of 1987, the value of imports subject to quantitative controls has been brought down to 20 percent of the total. Exporters enjoy the additional advantage of being able to import practically anything free of tariffs if they import goods temporarily, to re-export them after some degree of transformation. Tariffs have been drastically reduced as well.

The opening up of the economy has included the healthy restructuring of a number of industries and an unprecedented increase in nonoil, especially manufacturing, exports.

By 1982 the prices of public sector goods and services, mostly energy-related, had decreased to tiny fractions of their international levels. The loss in public revenues had been compounded by huge public investments required to satisfy the increased quantities demanded of the subsidized public goods and services. These prices have been gradually brought into line with some, like diesel, increasing several-fold in real and dollar terms.

The number of public enterprises was 1,155 at the beginning of 1983. Through liquidations, sales and mergers, this has been reduced to 746. The public sector has completely left sectors such as pharmaceuticals, secondary petrochemicals, and the automotive industry.

There were other structural changes, but as stated above, relatively more attention will be devoted to budgetary improvements. Here, as in many other fields, there are several ways to analyze the figures. One is to look at the ratio of noninterest expenditures and government income to GDP. As table 10.9 shows, noninterest public sector expenditures have fallen 9.8 percentage points of GDP from 1981 to 1987, while public sector income, despite the inflationary ravages on tax revenues (the Oliveira–Tanzi effect), has risen 4.2 percentage points of GDP.

Since the public sector's nominal deficit is largely endogenous when there is inflation, its numbers will not be analyzed. On the other hand, the primary (noninterest deficit) has fallen from a peak of 8.4 percent in 1981, to a surplus of 3.6 percent in 1985 and 2.9 percent in oil-shock year 1986. The 1987 expected figure was a surplus of 5 percent. Comparing 1981 with 1987, there has been a correction of 13.4 percentage points of GDP, despite steadily declining terms of trade (although part of the fall in the terms of trade experienced in 1986 has been recovered in 1987). It is hard to find elsewhere a budget correction of such a magnitude in such a short period.

But with net negative foreign resources over the crisis period, the country has had to depress its growth in order to pay. On the other hand, with no real growth and no net foreign resources available, the public sector can only finance its smaller real deficit by crowding out the private sector. But as table 10.7 showed, the public sector already took out 60 percent of M5 for its own uses in 1986. The figure estimated for 1987 was two-thirds of M5. With such a narrow breathing space, the remaining deficit has had to be balanced through the inflationary tax.

To see the rate of the inflationary tax, consider the operational deficit

Table 10.9 Public finances (% of GDP)

	1980	1981	1982	1983	1984	1985	1986	1987
PSBR	7.9	14.8	17.6	9	8.7	10	16.3	16.9
Noninterest public sector expenditures	31.3	36.2	37.7	29.9	28.4	29	28.9	26.4
Public sector income	28.1	27.8	30.1	34.3	33	32.6	31	32
Primary economic deficit	3.2	8.4	7.6	−4.4	−4.9	−3.6	−1.6	−5
Operational deficit	3.6	10.1	5.8	1.4	−0.1	1	2.7	2.7
Adjusted operational deficit	6.3	11.9	15.3	5.2	1.9	2.6	4	2.6

Source: Indicadores Economicos and Informe Anual 1986, Banco de Mexico

which has been in surplus or nil from 1983 onwards (table 10.9). Since the PSBR reflects the savings on interest expenditures transferred to the government by the Central Bank on its monetary liabilities, the PSBR corrected for inflation, the operational deficit, are lower than they would be if there were no inflation, but marginally higher because of the Oliveira–Tanzi effect (see Gil-Diaz and Ramos-Tercero, 1987, for a more detailed explanation). The net result of the operational deficit thus corrected is the adjusted operational deficit (AOD). The AOD has been brought down from 15.3 percent of GDP in 1982 to an estimated 2.6 percent in 1987, a substantial reduction, but still a high figure when there is no growth to create a demand for additional financial assets by the public, and where growth is stifled by the substantial transfer of resources that the country has been making abroad.

To realize the magnitude of interest payments abroad, it is interesting to compare them with the true structural budget deficit the country has sustained in the past few years, consider the figures presented in table 10.10.

Throughout the crisis years 1983–7, the peso equivalent of interest paid on Mexico's foreign public debt has exceeded the AOD by a wide margin.

Clearly, from whatever angle chosen to examine the budgetary problem and the foreign debt burden, the outcome is that, despite the already considerable adjustments undertaken by the Mexican government, the drain on public resources and on foreign exchange has proved heavy to bear.

Table 10.10 Ratio of interest paid abroad by Mexico's public sector to the adjusted operational deficit (AOD)

	Interest/ AOD		Interest/ AOD		
1965	49	1973	13	1981	18
1966	43	1974	15	1982	22
1967	23	1975	12	1983	129
1968	33	1976	17	1984	178
1969	34	1977	15	1985	129
1970	23	1978	21	1986	212
1971	36	1979	18	1987	139
1972	15	1980	17		

Source: Estadistica de Ingresos Gasto SHCP in Indicadores Economicos, Banco de Mexico and Informe Anual 1986, Banco de Mexico

7 What does the Future Hold in Store?

The organizers of this conference were interested in what they called a "forward looking" approach to this chapter. In a problem as serious and as complicated, because of the diversity and number of agents involved, it is absolutely necessary to be forward looking. To do this it will be useful to ask why the several efforts already initiated have been only partially successful. It has already been pointed out that Mexico experienced falling and, in 1986, plunging terms of trade. But even before then, and afterwards in 1987, it has become evident that as soon as barely marginal economic growth begins, the financial and currency markets start creaking and the country is led into a renewed balance of payments weakness with the exchange rate becoming volatile (see figure 10.2).

Some simple arithmetic explains this behavior. If financial intermediation represents 28 percent of GDP, and if no net foreign credit is available, annual growth of 10 percent in output will enable the economy to finance a deficit of only 3 percent of GDP without pressing the price level and/or the foreign exchange market. A still high rate of growth, by recent standards of 5 percent per year, will only provide financing for a dificit which is 1.5 percentage points of GDP. Growth itself does not provide the credit needs of the economy as long as there is a government deficit, however small (see Gil-Diaz and Ramos-Tercero, 1987, for an in-depth examination of this issue).

Evidently, a debt burden which, under zero inflation, would represent approximately 50 percent of the revenues of the federal government,

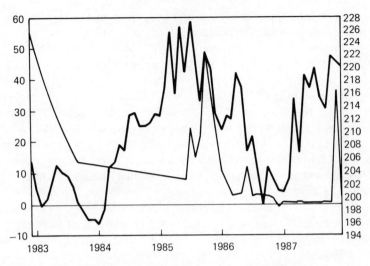

Figure 10.2 Industrial production and exchange rate differential

―――――― Differential between free and controlled rates
―――――― Industrial production (1970 = 100)

Source: Banco de Mexico

represents quite an obstacle for further deficit reductions. Remember that public expenditures have already been cut 7.3 percentage points of GDP over the past five years.

Given these numbers, the achievement of growth and stability seems to hinge on an agreement for debt relief, or an automatic provision of fresh money to finance part of the interest burden. Past programs, which provided one-off amounts of foreign resources are welcome if their intent is to enlarge the international reserves of the Central Bank, but they certainly do not provide even a temporary solution to growth-cum-stability. If the money provided in these programs so much in fashion recently in Latin America is spent, instead of storing it as international reserves, it will induce a balance of payments gap (or a smaller surplus) equal to the transfer during the period it is spent. When the party is over, the country will have to adjust to the "shock" of having lost its once and for all transfer of resources. The next typical step is the setting up of a new "package" which, after ardous negotiations, will again allow another economic spurt. Such stop–go arrangements are not conducive to growth, but rather lead economies into a trend of stagnation while in even greater debt.

Given these difficulties, some countries have fallen prey to the temptation of taking unilateral decisions, thus becoming international pariahs. An alternative to going it alone or with a few companions, is the temptation for debtor countries to coalesce and agree upon a multilateral one-sided escape to the debt burden. If this did happen, it would most probably work against the interests of everybody. Such a move would probably be motivated by the wish not to adjust at home, which would lead those economies again into crisis, even if they obtained a temporary breather by paying less or nothing at all. On the international front, a unilateral move would dry up suppliers' credits, letters of credit and other lubricants of international trade, lowering world economic welfare in general, but most particularly that of the isolationists. However, some banks and regulatory authorities of some creditor countries are not helping to find a solution, and are even actively standing in the way of finding one. Such stubbornness on both sides may lead to a situation neither side wanted but did little to avoid. Pious recommendations to perform structural changes and to adjust might be sincere, but unless it is understood that countries can only grow out of their burdens, the stalemate will be resolved by a crisis brought about by increasingly spreading default.

A crisis will resolve the stalemate, but not the problem. To see how an alternative may be worked out consider the meaning of growing out of the crisis.

To sketch a possible solution it will be helpful to analyze the behavior of the loan portfolios of the commercial banks of some of the leading industrial countries. Table 10.11 contains the dollar value at two dates, 1970 and 1986, of the loan portfolios of the commercial banks of the listed countries.

The average annual rate of growth of the loan portfolios of the listed countries was 13 percent, compared to an average interest rate of 10 percent for the prime interest rate in this period and to 9.7 percent for the LIBOR rate. These numbers indicate that the rate of growth of the loans was greater than the relevant interest rates, or that the present value of the bank's loans was growing through time.

This arithmetic has a profound meaning for the key to a possible formula which may contribute to solving or at least alleviating the debt problem. If the rate of growth of the loan portfolio is 10 percent and is equal to the rate of interest, and if banks lend (or capitalize) in fresh money 80 percent of the interest due to developing countries, in 20 years an initial 30 percent loan portfolio to LDCs will be worth only 21 percent of the total portfolio. If only half of interest due is re-lent, the LDC portfolio will be only 12 percent of the total, and so on.

Even if countries did not grow, banks would "amortize" in present value terms their current portfolios. But most countries would grow as the amount of real transfers abroad they are currently obliged to make diminished significantly. They would grow also because they would be able to

Table 10.11 Dollar value of the loans of commercial banks ($b)

	1970	1986	Annual rate of growth
United States	447	2093	10.1
Japan	125	1832	18.3
West Germany	114	832	13
Belgium	5	33	12
Denmark	6	37	12
Finland	4	40	15
France	60	558	9
Ireland	1.7	13	13
Italy	44	211	10
Norway	4	36	15
Spain	22	142	12
Sweden	15	59	9
Switzerland	12	126	16
Total	860	6012	13

Source: Main Economic Indicators, 1964–83, and May 1987, OECD

plan. Debt negotiations would no longer be the intermittent, drawn-out and inconclusive processes they are now.

The agreements could set a range for interest refinanced, from 1/3 to 8/10 of the total, depending on the countries' fulfillment of certain structural and budgetary goals.

It is true that some countries have not adjusted, but it is also true that others have made significant changes and have been rewarded mostly with sympathy. Others suffer, despite not having a true debt problem, because of the hospital-ward syndrome: they are neighbors to the sick. Clearly there is a need for a greater will to act on the three sides involved: the LDCs, the banks and the regulatory agencies of the creditor countries.

The zero coupon bond

A recent effort by Mexico to test the waters through a market scheme devised to lure banks into voluntarily discounting their portfolios, somewhat reduced Mexico's foreign debt at an advantageous price, but because of its relatively small size it is only just one more small step towards the solution of Mexico's debt problem.

The mechanics involved represent an example of ingenious financial engineering. Its broad elements were: (1) the purchase by Mexico of zero coupon US Treasury bonds with a nominal value at their termination date equal to the purchase price of the "old" debt Mexico purchased at an auction carried out for this purpose. These bonds guarantee the payment of the principal of the "new" debt issued by Mexico. (2) After surveying the bids submitted by the banks, Mexico decided, considering the discounts offered, the amount of its foreign debt it would accept to purchase giving in exchange "new" debt in the form of 20-year Mexican government bonds. The bonds will pay in interest 1 5/8 percent per annum over the LIBOR rate for six-month Eurodollar deposits. The bonds will not be subject to restructuring, nor will they be included as part of the portfolio of banks which is considered to calculate requests for new money.

While the result of the auction represents a discount slightly above 30 percent and a reduction in Mexico's foreign debt of $1.1 billion, figures which fall short of the maximum amount Mexico was willing to offer if the price had been right, the transaction does have various advantages. In order of importance, perhaps the first is that some small banks got rid of their Mexican portfolio. Since these banks require a disproportionate amount of effort on the part of Mexican authorities and the Bankers' Steering Committee every time a negotiation is conducted, their exit represents an improved situation for everybody: the Mexican government, the big banks and the financial authorities of lending countries. The second positive effect is that a new instrument has been successfully tested for debt renegotiation and third, but not least, a reduction in Mexico's debt was achieved at a discount advantageous for Mexico.

Some Concluding Remarks

Lenders and borrowers are involved in a Prisoner's Dilemma, or at least are acting as if they were. The refusal of banks to engage in an automatic, continuous refinancing mechanism limits or curtails the economic growth of debtors while contributing to the heavy discounts of their own portfolios. The more banks refuse to provide fresh money, the more heavily discounted their assets become on the margin, while debtors' growth prospects are further suffocated.

The difference between this situation and the Prisoner's Dilemma of course is that the agents involved can talk to each other and achieve the best solution for all involved. Debtors, regulators and creditors, specially the two latter, should start putting a credible and efficacious act together, before the outcome results in the worst possible solution.

NOTES

My appreciation to Juan Díez-Canedo for his comments and to Oscar Sanchez for his assistance. The views expressed here are the sole responsibility of the author.

1 At that time Secretary of the Treasury but who, for many years, had been engaged in the renegotiation of the debt.
2 The operational deficit is a proxy of the real deficit. It is calculated taking the real increase in the government's internal debt plus the net inflow of foreign credit to the public sector.
3 The internal peso debt is considered for this estimate because from 1983 onwards practically all the internal dollar denominated debt is matched by outside dollar liabilities of the Mexican banks who hold such credits.

REFERENCES

Bazant, Jan (1968), *Historia de la Deuda Exterior de México*. Centro de Estudios Historicos, Mexico: El Colegio de Mexico.
Dornbusch, Rudiger (1986), "External Debt Budget Deficit and Disequilibrium Exchange Rates". in R. Dornbusch, *Dollars, Debts and Deficits*, Cambridge, MA: MIT Press.
Gil-Diaz, Francisco and Ramos-Tercero, Raul (1987). "Lessons from Mexico". Presented at the Conference on Inflation Stabilization; The Experience of Israel, Argentina, Brazil, Bolivia and Mexico. Toledo, Spain: Fundacion Ortega y Gasset, June 1987. Dornbusch, R. and Fischer, S. (forthcoming).
Gil-Diaz, Francisco and Rubio, Luis (1987). *A Mexican Response*. A Twentieth Century Fund Paper, New York: Priority Press Publications.
Selowsky, Marcelo and Van der Tak, Herman G. (1986), "The Debt Problem and Growth". World Bank Reprint Series no. 399, Oxford: Pergamon.
Suarez, Eduardo L. (1965), *Memorias y Recuerdos*. Mexico: Editorial Porrua.
Tanzi, Vito (1980), *Inflation and the Personal Income Tax: An International Perspective*. Cambridge, MA: Cambridge University Press.

Comment

Francisco Rosende

Gil Diaz's chapter eloquently conveys the significance of the problem posed by external indebtedness that currently affects the Mexican economy, as well as the severity of the adjustment program undertaken in that country during the years 1986–7 in order to face the problem. Thus, the author points to the application of an important fiscal adjustment process and a tight wages policy, which has promoted a steep fall in real wages, estimated to be approximately 40 percent between 1981 an 1987 for the minimum wage, whereas the real exchange rate has undergone a 90 percent increase during the same period.

As part of this adjustment process, and in order to overcome macroeconomic imbalances, Mexican economic policy has promoted tariff decreases on various products and the privatization of a significant number of public enterprises. As a result, the price of public services has reached a level that is consistent with the efficient performance of the firms that are offering them.

One element of Mexico's economic policy that it is necessary to highlight is, precisely, the implementation of a vigorous program of domestic expenditure adjustment that has resulted in a significant increase in international reserves and nonoil exports. This is particularly important since an approach frequently cited in some Latin American countries concerns the need to have a more aggressive strategy with respect to creditor banks and multilateral agencies – like the IMF – by advancing formulae such as fixing maximum levels for interest payments. This strategy, however, only tends to slow down or delay the adjustment. This type of argument usually accompanies judgements on the bargaining power of these economies, either individually or as a cartel. It is significant, however, in the evaluation of the appropriate strategies to face the foreign debt problem, to realize that Mexico – in theory a privileged country among indebted economies with respect to its negotiating capacity – has taken on a harsh adjustment program, obtaining significant results within a short period of time, in matters such as accumulation of international reserves, fiscal adjustment, and export growth.

Beyond the adjustment program itself, the overall evaluation of the

Mexican economy makes it necessary to place the current developments in a longer-term perspective. In particular, a very important question that is not answered in Gil-Diaz's chapter relates to the depth of the reforms that are currently being undertaken in this economy. The evaluation will be different if the economic policy is just concerned with the current macro-economic imbalances, or if there is an intention to change to a significant extent the structure of economic incentives, in order to improve the general efficiency of the economic system.

In the study carried out, Gil-Diaz mentions that the Mexican economy's problem of excess expenditure began at the beginning of the 1970s, at the same time as a substantive improvement in the terms of trade, the well-known "oil shock" for nonoil exporting economies. Then, under very favorable external economic conditions that extended up to the beginning of the present decade, the Mexican economy was characterized by soaring inflation, high indebtedness and high government intervention in economic activity. Consequently, the question that is necessarily raised by any observer of the Mexican economy, is that of whether the process of adjustment is only addressing problems of expenditure imbalances or, rather, is a wider program directed to bring about a transformation in the structure of Mexico's economic institutions and productive structure. The answer to this question is as important as the evaluation of the efficiency of the expenditure adjustment policy, since it will provide information on the future of export promotion policies, or more generally, about the direction of the economic policy if, for example, the oil price suddenly increases.

Finally, Gil-Diaz points to the lack of support on the part of creditor banks and multilateral agencies for the Mexican adjustment process. Certainly, the continuity and efficiency of this kind of program necessitate an effective backing from the banks and multilateral agencies. An adverse selection-type behavior, or the adoption of protectionist measures in industrialized economies, will only discourage the adjustment efforts made in these economies and encourage the stance of those who foster more aggressive positions with respect to the solution of the debt problem.

11

Brazilian Debt: a Requiem for Muddling Through

Eliana A. Cardoso and Rudiger Dornbusch

1 Introduction

This chapter investigates the outlook for Brazilian debt after a five-year period of muddling through. The state of moratorium and the disarray in the Brazilian economy raise doubts about the strategy of the past five years. The rescheduling that is underway does not detract from the fundamental fact that willingness and ability to service the debt are in question. In addition, the rescheduling does not change the fact that the process over the past five years was highly undesirable from any longer-run perspective, even though it may have served the creditors' short-run interests.

We develop our discussion by first taking a look at Brazilian debt history. This is a useful exercise to give a sense of *déja vu*. From there, we proceed to a review of the period 1982–7 and an analysis of why the debt muddling-through strategy failed. That the process failed is not in question, since Brazil's debt–GDP ratio today is far higher than it was when the crisis first started.

The following section investigates the world macroeconomic outlook and uses it in the context of the debt dynamics model to analyze alternative scenarios. The chapter concludes by stating policy options more consonant than the current strategy, with the long-term interests of Brazil and its creditors.

2 Brazilian Debt Retrospective

While history cannot be depended upon to repeat itself, today's debt crisis runs parallel to earlier developments in the 1930s. First there was a plethora of capital available for loans in the decade preceding each of these crises – the 1920s as well as the 1970s. These two decades of economic

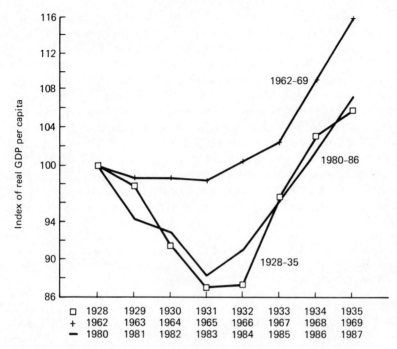

Figure 11.1 Three recessions (last peak before recession = 100)

prosperity were then followed by the deadly combination of terms-of-trade deterioration and cessation of capital flows both in the early 1930s and 1980s. In the 1930s crisis, there were 12 years of partial default before a permanent settlement could be reached. If the parallel is valid, years must pass before the current debt problem will be solved. Figure 11.1 shows the path of GDP per capita in the two periods. Included in the figure is an early 1960s crisis that pales in comparison with the other two.

Brazil went into debt in its very infancy. The history of the Brazilian empire is one of budget deficits, financed by external and domestic borrowing. Minister Ouro Preto's report on the budget situation at the time of the proclamation of the Republic shows that taxes and other revenues during the time of the empire covered only 30 percent of total expenditures. The rest was financed by debt which the Brazilian republic then inherited.

When the Brazilian Republic was declared in 1889, the external public debt already amounted to £33 million. Ten years later, with a debt of almost £50 million, the first debt crisis was brought about by falling commodity prices and halt to international lending in the aftermath of the Baring crisis.

The cessation of capital flows in 1889 meant that the deficit had to be financed by money creation. And the money supply was, indeed, increased. Where there is money, there is a feast, and the banquet lasted until 1892. Those were the years of the *Encilhamento*. With large inflation rates, financial instability and deterioration of the terms of trade, the situation could not last long. The whole affair culminated with the 1898 funding loan, the conditionality terms of which were no better than those imposed by an IMF agreement. Taxes were increased and the Finance Minister, Murtinho, rapidly went on to destroy paper currency.

The 1898 solution was the first of a series of reschedulings and "new money" packages which then were called "funding loans". By 1911 the debt increased to £145 million; the second debt crisis, as well as the second funding loan, was imminent. Finance Minister Rivadavia Correa noted:

> In finance the essential fact is that debts are paid with funds obtained from new loans. This has been the rule for us already many years. What is new is that this time the loan is made by the same people to whom we owe the overdue interest. (Campos (1946) our translation)

Brazil did not miss out in the twenties. The first American issue was sold in 1921, and prior to World War I, Brazil had raised her foreign loans in London. Sixty percent of the external obligations outstanding in 1930 were still denominated in sterling. By then, the external debt had risen to £250 million (more than US $1 billion) and it was time for yet another debt crisis, a moratorium, and shortly afterwards the third funding loan. But in the next few years regular debt service, even with restructuring, could not be maintained. As a result of the Depression, service was interrupted in 1931–2. Application of part of the reduced funds available for debt service to the market purchase of bonds, depreciated by the default, became common.

In barely 40 years, the bondholders were forced to accept three voluntary abatements of their contractual claims, marked by the fundings of 1898, 1914 and 1931. In February, 1934, a "readjustment plan" named after Finance Minister Osvaldo Aranha, was put into effect. It effected a unilateral scaling down of payments. In previous difficulties, a funding loan provided the extra resources to partially satisfy existing creditors. This was the first time that debt service terms were unilaterally reduced, and some payments suspended.

Starting in November 1937, there was a complete suspension of debt remittances. Brazil's Dictator, Getulio Vargas, explained:

> We stopped the service of the external debt, moved by circumstances beyond our control. This does not mean the rejection of earlier commitments. All we need is time to resolve difficulties that we did not create and to readjust our economy, transforming potential wealth in resources that will permit us to

repay, without sacrifices, our creditors. Gone are the days when our obligations were written abroad, at the discretion of banks and intermediaries. (Bouças, 1950, our translation)

Not until 1940, with the help of World War II, was partial debt service resumed under a modified version of the previous schedule. This involved a further cut in the original rates of payment.

In late 1943 Brazil implemented a unilateral exchange offer to consolidate debt service in a manner that is highly suggestive of possibilities today. The American press reacted with sympathy, as shown in an article in *Barron's*: "In retrospect, we find that Brazil always paid on its foreign obligations when it was able to do so" (*Barron's* National Business and Financial Weekly, April 20, 1942, p. 18).

Not everybody, however, would agree with such a statement. A notable exception appeared in the *Economist*:

> The whole story [of the Brazilian reschedulings] confirms the belief, expressed here more than once, that Brazil's intention has throughout been to escape from her obligations as lightly as possible and that she was enabled to do so by persistent disagreement between the representatives of America and Britain, and by the inability or unwillingness of the British authorities to play any effective part in securing reasonable terms. (*The Economist*, December 18, 1943, p. 817)[1]

The 1943 plan consolidated the entire Brazilian debt, stretched the maturities by 40–60 years, and adjusted downwards both principal and interest. Creditors were offered a choice between two plans:

Plan A: There would be no reduction of principal, but interest rates were reduced from more than 6.5 percent to 3.375 percent (and less) with a provision for a sinking fund. Debt service (interest plus sinking fund) amounted to between 2.9 to 5.1 percent.

Plan B: For every $1000 of original bonds, bondholders would receive a cash payment of between $75 and $175, a new bond with a face value of $800 (and $500 in some cases), and a coupon reduced to 3.75 percent. The bonds had no fixed maturity but were entitled to a sinking fund. Interest plus sinking fund amounted to a combined debt service rate of 6.4 percent. In addition, the Brazilian government guaranteed the service of state and municipal bonds assenting to plan B, should the individual obligors fail to make the required remittances.

Dollar issues constituted only about one-third of the foreign indebtedness of Brazil. The bulk of the obligations consisted of sterling loans, and the amount of service funds allotted to British creditors represented the 65.8 percent of total debt payments.

Once again, *Barron's* and the *Economist* disagreed as to which of the plans offered better terms. The *Economist* believed that option A, retaining the whole of the nominal capital, was the better option to take in the case of bonds with a low market value (*The Economist*, December 23, 1944, p. 852).

Barron's stated that much more favorable treatment was available under option B which could be accepted only through the last day of 1944. It also explained the reason why option A was offered at all, considering that option B was far superior. Since the creditors were given one unfavorable and one favorable choice with a time limit, the numbers of assents were probably higher than they would otherwise have been. And Brazil, no doubt, would find it worthwhile to offer better terms for its external creditors if the external debt could be cut down from $837.7 million to $521.5 million, assuming 100 percent acceptance of option B (*Barron's* January 31, 1944, p. 8).

By early 1946, 78 percent of bond holders had assented to the exchange offer. Plan A had been chosen by 22 percent of the bondholders and 56 percent had opted for Plan B. Figure 11.2 shows the monthly maximum price in New York of a Brazilian bond with original terms of 6.5 percent interest and 1957 maturity.[3] After 1943 the price refers to the same bond, now stamped for Plan A, interest adjusted to 3.375 percent and the maturity stretched to 1979. Throughout, the price is expressed as a ratio of the price of a 30-year US government bond with a 6.5 percent coupon. The interesting point here is that, after the 1943 downward adjustment in terms, with repudiation threats removed, the bond actually *increased* in value. From rock bottom in 1940, prices increased over the next 10 years more than sevenfold, yielding a compound rate of return (interest plus capital gains) of 125 percent per annum! As a result, Brazilian loans are seen as unusually attractive. This analysis, however, leaves out the financial consequences for widows and orphans who sold out at the bottom.

Brazil's debt problems did not end in 1943. New debt difficulties emerged in the early 1960s and again in the 1980s. Figures 11.3 and 11.4 show the real debt per capita and the debt–export ratio between 1929 and 1986 (sources are given in the appendix). The relatively low and decreasing levels of external debt recorded in the first postwar quinquennium are a legacy of the prewar experience. The 1943 plan helped reduce the size of the debt from its level of more than $1 billion in the early 1930s to some $600 million in 1946. In addition, a strong postwar recovery in Brazil's export prices postponed the need to explore new sources of external credit.

In the early 1950s, however, the country experienced huge trade deficits. They resulted primarily from the relaxation of import controls to permit stockpiling of materials during the Korean War. Those imports were

Figure 11.2 The price of a Brazilian bond (relative to price of a US long-term bond)

initially financed by commercial arrears which, in the following year, were refinanced by short- and medium-term loans. By 1953, the external debt had doubled to more than $1 billion.

By now, a new entry of capital in order to finance an ambitious indus-trialization drive had become necessary. Total capital inflows, both direct investment and loans, increased sharply after 1955, especially with sup-pliers' credits. At the end of 1961, a time of political unrest, the external debt stood at double its level in 1955 and the country was subjected to one more external crisis. As the economic situation deteriorated, capital in-flows virtually ceased. The World Bank, previously an important source of official resources for Brazil, did not authorize a single loan between 1960 and 1964.

Debt rescheduling and new credits became available after the military coup in 1974. (Bitterman (1973) provides a description of the 1961 and the 1963–4 consolidations.) Thereafter, the government consciously embarked on a policy of tapping private capital markets to underwrite rapid expan-sion.

Two main features distinguish the postwar evolution of Brazil's current account balance. First, this balance was almost continuously unfavorable. Between 1950 and 1986, there was a surplus in only eight of these 37 years.

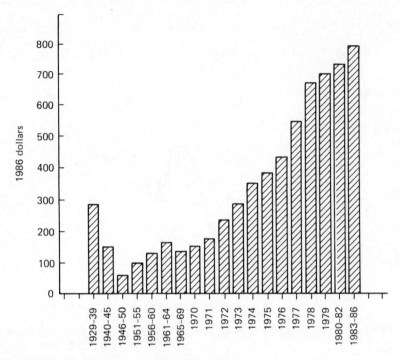

Figure 11.3   Real debt per capita 1929–1986

Second, the deficit on the current account, which was relatively small until 1969, increased sharply after 1970.

The existence of a large deficit on the current account up to 1983 was regarded as normal, since developing countries are importers of capital. The deficits rose sharply after 1970 and pointed to the problems that were starting to develop.

3   The Origins of the 1982 Crisis and Muddling Through

When the debt crisis erupted in Mexico in the summer of 1982, and shortly after in all of Latin America, the handling of the crisis was based on three premises:

1. The world economy was at an extraordinarily low level: economic activity was lower than at any time since the Great Depression. Interest rates were at their highest levels in decades. The real price of commodities was sharply depressed, and the dollar was overly strong.

Recovery of the world economy was certain. As a result, there was an

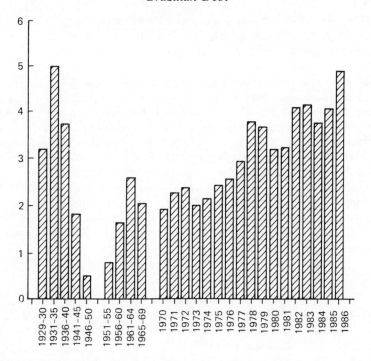

Figure 11.4 Debt–export ratio

expectation of cyclically rising manufactures exports, rising real commodity prices, declining real interest rates, and even of an early fall of the
dollar. This favorable perspective for the world economy suggested that
the burdens of debt service would almost certainly vanish.

2. Debtor countries had mismanaged their economies beyond belief;
overvalued exchange rates, pervasive budget deficits, unproductive spending and capital flight had absorbed scarce foreign exchange resources and
stood in the way of better trade performance and debt service ability.
Using resources more efficiently, of course, implied that debt service would
not necessarily be at the cost of reduced standards of living.

3. A return to voluntary lending could only be envisaged if debtor
countries made the best efforts to co-operate with the system, adjusting
and serving debts to the fullest extent possible. Debtor countries agreed to
do the utmost to promote a return to voluntary lending, so as to be in a
position to call on foreign saving for development finance. There was no
doubt that foreign lenders would unquestionably resume lending, once
creditworthiness (defined objectively in terms of debt ratios) was restored.

These three premises were quite uniformly the elements in the crisis diagnosis. Different observers disagreed, however, on weights assigned to each of these considerations. Characteristically, officials in the US saw the mess in the debtor countries as *the* cause of the debt crisis:

> The debt crisis just did not happen in 1982 or was not the result of the increase in the oil price shock of 1979–80 or the rise in the dollar exchange rate. The cause of the debt crisis had its domestic origins in the economic policies of the debtor countries and so what we are seeing and what we will continue to see is a change in these policies – budget deficits, excessive government spending, government interference in the markets, price controls and so on.[3]

Latin American observers, by contrast, gave far too little weight to their own dramatic mismanagement and the resulting debt accumulation. World macroeconomic developments, shown in table 11.1, are seen by them as the outstanding source of the problems.

The Brazilian case

Brazil's case is interesting in that it does not meet the image of capital flight, overvaluation or massive inefficiency in the public sector (see Dornbusch (1985), Simonsen (1986), Cardoso and Fishlow (1987)). Increased interest rates and sharply augmented debt burdens are the most immediate cause of the foreign exchange shortage. If it were not for the Mexican crisis, rolling over of debts and some domestic restraint and cleaning up might well have made the problems dissolve into the background.

Table 11.2 shows the impact of external shocks on the Brazilian external balance. Between 1978 and 1982 the current account shifted by $13 billion toward deficits. That shift is explained, for the most part, by the impact of the slowdown in exports, the increased real interest rate and higher real oil prices. These calculations do not even include the impact of reduced real commodity export prices or the interest on the extra debt due to the shocks.[4]

The table shows that between the years 1978 and 1982, a cumulative sum of $35 billion – three quarters of the total net debt accumulation – can be accounted for by the adverse external environment. The fact that external shocks can explain so much of the debt accumulation does not, of course, imply that there was no Brazilian policy mistake involved.

The policy mistake is well explained by Finance Minister Delfim Neto's memorable phrase: "Debts are not paid, debts are rolled." Nonetheless, relatively permanent shocks need adjustment, not financing. The Brazilian policy mistake, if any, was failure to adjust to external shocks. But then, in 1982, everybody was busily explaining how the world economic shock was transitory.

Table 11.1 Aggregate world macroeconomic indicators

	Real commodity prices (1980=100)[a]	LIBOR % p.a.	Inflation[b] % p.a.	World activity[c] % p.a.
1960–69	115	5.2	1.0*	6.2*
1970–79	115	8.0	11.4	3.4
1980	100	14.4	13.0	0.0
1981	96	16.5	−4.1	−7.0
1982	89	13.1	−3.5	−3.3
1983·	98	9.6	−3.3	3.3
1984	101	10.8	−2.5	6.5
1985	88	8.3	−0.4	3.0
1986	72	6.9	13.7	1.0
1987	63	6.8	12.8	2.2

[a] Measured in terms of manufactures' export prices of industrial countries.
[b] Rate of increase of industrial countries' unit export values.
[c] Industrial production

Source: IMF and Economic Commission for Latin America

Table 11.2 Contribution of external shocks to debt accumulation, 1978–1982 ($b)

	Oil (1)	Export volume (2)	Interest rates (3)	Total debt shock	Net debt outstanding
1978					36.2
1979	1.8		0.3	2.1	46.4
1980	5.7	0.6	1.1	7.4	57.7
1981	7.1	1.4	2.5	11.0	68.0
1982	6.1	2.4	5.9	14.4	83.5

The calculations are based on the 1978 oil price, 1978 real interest rates (in terms of the US deflator) and export performance based on deviations from an export regression.

Source: Cardoso and Fishlow, (1987), table 3.1.

What went wrong with muddling through?

The muddling-through strategy of 1982 was predicated, as discussed above, on a progress that would come fast, visibly and without extreme costs for either borrowers or lenders. Cline (1984), who was foremost in setting out

304 Country Studies

Table 11.3 Cline's 1983 forecasts for Brazil and actual outcome ($b, except as noted)

	Current account[a]	Non-interest current account	Interest[a]	Debt[b] increase	Debt–exports[c]
Cline forecast	–3.4	5.8	9.2	4.1	2.0
Actual	–3.0	8.0	10.8	27.3	4.2

[a] Annual average 1983–6 [b]Cumulative increase in total debt, $b, 1982–6
[c] Ratio of net debt to exports

Source: Cline (1984), Table 3.3, IMF and Banco Central

a framework and forecasts, saw Brazil, in particular, as one of the countries with a favorable outlook in its ability to return to creditworthiness. Table 11.3 shows forecasts for Brazil laid out by Cline (1984) in 1983. The baseline scenario assumed the following 1983–6 averages: a growth rate of industrial countries of 2.6 percent, $30 a barrel of oil, LIBOR at 9 percent, and a cumulative 10 percent dollar depreciation.[5]

Although the current account deficit averaged approximately what had been predicted, the debt accumulation and the increase in the debt/export ratio are far larger than forecast. Important differences in the debt accumulation arise from the fact that Brazil experienced large capital outflows (in part connected with debt–equity swaps) whereas the Cline scenario anticipated substantial inflows. More recently capital flight has become an additional source of capital outflows. The large discrepancy between the actual debt/export ratio and Cline's forecast arises from the fact that Cline assumed a doubling of the value of merchandise exports, while in fact the 1986 level is only 10 percent above that of 1982.

It is clear that Brazil's return to voluntary lending is not on schedule. Even though, in 1986, a return to the capital market seemed a possibility, at least in the rhetoric of the creditors, the chances today are once again quite remote. The state of moratorium and domestic disarray is one that would disabuse any lender of the notion that the debt strategy is on course.

Developments of the past five years evolved very differently from the 1982–3 expectations. Today the muddling-through strategy, even with Baker Plan enhancements, is widely considered a failure. Interestingly, the problem was not with growth in idustrialized countries. The 1982 IMF economic outlook, to use a specific benchmark, anticipated a growth rate in the base scenario of 2.2 percent on average in the period 1984–6, when the actual growth rate was in fact 3.1 percent. But there were four factors which clearly diverged from the 1982 scenario (see IMF *World Economic Outlook*, April 1982, for the initial scenario).

1. Real interest rates were expected to decline much further than they did. The outlook was for real interest rates to average only 2 percent in 1984–6 (using the US GNP deflator to measure inflation). In fact, however, they averaged 5.4 percent. Even in 1987 they still uncomfortably exceeded the early expectations. Given the sensitivity of major debtors to an increase in interest rates, this represents a major deterioration in the outlook. (This is compounded by the fact that Brazil's spreads did not in fact decline, unlike in other major debtor countries). The chief reason for high interest rates was seen to be the US budget deficit.

2. Real commodity prices were expected to recover from what was thought to be a cyclical low. In fact, however, they kept on falling even from their 1982 levels. By early 1987 the real price of non-oil commodities was at the lowest level since the 1930s. It had become increasingly clear that much of the decline was not cyclical, but rather an irreversible decline in real commodity prices due to capacity expansion, and to commodity-saving innovation and substitution on the demand side. In the case of agricultural goods in particular, the immense productivity growth and increasing self-sufficiency of many traditional importers, as well as price support policies in industrial countries, had led to worldwide oversupply.

3. There was the unexpected (but historically well-known) "transfer problem." This is the catchall phrase that describes problems that result from the attempt to transfer resources representing a significant share of GDP from debtors to their creditors.[6] There are three aspects of the transfer problem that deserve emphasis. First, the effort in the budget to service debts (including interest) rather than roll them over, strains budgetary resources and leads to inflationary money creation. If domestic debt is issued to acquire the resources for external debt service, then the domestic debt accumulation foreshadows debt and deficit problems that are merely postponed. Second, the effort to transfer resources abroad requires an improvement in competitiveness which is itself inflationary. The more sticky real wages are, the more inflationary it is. Moreover, these two factors interact: the need to depreciate the real exchange rate in order to transfer resources abroad, raises the real cost of debt service measured in terms of the domestic tax base.

The third aspect of the transfer problem concerns the manner in which the transfer is financed on the resource side: the required trade surplus may come out of reduced consumption (public or private) or out of reduced investment. When investment declines, as has been the case in Latin America, there is a concern about sustainable growth. The notion that the

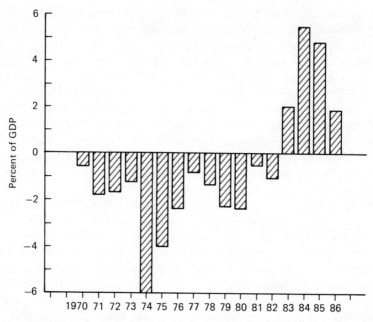

Figure 11.5   Real resource transfers (percent of GDP)

transfer could be financed by asset sales, thus apparently avoiding *any* crowding out, is an illusion, of course, as Simonsen (1985, 1986) has forcefully pointed out.

Finally, cartel fatigue is now pervasive. The precarious cohesion of the creditor cartel is increasingly being tested as rescheduling are becoming open-ended and the mirage of an early return to normal fades away. Differences between large and small banks, and now even between large and medium-sized banks, are becoming starker. Differences are also apparent between European banks, those in Japan and the major US banks. The US Congress increasingly takes the view that the current handling of the debt problem is not in the public interest. Staffs of the multinationals, though perhaps not management, admit openly to the implausibility of muddling through. Every new rescheduling is said to be the last that could possibly be done, but the next one is already on the calendar. Banks have openly declared that they are on the way out, that new money now has to come from the taxpayer:

> Official bodies and their controlling governments, should recognize that the roughly 50–50 split between private and official funds typical of many past new money packages for the debtor countries may not be a workable norm for the future, nor is indefinite reliance on "involuntary" lending by banks.

Realism demands an increased share of new money be furnished by official
sources during the next several years. (Morgan Guaranty *World Financial
Markets*, June/July 1987, p. 2)

While the previous four factors have undoubtedly worked to the detriment of a steady, smooth disappearance of the debt problem, there has
been one favorable factor, namely oil prices. Oil prices, in Brazil's case,
provided important good news to offset the bad. From the level of $34 per
barrel in 1982, world oil prices declined to an average of only $25 in
1983–6. By 1987 the $18 price remained far below the 1982 peak. The
favorable oil price helps explain how, in 1985, the entire Brazilian interest
bill could be paid out of trade surpluses.

The current situation

The situation today is well captured by the state of moratorium and by the
deep discount for Brazilian debts in the secondary market. Much of the
problem with the external debt today reflects the disastrous state of
domestic macroeconomics and an unwillingness to pay. The objective
ability to service debts, in the long run, is much less in question then the
willingness of the government to perpetuate the political and economic
mistake of continuing the muddling-through strategy.

Table 11.4   The discount in the secondary market for Brazilian debt (cents per
dollar, selling price)

7/85	1/86	7/86	1/87	5/87	7/87	9/87
75	75	73	74	64	57	39

Source: Salomon Brothers

One of the important questions in deciding on a debt strategy for the
next few years (assuming there is enough concentration and political
leeway) must involve, once again, an assessment of the world macroeconomic and trade policy outlook. We turn next to these issues.

4   Debt Dynamics and the World Macroeconomic Outlook

The model of debt dynamics, in the tradition of Domar and Avramovic,
can be used to assess the impact of world and country-specific developments on external debt. Feldstein (1986, 1987) has recently used this
framework to suggest that the case of Brazil is viable in the sense that a

noninterest surplus (as a fraction of GDP) of 2.5 percent would be fully consistent with a declining debt ratio.

The basic debt dynamics model focuses on the ratio of debt to GDP. The debt/GDP ratio evolves accordingly to the familiar equation:

$$x_t = \alpha x_{t-1} - \sigma - \delta; \qquad \alpha = 1+r+d-y \qquad (1)$$

where:

x is the ratio of debt to GDP

r is the effective real interest rate on debt adjusted for US inflation

d is the rate of real depreciation of the domestic currency

y is the growth rate of domestic income

σ is the noninterest current account surplus as a ratio of GDP

δ is the nondebt-creating capital inflows as a ratio of GDP.

The equation highlights three separate determinants:

The first factor (α) captures the automatic component of debt accumulation. The effective real interest rate is the LIBOR rate plus spread adjusted for US inflation. If the real interest rate plus the rate of real depreciation exceed the Brazilian growth, then the debt–GDP ratio will rise. The equation emphasizes high US real interest rates, large spreads, large real depreciation, and sluggish growth as sources of debt accumulation, relative to GDP. Of course, real depreciation and growth also affect the noninterest current account, which we will consider in turn.

The noninterest current account surplus, σ, is an essential determinant of debt accumulation. Other things being equal, the higher the noninterest surplus, the lower the rate of increase of the debt–income ratio. These results of course, depend in part on the external environment. The ease with which a country can generate a noninterest surplus consistent with domestic growth, moderate inflation, and high investment is the key issue in the debt discussion today.

Third, nondebt-creating capital flows can reduce the rate of debt accumulation. Direct investment inflows would reduce the rate of debt increase. By contrast, repatriation of foreign investment and capital flight add to the debt–GDP ratio.

The Feldstein (1986, 1987) analysis focused on a situation where a country with Brazil's characteristics sustains a noninterest current account surplus equal to 2.5 percent of GDP. With a debt–income ratio initially equal to 0.4 and a real interest rate of 6 percent, the debt–income ratio will steadily decline as long as there is some growth and nondebt-creating capital flows are zero. This argument seems to establish a rather strong presumption that the debt problem will vanish in time. But, of course, the basic assumption is that three conditions must be met: the country must

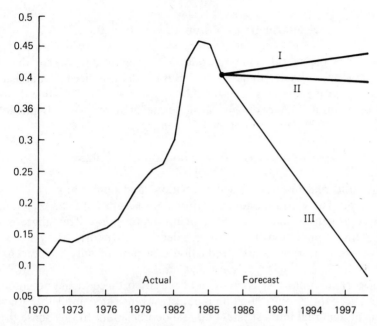

Figure 11.6 Debt–GDP ratio: alternative scenarios (percent)

generate noninterest surpluses, the real interest rate cannot be too high relative to output growth, and there needs to be a mechanism for financing the portion of interest payments that is not supported by the noninterest current account surplus.

Figure 11.6 shows the historical series for the Brazilian debt–GDP ratio, as well as three scenarios for the 1987–1999 period:

Scenario I: $\alpha = 0.03$ and $\sigma + \delta = 0.01$

In this outlook the combined real interest rate and real depreciation rate are high relative to the rate of growth of income. The scenario might be one where real depreciation is required, and growth is sluggish because of external constraints. The country, however, runs a surplus on the noninterest current account. The sum of this surplus and nondebt-creating capital flows equal 1.0 percent of GDP. Even so, the debt–GDP ratio rises from the 1986 level of 41 percent to 44 percent by 1999. This is a scenario where an unfavorable world economic environment leads to a deterioration of debt even with some efforts toward debt service. The debt service effort is simply not enough to make up for the bad environment.

Scenario II: $\alpha = 0.06$ and $\sigma+\delta = 0.025$

In this case the world economic outlook is significantly worse than in
scenario I, and α is accordingly higher. But the debt service effort added to
nondebt-creating flows is so substantial – 2.5 percent of GDP – that it more
than compensates. Accordingly, a moderate debt reduction is possible,
leading to a 1999 debt ratio of 39.4 percent.

Scenario III: $\alpha = 0$ and $\sigma+\delta = 0.025$

In this case real interest, real depreciation, and domestic growth offset
each other. The world economic environment is sufficiently favorable that
there is growth at home, and little or no depreciation. Thus there is no
automatic accumulation of debt. With a debt service effort of 2.5 percent of
GDP there is a dramatic debt reduction to a ratio of only 8.1 percent in
1999.

The simulations give some idea of the importance of the noninterest
current account surplus. High noninterest surplus can compensate for the
effects of high real interest rates and real depreciation. In that sense there
is no debt problem that must get fatally worse. The active issue, here, is
how difficult it is to generate noninterest surpluses large enough to finance
the debt effects of high real interest rates in the presence of capital
outflows. We return to this question below. In the meantime we consider
whether the world's macroeconomic outlook offers the perspective of an
improvement or deterioration.

The world macroeconomic outlook

The most recent IMF economic outlook is shown in table 11.5. The table
highlights a relatively flat external environment: sustained growth, a minor
improvement in real commodity prices, and no significant decline in real
interest rates. The general scenario in table 11.5 conceals the very substantial differences that arise under alternative assumptions about US fiscal and
external balance adjustment. We now explore two basic scenarios, one
favorable the other unfavorable from the point of view of a debtor country.

The favorable scenario involves a large decline in the dollar, continued
world economic growth, and a decline in real interest rates combined with
a rise in commodity prices. This scenario has become significantly more
plausible in the aftermath of the worldwide decline in asset markets which
exposed pervasive financial fragility.

The favorable scenario might come about as follows: contrary to early
expectations, the stock market decline does not bring about a major

Table 11.5 The 1987 IMF world economic outlook (average annual percentage change)

	1983–87	1987	1988	1989–91
Indust. countries' growth	3.2	2.4	2.6	2.9
Real LIBOR[a]	5.3	3.9	3.6	4.0
Manufactures prices	5.2	12.8	3.8	3.0
Oil prices	–8.2	27.6	3.5	3.0
Commodity prices	–0.9	–1.0	4.0	4.2

[a] Using the US GNP deflator

Source: IMF *World Economic Outlook*, October 1987

slowdown of the world economy. Congress and the President agree on a multi-year, significant deficit reduction package. The confidence effects of this program in asset markets bring about a rise in asset prices and a decline in long-term interest rates. The monetary authorities support the fiscal contraction by maintaining real interest rates at the current or lower levels. The reduction in interest rates leads to a massive decline in the dollar, the extent of which is arrested only when foreign monetary authorities likewise cut interest rates. Lower interest rates worldwide, continued growth, and a steep fall in the dollar would inevitably bring about a major increase in the dollar prices of commodities. If US fiscal correction includes a significant tax on gasoline, and OPEC feels weak, oil prices in dollars might show little increase.

Adding up all the aspects of this favorable scenario, Brazil could do very well. Commodity price increases would help export revenue, and continued growth would support growth of manufactures exports; lower interest rates (certainly in real terms) would reduce debt service burdens. This scenario has many of the features of 1973–4 which was immensely beneficial for debtors. It is worth noting that the dollar decline works through two separate channels. First it raises the dollar value of debt denominated in European currencies and in yen. But these debts account for only 30 percent of the total, and hence the effect is limited even for a major dollar decline. But there is also an increase in the dollar prices of primary commodities, and hence of export earnings.

A dollar depreciation would raise dollar prices of primary commodities by about half the depreciation. This would be a lasting increase in commodity prices, applying to at least half if not more of exports. This effect is accordingly very powerful because it is recurrent. If reinforced by lower interest rates it can bring about a major change in the international setting to slow debt accumulation directly and by greater ease in running noninterest surpluses. Interest rates are crucial because 75 percent of Brazilian debt service is geared to short-term money market rates.

The alternative scenario was more likely before the crash, but is not totally implausible even today. In this scenario concern over exchange rates leads the Federal Reserve to raise interest rates sharply. Growth slows down worldwide. Any fiscal correction would further aggravate this outlook. Moreover, high interest rates and the slowdown would exert a dampening effect on commodity prices in dollars.

In concluding on these scenarios associated with US adjustment, there are genuine possibilities for a major change in the international environment. Specifically the favorable scenario might lead to a melting away of debt income ratios if the world economy is willing to accept a fair amount of inflation. But there is an offsetting point that has not received much attention: that is the counterpart to US adjustment. Will Japan and Europe lose their surpluses? And if so, what is the impact on their imports from developing countries? Will debtor countries like Brazil have to make a major contribution? There is serious risk here of inconsistency. US trade improvement and a dramatic improvement of debtor country creditworthiness are basically inconsistent, unless extremely low real interest rates and high real nonoil-commodity prices become the central facts in the coming years.

The other important risk which remains is protectionism. There is no question, however, that in the context of protectionism any legitimacy of debt collection would simply evaporate.

5 Constructive Policy Alternatives

The discussion of the transfer problem highlighted the domestic costs of bringing about, in the budget and in the external balance, a premature transfer of real resources toward the creditors. The costs take the form of depressed living standards, hyperinflation, sharply reduced investment, and hence the perspective of reduced long-term growth opportunities. The insistence on cash collection of the past five years has aggravated these transfer problems to the maximum extent. Even in Brazil, where foreign resources had on balance been wisely invested, at least until the late 1970s, the costs are totally apparent. The trade-off between immediate growth and debt service is there for anyone to see.

Are there ways in which the long-term interests of debtors and creditors can be reconciled? The answer is yes. A scheme that recycles a large part of the interest payments into the country does away with the need for trade surpluses and the resulting crowding-out of investment. It thus makes it possible to have investment and growth, and yet provide creditors with debt service, albeit in investments that cannot be repatriated for the time being.

Practically, this could be achieved by adopting the following procedure. A much reduced trade surplus of perhaps 1 percent of GDP would be used to service a minor part of the debt, mostly to governments and multilateral agencies, and to provide resources to buy out (via auction) small banks who are willing to accept deep discounts.

The major part of the debt would be paid in Baker certificates – cruzados which are in part automatically re-lent to the government to finance public sector investment and in part are freely disposable to finance loans or acquisition of assets in Brazil. The only restriction on the disposal of Baker certificates or the investments they generate is that they cannot be transferred out of Brazil. In combination with a serious fiscal reform, this shift in debt servicing would restore normal growth and investment, and thus, provides maximum assurance of an ultimate transfer of resources to the creditors.

This scheme basically gives Brazil some years to restore a normal macroeconomy before resuming resource transfers abroad. It emphasizes that debt service is ultimately best guaranteed by investment and growth. The Baker Plan, while nominally committed to this target, failed because it overstressed early debt collection at the expense of investment.

NOTES

We are indebted to Tim Vogelsang for valuable research assistance.

1 "Squeezing the Lender." In the following issue, December 25, pp. 833–4, *The Economist* further criticizes the Brazilian settlement and states: "the British authorities were unwilling or unable to put any pressure on the Brazilian government in favour of a less inequitable settlement. And it is an open secret in the City that the reason for the authorities' reluctance was the fact that Washington would not permit it. . . . To put the question quite bluntly, the British holder of Brazilian obligations has been made to sacrifice to Pan-Americanism. . . . There are higher things at stake than Brazilian bonds. Least of any journal in the country would the *Economist* object to anything that smoothes the path of British–American co-operation, even it involves some sacrifice. If this is Washington's idea of a fair bargain, there is nothing to be done but to acquiesce."

2 Weekly prices of Brazilian bonds are found in the *Commercial and Financial Chronicle*.

3 Statement by Ciro DeFalco, US Treasury, at a conference cosponsored by the Joint Economic Committee and the Congressional Research Service, *Dealing with the Debt Problem of Latin America*, p. 76.

4 For an alternative calculation, broadly consistent with the estimates reported here, see Dornbusch (1985). It is shown there that in the period 1978–82 a $34.9 billion increase in debt, compared to the counterfactual scenario, can be attributed to higher oil prices and increased interest rates. This number is virtually identical to the estimate in the text, although arrived at in a very different fashion.

5 The actual 1983–6 averages are: 3.5 percent growth, $24.5 a barrel of oil, LIBOR at 9 percent and 8 percent cumulative dollar depreciation.

6 See Fraga (1986), and Dornbusch (1986, 1987a), for a discussion of the transfer problem in relation to debt service and for comparisons between the experience of Weimar Germany and Brazil.

REFERENCES

Abreu, M. de Paiva (1978), "Brazilian Public Foreign Debt Policy, 1931–1943," *Brazilian Economic Studies*. No. 4, IPEA: Rio de Janeiro.
Bittermann, Henry (1973), *The Refunding of International Debt*. Durham: Duke University Press.
Bouças, Valentim (1950), *História da Dívida Externa*, Rio de Janeiro.
Campos, Claudionor de Souza (1946), *Dívida Externa*, Rio de Janeiro.
Cardoso, E. and Fishlow, A. *Macroeconomics of Brazilian External Debt*. Chicago: University of Chicago Press, forthcoming.
Cardoso, E. (1988), "Lessons of the 1890s for the 1980s: Comments," in R. Findlay (ed.) *Debt, Stabilization and Development*, Oxford: Blackwell.
Cline, W. (1984), *International Debt*. Cambridge, MA: MIT Press.
Donnelly, J. T. (1973), "External Financing and Short-Term Consequences of External Debt Servicing for Brazilian Economic Development, 1947–1968," *Journal of Developing Areas*. April, pp. 411–30.
Dornbusch, R. (1985), "External Debt, Budget Deficits and Disequilibrium Exchange Rates," in G. Smith and J. Cuddington (eds.), *International Debt and Developing Countries*. Washington: World Bank.
Dornbusch, R. (1986), "Policy and Performance Linkage Between LDC Debtors and Industrial Countries," *Brookings Papers on Economic Activity*. no. 2.
Dornbusch, R. (1987a), "Stopping Hyperinflation: Lessons from the Experience of Germany in the 1920s," in R. Dornbusch, S. Fischer and J. Bosson (eds), *Macroeconomics and Finance: Essays in Honor of Franco Modigliani*. Cambridge, MA: MIT Press.
Dornbusch, R. (1987b), "Developing Country Debt: Anatomy and Solutions." Twentieth Century Fund.
Feldstein, M. (1986), "International Debt Service and Economic Growth: Some Simple Analytics." NBER Working Paper No. 2076.
Feldstein, M. (1987), "Latin America's Debt," *Economist*. June 27.
Fishlow, A. (1988), "Lessons of the 1890s for the 1980s," in R. Findlay (ed.), *Debt, Stabilization and Development*. Oxford: Blackwell.
Fraga, A. (1986), *German Reparations and Brazilian Debt: A Comparative Study*.

Princeton University: Princeton Studies in International Finance, International Finance Section.

Maddison, A. (1985), *Two Crises: Latin America and Asia 1929–38 and 1973–83*. Paris: OECD.

Marques Moreira, M. (1986), *The Brazilian Quandary*. Twentieth Century Fund.

Ministerio de Fazenda, Republica do Brasil (1987), "The Financing of Economic Development in the Period 1987–1991". Brasilia, March 31st.

Nogueira Batista, P. (1983), *Mito e Realidade da Divida Externa Brasileira*. Rio de Janeiro: Paz e Terra.

Simonsen, M. (1985), "The Developing Country Debt Problem," in G. Smith and J. Cuddington (eds), *International Debt and the Developing Countries*. Washington: World Bank.

Simonsen, M. (1986), "Brazil," in R. Dornbusch and L. Helmers (eds), *The Open Economy: Tools for Policy Makers in Developing Countries*. Washington: World Bank.

Appendix

Table A1 External debt

Period	Total debt (billions of current dollars)	Real debt per capita (in 1986 dollars)[e]	Debt–income[f] index 1970 = 100
1929–39	1.190[a]	287	582.3
1940–45	0.855[a]	153	255.8
1946–50	0.600[b]	60	81.9
1951–55	1.227[c]	96	107.4
1956–60	2.201[c]	131	123.5
1961–64	3.545[c]	168	133.5
1965–69	3.755[c]	138	103.1
1970	5.295[c]	156	100.0
1971	6.622[c]	179	105.9
1972	9.521[c]	239	129.4
1973	12.572[c]	291	141.3
1974	17.166[c]	355	162.2
1975	21.171[c]	389	173.1
1976	25.985[c]	438	181.9
1977	35.737[d]	551	224.2
1978	48.111[d]	675	268.4
1979	56.104[d]	706	268.2
1980	64.648[d]	712	254.0
1981	75.511[d]	742	280.7
1982	83.265[d]	751	288.6
1983	91.632[d]	779	314.8
1984	102.039[d]	815	319.3
1985	105.126[d]	795	294.9
1986	110.572[d]	798	280.6

Sources: [a] Marcelo de Paiva Abreu (1978), (table 1 figures were converted to dollars)[b] John T. Donnelly (1973), pp. 411–430.[c] Banco Central do Brasil: Long and Medium Term Debt.[d] Banco Central do Brasil, Long, Medium and Short-Term Debt.[e] Nominal debt deflated by US implicit price deflator for GNP, *The National Income and Product Accounts of the U.S.*, US Department of Commerce. Brazilian population before 1950 from Villela e Suzigan, *Politica de Governo e Crescimento da Economia Brasileira- 1889–1945*, IPEA/INPES, Rio de Janeiro, 1973. After 1950, IMF, *International Financial Statistics*. [f]Obtained by dividing the index of the real debt per capita by the index of the real GDP per capita.

Table A2 Brazilian debt and deficits (% of GDP)

	1982	1983	1984	1985	1986
PSBR[a]	15.8	19.9	23.3	27.5	10.8
Operational deficit[b]	6.6	3.0	2.7	4.3	3.7
Total debt/GDP	28.8	45.0	47.7	49.2	46.9
Resource transfer abroad	−1.4	2.0	5.4	4.8	2.3
Share of external debt in total debt (%)	55.5	64.1	60.4	59.3	59.11

[a] Public sector borrowing requirement, % of GDP, [b] % of GDP

Source: Banco Central and Minsterio da Fazenda

Table A3 Brazil: 1987 structure of the external debt

	$ bill	Percent
Total	110.4	100.0
Official institutions	28.3	25.6
Int'l organizations	13.7	12.4
Governments	14.6	13.2
Private lenders	82.1	74.4
Banks	75.0	68.0
US banks	(22.2)	(20.1)
Other	7.1	6.4

Source: Banco Central

Table A4 Debt–export ratio

Year	Ratio	Year	Ratio
		1965	2.3
1929	2.5	1966	2.1
1930	3.8	1967	2.0
1931	5.3	1968	2.0
1932	5.5	1969	1.9
1933	5.0	1970	1.9
1934	4.5	1971	2.3
1935	4.7	1972	2.4
1936	3.9	1973	2.0
1937	3.4	1974	2.2
1938	4.0	1975	2.4
1939	3.7	1976	2.6
1940	3.7	1977	2.9
1941	2.6	1978	3.8
1942	2.3	1979	3.7
1943	1.9	1980	3.2
1944	1.3	1981	3.2
1945	1.0	1982	4.1
1946–50	0.5	1983	4.2
1951–55	0.8	1984	3.8
1956–60	1.6	1985	4.1
1961–64	2.6	1986	4.9

Source: Table A1, Banco Central, and Malan et al., *Politica Economica Externa e Industrializaçao no Brasil*, Relatorio de Pesquisa, IPEA, Rio de Janeiro, 1977

Comment

William R. Cline

Cardoso and Dornbusch have provided a study that is informative in many of its analyses, yet somehow strays in deriving policy interpretations. At the outset, the authors present an uncanny resemblance between the impact on Brazilian per capital income from the Great Depression of the 1930s and the recession of 1980–6. The finding of *déjà vu* implies that a repeat of the default of the 1930s is likely, desirable, or both. Yet there are important reasons why the 1930s provide a highly misleading analogy. In the Great Depression, the dollar value of world trade collapsed to about one-half its previous level. In contrast, from 1982 to 1987 the dollar value of world trade rose by 28 percent. In the debt crisis of the 1980s, it has been infinitely more feasible for nations to grow out of the crisis through expanding their exports. Indeed, figure 11.1 may be read in a different way: this time Brazil has been able to do just as well in income recovery as in the 1930s while avoiding default (and by early 1988 Brazil had rejected even the partial moratorium of 1987 and returned to making interest payments).

The description of the muddling-through strategy since 1982 summarizes its central elements (global recovery, increased exports, the expectation of higher commodity prices, decline in real interest rates and the dollar, domestic policy reform) aptly if hyperbolically ("burdens of debt service would almost surely vanish . . . foreign lenders would unquestionably resume lending"). However, this strategy had not emerged as the consensus until at least late 1983; in April of that year my own simulations along those lines represented a minority view.

The authors are correct to stress external shocks in the origin of the Brazilian debt crisis, and to note that capital flight played a much smaller role than in several other countries. However, there is also room for considerable blame to be put on domestic policies. The government consciously adopted a risky high-growth strategy based on heavy foreign borrowing after the first oil shock. When Planning Minister Mario Simonsen began a process of adjustment in 1979, he was replaced by Delfim Netto who renewed stimulus in 1980 and limited devaluation to 40 percent when inflation turned out to be 100 percent.

Cardoso and Dornbusch compare my own projections made in 1983 with the actual outcome for Brazil through 1986. As their table indicates, my current account projections turned out to be close to the actual results. Yet the debt build-up was far higher. The authors attribute the difference to capital outflows and capital flight. But I suspect a considerable part of the problem was "debt discovery," the more complete coverage of official debt data over time (and thus overstatement of the increment). Thus, cumulative current account deficits were $10.1 billion, reserves build-up $2.8 billion, and direct investment $2.4 billion for 1983–6, so that debt should have risen by only $10.5 billion. The actual increase was $27 billion, and errors and omissions account for only $1.2 billion of the discrepancy. Moreover, the exchange rate regime was such that it is hard to believe that $15.3 billion disappeared in capital flight (and as for the recorded capital account, it showed a surplus of $8.7 billion over the period).[1]

The other projection that erred was for the net debt–export ratio, which reached 4.1 instead of 2.0 by 1986. But recall that through 1984 the expected improvement was on track: Brazil's exports rose from $20 billion in 1982 to $27 billion. If exports had risen from 1984 through 1986 at the same rate as achieved by developing country exporters of manufactures, by 1986 the level would have stood at $31 billion (instead of $22 billion), placing the net debt–exports ratio at 2.9; and if the mysterious excess debt of $16.5 billion had not arisen (if it really did), the ratio would have stood at 2.4. In policy terms, internal Brazilian mistakes derailed the export expansion; *haec mea culpa non est.*

A crucial measure of the debt burden does not appear in the authors' analysis: the ratio of interest to exports of goods and services. This measure of the debt burden incorporates not just volume (debt) but price (the interest rate), as economic analysis usually should, and it shows a much more favorable outcome. Brazil's ratio of interest to exports of goods and services declined from 52 percent in 1982 to 36 percent in 1986 (and improved further to 32 percent in 1987). By this measure, the qualitative thrust of my 1983 projections was confirmed in practice even for the relative size of the debt burden, despite domestic policy errors that kept improvement more modest than it might have been.

Cardoso and Dornbusch seek to explain what went wrong with the muddling-through approach. They argue that it forgot the problem of domestic fiscal transfer. As Chile has shown, however, it has proved possible to manage the debt on the mainstream approach and still achieve fiscal balance and low inflation. The authors also stress fatigue in the bank cartel. But the fact is that the banks have repeatedly agreed to new money packages when asked by countries entering into IMF agreements (and by early 1988 another package worth nearly $6 billion was agreed upon for Brazil itself).

In evaluating the current situation, Cardoso and Dornbusch correctly note the "disastrous state of domestic macroeconomics and an unwillingness to pay" as important factors in the decline of the secondary market price from 75 cents on the dollar to 39 cents (table 11.4). The authors could have been more explicit, however, and stressed that it was the distortions of excess demand, overvaluation through the freeze in the exchange rate, and fiscal imbalance under the Cruzado Plan that disrupted Brazil's progress toward recovery from the debt problem in 1986. It should also be emphasized that the problem stemmed primarily from domestic policy; after all, Brazil enjoyed a windfall gain of some $6 billion in 1986 from lower oil import prices and lower international interest rates.

The role of intent as opposed to capacity to pay is underlined by the partial recovery of secondary market prices of Brazilian debt after the country moved toward a rapprochement with creditors in early 1988. By the end of February, 1988, the secondary market price was back up to 47 cents on the dollar. In addition, the reversal of the Cruzado Plan distortions (especially on the exchange rate) that had caused a collapse of the trade surplus from an annual rate of $12 billion to zero by late 1986 brought a revival of the surplus to a rate of about $11 billion by the second half of 1987, providing the underpinnings for an end to the moratorium in early 1988.

The macromodel presented by Cardoso and Dornbusch accurately captures the key determinants of future debt prospects. I agree with the authors that in a scenario in which the noninterest current account generates a surplus of 2.5 percent of GNP, the debt burden declines steadily toward levels compatible with restored creditworthiness. I also agree with most of the authors' observations on global macro prospects (although on the impact of fiscal correction in the United States on the dollar it seems to me that because of improved expectations a further decline might not occur, and in any event a further real decline of the order of 10–15 percent seems all that is required rather than a "massive" decline).

The authors are relatively optimistic on the global macroeconomic environment, primarily because they expect a lower dollar (which should boost commodity prices) and a lower real interest rate (providing direct alleviation of the debt burden). They make a crucial qualification, however, arguing that US trade correction is incompatible with improved debtor country creditworthiness. This conflict is false. As long as Latin American countries keep their real exchange rates against the dollar unchanged, and the US external adjustment is achieved through the price effects of dollar depreciation rather than US recession, Latin American exports to the United States should remain steady while exports to Europe and Japan could actually increase from improved competitiveness as Latin American currencies depreciate in real terms relative to the yen and European currencies.

The final policy portion of the paper is where the authors seem to leap to a massive *non sequitur*. Having just outlined the likelihood of relatively favorable developments for Brazil's debt, they present what amounts to a scheme of quasi-forgiveness. Their Baker certificates redeemable in local currency only (and ineligible for transfer abroad) would sell in a secondary market at 25 cents on the dollar at best. Their plan would decidedly push Brazil away from a return to normal relations with capital markets, just at a time when the country's trade performance and return to co-operation with foreign banks holds promise for renewed progress towards that goal.

The authors seek to recycle interest. That goal is worthy but they would carry it too far and do so in a counterproductive way. They call for a cut of the trade surplus to 1 percent of GDP, or only about $2.5 billion, from its prospective rate of some $10 billion to $12 billion annually. It is almost certain that cutting exports by $10 billion would damage growth, as exports are a key center of growth. It is implausible that an increase of imports by $10 billion, or by 60 percent, would be required to attain the steady growth of 6 to 7 percent that represents Brazil's potential rate. The government's own Macroeconomic Control Plan of 1987 projected that the economy could grow at 6 percent annually while achieving a trade surplus of $9–$10 billion.

In part of Cardoso and Dornbusch seem to subscribe to the "policy bribe" thesis, that by radical relief foreign creditors can purchase large policy reforms in the debtor country. But it is at least as likely that the extra resources provided would go to such white elephants as President Sarney's proposed north–south railway from the capital to his home state. When the politicians are prepared to take corrective measures on large fiscal deficits and other distortions, they will do so for the country's own benefit, not as a capitulation to creditors who have finally made the price right.

Similarly, the authors' view that debt service forgone would be reallocated to increased domestic investment is probably too simplistic. Domestic investment will revive only when the domestic macroeconomic conditions are more stable. Inflation of 500 percent per year or more cripples the demand for investment by making it impossible to plan and likely that price controls and other interventions will turn profits to losses. Yet when more stable domestic conditions are present, the increased investment required for target growth probably can be financed by higher domestic savings, renewed direct foreign investment inflows, and new money packages from the banks. In this connection, it is curious that the authors do not provide any calculation of the increase in the domestic growth rate that could be purchased by the resources provided through their proposal, as opposed to the alternative strategy of muddling through.

In sum, Cardoso and Dornbusch provide several illuminating analyses of the causes of Brazil's debt problem and the outlook for its resolution. Their policy proposal seems more likely to make matters worse than better, however. Brazilian authorities appear to have reached the same general conclusion in early 1988 when they ended their moratorium, citing its costs (such as the losses on short-term trade credits), rather than continuing the moratorium to force more radical solutions on debt.

NOTE

1 The World Bank also appears to believe that official Brazilian data overstate the debt build-up from 1982 to 1988. The Bank places total end-1982 debt at $91.6 billion, in contrast to the government's figure of $83.3 billion. By 1986 the two sources both show $110 billion in debt. If the Bank's figure for 1982 is accepted, unexplained debt build-up shrinks from $15.3 billion to $7.4 billion. Note that my 1983 study used $88.2 billion as the 1982 debt figure (World Bank, *World Debt Tables*, 1987–8 edition, Vol. II, p. 38).

Index

Compiled by
Jackie McDermott